W9-DER-551

1175

Introduction to
International Economics

THE IRWIN SERIES IN ECONOMICS

Consulting Editor
LLOYD G. REYNOLDS
Yale University

Introduction to International Economics

DELBERT A. SNIDER, Ph.D.
Professor of Economics
Miami University

Fifth Edition
1971

Richard D. Irwin, Inc., Homewood, Illinois
Irwin-Dorsey Limited, Georgetown, Ontario

FIFTH EDITION

First Printing, March, 1971

Library of Congress Catalog Card No. 77–141397

Printed in the United States of America

To my father
and the
memory of my mother
and
to Helen, Suzanne, and Chris

PREFACE

Several major changes have been made in the present revision of this book. The pure theory of trade has been completely rewritten. The Heckscher-Ohlin theorem, which in previous editions held the central place, is now presented as merely a special case of the more general equilibrium model that is developed first. The reason for this, of course, is the increasing scepticism concerning the empirical relevance of the Heckscher-Ohlin model.

A second important change consists of the replacement of Part IV of the text with a concentrated presentation of the role of trade and aid in economic development. Two entirely new chapters have been added, while three former chapters have been deleted.

Nearly all other chapters have undergone revisions, to bring them up to date with respect to theoretical analysis as well as to data.

While the contributions of numerous persons continue to be reflected in the present edition, I am especially indebted to my colleague, Professor Chung H. Lee, for helpful comments, with the usual absolvement from responsibility for the final presentation.

Finally, I am grateful to my family for their gracious acceptance of having husband and father out of circulation during the period of work on the revision, and to Mrs. Treva Reiboldt for extraordinary efficiency in typing manuscript.

Oxford, Ohio   DELBERT A. SNIDER
February, 1971

CONTENTS

INTRODUCTION

The Significance of International Economic Relations. The Composition and Pattern of World Trade. Political Aspects of International Economic Relations. The Tasks of Theory.

PART I: THE THEORY AND EMPIRICAL FOUNDATIONS OF INTERNATIONAL TRADE AND FACTOR MOVEMENTS

Interregional and International Trade. The Proximate Cause of Trade: *Relative Price Differences. Converting Relative into Absolute Price Differences: The Rate of Exchange. Comparative Cost Differences.* The Underlying Causes of Trade: Classical Theory. The Underlying Causes of Trade: Modern Theory: *Equilibrium in Isolation. Opportunity Cost Differences. The Shape of Transformation Curves. Factor Proportions. Relative Factor Supplies. Pre-Trade Output Points. Summary of Modern Theory. The Heckscher-Ohlin Theorem. Identical Production Features. Factor Proportions. Economies of Scale. Demand Conditions.* Summary and Conclusions.

Specialization and Trade: *Constant-Cost Conditions. Decreasing Cost Conditions. Increasing Cost Conditions.* The Terms of Trade: *Limits of the Terms of Trade. The Equilibrium Terms of Trade. Reciprocal Demand.* The Economic Effects of Trade: *The Equalization of Goods and Service Prices and Costs. Factor Price Equalization.* The Gains from Trade: *The Gain from Specialization. The Gain from Exchange. Some Welfare Questions. Multicountry, Multicommodity Trade. Multicommodity Trade. Multicountry Trade. Multilateral Trade. General Equilibrium.* Appendix: A Diagrammatic Analysis of International Trade. *Production Functions, Resource Supplies, and the Production Transformation Curve. Demand and Pretrade Equilibrium Output. Production, Consumption, and Trade.*

1789–1934: *Tariffs for Revenue. Tariffs for Protection. Major Tariff Issues before 1934.* American Commercial Policy, 1934–62: *The Reciprocal Trade Agreements Program. The Proposed International Trade Organization* (ITO) . *The General Agreement on Trade and Tariffs. Tariff Reductions under the Reciprocal Trade Agreements Program. Weakening of the Trade Agreements Program. Other Aspects of U.S. Commercial Policy.* The Trade Expansion Act of 1962: *Authority to Reduce Tariffs. Escape Clause. Adjustment Assistance. Results of the Kennedy Round.*

PART IV: THE INTERNATIONAL ECONOMICS OF DEVELOPMENT

LIST OF TABLES AND FIGURES

xvii

Introduction

Chapter 1

THE SIGNIFICANCE AND SCOPE OF INTERNATIONAL ECONOMICS

The daily lives of most of us are largely confined to activities in our home communities. We are aware of the local economy, for this is the immediate provider of the goods and services we consume and the source of our employment opportunities. Most of us are also conscious, however, that the local economy is only a small part of a much larger national economy. Aside from personal services, by far the greatest portion of the goods and services we purchase are not the product of the local economy: the meat on the table may come from Texas via packing plants in Chicago, the clothing in the wardrobe from manufacturers in New York, the fruit in the bowl from Florida and California, the car in the garage from Detroit, and so on. At the same time, our jobs yield products which more than likely will be consumed outside the local economy.

The complex of interrelationships among the thousands of local communities, bound together through a vast volume of exchange of goods and services and the movements of people and capital, constitutes the national economy. Awareness of the national economy is sharpened by the presence of a federal government whose influence is felt, through its taxes, spending, and regulations, in every nook and corner of the country.

We live and work in a local economy and a national economy; but we also live and work in an international or "world" economy. Just as national economies are composed of local and regional parts, so the world economy is composed of national economies. The world economy is "looser" than the usual national economy, in the sense that the national members of the world economy are not as closely interrelated and interdependent as the local and regional parts of the typical national economy. However, for many national economies external economic relations are of paramount importance. And for nearly all countries, participation in the world economy could not be withdrawn without extremely serious adverse consequences which would be felt at every level in every community.

THE SIGNIFICANCE OF INTERNATIONAL ECONOMIC RELATIONS

There are different ways of assessing the significance of international economic relations. The broadest measure is the volume of economic transactions among countries. The principal international economic transaction is the exchange of goods and services among countries. Recent data on the volume of world merchandise trade are presented in Table 1.1. In addition, there are annually

TABLE 1.1

WORLD MERCHANDISE EXPORTS, SELECTED YEARS

Year	Value (In Millions of Current Dollar Equivalents)	Quantum Index (1963 = 100)
1938	22,700	38
1950	61,200	45
1960	127,900	83
1966	203,400	126
1968	238,700	149

SOURCE: United Nations, *Statistical Yearbook*, 1969.

billions of dollars of service transactions—shipping and passenger transportation, insurance, tourism, and so on.

Besides trade in goods and services, an important second category of international economic relations consists of the movement of capital, in the form of loans, grants, and investments, and of persons who migrate across national boundaries. Later, we shall call these "factor movements" and identify the significant role they have in the world economy.

Aggregate data conceal the position of individual components. In the case of trade and factor movements, the position of different countries varies by wide margins. The best single indicator of how important international trade is for a particular country is the proportion of its national income accounted for by its exports or consumed in the form of imports. The latter proportion—the ratio of

imports to income—is called the *average propensity to import.* The
average propensity to import ranges from a high of nearly 50 percent for the Netherlands to a low of 3 or 4 percent for the United
States.

The chief explanation of the large differences in the role of imports (and of foreign trade in general) for individual countries lies
in the size and diversity of national economies. The huge amount
of trade between the eastern and western regions of the United
States is labeled "domestic trade," but if the Mississippi River were
a national boundary dividing the country into two separate national states, the same trade would be "international." (This suggests that interregional trade within countries and international
trade have fundamentally the same bases—a point that will be
elaborated upon shortly.) Small countries, with limited amounts
and kinds of resources, tend generally to participate more extensively in foreign trade than do larger and more diversified countries.

However useful the figures on the trade of the world and of individual countries are, they do not fully reveal the significance of international economic relations. For some countries, existing populations could not be sustained, or, if so, only at severely reduced
standards of living, in the absence of international trade. A prime
example is the United Kingdom, whose population of 30 percent
and area of 3 percent that of the United States would not permit
her to provide anything like her present standard of living out of
domestic resources alone. By importing foodstuffs and raw materials
in exchange for highly manufactured goods and international services, she is able to maintain a relatively high standard of living.

For most of the countries that take advantage of the benefits realizable from geographic specialization on a worldwide basis, the internal economy is integrally tied into the world economy. External
and internal economic conditions and relations are not separated
into compartments that can be sealed off from one another without
vitally affecting the content of each. They are, rather, different
components of the same organic whole. As a consequence, it is not
legitimate to conclude that, for example, if the imports of a given
country are 15 percent of its national income, the latter would be
affected only to this extent if trading relations with other countries
were cut off. Imports may be a vital, even though, quantitatively, a
relatively small, proportion of the total national economy. An analogy might be the role of, say, steel output in the total national pro-

duction of the United States. Steel has a much greater significance for the economy than the ratio of steel output to total production would indicate. Just as, for instance, a strike in the steel industry can create a "bottleneck," slowing down overall production, so a cutting-off of the external trade of a country could cause a bottleneck effect on its national economy.

The above remarks are applicable, though to a much lesser extent than for most countries, even to the United States. Having a vast territory, rich in a wide variety of resources, and possessed of a huge internal market, America, unlike a country such as Great Britain, could maintain its present population at a relatively high standard of living even though economic contact with the outside world were completely cut off. Nevertheless, the American standard of living would be significantly lowered and its potentiality for continued growth and development reduced, perhaps seriously, were the United States to become economically isolated. Americans would have to forego or drastically reduce the consumption of such items as coffee, tea, and cocoa, the domestic supply of which is now totally imported, and of numerous other consumer goods which are now imported in large quantities. More important, notwithstanding the wide variety of raw materials found within the United States, there are many strategically important minerals and other primary products for which she is largely or entirely dependent on foreign sources—such as crude rubber, tin, asbestos, chromite, jute, nickel, and newsprint. Indeed, there are only two metals (magnesium and molybdenum) used by U.S. industry for which it is not partially or wholly dependent on foreign supplies. The United States has become the world's largest importer of copper, lead, and zinc, whereas she was once an exporter of these metals; and she has even begun to meet from foreign sources a growing portion of her needs for petroleum and iron ore, in which she has traditionally been self-sufficient. In general, as compared to the beginning of this century, when the United States produced some 15 percent more raw materials than she consumed (excluding foodstuffs), by mid-century she was using 10 percent more materials than she produced.

It might be correctly argued that, were the United States cut off from all foreign supplies, she should be able in most cases physically to replace them by increased domestic output of the same or substitute commodities. But this argument misses the real point. It is not so much a question of physical incapability of producing at home what is now imported, though in some instances, such as certain minerals, this may be the case, but rather that the real cost of the home-substituted output would be so much higher than the real cost of imports. The chief consequence for the United States of economic isolation, in other words, would be a lowering of the standard of living.

On the export side of the American economy, production and employment in many important sectors depend significantly upon foreign markets. The export of agricultural commodities such as rice, cotton, wheat, tobacco, soybeans, lard, and dried fruits usually amounts to from 20 to 40 percent and more of U.S. production of these commodities. From 15 to 30 percent of the domestic output of such industrial goods as machine tools, tractors, textile machinery, printing machinery and equipment, office appliances, motor trucks and coaches, and oil-field machinery and tools are exported.

In general, we may conclude that for nearly all countries—with the exception of those that are in a primitive state of economic development and those, like the Soviet bloc countries, that deliberately minimize external economic relations on political grounds—international trade is a highly significant and integral part of the national economy. Adam Smith long ago enunciated a principle that has since become famous and accepted everywhere as a fundamental economic maxim: when production is organized on the basis of specialization, total output is much greater than it would be if production were carried on by self-sufficient, economically isolated production entities. The volume of international trade—the result of geographic specialization—is eloquent empirical evidence of the seriousness with which Adam Smith's principle has been accepted.

THE COMPOSITION AND PATTERN OF WORLD TRADE

There are hundreds of articles that enter into world trade, including products of all types and of virtually every country. For purposes of data collecting and international comparisons, the United Nations has classified the commodities traded internationally into 177 groups (containing, in all, 1,312 items), and these groups are consolidated for summary presentation into 10 broad sections.[1] A still broader, though much less accurate, classification

---

[1] See United Nations, *Standard International Trade Classification* (rev. ed.; New York, 1960).

would embrace just three groups: food (including tobacco and beverages), raw materials, and manufactured goods.

In the prewar years, world trade was divided up among the three broad groups of items roughly as follows (each as a percentage of total trade).[2]

Foodstuffs...................... 25%
Raw materials.................. 35
Manufactured goods............. 40

Since the prewar days, these proportions have changed, with manufactured goods exports rising in recent years to over 60 percent of total commodity trade.

A relatively few items account for the great bulk of world commodity trade. Of foodstuffs and related items, wheat, meat, fruits, sugar, edible oils, coffee, cocoa, tea, alcoholic beverages, and tobacco are examples of leading trade items. Petroleum, wool and cotton, wood pulp, timber, coal, copper, rubber, jute, tin, lead, and zinc are examples of leading raw materials traded internationally. Of manufactured goods, machinery, iron and steel products, transport equipment, chemicals, and textiles account for a very large proportion of total world trade in manufactured goods.

As we would expect, agricultural countries are largely exporters of foodstuffs and raw materials and importers of manufactured goods, while the highly industrialized countries follow the reverse pattern. This does not mean, however, that trading relations among countries with the same general type of economy are unimportant. Indeed, about two thirds of the trade of the main industrial countries of the world is among themselves. There is a very wide range of useful specialization possible, and, even though two national economies are both highly industrialized, there still are specialty manufactures of each that are traded. The same thing is true, though probably to a lesser extent, of agricultural countries.

One of the most important determinants of the overall size of a country's foreign trade is the level of its real income, aggregate and per capita. Countries with very low incomes cannot import much because of their limited purchasing power. The distribution of world income among different countries is markedly unequal. The United States has the lion's share—over one third. Western Europe accounts for about one fifth, and the Soviet Union about one

---

[2] League of Nations, *The Network of World Trade* (Geneva, 1942), pp. 23–24.

eighth.[3] Together, these countries enjoy over two thirds the world's income, yet have less than one quarter the world's population.

It is not surprising, therefore, to find that the largest part of world trade is conducted by relatively few countries in the higher range of incomes. The exports of the developed countries account for about 80 percent of world exports. Indeed, a few countries—the United States, Canada, the United Kingdom, industrial Europe, and Japan—are responsible for over two thirds of total world exports. These figures do not mean, of course, that international trade is not important to other countries. Relative to their size and national incomes, foreign trade, as we indicated earlier, is very important to most countries of the world.

POLITICAL ASPECTS OF INTERNATIONAL ECONOMIC RELATIONS

Up to now the discussion has centered on the economic aspects of international relations, and this indeed will be the focus throughout. But a word is in order at this point on other, closely related facets of the world economy. International economic relations are conducted within a framework of national and international law, institutions, and practices which influence, and are influenced by, economic relations. Political influences and effects are the most obvious, and probably the most important, of these extraeconomic aspects.

The international economy is a reflection of the political division of the world into separate, sovereign states, each of which has its own set of institutions and policies. National boundaries constitute obstacles in various ways to international economic relations. The most obvious of these obstacles are tariffs and quantitative restrictions on the movement across national frontiers of goods and services and limitations on the movements of persons and of capital. Less direct but nonetheless potent barriers exist by reason of separate national monetary systems, giving rise to the complex problems of international monetary relations. The not infrequent use of economic measures as instruments of political policies adds to the special difficulties which beset foreign trade and factor movements.

The vitality of the forces underlying international economic re-

---

[3] See P. N. Rosenstein-Rodan, "International Aid for Underdeveloped Countries," *Review of Economics and Statistics*, May, 1961, p. 118.

lations is attested to by the large volume and continuing growth of these relations notwithstanding the obstacles encountered. Evidently, the benefits of trade and factor movements are great. Recognition of this fact has led to an increasing degree of international cooperation to reduce the barriers to economic relations among countries. Various agreements and institutions relating to trade and investment and monetary arrangements have considerably changed the environment within which international economic relations are conducted. Nevertheless, as compared to interregional relations within national boundaries, international economic relations are subject to a special set of restraints.

On the other side of the coin, international political relations are strongly influenced by economic relations. Politics may be defined in terms of *power* relationships, while economics deals with the use of scarce resources. A major ingredient of power is command over resources. The dominant power position of the United States and of the Soviet Union, and the potential threat posed by Communist China, are the most obvious examples of the relationship between command over resources, actual or potential, and international politics.

The economic strength of a country, however, depends upon more than the mere physical inventory of its resources; it also depends upon how efficiently its resources are employed. International economic relations provide the opportunity significantly to increase the efficiency of resource use. There is, therefore, a strong motive for countries to construct an international political framework within which economic relations with other countries are fostered. Friendly and stable political relations promote economic relations; beneficial economic relations encourage friendly and stable political relations.

The mutually supporting interconnections between international economics and politics are most sharply brought out by regional movements toward economic integration, of which the European Common Market is the outstanding example. The Common Market in Europe had its origins in the desire to achieve political integration. Rather than approaching the latter goal directly, European statesmen concluded that it would be more feasible to proceed indirectly via the route of economic integration. The thinking was that if countries become closely tied together economically they can hardly avoid parallel political cooperation. Whether this is an entirely valid conclusion remains to be seen, though the presumption in its favor is strong.

THE TASKS OF THEORY

Economics has its ultimate justification in providing guidelines for rational and intelligent policy making. The prime prerequisite for fulfilling this function is to find a satisfactory explanation of observed phenomena—the why's and wherefore's in the case at hand of international economic relations. Unless the causes and effects of international trade and factor movements are known, the bases for policy formation, which requires prediction of the effects of various measures, would be extremely weak and shaky.

More specifically, the major and basic questions in international economics which need to be answered are as follows:

1. Why do international specialization and exchange and, parallel to this, international movements of labor and capital, occur?
2. What determines which commodities and services and factors of production will be exported and imported by each country and in what quantities?
3. What economic effects follow from free international trade and factor movements? In particular, how are the efficiency and structure of national economies and the distribution of real income affected?

Part I of this book is devoted to finding answers to these questions, calling for an examination of the so-called "pure theory" of international trade.

Part II is devoted to what might be called "deviations from the pure model of international trade." This would be an unnecessarily formidable title, however, for what are, after all, rather commonplace phenomena. As in all sciences, the pure theory of international economics makes certain simplifying assumptions; one is that there are no artificial barriers erected by either governments or business firms to the free flow of goods and services from country to country. In actuality, however, this assumption is unrealistic. National governments impose tariffs and quotas against foreign goods and sometimes even interfere with the export of home-produced goods and services. And business firms sometimes are able, either because of their economic position in an industry or as a result of collusive agreement, to interfere with the free flow of goods and services, such as would occur in fully competitive markets. The reasons for and consequences of such actions by either governments or private groups are an important part of international economics.

A third major part of international economics has to do with the *mechanisms* rather than the substance of intercountry economic relations. Especially important in this connection are international monetary relations. Since each country has its own monetary system, what are the instruments for making payments from one country to another? Where and how does a country obtain the means of making international payments? What are the causes and the effects of an imbalance between a country's current international payments and current international receipts? A description of institutional arrangements, as well as a theoretical analysis, is required to answer these important questions, and both are provided in Part III of this book.

A related task of international economics, also undertaken in Part III, is to analyze the processes that bring the national economies of different countries into a set of balanced international relationships. In view of the political right of each country to determine its own policies and the consequent possibility of conflicts in national economic policies, the problems of keeping equilibrium relationships internationally or of restoring such relationships, if disturbed, are of prime importance.

Finally, in Part IV we discuss the international economics of the special problems of less-developed countries.

RECOMMENDED READING

BROWN, A. J. *Introduction to the World Economy*. New York: Rinehart & Co., Inc., 1959.

ELLIOTT, WILLIAM Y. (ed.). *The Political Economy of American Foreign Policy*. New York: Holt, Rinehart & Winston, Inc., 1955.

LEKACHMAN, ROBERT (ed.). *National Policy for Economic Welfare at Home and Abroad,* chaps. v and vi. New York: Doubleday & Co., Inc., 1955.

MYRDAL, GUNNAR. *An International Economy*. New York: Harper & Row, Publishers, 1956.

The student is well advised to become familiar early with the following principal primary sources of international trade and monetary statistics.

Prewar Data

LEAGUE OF NATIONS, Geneva. *International Trade Statistics.*
————. *Review of World Trade.*
————. *Industrialization and Foreign Trade.* 1945.
————. *International Statistical Yearbook.*
————. *The Network of World Trade.* 1942.

Postwar Data

FOOD AND AGRICULTURAL ORGANIZATION (FAO), Rome. *Yearbook of Food and Agricultural Statistics.*
————. *Yearbook of Forest Products Statistics.*
INTERNATIONAL LABOR OFFICE (ILO), Geneva. *Yearbook of Labor Statistics.*
INTERNATIONAL MONETARY FUND, Washington. *Balance of Payments Yearbook.* Issued annually, with loose-leaf sections issued more frequently.
————. *International Financial Statistics.* Issued monthly. The best source of current data on trade, exchange rates, production, and other economic and financial conditions for the principal trading countries of the world.
UNITED NATIONS, NEW YORK. *Demographic Yearbook.*
————. *Monthly Bulletin of Statistics.*
————. *Commodity Trade Statistics.*
————. *Yearbook of International Trade Statistics.*
————, jointly with the INTERNATIONAL MONETARY FUND and the INTERNATIONAL BANK FOR RECONSTRUCTION AND DEVELOPMENT. *Direction of International Trade.*
————. *World Economic Report.* Economic surveys are also made for various regions of the world—Europe, Latin America, and Asia and the Far East.
U.S. DEPARTMENT OF COMMERCE, Washington, D.C. *Foreign Commerce Yearbook.*
————. BUREAU OF THE CENSUS. *Historical Statistics of the United States, 1789–1945.* 1949.
————. *Statistical Abstract of the United States.*
————. *Survey of Current Business,* monthly. Best source of current data on the international economic and monetary transactions of the United States. Special supplements are occasionally issued on particular subjects, such as *Balance of Payments of the United States, 1919–1953* (1954) .

————. *The United States in the World Economy.* 1949.

————. *Foreign Commerce Weekly.*

STUDY QUESTIONS

1. See how many of the items which you consume that you can separate out according to their origin as provided by the local, national, and international economy.
2. Identify the major categories of international economic relations.
3. Define the average propensity to import and assess its significance as a measure of the importance of foreign trade to a country.
4. Explain the low propensity to import of the United States and of the Soviet Union.
5. What is meant by the statement in the text that cutting off foreign trade would have a "bottleneck" effect on national economies?
6. Why is the cost, rather than the physical capability of producing goods and services, the critical consideration in determining a country's imports?
7. How does the existence of separate national states affect the world economy?
8. Distinguish between international political and international economic relations.
9. Give some concrete examples of the mutual interrelationships between international political and international economic relations.
10. Review the basic questions with which international economics as a field of study is concerned.

PART I

The Theory and Empirical Foundations of International Trade and Factor Movements

The five chapters which follow seek to lay the theoretical foundations and describe the empirical basis of international trade and factor movements. While these chapters are perhaps the most difficult in the book, they are essential to an understanding of the fundamental causes and effects of international economic relations and give indispensable background for the subsequent analysis.

Chapter	THE PURE THEORY OF
2	INTERNATIONAL TRADE

The so-called "pure theory" of international trade seeks to explain the underlying causes and major effects of the international exchange of goods and services. The theory is based on certain simplifying assumptions, and relates to "real" economic variables, abstracting from any independent influences which may be produced in actuality by monetary factors. (The role of monetary factors is considered in Part III of this book.)

It may reasonably be asked why a separate theory of trade is necessary or desirable. The question is all the more pointed in view of the essential similarity between the trade that occurs among the various regions of any given national economy and that which occurs among countries.

INTERREGIONAL AND INTERNATIONAL TRADE

The exchange of goods and services is one of the most salient characteristics of economic life. Only if economic activities were compartmentalized into self-sufficient entities at the individual or family level would there be no exchange. In the modern economy, the exchange of goods and services is extensive at nearly all levels of economic activity. The individual worker, for example, in helping to produce a good for which he collects wages that are spent in the marketplace in effect exchanges his output for the output of hundreds or thousands of other producers. This type of exchange is the kind that is encompassed in the ordinary general theory of value that students encounter in their first course in microeconomics.

At another "higher" level, a huge volume of trade occurs among the *regions* of the typical national economy—such as, for example, the exchange of the manufactured goods of the northern and eastern parts of the United States for the agricultural products of the southern and western areas. With respect to such *interregional* trade, the ordinary general theory of microeconomics remains valid but requires some extensions and modifications to make it applicable.

The chief difference between economic relations within a given region and such relations among different regions is that in the former there is a single, integrated market for each good and productive factor, whereas in the latter markets are to some extent separated. Indeed, this is precisely the basis for defining the boundaries of economic regions.

Separate markets do not necessarily mean isolated markets. On the contrary, there may be a vast amount of contacts among markets, as is typically the case in interregional and international trade. The major sign of market separation is the presence of differences in prices. In a single market, there is a single price for any given good or service.

Two reasons may be cited for differences in interregional prices. The first is transportation costs owing to spatial separation. For some products, the costs of transport are so high, relatively to their value, that they do not ordinarily move across regional boundaries. Such products are called "local" or "home" goods, as distinguished from traded goods. Traded goods move across regional boundaries notwithstanding costs of transport, but the latter may then be responsible for interregional differences in their prices.

A second important reason for interregional price differences lies in the partial or complete immobility of the factors of production. Product prices reflect factor prices. If given productive factors have the same prices in different regions, there is a strong presumption (though no absolute certainty) that given products will have the same prices. A particular factor will tend to have the same price throughout any area within which the factor is completely mobile. If, however, there are obstacles to factor movement from one area to another—because of costs of moving, psychological or cultural impediments, and so on—factor prices in the two areas may differ. In other words, interregional factor immobility leads to the separation of factor markets, just as barriers to the interregional movement of goods results in the separation of goods markets.

The separation of markets because of spatial distance and factor immobility accounts for the need to modify and extend the theory of the "domestic" economy—based on the assumption of single, in-

tegrated goods and factor markets—to render it applicable to inter-
market relations.

If a special theory of *interregional* economic relations is justified,
the justification clearly extends to *international* economic relations.
The same forces causing the separation of regional markets are responsible for the separation of national markets. If there is a difference between the two cases, it is mainly one of degree rather than
of kind. Transport costs are frequently, though not always, greater
internationally than interregionally, depending upon, among other
things, the distances involved. The obstacles to factor movements,
however, are usually considerably greater internationally than interregionally, not only because of national controls but also because
of greater psychological and cultural impediments.

The essential similarity between interregional and international
economic relations has resulted in the development of a theory of
trade which, in its most general and abstract form, is equally applicable to regions and countries. If one confines himself to the basic
economic essence, there is no difference in principle between trade
across regional boundaries within countries and trade across national boundaries. After all, national boundaries are only imaginary
lines drawn on the basis of historical, political considerations. As
such, these boundaries have no economic significance.

When one moves from abstract theory to real-world relations, of
course, political boundaries emerge as the sources of special operating problems in international economic relations not normally
found in interregional relations. Especially important are the artificial barriers to international trade which national governments impose, and the problems created by the existence of separate national
monetary and fiscal systems. Both these special aspects of international economic relations we ignore at first, but they are given all
the attention they deserve in the theory of commercial policy (in
Part II of the book) and in the theory of international monetary
relations (in Part III).

One last remark introductory to the study of the pure theory of
trade remains to be made. Even though, as we have noted, national
economies in fact are each composed of separate economic regions,
to isolate the phenomena of international trade and simplify the
analysis we shall treat national economies as if each were a single
economic region. This fits in, of course, with the conclusion reached
above that the pure theory of international trade is identical with
the theory of interregional trade.

THE PROXIMATE CAUSE OF TRADE

If you were to ask an importer why he purchases a certain product abroad instead of domestically, he would probably answer that the product can be obtained at a lower price in the foreign country than at home. Assuming the existence of a market system and the profit motive, the proximate cause of trade is rather obviously the presence of international price differences which provide private traders with the opportunity to make a profit. To stop the analysis at this point, however, would be an example of a trivial and superficial "theory" of trade. Our task is to go behind differences in international prices and find the underlying causes of these differences. To make the exploration as simple as possible, it is proposed to proceed by stages. In the first stage, we shall see that immediately behind international differences in *absolute* prices lie differences in *relative* prices. It is to this first proposition that we now turn.

Relative Price Differences

Absolute price comparisons refer to those made in terms of a common monetary unit. If the price of good X is $1 and of good Y $2, X is absolutely cheaper, as measured in terms of dollars, than Y. By contrast, *relative* prices are measured in terms of each other, rather than expressed in a common unit of measurement. In the above example, the price of X relative to that of Y is 1:2 (and of Y relative to X, 2:1).

Absolute price comparisons cannot be made if different prices are stated in different monetary units, unless there is some way of converting all the prices into a common monetary unit. As we shall see presently, the foreign exchange market provides a way of making such conversions.

Relative price comparisons, on the other hand, do not require the presence of a common monetary unit or means of converting different monetary units onto a common base. For example, if the prices of goods X and Y are, respectively, $1 and $2 in the United States and 5 francs and 15 francs in France, it can be seen that the relative price of X in terms of Y is 1:2 in the United States and 1:3 in France, and that therefore X is *relatively* cheaper in France and Y is *relatively* cheaper in the United States.

In investigating the origins of foreign trade, we cannot point to international differences in absolute prices, even though these are the immediate basis for importing and exporting decisions, for until trade has actually begun, there is no way of making absolute price comparisons across national monetary boundaries. But *relative* price comparisons *can* be made even when countries are in a hypothetical state of pretrade isolation. What needs to be shown is that pretrade relative price differences internationally constitute the basis for the emergence of absolute price differences, hence to trading relations. A very simple model will suffice for the demonstration.

Assume that there are only two countries, the United States and Argentina, each of which produces both of only two standardized goods, cloth and beef. Suppose that in pretrade isolation the price of cloth is $4 (per yard) in the United States and 200 pesos in Argentina, while the price of beef (per pound) is $1 in the United States and 20 pesos in Argentina. This information is summarized in tabular form as follows:

	United States	*Argentina*
Cloth........................	$4.00	P.200
Beef........................	1.00	20

No comparison of absolute prices between the two countries is possible as yet. It is not legitimate, for example, to conclude that either or both products are absolutely cheaper in the United States because it takes fewer dollars than pesos to buy them, for these currencies are different units of measuring price and there is no established relationship between them. Were Argentina to issue a new currency, converting old pesos into new ones at a ratio of 100 old for one new, both products would then sell for fewer pesos than dollars, even though no change in the real situation has occurred.[1] This has illustrated the futility of attempting direct absolute price comparisons.

Fortunately, however, it is easy to compare relative prices. Based on the hypothetical figures given above, the ratio of the price of cloth to that of beef is 4:1 in the United States and 10:1 in Argentina. Hence, the relative price of cloth is lower in the United States

---

[1] France performed precisely the kind of operation referred to in 1960, exchanging 1 new franc for 100 old ones. The consequence was only to lower all prices to 1/100 their previous levels.

than in Argentina, while the relative price of beef is lower in Argentina than in the United States.

It would not be difficult to show how private traders would have a motive to engage in barter deals, with U.S. cloth being exchanged directly for Argentina beef. But it is closer to reality and more revealing of other important aspects of trade to let money serve its usual function of medium of exchange.

In order for traders to deal in monetary rather than barter terms, a connection between the dollar and peso must be created. The connection is provided if a *rate of exchange* between the two currencies is established. A rate of exchange is the price of a foreign currency unit expressed in domestic currency units. If there were a rate of exchange between the dollar and the peso at which traders in each country could purchase the currency of the other, a direct and absolute price comparison for each good could be made.

Converting Relative into Absolute Price Differences: The Rate of Exchange

One way of establishing an exchange rate is for the governments concerned to agree upon monetary arrangements under which foreign currencies are bought and sold to private traders at some specified price. However, in our present model we want to exclude government and confine ourselves to the assumption that a laissez-faire market price system is operative. In this case, whether or not an exchange rate is established depends entirely upon whether or not a private *market* for foreign exchange develops in which an equilibrium price emerges.

In order for a free-market price for anything to come into existence, there must be some price range over which there are both demanders and suppliers, so that at some particular price the total quantity of the item in question demanded is equal to the total quantity offered for sale (supplied). Now let us see how these conditions are fulfilled with respect to dollars and pesos, given the assumptions made above as to the pretrade prices of cloth and beef in the two countries.

A foreign exchange market in dollars and pesos will tend to develop in each of the countries, but we need observe the market in only one, say, the United States, since whatever conclusions arrived at will be equally applicable to the other country's market. The immediate question, then, is whether there will emerge a market demand and supply for pesos in the United States.

Looking at the demand side first, we observe that private traders will want to buy pesos if they can be obtained at any price (rate of exchange) *less* than 5 cents per peso. Why? Simply because in this case beef is *absolutely* cheaper in Argentina than in the United States. For example, suppose that pesos could be purchased at a rate of exchange of 4 cents. The Argentina price for beef of 20 pesos is then the equivalent of $0.80, compared to the United States price of $1. Traders would want to buy pesos in order to be able to buy beef to import into the United States.

Turning next to the supply side of the foreign exchange market, we note that private traders would be happy to *sell* pesos at any rate of exchange *above* 2 cents per peso. The reason? At any such rate cloth could be exported to Argentina, sold for pesos, the pesos in turn sold for dollars, and a profit realized. For example, if the exchange rate were 3 cents per peso, a yard of cloth costing the exporter $4 would yield 200 pesos which could be sold for $6 on the exchange market.

Combining the demand and supply sides, we observe that there is a common range in the dollar exchange rate on the peso over which there are quantities of pesos both demanded and supplied—the required condition for the emergence of an *equilibrium rate of exchange.*

The equilibrium rate of exchange is the particular dollar price of pesos at which the total quantity of pesos demanded is equal to the total quantity supplied. This is the rate that will in fact tend to prevail under competitive conditions.[2]

We know that the equilibrium rate of exchange in our example must lie somewhere between 2 cents and 5 cents per peso.[3] Where exactly the rate will ultimately tend to settle will be considered later. The main point now is this: at any rate of exchange within the range 2 cents–5 cents per peso, the *absolute* price of cloth is lower in the United States than in Argentina, while the *absolute* price of beef is lower in Argentina than in the United States. Hence, traders are motivated to import beef from Argentina and to export cloth from the United States. The beginning proposition that *relative* price differences in pretrade isolation become differences in

---

[2] The ordinary law of supply and demand studied in principles of economics is the basis for this conclusion.

[3] The student is invited to work out the reason why the rate of exchange cannot, initially at least, be outside the range. *Hint:* Assume that the rate is outside the indicated range, for example, 6 cents per peso or 1 cent per peso. Now see whether there would be *both* a demand *and* a supply of pesos at the assumed rate.

absolute prices upon the opening of trade relations is thus illustrated by our example.

A corollary to this proposition is that if relative prices are the *same* internationally in pretrade isolation, no trade will occur. The reader can convince himself that this is the case by assuming the same pretrade relative prices of cloth and beef in the United States and Argentina (say $4 and $1 in the United States, 200 pesos and 50 pesos in Argentina for cloth and beef, respectively) and observing that there is no rate of exchange at which there are both a demand and supply of pesos.

As indicated earlier, we want to know not only under what conditions international trade will occur but also what determines its pattern. In the hypothetical case discussed in the preceding pages, a specific pattern of trade was established: the United States exported cloth and imported beef, Argentina exported beef and imported cloth. Was this an arbitrary pattern of trade or a necessary result of the assumed price data? If it was the latter, what is the general principle involved?

First, the pattern of trade we deduced was *not* arbitrary. Given the assumed pretrade price data, it would not be possible at any equilibrium rate of exchange for the absolute price of beef to be lower in the United States than in Argentina or for the absolute price of cloth to be lower in Argentina than in the United States. In verifying this conclusion, the student need only remember that the equilibrium rate of exchange on the peso must fall within the limits of from 2 to 5 cents.

Cloth becomes the absolutely cheaper good in the United States and beef the absolutely cheaper good in Argentina because each was the respective country's *relatively* cheaper product before the opening of trade relations. The general principle, then, is as follows:

> *A country tends to export the product the relative price of which is lower in pretrade isolation at home than abroad, and to import the product the relative price of which is higher at home than abroad.*

Comparative Cost Differences

We have seen that if the relative prices of goods differ from one country to another in economic isolation, free and competitive market forces can be expected to establish a rate of exchange between the currencies of the countries at which absolute prices of the goods differ, thereby leading to trade. The analysis could be halted at this point, with the conclusion that the cause of international trade is relative price differences in isolation. However, we would have to admit that the probe is shallow, penetrating only slightly below the surface and leaving unexplored the question of what accounts for pretrade relative price differences. To arrive at a more fundamental understanding of the reasons for trade, we must explain the reasons for relative price differences.

In purely competitive markets, which we are assuming throughout the present discussion, the equilibrium price of a good is equal to its marginal (and average) cost of production. Relative prices are therefore reflections of relative costs, so that the general principle stated above in terms of relative prices may be restated in terms of relative—or *comparative*—costs as follows:

> *A country tends to export the product the comparative cost of which is lower in pretrade isolation at home than abroad, and to import the product the comparative cost of which is higher at home than abroad.*

As thus stated, the principle is in the form known traditionally in economics as the *law of comparative advantage,* where "advantage" is based on costs.

We have now completed the second stage in the explanation of trade. Behind absolute price differences lie relative or comparative cost differences, giving each country an advantage in certain products and disadvantage in others. The third stage in the search for the basis of trade leads us into the underlying causes of international differences in comparative costs.

THE UNDERLYING CAUSES OF TRADE: CLASSICAL THEORY

The classical theory held that the value of a good is determined by the amount of labor time required to produce it. Within a given market, if good X requires per unit of output 10 hours of labor, while good Y requires per unit of output 30 hours of labor, the value (and price) of Y will be three times the price of X.

The British economist David Ricardo (1772–1823) applied this labor theory of value in his formulation of the doctrine of comparative cost to explain international trade. The value of goods is determined in each country by the amount of labor required to produce them, but this need not be the same in different countries. Labor may be more productive in one country than in another, so that different amounts of labor are required to produce given goods. However—and here is where Ricardo made his major contribution to trade theory—it is not absolute but *comparative* differences in labor costs that underlie international trade.

The doctrine of comparative cost differences as the basis for trade is, as we have seen, still as valid today as it was in Ricardo's time. But Ricardo's explanation of comparative cost differences is *not* generally accepted today.

The first reason is the modern rejection of the labor theory of value. While labor is nearly always the largest component of cost, it is rarely the sole component. Output is the joint product of several different factors of production rather than of labor alone. This would not matter in determining relative costs provided that other factors of production were always combined with labor in the same proportions. An American economist, Frank Taussig, writing about a century after Ricardo, believed this to be a sufficiently valid generalization to save the labor theory of value. However, few economists today would agree.

A similar objection to the labor theory of value is its assumption that labor in each country is homogeneous, so that comparisons of the labor time required for the production of various goods yield a true measure of their relative values. In fact, labor (as well as other factors) is not homogeneous; it consists of numerous qualitatively different subgroups, known as "noncompeting" groups. Again, Taussig attempted to circumvent this objection by postulating a similar hierarchy of noncompeting groups in different countries, leaving the *relative* wages of various groups about the same in all countries. Whether this is true is an empirical question that has not been settled. Until it is, the assumption must be treated with extreme caution.

Finally, the clinching objection to the labor theory of value is that a much better theory, free of the chief weaknesses noted above, has evolved since Ricardo's day. The modern theory of value takes into account on the cost side all factors of production, not just labor alone, and defines cost in terms of sacrificed alternatives instead of in terms of the absolute quantity of inputs required in production. In the minds of most economists today, this concept of *opportunity* cost is much more significant and relevant than the notion of costs as equated to labor time.

There is a second objection to the classical theory of trade: it never really explains why comparative cost differences exist. If it requires relatively less labor to produce a given good in one country than in another, why is this? The answer of the classical economists is vague and general, put usually in terms of differences in economic "climate." But one must be more specific than this if the fundamental basis for trade is to be meaningfully identified. The modern theory at least boldly makes the effort to identify the specific bases of trade.

THE UNDERLYING CAUSES OF TRADE: MODERN THEORY

As mentioned above, in modern thinking opportunity cost is the most meaningful and significant concept of cost, and it is a concept which lends itself readily to analysis of the causes of trade. We have seen that a basis for trade exists if in pretrade isolation comparative costs differ internationally. Cast in terms of opportunity costs, the equivalent statement is that a basis for trade exists if opportunity costs differ internationally.

Different opportunity costs imply different comparative costs. This is because opportunity costs are defined, as are comparative costs, in relativistic terms. The opportunity cost of good X is the amount of good Y that must be sacrificed in order to produce X. Say that the output of Y must be reduced by two units in order to release the resources required to produce an extra unit of X. In this case, the marginal opportunity cost of X is $2Y$. In a perfectly functioning price system, such as we are assuming to exist, the market price and money cost of X would be twice that of Y, so that the comparative cost of X is $2Y$, the same as opportunity cost. Hence, if opportunity costs differ internationally, so too do comparative costs, and the basis for trade is present.

Our objective now is to discover what may account for international differences in opportunity costs according to modern theory.

Equilibrium in Isolation

It is convenient to begin our search by observing the equilibrium conditions prevailing in each country in pretrade isolation. To keep the analysis manageable at a simple level, we assume that there are only two goods, X and Y. It is also assumed that a perfectly functioning, competitive market system is operative in each country.

In each country in pretrade equilibrium, the marginal opportunity cost of X in terms of Y (and, reciprocally, of Y in terms of X) is at a certain level. (*Marginal* opportunity cost is the *additional* cost of producing one *extra* unit of output.) In equilibrium, the relative market prices of the goods are equal to their marginal opportunity costs, and at these prices the total quantity of each good demanded by consumers is just equal to the quantity being produced.

These equilibrium conditions are easily illustrated graphically, and in a manner that will prove helpful to our subsequent analysis.[4] The basic device used is the *production transformation curve,*

FIGURE 2.1

THE PRODUCTION TRANSFORMATION CURVE

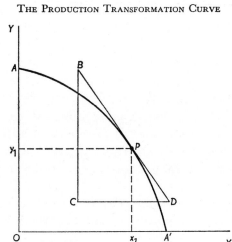

familiar to students from their first course in economics, where the curve usually goes under the name of *production possibilities curve.*

As will be recalled, the production transformation or possibilities curve shows the alternative combinations of output which an economy is capable of producing with its given stock of resources fully employed in the technically most efficient manner. The *slope* of the curve at any point measures the *marginal opportunity costs* of production when the output combination is at that point. To illustrate, refer to Figure 2.1.

AA' is the assumed transformation curve of country A. Each

---

[4] The graphical techniques employed in the remainder of this chapter and in the next chapter are extended in a complete graphical model in the Appendix to Chapter 3.

point on the curve represents a possible output combination of goods X and Y. At point P, for example, $O(x_1)$ of X and $O(y_1)$ of Y are produced. The marginal opportunity cost of X at point P is measured by the slope of the curve at that point. The slope of the curve is given by the ratio of the vertical to the horizontal distances covered by any movement along the straight-line *tangent* to the curve. In Figure 2.1, BD is the line tangent at point P, and has a slope equal to BC/CD. This ratio represents the marginal opportunity cost of X, for it shows the rate at which good Y (measured vertically) must be sacrificed as the output of X (measured horizontally) is increased. Conversely, the reciprocal of the slope—CD/BC—measures the marginal opportunity cost of Y, since it shows the rate at which X must be sacrificed as the output of Y is increased. (The slope of the curve is a valid measure of marginal opportunity costs only for very small changes in output, for each point on the curve has a different slope.)

If P is an equilibrium output point, the slope of tangent line BD measures not only marginal opportunity costs but also the *relative prices* of X and Y. For example, suppose that the ratio BC/CD equals 1.5. Then we know that the marginal opportunity cost of X is $1.5Y$ (and the marginal opportunity cost of Y is $2/3X$). For equilibrium to prevail, the price of X must therefore be 1.5 times that of Y.

To determine whether there is a basis for trade, the same procedure as above is followed for country B. The necessary condition is that pretrade equilibrium marginal opportunity costs and relative prices of X and Y are different from those in country A. In diagrammatic terms, the slope of B's transformation curve at the pretrade equilibrium output point must be different from A's if trade is to occur.

Opportunity Cost Differences

If, as we have concluded, trade is in response to pretrade international differences in opportunity costs, the next question to pursue is what accounts for these differences. The clue to the search for the answer is provided by the above discussion. In each country, opportunity costs are determined by the conjunction of two sets of forces: those determining the *shape* of the transformation curve and those determining the equilibrium *location* on the curve. *Differences in opportunity costs, therefore, arise as a result of either dif-*

ferently shaped transformation curves or different equilibrium lo-cations on the curves, or both. (As we shall see, however, it is possible for differences in one respect to be offset by opposite differences in the other respect.) Our investigation shall proceed accordingly, with the shape of transformation curves being considered first.

The Shape of Transformation Curves

A transformation curve is the expression of the conditions of production in an economy. Its shape (and position) are determined by the amounts and kinds of resources available and, given the state of technology, the technical possibilities of converting the output of one good into the output of another good through reallocating the given resources. It follows that if all countries possessed identically the same quantities and kinds of resources and produced under identical technical conditions, they would have identical transformation curves. Differences in the shapes of transformation curves must therefore be attributed to differences in one or more of these conditions.

Factor Proportions

Let us first consider how the technical conditions of production affect the shape of the transformation curve. Following this we shall look at the influence of resource supplies.

Technical conditions of production are revealed in the *production function,* which is the relationship between factor inputs—land, labor, capital—and output of the good. The characteristic of the production function centrally important for the purpose at hand relates to the proportion in which inputs are employed in producing a good.

Usually a good can be produced by any one of numerous different combinations of factors. This is because, within limits, different factors can be substituted for each other in the production process. However, the rate at which any factor can be substituted for another without reducing output *diminishes* the more extensive the substitution is. As a consequence, ever-increasing quantities of the factor being substituted for another are required to maintain any given level of output as the substitution proceeds.

While the substitutability of factors permits a possible wide

range of choice among alternative technically feasible factor proportions, the economically most *efficient* (least-cost) combination depends upon relative factor prices. The relatively cheaper a given
factor is, the greater is the proportion in which it is used in the factor mix.[5]

With relative factor prices given, different goods usually have
different least-cost factor proportions, owing to different production
functions. Accordingly, commodities may be classified on the basis
of the factor used in the relatively greatest proportion. For example, if in producing X and Y each in the most efficient manner the
ratio of labor to capital (L/K) is always greater for X than for Y at
given factor prices, we call X a relatively *labor-intensive* good and
Y a relatively *capital-intensive* good.

With the above remarks as background we are enabled to arrive
at a fundamental proposition concerning the shapes of transformation curves:

> *Different factor intensities for different goods give rise to in-*
> *creasing marginal opportunity costs and a concave transforma-*
> *tion curve. The same factor intensities for different goods lead*
> *to constant marginal opportunity costs and a linear transfor-*
> *mation curve.*

Figure 2.1 is an example of a *concave* transformation curve—
that is, a curve bowed outward as viewed from the origin. Such a
curve reflects *increasing* marginal opportunity costs. As shown earlier, marginal opportunity costs at any point on the curve are measured by the slope of the curve at that point. It will be observed
that as the output of X is increased (and of Y decreased), the output point moves down the curve to *increasingly steeper sections,*
indicating increasing marginal opportunity costs of X. Conversely,
as movement occurs along the curve in an upward direction, signifying the increasing output of Y, the slope becomes less and less
steep. This, too, indicates increasing marginal opportunity costs for
Y, since the latter are measured by the *reciprocal* of the curve's
slope.

Let us return now to the proposition that different factor intensities for goods lead to increasing marginal opportunity costs and a
concave transformation curve. To see why, suppose that the output

---

[5] The general principle for achieving the least-cost factor combination is that the
marginal rate of technical substitution of factors be equalized with the ratio of factor prices.

of Y, a capital-intensive good, is reduced by one unit. Labor and capital are released from the Y industry (for convenience we assume that these are the only factors employed) and transferred to the X industry. However, the proportion of labor to capital released from the Y industry is smaller than the proportion used in the labor-intensive X industry. This means that there must be some substitution of capital for labor in the X industry, and the extent of this substitution becomes greater the greater is the transfer of factors from Y to X. But capital has a diminishing effectiveness as a substitute for labor, with the consequence that increasingly larger reductions in the output of Y are required to achieve *equal* increments in the output of X as the transfer of resources progresses. Increasing marginal opportunity costs therefore prevails. The same phenomenon, operating in reverse with labor substituted for capital, causes the marginal opportunity cost of Y to rise as its output is increased.

We pause briefly to note an implication of the above analysis: if factor proportions were always the *same* in the X and Y industries, opportunity costs would tend to be *constant*. Graphically, this would be shown by a *linear* (straight-line) transformation curve—that is, a line with constant slope. However, empirical observation clearly reveals that different goods are normally subject to different production functions with respect to factor proportions, so that we may henceforth omit further reference to the constant-opportunity cost model.[6]

The preceding discussion points to the conclusion that, owing to different production functions for different goods, transformation curves are normally concave. (The possibility of a curve being convex will be briefly examined at a later point in this chapter.) Since we are considering a given pair of goods, X and Y, does this mean that the transformation curve can be expected to have the same shape in country A as in country B, in the sense that for any given output combination the marginal opportunity costs are the same in the two countries? Even though the transformation curves are concave in both countries, they may still not be of identical shape in the sense indicated, for either of two reasons.

The first possibility is that production functions differ between countries, as well as between goods. If, for example, the production

---

[6] By contrast, the classical theory was based on the assumption of constant opportunity cost. This was the consequence of a one-factor (labor) model, in which case the issue of factor proportions, of course, does not arise.

function for X is different in country A from that in country B, and possibly also different in the two countries for good Y, this might well cause different slopes of the transformation curves at given relative output levels.

The second possibility has attracted more attention in the literature. Even if the production function for each good is the same in both countries (though different as between the two goods), the transformation curves will nevertheless be different *if relative factor supplies are not the same in the two countries*. Since relative factor supplies are obviously and markedly different as between countries in the real world, this is a highly relevant proposition in trade theory, deserving elaboration.

Relative Factor Supplies

Suppose that country A, as compared to country B, has relatively a large supply of labor and small stock of capital. We may then designate A as a relatively *labor-abundant* country and B as a relatively *capital-abundant* country, irrespective of the *absolute* size of their factor supplies.

Now assume as before that good X is a relatively *labor-intensive* product, good Y a relatively *capital-intensive* product. This means, as we saw previously, that the proportion of labor to capital is always greater in the production of X than in the production of Y. As a consequence, the labor-abundant country, A, will be able, as compared to country B, to produce relatively more of the labor-intensive product, X, than the capital-intensive product Y. In diagrammatic terms, the production transformation curve of country A will be stretched out relatively farther on the X-axis and be relatively shorter on the Y-axis than the curve for country B. This is illustrated in Figure 2.2, where AA' is the transformation curve of country A and BB' is that of country B. It is clear from the figure that, *for any given output combination*, the marginal opportunity cost of X is lower in A than in B. Along any ray from the origin, such as OR or OR', the ratio of the output of Y to that of X is the same. Hence, at A_1 on A's transformation curve and B_1 on B's curve, the output ratio is the same in the two countries. Similarly, points A_2 and B_2 on the ray OR' represent the same output ratio. In these and all other cases, it is observed that the slope of A's transformation curve is less than the corresponding point on B's, indicating lower marginal opportunity costs of X in country A.

The economics underlying this is as follows: *Because* A *is a labor-abundant country and* B *a capital-abundant country, wage rates, compared to the price of capital, will tend to be lower in* A *than in* B. The principle here is that, other things being equal, the greater the amount of other factors of production available for a given factor to work with, the greater is the marginal productivity of the factor. Under competitive conditions, the price of a factor service is equal in equilibrium to its marginal product. Thus, the marginal product of labor and the wage rate can be expected to be lower in *A* than in *B,* while the marginal product of capital and the

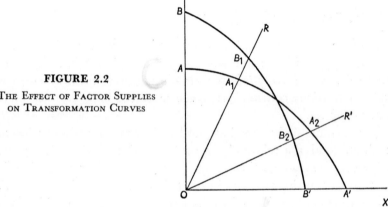

FIGURE 2.2

THE EFFECT OF FACTOR SUPPLIES
ON TRANSFORMATION CURVES

rental price of capital can be expected to be lower in *B* than in *A.* Now relatively low wage rates clearly cause relatively low costs of production for labor-intensive goods, while relatively low rental prices of capital lead to relatively low costs of production for capital-intensive goods. Hence, the relative abundance of labor in country *A* and of capital in country *B* imposes a bias in the direction of a comparative advantage for *A* in the labor-intensive commodity *X* and for *B* in the capital-intensive commodity *Y.*

In summary, *different factor intensities for commodities, in combination with different relative factor abundance, are responsible for concave transformation curves of different shapes.* In concluding this section, it must be emphasized that differences in *both* relative factor intensities and in factor supplies are required to produce this result. If factor intensities are the same for all commodities in all countries, differences in factor supplies (and hence in relative factor prices) will not be a cause of comparative cost differences, since all goods will have the same opportunity cost in each country, though different costs in different countries. In similar fashion, different factor intensities do not lead to comparative cost differences if relative factor supplies (and factor prices) are the same everywhere, since in this case the costs of commodities will bear the same proportion in all countries.

Pretrade Output Points

We noted some pages back that international differences in opportunity (and comparative) costs arise as a result of either differently shaped transformation curves or different equilibrium locations on the curves, or both. Having examined the possible reasons for differently shaped transformation curves, we need now to show the relevance of pretrade locations on the curves to opportunity cost differences.

In what we have come to regard as the normal case of concave transformation curves, the reason for the relevance of locations on the curves is readily apparent: marginal opportunity costs are different at different output points. The same thing is true if the curves are convex (attributable to economies of scale, discussed later). Only in the classical case of constant marginal opportunity costs, reflected in linear transformation curves, are output points irrelevant, since marginal costs are invariant with respect to output.

We have seen that with increasing costs and concave curves, there may be a bias in the direction of lower marginal opportunity costs for certain goods (one particular good in the two-goods model) in one country. Such is the case illustrated in Figure 2.2, where the transformation curve of country A is "stretched out" in comparison to that of country B, as the result of A's assumed relative labor-abundance in conjunction with the assumption that X is a labor-intensive good.

However, the bias imparted by different cost conditions can be either reenforced or counteracted by differences in pretrade output combinations. An extreme instance of the latter effect is illustrated in Figure 2.3, which reproduces the transformation curves of Figure 2.2

As noted previously, for the same output combination in A and B, marginal opportunity (and comparative) costs are lower in A

than in B. Suppose, however, that pretrade output is at point B_1 in country B and at point A_2 in country A. In this case, marginal opportunity costs are the *same*, as evidenced by the fact that the line B_1A_2 is tangent to both curves at the indicated output points.[7]

The question to be investigated now is what determines different locations on transformation curves. The question is equivalent to asking what determines the pretrade allocation of resources.

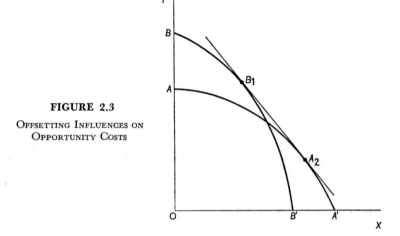

FIGURE 2.3

OFFSETTING INFLUENCES ON
OPPORTUNITY COSTS

In a competitive market system, the allocation of resources among alternative uses is determined by *demand*. If the demand for good X, compared to that for good Y, is relatively greater in country A than in country B, resources in A will be drawn more extensively into the X industry than is the case for B. If increasing costs prevail, this difference in demand conditions works in the direction of making the opportunity cost of X higher in A than in B, thus counteracting, partially or wholly, the bias on the production side toward lower opportunity costs of X in A. If the pattern of demand were the reverse, the effect would be the opposite: to increase the comparative cost advantage of A in good X.

The pattern of each country's demand is based principally upon

---

[7] The student is invited to demonstrate for himself that different output combinations can serve to *widen* opportunity cost differences. An extreme case—the polar opposite of that illustrated in Figure 2.3—is where different output combinations cause opportunity cost differences even though transformation curves are of identical shape.

the community's consumer preferences or tastes, and the level and distribution of real income. The demand for X may be relatively greater in A than in B because consumer tastes in A more heavily favor X while consumers in B have a stronger preference for Y. Or it could be that X is regarded as a necessity and Y as a luxury, and that the level of real income in A is lower than in B or less unequally distributed in A than in B. In short, demand would have a neutral role in determining comparative costs under increasing (or decreasing) cost conditions only if consumer preferences, real income levels, and the distribution of income happen to be such as to cause the same pattern of relative demand in different countries.

Summary of Modern Theory

It may be useful briefly to summarize the rather extended discussion of the modern theory of trade. Beginning with the proposition that trade occurs as the immediate result of relative price differences internationally, we proceeded to investigate the causes of the latter. Since in competitive equilibrium relative prices in each country equal marginal opportunity costs, our attention turned to the determinants of opportunity cost differences. In terms of the production transformation curve, we sought to explain the possible reasons for international differences in the slopes of the curves at pretrade equilibrium output points.

We found that transformation curves are normally concave, reflecting increasing opportunity cost conditions, owing to the presence of different factor intensities for different goods. But the presence of different relative factor supplies in different countries prevents transformation curves from having identical shapes. (International differences in production functions might also be responsible for this.) The relative abundance of a particular factor imparts a bias, on the production side, toward lower opportunity costs for the good relatively intensive in that factor.

However, actual opportunity costs depend not only upon the shapes of transformation curves but also upon output locations on the curves. The latter we found to be determined by demand conditions. International differences in the pattern of demand may either widen or narrow opportunity cost differences.

In capsule summary, the search for the underlying causes of trade leads to international differences in factor supplies or production functions, in conjunction with the pattern of demand.

The Heckscher-Ohlin Theorem

There is one rather unsatisfying aspect of the modern theory of trade as presented in the preceding pages: it is too general to allow more than a rather vague and amorphous impression of the underlying causes of trade in the real world. Technical conditions of production, as revealed in production functions, resource supplies, and the pattern of demand are all involved.

The mark of a "good" theory is its ability to explain a phenomenon in the most simple terms and with the fewest variables possible. Can the modern theory be simplified in this manner? Two Swedish economists, Eli Heckscher and Bertil Ohlin, attempted to do so several years ago in formulating a theorem bearing their names.[8]

The Heckscher-Ohlin theorem may be stated as follows:

> *Comparative cost differences are based on relative differences in countries' factor endowments; each country tends to have a comparative advantage in, and to export, those goods requiring in their production the factor in relative greatest supply in that country, and to have a comparative disadvantage in, and to import, those goods requiring in their production the factor in relative scarcest supply in that country.*

It will be noted that this theorem is simply a special case of the more general modern theory expounded in the preceding pages. For the special case to hold, two major assumptions are necessary: (*a*) the production function is the same in all countries for each good, though different in each country for different goods with respect to factor intensities, and (*b*) differences in demand conditions internationally do not offset the influence of production conditions on costs. Given these assumptions, the modern theory of trade leads to the Heckscher-Ohlin theorem as a special case, since the effect of the assumptions is to eliminate all determinants of comparative cost differences *except* for differences in relative factor supplies.

Because of its simplistic character, the Heckscher-Ohlin theorem is extremely attractive and has, until fairly recently, commanded wide support among economists. However, as we shall see in a later

---

[8] Ohlin, basing himself on earlier work by Heckscher, presented a complete statement of the theorem in his *Interregional and International Trade* (Cambridge, Mass.: Harvard University Press, 1933).

chapter, recent empirical studies have cast doubt upon the validity of the theorem. Though the outcome is far from being settled, the uncertainty generated warrants our examining the key assumptions of the theorem to see what consequences their possible invalidity would have.

Identical Production Functions

The assumption that each good is everywhere subject to the same production function seems reasonable, since input-output relationships are based on technical, physical characteristics of the production process which are presumably universal. However, technical knowledge is not necessarily the same or equally adaptable in all countries.

Whether or not in fact production functions are the same in different countries is an empirical question, and one study has reached the conclusion that they are not, at least in the countries and for the industries investigated.[9]

As we observed earlier, if different production functions exist, they are likely to have an independent effect on the shapes of different countries' transformation curves, and thus on comparative costs. Theoretically, therefore, differences in production functions must be admitted as one of the possible underlying bases of trade. (Caution: Keep in mind that it is differences *as between countries* for *given* goods referred to; differences in functions for different goods are not called in question.) Unfortunately, however, in the present state of knowledge no generalized conclusion on the specific influence of such differences on the actual pattern of trade can be reached.

Factor Proportions

A second key assumption of the theory of trade developed above relates to another aspect of production functions: that commodities can be unambiguously classified according to their factor intensity. This means, it will be recalled, that if a commodity is classified as, say, labor-intensive, the proportion of labor to other factor inputs used in producing the commodity is always greater than for those goods designated as capital-intensive or land-intensive. Such an as-

---

[9] K. Arrow, H. Chenery, B. Minhas, and R. Solow, "Capital-Labor Substitution and Economic Efficiency," *Review of Economics and Statistics,* August, 1961.

sumption is critical for the conclusion that relative factor supplies are the primary basis of comparative cost differences.

It is theoretically possible, however, for factor intensities to switch at some factor price relationships—a phenomenon called *factor reversal.* Factor reversal occurs if at some factor price ratio a good changes from being, say, labor-intensive to being capital-intensive. The reasons for such switching are too technical to be appropriately discussed here,[10] but its consequences for the theory of trade deserve to be pointed out. (It also has other important implications, especially for factor pricing, that will be discussed in due course.) If factor reversal occurs (it may occur once or more than once), there is no longer a definite relationship between comparative cost advantage and relative factor abundance. A labor-abundant country, for example, may have a comparative advantage in either labor-intensive or capital-intensive goods.

Factor reversal is clearly devastating to any theory of trade along the lines previously presented here, and especially to the Heckscher-Ohlin version. It may provide some comfort to note that factor reversal in some cases *cannot* occur, for technical reasons, and in other cases *will* not occur. The probability of factor reversal appears to be significant only when there are large differences between countries in relative factor prices. However, empirical evidence has been gathered that factor reversal *does* occur in particular cases,[11] and this should be sufficient to warn us that a contrary assumption risks conclusions of doubtful general validity.

Economies of Scale

A third assumption implicitly made in the discussion to this point is the absence of internal or external economies of scale. This may not always be a legitimate assumption, and we should be aware of the consequences when it is not.

The absence of internal economies of scale is essential for any model based on competition, for the presence of such economies leads to some kind of monopolistic market structure. (External

---

[10] The interested reader may consult Harry Johnson, "Factor Endowments, International Trade, and Factor Prices," *Manchester School of Economic and Social Studies,* September, 1957; reproduced as Chapter 1 in Johnson's *International Trade and Economic Growth* (Cambridge, Mass.: Harvard University Press, 1961.)

[11] See B. S. Minhas, "The Homohypallagic Production Function, Factor Intensity Reversals, and the Heckscher-Ohlin Theorem," *Journal of Political Economy,* April, 1962.

economies, however, are perfectly consistent with pure competition.) The effects of monopoly on trade will be considered in a different context in a later chapter, but it may be briefly noted with reference to the present subject that internal economies can be a source of comparative cost advantage.

Where internal economies of scale are present, the average and marginal costs of production decline as firms increase their scale of output. A country may therefore have a comparative cost advantage in industries where there are economies of scale because, owing to a larger market, the scale of production is larger than in other countries. A country with a large market for automobiles, for example, may have considerably lower costs of production than a small country with a limited market.

External economies of scale depend not upon the size of individual firms, but rather upon the size of a whole industry. Where present, such economies lead to *decreasing* marginal opportunity costs and *convex* transformation curves. Comparative cost differences are therefore as likely to be present in this case as when marginal opportunity costs are increasing and the transformation curves are concave. However, there is this difference: a comparative cost advantage may develop, or become greater, as a *result* of trade when decreasing costs prevail. Even if initially comparative cost differences were negligible, once trade opens up, each country may develop a cost advantage in a particular product in which there are economies of scale realizable through specializing in that product.

In sum, economies of scale are a potentially important cause of trade in addition to the other possible causes previously identified.

Demand Conditions

Finally, the assumption of no large international differences in the pattern of demand, especially important in the Heckscher-Ohlin theory, should be examined.

On the basis of the general principles determining economic values, the presumption against ignoring demand or assigning to it a subsidiary role is strong. Demand and supply jointly operate to determine price, with no a priori basis for imputing dominance to the one or the other. As we observed earlier, it is quite possible theoretically for differences in the pattern of demand to exert an influence on comparative costs *counter* to that exerted by relative factor endowments considered alone. If such happens to be the case, the explanation of trade according to the Heckscher-Ohlin theorem, of course, requires major amendment.

As with respect to many other issues, the proper settlement of the role of demand in trade theory can be made only on the basis of empirical evidence. Unfortunately, the available evidence is rather meager. What evidence we have suggests that whereas the pattern of demand tends to be rather similar between countries of similar per capita income levels, it varies widely between countries with large differences in per capita income.[12] We must conclude, therefore, that the more general theory earlier presented, in which demand was admitted into the model, is safer, even though more complicated, than the Heckscher-Ohlin theorem.

SUMMARY AND CONCLUSIONS

The main thrust of this chapter has been to identify the chief possible bases of international trade and the determinants of its pattern, mainly in the context of modern theory. Cast in the most general and comprehensive terms, modern theory identifies production functions, resource supplies, and demand conditions as the major underlying elements determining comparative cost differences. By making certain assumptions, the theory can be simplified and the bases of trade narrowed to a few dominant variables. The Heckscher-Ohlin theorem is the most ambitious attempt to reduce the reasons for trade, with international differences in relative factor supplies emerging as the central cause.

Unfortunately, there is the risk that in gaining simplicity and specific lines of causation, the operational usefulness of theory will be compromised. Although definitive conclusions remain to be reached as to the operational validity of the Heckscher-Ohlin theorem, we briefly noted some of its more vulnerable points. The possibilities that production functions are not everywhere identical for the same commodity, that factor reversals may occur, that economies of scale may be significant in determining costs, and that relative demand may exert an important influence, must all be admitted. Whether or not any or all of these possibilities are in fact elements to be reckoned with is an empirical question, with the final effect on the theory of trade having to await the verdict of definitive evidence.

---

[12] See H. Robert Heller, *International Trade, Theory and Empirical Evidence* (Englewood Cliffs, N.J.: Prentice-Hall, Inc., 1968), p. 58.

RECOMMENDED READING

See the end of the next chapter.

STUDY QUESTIONS

1. What is required for absolute price comparison to be made?
2. Why can relative, but not absolute, price comparisons be made between countries?
3. In what sense is the rate of exchange simply a price?
4. What is required for the emergence in a free market of an equilibrium price?
5. On the basis of the assumptions made in the text, what is the only source of demand for exchange? The only source of supply?
6. Define the equilibrium rate of exchange.
7. Referring to the Argentina–United States example in the text, prove that the dollar-peso rate of exchange must fall somewhere within the range of 2 to 5 cents.
8. Explain why *relatively* lower prices in pretrade isolation become *absolutely* lower prices with trade at an equilibrium rate of exchange.
9. What is the basis for saying that relative prices reflect comparative costs?
10. State succinctly the law of comparative advantage.
11. What are the principal defects of the classical theory of trade from the perspective of modern theory?
12. Review the meaning and construction of the production possibilities or transformation curve.
13. Show how differently shaped transformation curves reflect different cost conditions.
14. Prove that differences in marginal opportunity costs in different countries are equivalent to differences in comparative costs.
15. Why do pretrade output points have no influence on comparative costs if constant-cost conditions prevail?
16. If there are increasing or decreasing marginal opportunity costs, why must pretrade output points be specified in order to determine comparative costs?
17. In what sense can it be said that differently shaped transformation curves exhibit a *bias* toward a comparative cost advantage in one product?

18. Construct an example in which comparative costs differ even though transformation curves are identical.

19. Factor inputs are usually substitutable, but only at diminishing rates. Explain.

20. Clearly explain the meaning of factor intensity.

21. Explain how different factor intensities for different commodities lead to increasing marginal opportunity costs.

22. On what basis may countries be classified with respect to their factor endowments?

23. What effect does a relative abundance of labor have on the shape of the transformation curve when a labor-intensive good is measured vertically?

24. Through what economic mechanism does relative factor abundance affect relative factor prices and comparative costs?

25. Prove to your own satisfaction that both different factor intensities and different relative factor supplies are necessary for either one to cause comparative cost differences.

26. Specify the principal determinants of pretrade output points.

27. State the conclusions of the Heckscher-Ohlin theory. What simplifying assumptions does it make, and on what grounds?

28. What consequence for the theory of trade would follow from the presence of international differences in the production functions?

29. Explain the meaning of factor reversal and indicate its significance for trade theory.

30. How may economies of scale serve as an independent basis for international trade?

31. Under what conditions can relative demand be expected to differ most internationally?

32. What are the advantages and the risks of simplifying assumptions in the construction of a theory?

| Chapter 3 | THE PURE THEORY OF INTERNATIONAL TRADE (CONTINUED) |

In the preceding chapter, attention was focused on two primary questions: What are the ultimate causes of international trade, and what determines its pattern? Two additional related questions remain for exploration before we turn to the major economic effects of trade, and extend the analysis beyond the two-country, two-commodity model so far employed. These two questions relate to the degree of specialization in production, and the terms on which goods exchange for each other in trade.

SPECIALIZATION AND TRADE

Exchange of goods and services, with minor exceptions, is the consequence of specialization in production. With international trade, each country specializes in the production of those goods and services in which it has a comparative advantage, exporting the surplus of domestic output over domestic consumption in exchange for the similar surplus output of its trade partners. The mechanism leading to specialization consists of the increase in demand for the goods in which a country has a comparative advantage, accompanied by a decrease in the domestic output of the goods in which the country has a comparative disadvantage.

How far does the reallocation of resources toward export industries go? Does each country end up producing only export goods, with domestic consumption of other goods provided entirely by imports? If so, we say there is *complete specialization*. Or does each country continue to produce domestically, though on a reduced scale, goods and services which it also imports? If so, the reallocation of resources to export industries stops short of being complete, and we say there is *partial specialization*.

Whether specialization is complete or partial depends, in the first instance, upon cost conditions. Constant- and decreasing-cost conditions each favors complete specialization, while increasing costs are associated with partial specialization. The reasons are easy to perceive.

Constant-Cost Conditions

Consider first the constant-cost case. If country *A* has an initial comparative cost advantage in, say, good *X*, the advantage will be maintained at all output levels. That is, as the output of *X* is increased to meet foreign as well as domestic demand, its marginal (and average) opportunity cost remains constant *at a lower level* than the cost abroad. Foreign producers are thus unable to compete in the market for *X* and will cease to produce the good at home. At the same time, if good *Y* is also produced at constant costs, the initial advantage of country *B* in that good is maintained as its output is increased, so that country *A* ceases to produce it. The final outcome is that the production of *X* is confined to country *A*, while the production of *Y* is confined to country *B*.

An exception arises if either country, though completely specialized, is unable to supply both the home and foreign demand for its export product. In this event, imports in the other country would be supplemented by some home production—at a price equal to the domestic cost.

Decreasing-Cost Conditions

The tendency toward complete specialization is even stronger with decreasing costs than with constant costs. Suppose again that country *A* has a comparative advantage in good *X* and country *B* in good *Y*, each good being subject to decreasing costs. As *A* expands the output of *X* in response to *B*'s import demand, the marginal cost of *X* falls. As *B* contracts the production of *X*, its marginal cost rises. Hence, the initial differential in the cost of *X* in *A*'s favor increases. The same result occurs with respect to good *Y*, the cost advantage of country *B* in good *Y* increasing as its output expands.

Increasing-Cost Conditions

Finally, under what is perhaps the most common cost conditions, specialization tends to be partial. Let us see why.

Assume that X and Y are each produced under increasing costs, and that country A has a comparative advantage in X, country B in Y. As A expands the output of X and contracts the output of Y, the marginal cost of X increases and of Y decreases. The opposite occurs in country B—the marginal cost of Y increases and of X decreases. The initial comparative cost advantage of A in good X and of B in good Y therefore narrows as specialization proceeds, until at some output point the initial differential in marginal opportunity costs disappears. At this point, A ceases to expand further the output of X and to contract further the output of Y, and B likewise halts the further reallocation of resources toward the Y industry. Each country ends up producing both goods, though in quite different proportions than before trade began.

THE TERMS OF TRADE

A very important aspect of international trade which we have ignored to this point is on what terms trade is conducted.

By the "terms of trade" is meant the ratio at which goods are exchanged. When there are only two goods being traded, as in the model we have been using, the terms of trade are given simply by the ratio of the goods' international prices. If, for example, with trade at an equilibrium rate of exchange the international price of X is \$1 and of Y \$2, the terms of trade are $1X = \frac{1}{2}Y$, or $1Y = 2X$. In reality, of course, numerous goods enter into international trade, and the terms of trade then must refer to the international price ratios of a country's "bundle" of exports and its "bundle" of imports.[1]

The terms of trade are clearly important to a country, for they determine what quantity of imported goods any given quantity of exports will exchange for. Especially the less economically developed countries of the world are sensitive to their terms of trade. Many of these countries depend upon imports to help feed their people and to provide essential raw materials and manufactured goods. If their terms of trade deteriorate—that is, become less favorable because import prices on the average rise relatively to export prices—their ability to pay for imports with exports is de-

---

[1] The terms of trade are usually measured as the ratio of the weighted index of import and export prices. This yields, not the absolute terms of trade (which do not have too much meaning with many commodities involved), but *changes* in the terms as compared to some base period.

creased, thereby posing a threat to an already low standard of living.

If one country's terms of trade improve (import prices fall relatively to export prices), clearly one or more of its trading partners' terms of trade must deteriorate. As a consequence, the *division of the gain* from trade among trading countries depends upon the terms of trade, as we shall see later. Further, the possibility is thus raised that each country may attempt to obtain a larger share of the gain from trade through various devices to improve its terms of trade. This prospect of economic warfare will be examined in our later discussion of tariffs and quotas in Chapter 7.

Let us now turn to the question of what determines the terms of trade in a competitive market setting.

Limits of the Terms of Trade

First of all, *the possible range within which the terms of trade can fall is limited by the pretrade marginal opportunity cost ratios* in the trading countries. To understand why this is so, let us revert to an earlier example of trade between Argentina and the United States in cloth and beef. The same pretrade cost situation in the two countries as assumed in the earlier discussion will be retained for the present purpose, summarized as follows:

	United States	*Argentina*
Cloth....................	$4	200 pesos
Beef....................	$1	20 pesos

The pretrade cost ratios of cloth to beef are 4:1 in the United States and 10:1 in Argentina. The terms of trade must then fall somewhere between 1 cloth = 4 beef and 1 cloth = 10 beef, for a very simple reason: *On any terms outside this range, one of the countries would not be willing to trade.*[2] For example, on terms of 1 cloth = 3 beef, the United States is unwilling to export cloth for beef, since 4 beef can be obtained at home at the marginal opportunity cost of 1 cloth. On the other hand, the United States *would* be willing to export beef for cloth, but Argentina would refuse to trade, since 3 beef can be obtained domestically at a cost of less than

---

[2] To state the point in a different, though equivalent, manner, no equilibrium rate of exchange can be found outside the range of 2 cents to 5 cents per peso. At an exchange rate of 2 cents per peso, cloth exchanges for beef on terms of 1:10, and at an exchange of 5 cents per peso, the terms are 1:4.

1 cloth. The reader can satisfy himself that similar situations in reverse apply if the terms of trade are anywhere above 10 beef for 1
cloth.

The Equilibrium Terms of Trade

Within the limits set by pretrade domestic cost ratios, *the terms
of trade tend to settle at an equilibrium level at which the total
value of each country's imports equals the total value of its exports.*
(The equality of imports and exports is an equilibrium requirement only when nontrade transactions—such as loans, gifts, and
other capital transfers—are excluded from the model, as in the present discussion.) Should exports not equal imports on given terms
of trade, a change in the terms would occur until equality is established. The change in the terms of trade would be brought about
through a movement in exchange rates, or in commodity prices, or
both.

To illustrate with our United States–Argentina example, suppose that equilibrium is initially reached with the rate of exchange
at $2\frac{1}{2}$ cents per peso, the cost and price of cloth at \$4, and of beef
at 20 pesos. The terms of trade are therefore 1 cloth = 8 beef. (The
20-peso price of beef is equivalent at the assumed rate of exchange
to \$0.50, so that the ratio of the price of cloth to the price of beef
is 1:8.)

Now suppose that U.S. demand for Argentina beef rises, the Argentina demand for U.S. cloth remaining constant. The immediate result is an increase in the rate of exchange on the peso in response to the increased U.S. demand for pesos to purchase more
beef. As the rate of exchange on pesos moves upward, the *dollar*
price of beef rises, and the *peso* price of cloth falls. For example, at
an exchange rate of 3 cents per peso, the dollar equivalent of 20
pesos is \$0.60, and the peso equivalent of \$4 is $133\frac{1}{3}$ pesos, whereas
at the previous exchange rate, the prices were respectively \$0.50
and 160 pesos. The higher dollar price of Argentina beef reduces
the quantity the United States wishes to import, while the lower
peso price of U.S. cloth increases the quantity Argentina wishes to
import. At some rate of exchange, then, equality between the values of imports and exports is restored, and equilibrium is reestablished. If the new equilibrium rate of exchange is 3 cents per peso,
the terms of trade will be 1 cloth = $6\frac{2}{3}$ beef, assuming that the
prices of cloth and beef remain \$4 and 20 pesos, respectively. The

increase in the U.S. demand for the import good has therefore resulted in a deterioration in her terms of trade and an improvement in Argentina's terms of trade.

The same kind of result would follow if the assumption that the prices of cloth and beef in the exporting countries remain constant were dropped. Under increasing-cost conditions, the Argentine price of beef would rise in response to the greater demand for beef imports by the United States. The cost of beef to the United States thus increases, and her terms of trade move adversely not only because of a rise in the rate of exchange on the peso but also because of the higher peso price of beef. However, to the extent that the peso price of beef goes up, the rise in the equilibrium rate of exchange is moderated, since each performs the same function of reducing the quantity of beef demanded by the United States.

In summary, the terms of trade are determined by the forces of international demand, in conjunction with internal cost conditions in each country and the equilibrium requirement that, in the absence of all economic relations other than commodity trade, the total value of each country's imports equal the total value of its exports.

Reciprocal Demand[3]

The foregoing discussion points to the conclusion that it is the demand of each country for the other's export product that mainly determines the terms of trade. *Import* demand, however, is a function not only of demand for the import good but also of domestic supply of that good. For instance, if the quantity of beef demanded in the United States at a price of $0.60 per pound is 100 million pounds per day, the import demand for beef depends upon the quantity *domestically* supplied at that price. If none is produced domestically—because of complete specialization under constant-cost conditions—the entire domestic demand becomes import demand. But if, say, 40 million pounds of beef are domestically produced at $0.60 per pound, the import demand will be 60 million pounds.

A technique for explaining the terms of trade which embodies all the relevant variables—demand, supply, and equilibrium requirements—is provided by *reciprocal demand* analysis.

---

[3] This section can be skipped without loss of continuity.

The reciprocal demand of a pair of countries for each other's export products can be shown through the construction of international *offer curves* for each of the countries.

A country's offer curve represents the quantity of export goods which it is willing to exchange for a specified quantity of import goods on each of various terms of trade. The characteristics of typical offer curves are revealed in Figure 3.1.

FIGURE 3.1

RECIPROCAL DEMAND AND THE TERMS OF TRADE

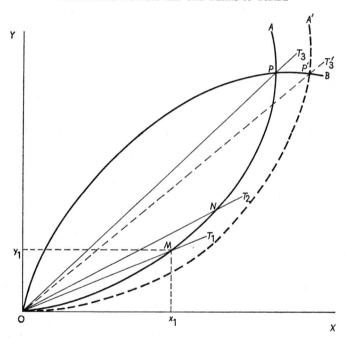

$OMNA$ is the offer curve of country A, OPB of country B. A's export good is X, measured on the horizontal axis, its import good is Y, measured on the vertical axis, while B's export good is Y and its import good is X. Each point on an offer curve represents the quantities of export and import goods which the country is willing to exchange. Thus, point M on A's offer curve indicates that country A is willing to exchange $O(x_1)$ of X for $O(y_1)$ of Y. How much of its export good a country is willing to trade for any given amount of imports is a function of the terms of trade. At point M on A's curve, the terms of trade are measured by the slope of the ray OT_1, equal to $O(y_1)/O(x_1)$. On more favorable terms of trade (from A's point of view), shown by a steeper terms-of-trade line such as OT_2, A is willing to offer a larger quantity of its export good in return for a larger quantity of imports (point N). However, as the volume of exports A gives up and imports she receives increases, her terms of trade must become increasingly more favorable to induce her to continue this process. This is why A's offer curve bends upward (and B's curve bends downward).

The reasons for the decreasing willingness to trade without a price inducement as the volume grows are twofold: the relative marginal utility of the import good compared to the export good declines as the domestic availability of the first increases and of the second decreases; and the marginal opportunity cost of the export good increases as its output is expanded, assuming increasing-cost conditions. At some point, these forces may become strong enough to make A unwilling to offer any greater amount of her export good regardless of the terms of trade, though, of course, the quantity of imports desired continues to increase as their price (the terms of trade) becomes more favorable. Such a point is indicated when A's offer curve becomes vertical. If her curve beyond that point turns backward to the left, this indicates that she is willing to offer only an increasingly *smaller* quantity of exports for greater quantities of imports.

Precisely the same considerations apply to country B, explaining the tendency for her offer curve to bend rightward, and perhaps eventually downward.

Equilibrium requires that the amount of X which country A offers in exchange for a given quantity of Y be equal to the quantity of X which country B is willing to accept in exchange for the given quantity of Y. This condition is fulfilled only when the offer curves of the two countries intersect. In Figure 3.1 the curves intersect at P, so that P is the equilibrium point, and OT_3, on which P is located, represents the equilibrium terms of trade.

It can now be shown how changes in reciprocal demand affect the terms of trade. Suppose that A's demand for Y increases, B's demand for X remaining constant. In graphical terms, A's offer curve moves to the right, becoming the broken line OA', indicating that A is willing to offer a larger quantity of X than before for any given quantity of Y (or is willing to accept a smaller quantity of Y for any given quantity of X). OA' intersects B's offer curve at point P', and the equilibrium terms of trade become OT'_3. The slope of OT'_3 is less than that of OT_3, showing that the terms of trade have become less favorable for A, and more favorable for B, as the result of A's increased demand for imports.

THE ECONOMIC EFFECTS OF TRADE

We have completed our discussion of the causes of trade, the determinants of its pattern, including the degree of specialization, and the terms on which it occurs, all within the framework of a two-country, two-goods model. We are now ready, while retaining this useful though simplified model, to consider the important question of what major economic effects are produced by trade.

The Equalization of Goods and Service Prices and Costs

As a prelude to exploring the less obvious and more fundamental effects of trade, let us begin with the observation that, under the assumptions we have adopted, trade results in the elimination of the price and cost differentials which are initially responsible for its occurring. Ignoring transportation costs and assuming the operation of free and competitive market forces, every article entering into international trade must have the same price in all countries at prevailing rates of exchange. This is simply the consequence of there being created a *single international market* in place of the separate national markets in existence before trading relations are begun. The common international price of each traded good will in equilibrium be at that level at which total world demand equals total world supply.

Not only are prices equalized by trade, so too are marginal (and average) costs. For each good price is equal to marginal cost in competitive equilibrium, so that the international equalization of prices carries with it the equalization of costs in the countries producing the goods. This is the reason why with constant-cost conditions specialization tends to be complete: The international price of the good, equal to its cost of production in the country with the comparative cost advantage, is below its cost, at all output levels, in the other country, which does not, therefore, produce it. Under increasing-cost conditions, however, some of the import commodity may be produced at home, since, at a reduced output level, domestic cost falls to the level of the international price, equal to the cost of production in the export country.

The international equalization of costs and prices as the result of trade raises this apparent paradox: Why should a commodity be exported or imported if its domestic price and cost are the same at home as abroad? The solution to the paradox is, of course, that the *reason* why the price and cost are the same is *because* there is trade. Were trade to stop or be reduced below the volume at which the price is the same in all countries, a differential in price would appear and cause trade to start up again or to increase in volume until the differential disappeared.

The Role of Transportation Costs. It is worth reiterating that the equalization of the prices and costs of goods as the result of trade is dependent, among other things, upon the absence of transportation costs. In reality, of course, transportation costs always are present, with consequences for trade which deserve at least brief discussion.

The first point to make is that transportation costs constitute a natural barrier to international trade that cannot be hurdled in all cases. The price of a good to an importing country includes the costs of freight, insurance, and handling. If these exceed the difference in the domestic price of the good abroad and at home, trade does not occur. Many goods and services are practically excluded from international trade for this reason. Bricks, for instance, are produced for highly localized markets because of the cost of transporting them in relation to the cost of producing them.

Where transport costs do not remove the advantages of trade, they quite often exert a determinative influence on the pattern of specialization and trade. Consider, for example, a particular industry requiring various raw materials available only in different geographic regions. Clearly, there will be a tendency for trade to occur, but what will be its pattern? For example, which region will bring all the required raw materials together for fabrication of the finished product? Other things being equal, the location will be where *transport costs are minimized.*

A classic example is the steel industry in the United States. The tendency to locate near the coal supply rather than the iron ore ranges stems from the fact that, per ton of steel, a greater tonnage of coal than of iron ore is used. Similar considerations apply to most industries requiring large amounts of fuel—cement, glass, calcium carbide, etc.[4] In other cases, nearness to the market for the product, differential freight rates (based on the type of material or com-

---

[4] See Edgar M. Hoover, *The Location of Economic Activity* (New York: McGraw-Hill Book Co., 1948), pp. 32 ff.

modity, the volume of traffic, the type of transportation means available, etc.), and similar elements enter into the determination of the best location of particular industries from the standpoint of minimizing transport costs.[5]

In general, transport costs reduce the volume of trade below the level it would be in their absence and in some instances significantly modify the pattern of geographic specialization.

Factor Price Equalization

One of the most interesting and important effects of international trade is in the direction not only of equalizing goods' prices internationally but, under certain circumstances, *factor prices* as well.

The most convenient starting point for showing a tendency toward factor price equalization as the result of trade is the Heckscher-Ohlin trade model, described in Chapter 2. It will be recalled that in this model each country specializes in the production of the good which uses a relatively large quantity of the country's relatively abundant factor. The relatively abundant factor is also the relatively *cheap* factor, since a factor's price is equal to its marginal productivity, and relative abundance implies low marginal productivity.

The effect of trade is to reduce the relative abundance of a country's abundant factor and to reduce the relative scarcity of its scarce factor. This occurs even though the *physical* supplies of the factors remain constant. The relatively abundant factor becomes economically less abundant (scarcer) *because of the increased demand for it,* while the relatively scarce factor becomes economically less scarce (more abundant) *because of the decreased demand for it.* These changes in relative factor demand are the direct consequence of the country's specializing in the product in which it has a comparative cost advantage, together with the assumption that different goods have different factor intensities.

Suppose, for example, that country A is labor-abundant and capital-scarce, and that good X is labor-intensive and good Y capital-intensive. As the result of trade, A increases its production of X (in which it has a comparative advantage) with resources released from the Y industry (in which it has a comparative disadvantage). The resources released from the production of Y consist, by assumption,

---

[5] For a detailed description, see *ibid.*

of a greater proportion of capital to labor than used in the production of X. Hence, for full employment of capital to be maintained (also assumed in the model), the "extra" capital released from the Y industry must be absorbed in the X industry. The *ratio* of capital to labor is thereby increased in the X industry. It is in this sense that labor becomes relatively scarcer and capital relatively less scarce.

Since a factor's marginal productivity and price increase as its relative scarcity increases, wage rates rise and the rental price of capital falls as A shifts resources from the Y industry to the X industry. The same phenomenon can be observed from another point of view. Since the demand for X has increased and that for Y has decreased, the demand for the principal factor (labor) used in producing X increases, while the demand for the principal factor (capital) used in producing Y falls. As far as individual firms are concerned, it is the consequent rise in wage rates relatively to the rental price of capital that induces a substitution of capital for labor to maintain the least-cost combination of inputs. It should be noted that the substitution occurs in the Y industry as well as in the X industry, since the wage rate is relatively higher in all employments.

The same kind of changes in relative factor scarcities and prices occur in other countries. In country B, labor-scarce and capital-abundant, wage rates tend to fall and the rental price of capital to rise as resources are shifted from the labor-intensive X industry to the capital-intensive Y industry.

These changes in relative factor prices serve, of course, to reduce the initial disparity in the international prices of factors. Before trade, wage rates were low in country A and high in country B, with the reverse relationship in the rental price of capital. As the result of trade, wage rates rise in A and fall in B, while the rental price of capital falls in A and rises in B.

Given the assumptions of the Heckscher-Ohlin model, the tendency toward factor price equalization is inevitable. By adopting certain additional assumptions, it can be shown that not only are factor price differences reduced by trade, they are *eliminated,* leaving each factor with the *same* price in all trading countries. The conditions necessary for this extreme result to follow, however, are highly restrictive and never encountered in reality.[6]

---

[6] For a description of the conditions referred to, see J. E. Meade, *Trade and Welfare* (London: Oxford University Press, 1955), chaps. xix–xxiii.

Even the much weaker proposition that factor price differences are merely reduced without being completely eliminated depends upon the validity of the assumptions underlying the Heckscher-Ohlin theory of trade. We observed earlier (see Chapter 2, page 39 ff.) several assumptions of the theory concerning which doubt has been raised. One of these doubtful assumptions was shown to be especially critical for the theory of trade—namely, the assumption that each commodity is produced with the relatively intensive use of a particular factor resource, and that this factor intensity remains intact at all factor price ratios. So-called "factor reversal," in which a good switches intensity in one factor to another, removes the basis for predicting the pattern of trade according to relative factor supplies. More than this, *factor reversal also destroys confidence in the effects of trade on factor prices.* Instead of being able confidently to predict that trade will narrow factor price differences, with factor reversal present we can only say that, though probably factor prices will be affected by trade, *the effect may be either to widen or reduce differences.*

Regardless of the specific effects of trade on factor prices, depending upon such things as the absence or presence of factor reversal, one general observation seems fairly secure: *trade affects the distribution of income within each trading country.* If a tendency in the direction of factor price equalization holds, in each country the relative and absolute income share of the abundant factor is increased. If, on the other hand, there is factor reversal, the share of the scarce factor may either increase or decrease relatively to that of the abundant factor. But in any event, some factor owners are very probably adversely affected by trade, while others are benefited. This has important implications for trade policy, as we shall see.

THE GAINS FROM TRADE

The culminating question we must examine are the *welfare effects* of international trade. The ultimate purpose of descriptive, or "positive," economic theory is to furnish the basis for arriving at rational and intelligent judgments on policy issues. This leads into the area of *prescriptive,* or "welfare," economics in which value judgments cannot be avoided. It will be our intent, however, to keep the welfare evaluation of trade as free of value judgments as possible.

The Gain from Specialization

International trade is the result of extending on a wider scale the specialization in production characteristic of all modern, developed economies. Just as specialization within a country increases efficiency and real income, so for the same reasons does specialization on an international scale increase the efficiency and output of the world economy.

World Output and Welfare. The opportunity for the world to reap the benefits of specialization is present whenever the marginal rate at which any pair of goods can be transformed into each other is not the same in different countries. The marginal rate of transformation between goods is indicated by their marginal opportunity costs. Say the marginal opportunity cost of good Y is $2X$. This tells us that an extra unit of Y can be produced with the resources used to produce two units of X, or that an extra unit of X can be produced with the resources used to produce one-half unit of Y. It is in this sense that one good can be "transformed" into another at a rate given by their marginal opportunity costs. We have seen that differences in marginal opportunity costs lead to specialization and trade. Let us now observe how this results in an increase in *total world productivity*.

Suppose that the marginal opportunity cost of Y is $10X$ in country A and $2X$ in country B. Let country A reduce its output of Y by one unit and country B increase its output of Y by one unit. The combined output of Y by the two countries thus remains constant. What happens to the combined output of good X? Country A is able to increase its production of X by 10 units. Country B is forced to reduce the production of X by two units. Hence, the combined output of X increases by a net amount of eight units. The "world" $(A + B)$ has available for its use the same amount of Y as before but eight units more of X. It is also possible for the world to have more of Y and the same amount of X, or more of *both* goods. For instance, if A reduces its production of Y by one unit and B increases its output by two units, the combined production of Y increases by one unit and of X by six units (plus 10 in A, minus 4 in B).

It is to be noted that world production is expanded in the above example without any change in the quantity or quality of productive resources. The source of gain in output is the greater *efficiency* in the use of given resources.

Observe further that the opportunity to increase world output through reallocating resources continues to exist as long as marginal rates of transformation or marginal opportunity costs of any pair of commodities are not the same in different countries. The possibility of further gains is exhausted only when either the countries become completely specialized or marginal rates of transformation have become equalized.

The result of the world's resources being reallocated until marginal rates of transformation are equalized everywhere can be simply put in another way: *the world's production and consumption possibilities are maximized.* It is in this sense that the world's *welfare* is improved by free international trade. As our earlier analysis showed, free trade leads precisely to the reallocation of resources postulated above. Differences in marginal rates of transformation are equivalent to comparative cost differences, and in trade equilibrium comparative costs, and therefore marginal rates of transformation, are equalized. Hence, free trade yields to the world the opportunity of consuming more of all goods, or of consuming more of some and no less of others. It would be difficult to find a less ambiguous criterion of welfare improvement.

National Output and Welfare. It is conceivable for the world's welfare to be advanced by trade while the welfare of a particular country is decreased. Since attitudes and policies are usually based on each country's conception of its own national interests, it is important to view the welfare effects of trade from the individual country's point of view.

Let us presume, as the theory of trade informs us, that each country specializes in the production of the good in which it has a comparative cost advantage and exchanges that good for another on terms of trade more favorable than the domestic marginal rate of transformation.

To fix ideas, assume that a country has a comparative advantage in Y whose marginal opportunity cost at home is $2X$, and that the opportunity to trade on terms of $1Y = 5X$ is opened up. This is equivalent to saying that the country can transform Y into X at a lower marginal opportunity cost through trade than in economic isolation. As a consequence, through specializing in Y and trading some of it for X the country's consumption frontier is pushed outward beyond its domestic production boundary. In pretrade isolation, the country's consumption possibilities were limited to its production possibilities; with trade, its consumption possibilities extend beyond its pretrade production possibilities.

To illustrate, suppose that before trade began, the country pro-

duced and consumed 100Y and 50X. With trade, the output of Y
is increased, say, to 101 units, at the opportunity cost of decreasing
the production of X to 48 units. Now the extra unit of Y is traded
for 5 units of X, leaving the country with 100 units of Y and 53
units of X for home consumption. Net result: the same consumption of Y as before trade plus three additional units of X. This is
not, of course, the only possibility. More of *both* goods would be
made available if, for example, *half* the extra unit of Y produced

FIGURE 3.2

CONSUMPTION POSSIBILITIES WITH TRADE

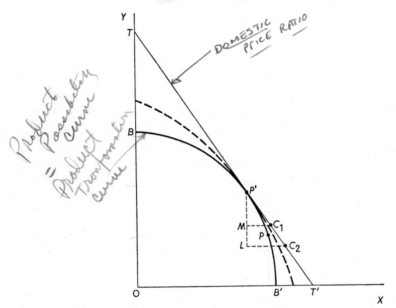

were exported for 2½ units of X, leaving posttrade consumption
at 100½ Y plus 50½ units of X.

The above plus all other consumption possibilities with trade as
compared to the pretrade situation can be shown diagrammatically,
as in Figure 3.2. *BB'* is the country's production transformation or
possibilities curve. Point *P* is assumed to be the pretrade production and consumption point. The opportunity to trade is shown by
the terms of trade line *TT'*, the slope of which measures the terms
of trade. The equilibrium output point with trade is *P'*, where the
transformation curve is tangent to the terms of trade line, and

therefore the marginal opportunity cost ratio of the goods is equal to their international price ratio.[7] The movement of the output point from P to P' represents the extent to which the country specializes with trade in the production of good Y.

The terms-of-trade line TT' now represents the country's consumption possibilities. If MP' of Y is exported, MC_1 of X is received in exchange, so that point C_1 is reached in consumption. LC_2 of X can be obtained by exporting LP' of Y, bringing the country to point C_2 in its consumption. Any other point on TT' can be reached in a similar manner.

That the country benefits from trade in the same sense that the world as a whole was shown to gain is clearly demonstrated. If the country chooses the combination of X and Y represented by point C_1, more of *both* goods is available for consumption than was true in isolation at point P. (This is shown by the position of C_1 above and to right of P.) The country's welfare can therefore safely be said to have improved as the result of trade. The same conclusion holds even if the consumption of one of the goods with trade is less than in isolation, such as at point C_2. Since C_1, with more of both goods available, is an alternative option open to the country, C_2 must be presumed to yield at least as much total utility to the community as C_1.[8]

Three subsidiary comments on the above discussion remain to be made. The first is that, other things being equal, a country's gain from trade is greater the more favorable are the terms of trade; that is, the higher the ratio of export prices to import prices. In Figure 3.2, if the terms of trade were more favorable, the terms-of-trade line would be less steeply sloped, swinging the country's consumption possibilities frontier further outward on the X-axis. Any given amount of Y exports would thus exchange for a larger quantity of X imports. By the same token, of course, the gain realized by B's trading partners, whose terms of trade are less favorable, would be smaller.

The second comment is that the potentiality of gain from trade depends upon the opportunity to trade on terms *different* from pre-

---

[7] At the point of tangency the slopes of the transformation curve and of the terms of trade line are equal. The slope of the former measures the ratio of the marginal cost of X to the marginal cost of Y, while the slope of the latter measures the ratio of the price of X to the price of Y.

[8] For the use of consumption indifference curves to show the gain from trade, see the Appendix to Chapter 3.

trade marginal opportunity costs. If, for example, with reference to Figure 3.2, the pretrade output point had been P' instead of P, the country would have been consuming the same quantities of X and Y before trade as after trade. In this case, there would be no point in trading—a conclusion in accord with our earlier analysis which showed that the terms of trade must fall within the limits set by domestic cost ratios in the trading countries.

Finally, it should be noted that the terms of trade can be expected to remain the same at all volumes of trade, as assumed above, only under special circumstances. If a country's exports and imports are each an insignificant fraction of total world exports and imports, the terms of trade will be unaffected by that country's demand for imports or supply of exports. On the other hand, if the country's trade is an important part of world trade, its terms of trade will respond to shifts in its own demand for imports and supply of exports, as concluded in our earlier discussion of reciprocal demand. In this latter case, there is not a fixed term-of-trade line, such as TT' in Figure 3.2, but a whole series of different lines associated with different volumes of exports and imports. However, this makes no essential difference to our analysis of the gain from trade. As before, the country's consumption possibilities curve lies outside its transformation curve, except at a point of tangency with it. The difference is that the consumption possibilities curve will be concave instead of linear, illustrated in Figure 3.2 by the broken line lying just below TT'.

The Gain from Exchange

The gain from trade discussed above arises out of two sources: the greater efficiency of resource use as the result of specialization and the greater utility enjoyed by consumers as the result of a different set of consumption opportunities. For convenience, we may call the latter the *gain from exchange*.

To isolate the exchange benefits from the specialization benefits, let us assume that for some reason resources are not reallocable, so that each country continues to produce the same "mix" of goods and services after trade as in isolation. The potential gain from specialization is therefore left unexploited. What, then, are the possible benefits from engaging in trade?

Suppose that in pretrade equilibrium the price of good X is \$1 in country A and 100 lira in country B, while the price of good Y is \$2 in A and 500 lira in B. The assumed situation is as shown in the accompanying table.

	Good X	Good Y
Country A.......	$1	$2
Country B.......	L.100	L.500

Since relative prices, and therefore comparative costs, differ, we know that there is a basis for mutually beneficial specialization and trade. But we are assuming that specialization in production does not occur. Nevertheless, the potentiality for exchange benefits from trade is present because of the differences in relative prices.

In equilibrium, consumers in each country purchase that combination of goods which yields the same marginal utility or satisfaction per dollar's expenditure for each good consumed. Were this not the case for any consumer, he could increase his total utility from a given expenditure by rearranging his purchases until the indicated relationship was established. In terms of our example, then, we see that for consumers in country A the marginal utility of Y is twice that of X (since the price of Y is twice that of X), while for consumers in country B the marginal utility of Y is five times that of X.

Consumers in both countries can obtain greater total utility from a given amount of expenditure by trading on terms of trade anywhere between $1Y = 5X$ and $1Y = 2X$. For instance, let the terms of trade be $1Y = 3X$. A consumer in A exchanges a unit of Y for three units of X with a consumer in B. But prior to the exchange the marginal utility of the unit of Y to the consumer in A is equivalent to the extra utility yielded by two units of X. Therefore, A's consumer is giving up (exporting) a good worth to him the equivalent of *two* units of X and receiving in return (importing) *three* units of X. In effect, he is gaining a "bonus" of one unit of X by trading.

Looking now at B's consumer, three units of X are given up in return for one unit of Y. But the extra unit of Y has a marginal utility for him equivalent to that of *five* units of X. So he, too, gains a bonus, in his case amounting to two units of X.

Both sets of consumers continue to gain from further exchanges until, as the result of diminishing marginal utility, the ratio of the marginal utilities of X and Y is the same for consumers in both countries. This automatically becomes the situation when the equilibrium relative prices of X and Y are the same in both countries— a condition brought about by free trade.

It will be observed that the exchange gains from trade result from the reallocation of consumption expenditures, whereas the specialization gains from trade flow from the reallocation of productive resources. Even though these are separate and distinct sources of benefits, they are clearly parallel phenomena, each springing from the wider set of feasible alternatives afforded by trade. Maximum benefits are realized if *both* sources of gain are exploited, though either alone justifies trade.

Some Welfare Questions

That trade provides the opportunity for the world and for each trading country to obtain a greater quantity of goods and/or to obtain greater total utility from the consumption of given quantities of goods has been demonstrated. However, we have *not* concluded that *every individual's welfare* is improved by trade. Indeed, the probability is very strong that some individuals will in fact be *harmed* by trade unless deliberate steps are taken to avoid it.

One group of individuals adversely affected by trade are those whose tastes happen to favor heavily the goods which his country exports. The usual effect of trade is to *increase* the domestic prices of export goods and to *decrease* the domestic prices of import goods. This follows from the pretrade international differences in relative prices which are eliminated as the result of trade. Unless, therefore, the income of the individual with a strong preference for the export good is increased, he may be worse off with trade than without it. Note, however, that the probability of this kind of ill effect diminishes as the number of goods entering into trade increases, for the chances of having the adverse effects of higher prices on preferred exports goods being offset by the beneficial effects of lower prices on preferred import goods are then greater.

A second kind of adverse welfare effect is suffered by those whose *incomes* are reduced by trade. As observed earlier, trade is nearly certain to cause a redistribution of the national income of each trading country. If the Heckscher-Ohlin theorem holds, it is specifically the owners of the relatively scarce factor whose income is reduced by trade. But in any event, a depressive effect of trade can be expected for certain factor owners.

If some people are hurt, even though others reap benefits, how can it be concluded that the *general welfare* is advanced by trade? There is no objective method of making interpersonal utility comparisons. But modern welfare economics has come up with a resolution of the dilemma thus posed.

The principle appealed to is as follows: the general welfare is improved if those who benefit from trade could compensate those who lose from trade, while leaving the first group with a net gain and the second group in at least a no worse position than before trade. On the basis of this criterion, trade can be said unambiguously to promote the general welfare. Trade increases the real national income of each participating country. Clearly, therefore, everyone *could* have a larger real income, or some people could have a larger income without others having a smaller income. Whether, in fact, the national gain from trade is so distributed as to produce either of these results depends upon whether the machinery possessed by the state for redistributing income (monetary and fiscal measures) is employed to that end.

As a matter of practical policy, there is very little chance that redistributive measures would, or could, assure that in fact no one is harmed by trade. From a strict purist point of view, therefore, we could only say that trade offers *potential* gain to a society. But it is worthwhile to point out that the same thing is true of nearly *all* economic events and actions which we are pleased to regard as contributing to progress, for hardly any economic change occurs without in some respects adversely affecting particular individuals. Economic advancement would indeed be difficult to achieve if every step had to be accompanied by some deliberate redistribution of benefits to compensate those individuals harmed.

MULTICOUNTRY, MULTICOMMODITY TRADE

We have completed the discussion of the theory of international trade as viewed within the simplified context of a two-commodity, two-country model. It is time now to investigate what modifications are required when the more complicated actual situation of trade in thousands of commodities among a large number of countries is approached.

Multicommodity Trade

First, consider the case of more than two commodities, while re-taining the assumption of only two countries. Assume that in pre-trade isolation the price (and cost) relationships shown in the accompanying table prevail. The question is, which country has a

	United States	Argentina
Beef.....................	$ 1.00	P. 20
Cloth....................	4.00	200
Wheat...................	0.50	15
Bicycles................	20.00	1,200
Tractors...............	1,000.00	80,000

comparative advantage in which commodities? In a two-goods model, there is no difficulty in finding comparative costs; not so in the present case. The first problem is that different answers are ob-tained depending upon the pair of goods chosen for comparison. For instance, cloth is relatively cheaper in the United States than in Argentina when compared to beef and also when compared to wheat. But in comparison to either bicycles or tractors, cloth is relatively cheaper in Argentina!

To resolve this problem, let us calculate the ratio of Argentine prices (in pesos) to the United States prices (in dollars) for each good. The result is:

Beef.................... 20:1
Cloth................... 50:1
Wheat.................. 30:1
Bicycles................ 60:1
Tractors............... 80:1

Now the commodities may be ordered on a scale of comparative costs, from lowest to highest, with the direction measured from left to right for the United States and from right to left for Argentina:

U.S. → tractors—bicycles—cloth—wheat—beef ← Argentina

This shows that for the United States tractors have the *least* com-parative costs, while the opposite is true for Argentina. We can therefore identify tractors as the good in which the United States has a clear-cut comparative advantage, and beef as the commodity in which Argentina has an unmistakable comparative advantage. The United States will certainly tend to export tractors and import beef. But what are we to conclude with respect to the other three commodities?

The answer depends upon reciprocal demand and the terms of trade as these are reflected in the equilibrium rate of exchange between the dollar and the peso. Suppose that the equilibrium rate of exchange is 1.8 cents per peso. Referring to the assumed price data given above, we see that at this rate of exchange beef, wheat, and cloth are all absolutely cheaper in Argentina than in the United States, while bicycles and tractors are cheaper in the United States than in Argentina. If, then, 1.8 cents per peso is the equilibrium rate of exchange, the total value of Argentina's exports of beef, wheat, and cloth is equal to the total value of its imports of bicycles and tractors, and similarly for U.S. exports and imports. Thus, in the scale of comparative costs, the dividing line in this case lies between bicyles and cloth, with the United States having a comparative advantage in the goods to the left of the line and Argentina in the goods to the right of the line.

However, the dividing line is not fixed. Suppose, for example, that at the rate of 1.8 cents per peso the total value of imports demanded by the United States exceeds the total value of U.S. expors demanded by Argentina. As a consequence, the dollar rate of exchange on the peso will rise until an equilibrium rate is reached. If the equilibrium rate happens to be 2.0 cents per peso, cloth will disappear as a traded item, for its price will then be the same in both countries. Were the equilibrium rate to rise above 2.0 cents, cloth would switch from being an import of the United States to becoming an export along with bicycles and tractors.

In general, the commodities falling in the middle range of the scale of comparative costs have an indefinite status until reciprocal demand and an equilibrium rate of exchange are known. However, no matter where the dividing line between exports and imports falls, *the comparative costs of the commodities exported are always less than the comparative costs of the goods imported.* In this most important respect, the multicommodity model yields essentially the same results as the two-country model.

Multicountry Trade

The analysis of multicountry trade follows lines similar to that of multicommodity trade. Again, we may be sure that each country will export those commodities the costs of which are relatively lower at home than abroad and import others that are relatively lower in cost abroad. But which specific goods will be exported and imported by each country cannot be determined in advance without specification of reciprocal demand and the terms of trade.

To illustrate, assume the pretrade price data shown in the accompanying table. From the ratio of the price of cloth to the price

	United States	Argentina	Italy	France	Japan
Price of beef...............	$1	20 pesos	50 lira	10 francs	40 yen
Price of cloth..............	$4	200 pesos	150 lira	60 francs	80 yen
Ratio of cloth price to beef price...............	4:1	10:1	3:1	6:1	2:1

of beef given in the last row, the comparative cost positions of the countries can be ordered on an ascending scale, as follows:

Comparative cost of cloth in terms of beef
$\rightarrow$ Japan—Italy—U.S.—France—Argentina
$\leftarrow$ Comparative cost of beef in terms of cloth

This shows that Japan has the greatest comparative advantage of all countries in cloth and the greatest comparative disadvantage in beef, while Argentina is in the reverse position. The countries in between may export or import either commodity, depending upon reciprocal demand and the terms of trade. For example, if the terms of trade are 1 cloth = 5 beef, Italy and the United States would join Japan as exporters of cloth and importers of beef; if the terms were 1 cloth = 3.5 beef, Italy would still export cloth, but the United States would join Argentina in exporting beef; if the terms of trade were less than 3 (but more than 2) beef for 1 cloth, all countries, except Japan, would export beef in return for cloth.

Wherever the dividing line between cloth-exporting and beef-exporting countries is, all countries to the left of the line export cloth, and all to the right of the line export beef. Further, whichever good a given country exports, its comparative cost is less than in other countries, while the good it imports has a lower comparative cost abroad than at home.

Multilateral Trade

We have seen that, in the two-country model, equilibrium requires that each country's exports to the other be equal in value to the imports from the other. Does the same principle apply between each pair of countries when there are many countries trading with each other? That is, does equilibrium require that trade be *bilaterally* balanced? The answer is no—fortunately; for there is no reason to expect reciprocal international demand in a free market to produce such a pattern of trade.

Equilibrium, under our assumption of relations confined exclusively to commodity trade, requires only that each country's total exports be equal to its total imports. A country may fulfill this equilibrium condition even though its trade is unbalanced bilaterally with each of its trading partners, provided only that the sum of its bilateral import surpluses is matched by the sum of its bilateral export surpluses. If this holds for each trading country, we say that there is multilateral trade equilibrium. To illustrate this point, there is presented below a hypothetical trade matrix for five countries, each of which is in bilateral imbalance but multilateral balance.

Exports from ↓ \ Exports to →	Japan	Italy	United States	France	Argentina	Total Exports
Japan	—	80	100	5	5	190
Italy	50	—	80	40	20	190
United States	60	30	—	90	50	230
France	25	65	40	—	15	145
Argentina	55	15	10	10	—	90
Total Imports	190	190	230	145	90	845

The exports of each country listed in the left-hand column are shown horizontally; the imports of each country listed in the top row are shown vertically. From the data given, we may summarize each country's bilateral trade balance as in the accompanying tabulation (a plus sign indicating an export surplus, a minus sign, an import surplus).

Bilateral Trade Balance of ↓ \ With →	Japan	Italy	United States	France	Argentina
Japan	—	+30	+40	−20	−50
Italy	−30	—	+50	−25	+ 5
United States	−40	−50	—	+50	+40
France	+20	+25	−50	—	+ 5
Argentina	+50	− 5	−40	− 5	—

Each country is enabled to pay for its import surpluses from one or more other countries with its export surpluses to the remaining countries. Thus Japan pays for its import surpluses from France and Argentina with its export surpluses to Italy and the United States, etc.

General Equilibrium

Since there are, in fact, many countries producing many goods and services, very little can be said a priori concerning the *specific* composition and pattern of trade or the international value of any one commodity. Demand and supply, price and cost conditions, and exchange rates are mutually dependent in a set of complex general-equilibrium relationships. In the simple model of two countries and two commodities, the composition and pattern of trade can be directly determined from the comparative cost data, though the terms of trade and international values of the traded commodities cannot be arrived at without bringing in reciprocal demand. In the multicountry, multicommodity model, there is no such simple and direct line of causation. Indeed, as we have seen, the term "comparative costs" loses much of its meaning in this case, except within the context of an already established general equilibrium. With given demand and supply conditions in each country and with given international demand, a particular country will have a comparative cost advantage in certain commodities and a comparative disadvantage in others. Let international demand shift, and the comparative cost situation of the country will change, with some articles formerly exported now being imported or vice versa.

Within the framework of general equilibrium, each traded commodity will tend to have the same price, at equilibrium rates of exchange, in all countries (except for transportation costs), the price being at that point which equates world demand and supply. Whether a given country will export or import a particular commodity depends upon the domestic demand and supply at the prevailing world price. If the quantity demanded at home exceeds the quantity supplied domestically, the excess quantity demanded will be imported; if the quantity supplied exceeds the quantity demanded, the excess will be exported; if the quantity produced at home at the world price just equals the domestic demand, the commodity will be neither exported nor imported. But the domestic equivalent of the world price depends upon the rate of exchange, which, in turn, in a free market, will be such as to equalize the *aggregate* exports and imports of the country.

General equilibrium, then, involves a balancing of numerous interrelated forces, international and domestic. One basic point, however, emerges: with given demand and supply conditions, both at home and abroad, each country will have a comparative advantage in certain commodities, which are exported, and a comparative disadvantage in others, which are imported. Many commodities will tend to be on the margin between an export and import status, falling to one side or the other or remaining in the middle, depending upon international demand. Some commodities, in which the comparative advantage is greatest, will tend always to be exported, while others, in which the comparative disadvantage is greatest, will tend always to be imported. Irrespective of the exact composition of trade, any imported commodity will have a lesser opportunity cost, measured by the amount of exports required to obtain it, than it would have if produced at home. International trade therefore makes available more goods and services to each country than does economic isolation.

RECOMMENDED READING

CORDEN, W. M. *Recent Developments in the Theory of International Trade,* chaps. ii and iv. Princeton University, International Finance Section, Special Papers in International Economics No. 7, 1965.

ELLSWORTH, P. T. *The International Economy,* Part II. 3d ed. New York: Macmillan Co., 1964.

A clear exposition of the modern theory of trade, including a brief description of classical theory.

HABERLER, GOTTFRIED. *The Theory of International Trade,* chaps. ix–xii. New York: Macmillan Co., 1937.

Notable for its introduction of the opportunity cost concept into trade theory.

———. *A Survey of International Trade Theory,* chaps. ii–iv. 2d ed. Princeton University, International Finance Section, Special Papers in International Economics No. 1, 1955.

HELLER, H. ROBERT. *International Trade, Theory, and Empirical Evidence,* chaps. i–vi, viii. Englewood Cliffs, N.J.: Prentice-Hall, Inc., 1968.

A concise presentation of trade theory, on a considerably more advanced level than the present text.

JOHNSON, HARRY. "Comparative Costs and Commercial Policy," in *Money, Trade, and Economic Growth,* pp. 28–40. Cambridge, Mass.: Harvard University Press, 1962.

An excellent brief summary of the modern theory of the causes and effects of international trade, including the phenomenon of factor reversal.

OHLIN, BERTIL. *Interregional and International Trade,* Parts I and II and chaps. xii–xiv. Cambridge, Mass.: Harvard University Press, 1933 (reprinted 1952) .

The complete statement of the Heckscher-Ohlin theory.

ROBINSON, ROMNEY. "Factor Proportions and Comparative Advantage," *Quarterly Journal of Economics,* Vol. 70 (May–August, 1956) .

A sharp criticism of the Heckscher-Ohlin theory.

SAMUELSON, PAUL A. "The Gains from International Trade," in American Economic Association, *Readings in the Theory of International Trade* (eds. Howard S. Ellis and Lloyd A. Metzler) , chap. xi. Homewood, Ill.: Richard D. Irwin, Inc., 1949.

———. "International Trade and the Equalization of Factor prices," *Economic Journal,* June, 1948.

STUDY QUESTIONS

1. Identify the mechanism which operates in a market system to reallocate resources as a result of international trade.

2. Why, under constant- or decreasing-cost conditions, does specialization tend to become complete? Under what circumstances would there be an exception to this tendency?

3. Explain why increasing-cost conditions favor partial specialization.

4. Define the terms of trade. Why are they important?

5. Why do pretrade cost ratios set limits to the terms of trade?

6. What is meant by the "equilibrium" terms of trade?

7. What is the effect on a country's terms of trade if its demand for imports increases? If the foreign demand for its export goods increases?

8. How does a rise in the rate of exchange on foreign currencies promote exports and decrease imports?

9. Why is import demand for a good partly dependent upon domestic supply of the good?

10. Define the international offer curve and explain its construction.

11. What accounts for the usual curvilinear shape of offer curves?

12. In terms of reciprocal demand analysis, what determines the equilibrium terms of trade?

13. Why does trade eliminate international cost and price differences?

14. What kinds of influences on trade do transportation costs have?

15. Explain the effects of trade on the relative abundance and scarcity of factors of production. What implications does this have for factor prices?

16. How does factor reversal affect the tendency toward factor price equalization as the result of trade?

17. Why does trade nearly inevitably adversely affect some individuals?

18. Distinguish between the nature and sources of the specialization and the exchange gains from trade.

19. In what sense can it be said that the world's welfare is advanced by international trade?

20. What limits the consumption possibilities of an economy in isolation? How are these limits enlarged through trade?

21. How does trade make possible an increase in the total world output of goods with the same quantity of inputs employed?

22. What influences do the terms of trade have on a country's share of the gain from trade?

23. What particular individuals or groups are likely to be worse off with trade than without?

24. Describe the welfare principle that underlies the conclusion that society benefits from trade even though some individuals are harmed by trade.

25. Show the modifications required in the two-commodity trade model to predict the composition and pattern of trade in a multi-commodity world.

26. What determines whether a country will export or import a good the comparative cost of which is in the middle of the scale of comparative costs?

27. What general conclusion holds in the multicommodity case as to the relationship between the comparative costs of export goods and import goods?

28. Analyze the comparative cost situations of several countries trading two commodities.

29. Distinguish between bilateral and multilateral trade balance. Why is only the latter relevant in multicountry trade?

30. Why is a general equilibrium approach necessary in a multicommodity, multicountry model?

APPENDIX: A DIAGRAMMATIC ANALYSIS OF INTERNATIONAL TRADE

The theory of international trade can be very succinctly presented with the use of diagrammatic techniques. In the text of Chapters 2 and 3, a limited number of diagrams is employed to illustrate some of the basic relationships in trade theory. In this appendix, it is proposed to extend the diagrammatic method for the benefit of those students who find such an approach helpful in understanding complex relationships.

In Chapter 2 it was shown that comparative cost differences, which underlie international trade, are determined by production functions, resource supplies, and demand conditions. The first two of these elements together are responsible for the shapes of production transformation curves, while demand determines the equilibrium location on the curves. Our first task is to show diagrammatically how production functions and resource supplies generate transformation curves. Throughout it will be assumed that X and Y are the two commodities each of two countries, A and B, produce; that labor (L) and capital (K) are the only factors of production and that they are substitutable for each other, though at diminishing marginal rates; that X is labor-intensive and Y capital-intensive at all factor price ratios; that there are constant returns to scale in both industries; and that A is a labor-abundant and B a capital-abundant country.

Production Functions, Resource Supplies, and the Production Transformation Curve

The production function for a good can be represented, under our assumptions, by an isoquant. An isoquant shows the alternative combinations of labor and capital which are physically capable, employed in the technically most efficient manner, of producing a *given* quantity of output.

In Figure 3.3, $q_x q_x$ represents the isoquant for good X, $q_y q_y$ the isoquant for good Y. Each isoquant is convex to the origin, reflecting the presence of a diminishing marginal rate of technical substitution (MRTS) between labor and capital. This means that as more of either input is substituted for the other, increasing amounts of the substituted input are necessary to keep output constant as successive units of the other input are withdrawn. The

MRTS at any point on an isoquant is measured by the slope of the isoquant at that point. Hence, the diminishing MRTS of labor for capital is reflected in the diminishing slope of the isoquant as movement down the curve occurs, signifying an increase in the ratio of labor to capital.

It will be noticed that the isoquant for X is drawn so that it intersects that for Y, lying above Y's isoquant to the left of the intersection point and below to the right of the intersection point. The significance of this is its indication that X is always relatively labor-

FIGURE 3.3

PRODUCTION ISOQUANTS AND FACTOR PROPORTIONS

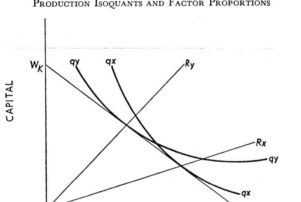

LABOR

intensive and Y relatively capital-intensive. The least-cost (economically most efficient) proportion of labor to capital to employ is attained when the MRTS of labor for capital is equal to the ratio of the price of labor to the price of capital. The latter ratio is represented by the slope of a straight line connecting the two axes. One possible ratio of the price of labor to the price of capital is given by the slope of the line W_kW_L in Figure 3.3. At this factor price ratio, the least-cost combination is shown by the point of tangency between W_kW_L and the isoquant, for at this point the MRTS between labor and capital (equal to the slope of the isoquant) is equal to the ratio of the price of labor to the price of capital. It will be observed that the least-cost combination for good X requires a larger proportion of labor to capital than for good Y. This is indicated by the steeper slope of the ray OR_y than of ray OR_x, each of which shows by its slope the proportion of capital to labor employed at the given factor price ratio. The student is invited to demonstrate for himself that at any other assumed factor price ratio, X will be produced with a greater proportion of labor to capital than employed in producing Y.

The next step is to construct a so-called "box diagram." Before undertaking this, it is first necessary to explain that for each good there exists a "map" of isoquants, consisting of as many isoquants one wishes to draw. Each isoquant represents a given level of output, so that different isoquants for the same good represent different

FIGURE 3.4

THE EFFICIENCY LOCUS

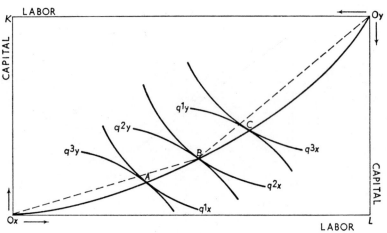

levels of output. (Under our assumptions, however, all isoquants for a given good have the same shape.) Second, in equilibrium, although the factor proportions employed differ for X and Y, the MRTS of labor and capital is the *same* for the two goods. The reason for this is that in each case the least-cost combination requires equality between the MRTS and the price ratio of labor and capital, so that at any given factor price ratio the MRTS must be the same for the two goods.

We proceed to draw a box diagram, as in Figure 3.4. The dimensions of the box show the factor endowments of the country. The width of the box (O_xL or O_yK) measures the country's labor endowment, the height (O_xK or O_yL) its stock of capital. Factor supplies may be measured either from the lower left-hand origin

O_x or from the upper right-hand origin O_y. If the O_x origin is used, labor is measured from left to right, capital from bottom to top. If the O_y origin is used, labor is measured from right to left, capital from top to bottom. Two different origins are designated because the factors are allocated between the X and Y industries. Hence, that part of the labor force used in the X industry (measured from O_x) must be subtracted from the total labor force to give the amount of labor employed in the Y industry (measured from O_y), and the same for capital.

The isoquant maps for X and Y may now be inserted into the box, but to avoid clutter only three pairs are shown. The X-isoquants are drawn from the O_x origin and therefore have the usual shape. But since O_y is the origin for the Y industry, its isoquants are flipped over from their normal position. The location of isoquants in the box indicates the level of output. The farther an X-isoquant is from the O_x origin in the northeast direction, the greater is the output of X; the farther a Y-isoquant is from the O_y origin in a southwest direction, the greater is the output of Y. The level of each good's output is indicated by the superscript of the isoquant. Because of limited resources, assumed to be fixed in amount, the greater the output of either good, the smaller is necessarily the output of the other good. Thus, when the output of X is q_x^1, the output of Y is q_y^3, while if X output is q_x^2, the output of Y is q_y^1.

The equilibrium requirement that the MRTS of labor and capital be the same in both industries is satisfied only at the points where X- and Y-isoquants are tangent (since MRTS is measured by the slope of an isoquant and at the point of tangency the slopes of the two isoquants are the same). In Figure 3.4 the three pairs of isoquants shown are tangent at points A, B, and C. All the other points of tangency between the isoquants not drawn are assumed to lie on the line $O_x ABCO_y$, which is known as the *efficiency locus*. Hence, whatever the allocation of resources between the X and Y industries, it will be somewhere on the efficiency locus.

It will be observed that the efficiency locus has been drawn to bend below a straight-line diagonal connecting O_x and O_y. This particular shape of the curve is a reflection of our assumption that X is a labor-intensive good and Y a capital-intensive good. The indication that this is the case is given by the different slopes of the rays from the two origins to any point on the efficiency locus. For example, at point B on the locus, the ray $O_x B$ has a less steep slope than the ray $O_y B$. In each case, the slope of the ray measures the ratio of capital to labor. At every point on the efficiency locus (except at the terminals O_x and O_y), the slope of the ray from O_x is less than that from O_y.

Since the efficiency locus shows the various possible maximum output combinations of X and Y, it provides the information required to construct a production transformation curve. The generation of a transformation curve from an efficiency locus is illustrated in Figure 3.5. It will be observed that the downward-bowed effi-

FIGURE 3.5

Transformation Curve Derived from the Efficiency Locus

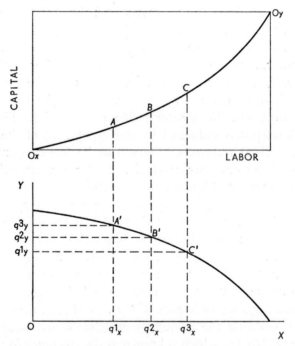

ciency locus has its counterpart in the concave shape of the transformation curve. In economic terms, the different factor intensities of X and Y—reflected in the shape of the efficiency locus—cause increasing marginal opportunity costs, reflected in the concave shape of the transformation curve, as explained in the text.

Demand and Pretrade Equilibrium Output

Now that the transformation curve has been established, we may proceed to determine the equilibrium output point in pretrade isolation. Given the conditions of production summarized in the production transformation curve, output is determined by demand. The conditions on the demand side are shown by a *consumption indifference map.*

With a given distribution of income, a community consumption indifference curve shows the various combinations of goods among which the community is indifferent, in the sense that consumers as a group have no preference for one combination as over against another. Suppose, for example, that the total satisfactions or utility enjoyed by the community from the consumption of 100 units of X and 200 units of Y is designated U_1. It may be presumed that there are numerous combinations of X and Y that would also yield utility U_1. A few other such combinations might be $110X + 180Y$, $120X + 155Y$, $130X + 120Y$. These and all other combinations giving the same level of utility would lie on the community indifference curve which represents total utility U_1.

Each consumption indifference curve can be expected to have a convex shape, as illustrated in Figure 3.6. The convexity of the

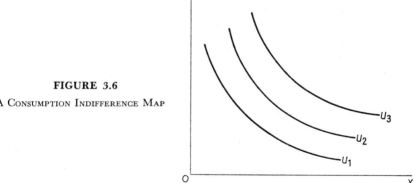

FIGURE 3.6

A CONSUMPTION INDIFFERENCE MAP

curve is a reflection of the phenomenon of diminishing marginal utility, or, in the terminology we shall use, *diminishing marginal rate of substitution in consumption.* The principle involved is that the greater the consumption of one good compared to another, the less is the marginal utility of the first good compared to that of the second good. Hence, the marginal rate of substitution in consumption of X for Y, with total utility remaining constant, diminishes as X is substituted for Y. In a like manner, the marginal rate of substitution of Y for X diminishes as Y is substituted for X. In order, therefore, for total utility to remain constant, increasing amounts of X must be obtained to compensate for successive one-unit losses of Y, and vice versa. The convexity of the indifference curve is the geometric expression of this.

If more of *both* X and Y are consumed, the total utility of the community is greater. Indifference curve U_2 in Figure 3.6 thus represents a higher level of community satisfaction than curve U_1, and so on for successively higher curves.[9] The assumption is that the community *seeks to get to the highest-level indifference curve possible.*

FIGURE 3.7

EQUILIBRIUM OUTPUT AND CONSUMPTION IN PRETRADE ISOLATION

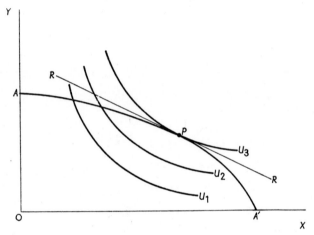

A community's consumption possibilities, however, are limited. In isolation, consumption is limited to production. In diagrammatic terms, a community in isolation cannot reach an indifference curve that lies beyond its production transformation curve. The highest attainable consumption indifference curve, therefore, is the one tangent to the production transformation curve. In Figure 3.7, U_3, is the highest attainable indifference curve.

---

[9] There are difficulties involved in constructing a map of community indifference curves which we are ignoring. The chief problem is that changes in income distribution—which normally occur as a result of engaging in trade—lead to different community indifference curves, so that there is no uniquely determined set. It is possible to circumvent this difficulty through various assumptions, but for the purpose at hand we may accept the indifference map as given.

To reach U_3, it is clear that production must be on the transformation curve AA' at the point of tangency, P, with the indifference curve. At this point of tangency, the two curves have the same slope, so that the marginal rate of technical substitution is equal to the marginal rate of substitution in consumption—the condition for an optimum allocation of resources.

In equilibrium, both the marginal rate of technical substitution and the marginal rate of substitution in consumption are equal to the ratio of the price of good X to the price of good Y. This is shown in Figure 3.7 by the price line RR, the slope of which measures the ratio of the price of X to the price of Y. We have thus determined the equilibrium ratio of commodity prices in isolation in country A.

Precisely the same procedures are followed in arriving at the ratio of commodity prices in country B. The only requirement for a trade potential to exist is that the ratio of prices be *different* in different countries. In what follows, we shall assume that the pre-trade ratio of prices in country B differs from that in A, specifically, that the relative price of X is lower in A than in B. A's comparative advantage in X may be thought of as the result of her being a labor-abundant country, with X a labor-intensive good, creating a cost bias in favor of X that is not offset by demand.

Production, Consumption, and Trade

Reciprocal demand determines the terms of trade between X and Y. The terms must fall somewhere within the range set by pre-trade cost ratios in A and B, but in any event the relative price of Y will be lower with trade in country A than in isolation. This is shown in Figure 3.8 by the terms-of-trade line TT, the slope of which is greater than A's pretrade price line RR.

As a result of being able to trade on the terms given by TT, country A expands the output of X until the ratio of the marginal cost of X to the marginal cost of Y equals the international price ratio of X and Y, given by the slope of the terms-of-trade line. A's equilibrium output point with trade is therefore at Q, where the terms-of-trade line is tangent to the production transformation curve. However, A will wish to consume X and Y at point C, where the terms-of-trade line is tangent to consumption indifference curve U_4. A is enabled to consume at point C by exporting VQ of X in exchange for VC of Y. The result of specialization and trade is to move

FIGURE 3.8

INCREASED CONSUMPTION POSSIBILITIES WITH TRADE: COUNTRY *A*

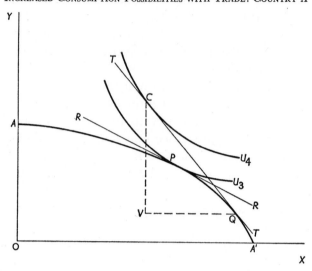

A off its highest consumption indifference curve without trade (U_3) to a higher curve (U_4).

The same analysis, with the same general effects is applicable to country *B*. In Figure 3.9, *B*'s equilibrium output in pretrade isolation is at P', where the highest consumption indifference curve *U* is tangent to the production transformation curve *BB'*. The equilibrium pretrade ratio of the price of *X* to the price of *Y* is given by the slope of the line *R'R'*. *R'R'* has a steeper slope than *RR* in the preceding figure, indicating that the relative pretrade price of *X* is higher in *B* than in *A*.

Now the possibility of trade opens up, on terms given by *TT*, which is of precisely the same slope as for country *A*. The production point in *B* is moved to point *Q'*, where the terms-of-trade line is tangent to the transformation curve. Consumption, however, is at *C'*, where the terms-of-trade line is tangent to *B*'s highest consumption indifference curve *U'*. This consumption point is reached by *B*'s exporting *Q'V'* of *Y* in exchange for *V'C'* of *X*.

It will be observed that for *TT* to be the equilibrium terms of trade, the quantity of *A*'s export of good *X* must be equal to the quantity of *X* that *B* wishes to import, and similarly for *B*'s export

FIGURE 3.9

<small>INCREASED CONSUMPTION POSSIBILITIES WITH TRADE: COUNTRY *B*</small>

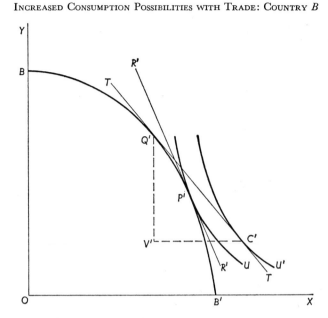

of Y and A's import demand for Y. In terms of Figures 3.8 and 3.9, CV must equal $Q'V'$ and VQ must equal $V'C'$.

The net result of trade, then, is a reallocation of resources in each country toward the product in which it has a comparative advantage, and the movement of each country onto a higher consumption indifference curve, indicating a higher level of welfare.

Chapter 4

THE EMPIRICAL FOUNDATIONS OF INTERNATIONAL TRADE

not Classical + H.O.

In our study in Chapter 2 of the ultimate bases of international trade, we learned that international differences in production functions, in resource supplies, and in demand theoretically can be, either separately or in combination, the primary cause of trade. Such an approach, while extremely helpful in identifying the major possible causes of trade, is too general, we concluded, to be very useful. The great virtue of both the classical theory and the Heckscher-Ohlin theory is their directness and simplicity, cutting through the numerous layers of variables having some influence on trade to those identified as the central and dominating ones. In the case of the classical theory, it is differences in relative labor productivity; in the Heckscher-Ohlin theory, it is differences in relative factor endowments that are the primary elements.

We have expressed a preference for the Heckscher-Ohlin theory over the classical theory, mainly because the former is consistent with—indeed, an extension of—modern economic thinking while the latter is based on an outmoded theory of value, and because the Heckscher-Ohlin theory attempts to probe more deeply than the classical theory into the causes of trade.

THE PROBLEMS OF EMPIRICAL VERIFICATION

The ultimate test of a theory, however, rests upon its reliability as a predictor as revealed in empirical studies. Unfortunately, empirical testing may be extremely difficult. A major obstacle to the testing of trade theory is the absence of pretrade situations which can be compared to posttrade situations. While trade theory seeks to identify the conditions in pretrade isolation which give rise to trade upon the opening of economic relations with other countries, in the actual world each country's economy has been importantly shaped by its long-time participation in the world economy.

Moreover, while trade theory is cast in terms of an ideal, competitive, and frictionless model in which artificial barriers to the flow of goods and services are absent, the actual pattern of observed trade is heavily influenced by the presence of tariffs, quotas, exchange controls, subsidies, imperfectly competitive markets, and so on, as we are going to see in subsequent discussions.

The paucity of complete and accurate data adds to the difficulty of empirical testing. Our empirical knowledge of all the important ingredients in the mix of influences on trade is extremely limited, though increasing.

Finally, there are problems of finding the appropriate empirical counterparts of theoretical concepts. A major example is the concept of "factor of production." Theoretically, units of resource belong to the same factor category only if these are perfectly substitutable for each other in production processes. But on this basis there would be hundreds or thousands of separate factors, thereby rendering the concept of relative factor supplies nearly meaningless. On the other hand, if the trichotomy of land, labor, and capital is adopted, unrefined for qualitative differences, a misleading picture may be drawn.

Notwithstanding the above difficulties, empirical studies of the classical and Heckscher-Ohlin theories of trade have been made. The results may be briefly reported.

TESTS OF THE CLASSICAL THEORY

The pioneering empirical study of the classical theory of trade was made by G. D. A. MacDougall.[1] Subsequent studies by Balassa and Stern lead to essentially the same conclusions as MacDougall's.[2]

MacDougall started from the observation that average wages in U.S. manufacturing were approximately twice as great as wages in the United Kingdom in the year 1937, the date chosen for the study. On the basis of the classical theory, one would expect that the United States would have a comparative cost advantage—and therefore export advantage—over the United Kingdom in those industries where labor productivity in the United States was more than

---

[1] "British and American Exports: A Study Suggested by the Theory of Comparative Costs." *Economic Journal,* Part I (December, 1951) and Part II (September, 1952) .

[2] See Bela Balassa, "An Empirical Demonstration of Classical Comparative Cost Theory," *Review of Economics and Statistics,* August, 1963, and Robert Stern, "British and American Productivity and Comparative Costs in International Trade," *Oxford Economic Papers,* October, 1962.

twice as great as in the United Kingdom. On the other hand, in those industries where labor productivity in the United States was less than twice that of British labor, the cost—and export—advantage would lie with the United Kingdom. MacDougall then examined actual trade data to see if United Kingdom and U.S. exports reflected the expected pattern. He found that they did in general.

While the empirical tests of the classical theory seem to support its validity, some doubt has been cast on this conclusion by a later study using the same data but a more sophisticated statistical technique.[3] Moreover, there is no necessary inconsistency between the classical theory and the Heckscher-Ohlin theory in their predictions of trade patterns. Hence, neither confirmation nor rejection of the classical theory implies either the validity or the invalidity of the Heckscher-Ohlin theory. In short, regardless of the outcome of empirical testing of the classical theory, the testing of the Heckscher-Ohlin theory is warranted on the basis of its own merits.

TESTS OF THE HECKSCHER-OHLIN THEORY

Unfortunately, the empirical testing of the Heckscher-Ohlin theory is considerably more complicated than for the classical theory. In part this is due to the simpler nature of the classical theory, which focuses on relative labor productivity as the origin of comparative cost differences, while the Heckscher-Ohlin theory finds differences in the relative supplies of all factors as relevant. Conceptual and empirical difficulties, as noted above, in defining and identifying relative factor supplies are thus encountered in testing the Heckscher-Ohlin theory but not in testing the classical theory. The greater complications of the Heckscher-Ohlin are also partly attributable to the deeper probe into the ultimate bases of trade which it attempts as compared to the classical theory. For the above reasons, tests of the Heckscher-Ohlin theory have so far been limited in number and in generality, with no firm bases provided for a definitive assessment.

Five attempts at testing the Heckscher-Ohlin theory have been made to date. The pioneering study was made by Professor W. W. Leontief.[4] Leontief made use of his well-known input-output table

---

[3] See Jagdish Bhagwati, "The Pure Theory of International Trade: A Survey," in the American Economic Association and the Royal Economic Society, *Surveys of Economic Theory* (New York: St. Martin's Press, Inc., 1965), Vol. II, pp. 165–72.

[4] "Domestic Production and Foreign Trade: The American Capital Position Reexamined," *Proceedings of the American Philosophical Society*, September, 1963; and

for the United States to determine the capital and labor requirements for a given bundle of exports and for a given bundle of imports. On the presumption that the United States is clearly a capital-abundant country, the Heckscher-Ohlin theory would predict
that her exports would be relatively capital-intensive and her imports relatively labor-intensive. The results of the study indicated
the reverse: United States exports are labor-intensive and imports
are capital-intensive, thus contradicting the Heckscher-Ohlin theory.

Leontief-type tests made by other investigators for other countries have shown mixed results. Some reinforce the inference from
Leontief's study that the Heckscher-Ohlin theory is defective, while
others confirm the theory.[5] In general, however, it certainly can be
said that the Heckscher-Ohlin theory has not been verified by the
tests so far applied.

On the other hand, the evidence gathered to date is far too thin
to justify the rejection of the Heckscher-Ohlin theory. Besides
weaknesses in the testing techniques employed and the limited
number and scopes of tests made, there are several doubtful aspects
of the tests which make one less than completely confident in the
significance of the results.[6]

Definitive, or at least more confident, judgment of the Heckscher-Ohlin theory must await more exhaustive and more thorough
empirical testing. We might be permitted to guess that as more evidence accumulates, some modifications in the Heckscher-Ohlin
theory will be indicated.[7]

Whatever the ultimate verdict on the Heckscher-Ohlin theory
turns out to be, it is highly probable that relative factor endowments will continue to hold an important place as one of the major
influences on trade, even if demoted to a less central role. It is
therefore of interest to observe the differences in factor endowments which actually prevail in the world. Working with what data
are available, and making broad qualitative distinctions with respect to factors when they are obviously called for, a classification

---

"Factor Proportions and the Structure of American Trade: Further Theoretical and
Empirical Analysis," *Review of Economics and Statistics,* November, 1956.

[5] The studies referred to are references one, two, six, seven, and eight in the Recommended Reading list at the end of this chapter.

[6] For some of the criticisms of Leontief's test, see Richard E. Caves, *Trade and
Economic Structure* (Cambridge, Mass.: Harvard University Press, 1960), pp. 273 ff.

[7] Especially important is the possibility that factor reversal and demand conditions may turn out to be empirically significant enough to require amendments to
the theory. See page 39 ff. for a discussion on these aspects.

of countries according to their relative factor endowments is attempted in the following pages. This is followed by a comparison of actual trade patterns with those to be expected on the basis of the Heckscher-Ohlin hypothesis. While such "casual empiricism" cannot be regarded as a substitute for more rigorous procedures, nevertheless it allows interesting tentative impressions to be gained.

THE SOURCES OF FACTOR SUPPLIES

As noted above, there are numerous different kinds and qualities of land, labor, and capital. Labor may be classified into categories such as professional, skilled, semiskilled, and unskilled; even so, there would remain considerable differences within each of these subclassifications. Similarly, land varies in numerous important respects: fertility, nature of the soil, temperature, rainfall, topography, location. Moreover, land, as a broad category, includes mineral resources, waterways, and all other natural appurtenances and qualities. Capital, by which is meant the stock of goods in existence that are useful in helping to produce other goods and services, includes such diverse instruments of production as ox-drawn wooden plows and tractor-drawn gang plows, hand sickles and modern combines, the distaff and the modern spinning frame, the mulepack and the airplane. While these qualitative differences cannot be ignored in a refined analysis, we shall largely do so in the pages that follow.

The factor supplies of the world or of any one country are not unchanging and immutable, although, in the absence of unusual events or catastrophes, large changes occur only over relatively long periods of time.

Labor

Labor, in its broadest sense of human productive energy, is limited in its ultimate supply by the size of population. Changes in population depend upon the relationship between the birth rate and the death rate, both of which, in turn, are determined by a complex of social, economic, and political considerations.

The population of the world as a whole has grown from slightly more than a half-billion persons in 1650 to nearly 3.5 billion in 1968. Table 4.1 gives some idea of the growth of population since 1650, by continents. It is evident from Table 4.1 that the rate of growth of population varies a great deal in different areas and at different times.

More significant than the absolute size of population or its rate of growth is its rate of growth in relation to changes in the supply of capital and land. There is cogent evidence, however, that population growth is in some measure related to changes in the supply of other means of production. Especially in young countries with a large supply of land and natural resources, such as Canada, for example, a growing population may serve as a stimulus to rapid economic development, including the formation of capital. In certain

TABLE 4.1

ESTIMATED POPULATION BY CONTINENTS, 1650–1968

(in millions)

Continent	1650	1750	1800	1850	1900	1968
Europe	100	140.0	187.0	266	401	693*
North America	1	1.3	5.7	26	81	309
South America	12	11.1	18.9	33	63	180
Oceania	2	2.0	2.0	2	6	18
Africa	100	95.0	90.0	95	120	336
Asia	330	479.0	602.0	749	937	1,946†
World Total	545	728	906	1,171	1,608	3,483

SOURCES: Data for 1650–1900 from A. M. Carr-Saunders, *World Population* (Oxford: Clarendon Press, 1936), p. 42; data for 1964 from United Nations, *Statistical Yearbook*, 1969, p. xvii.

* Including Soviet Union.
† Excluding Soviet Union.

other countries, notably, India, China, and the Near East, where the population is extremely large in comparison to the supply of land and capital, there is a strong tendency for any increase in capital supply to be accompanied by a corresponding increase in population, for any temporary improvement in per capita productivity and real income has the result of reducing the death rate and may even lead to an increase in an already high birthrate.

In determining the supply of labor, the size of the population is a very inadequate measure unless its *quality* is also taken into account. This has very little to do with innate abilities, racial characteristics, or other real or imagined "biological" differences between national populations; rather, it would appear mainly to be a question of training and environment.[8]

In a society with highly developed and widely available educational facilities, the labor supply will obviously be of a higher economic quality than in those societies with a high incidence of illit-

---

[8] It is not suggested that there are no innate differences in persons, but only that these differences must be presumed to be randomly distributed in essentially the same pattern in all countries.

eracy or inadequate training facilities. Similarly, if the standard of living and health conditions are favorable, the productivity of labor is certain to be greater than if the population is impoverished and disease-ridden. If the social and economic organization permits an easy movement from lower to higher strata in the hierarchy of occupations, average productivity is likely to be greater than is the case if, because of laws, customs, labor unions, etc., occupational mobility is severely limited. Other factors—such as the influence of different climates on energy and ambition—could be mentioned, but enough has been said to make it clear that mere comparisons of population sizes gives only a very rough index of the supply of labor.

Land

The area and the population density of the world and the major continental divisions are shown in Table 4.2.

TABLE 4.2

WORLD'S AREA AND POPULATION DENSITY, BY CONTINENTS, 1968

Continental Divisions	Approximate Area (In Thousands of Square Kilometers)	Approximate Population per Square Kilometer
Africa....................................	313	11
North America............................	24,247	13
South America............................	17,833	10
Asia (excluding U.S.S.R.)..................	27,532	71
Europe (excluding U.S.S.R.)	4,929	92
Oceania..................................	8,511	2
Soviet Union (U.S.S.R.)....................	22,402	11
World....................................	135,767	26

SOURCE: United Nations, *Statistical Yearbook*, 1969, p. xxvii.

Quantitatively, the area of the world presumably may be regarded as fixed, although, of course, its distribution among political powers may be drastically changed through conquest or agreement. Even more than in the case of population, however, quantitative statistics are devoid of significance if not qualified. Particularly important with respect to land are the qualifications relating to (*a*) the characteristics of the soil, climate, and topography; (*b*) the amount and accessibility of mineral and power resources; and (*c*) the degree to which potential resources are economically usable.

Soil, climate, and topography are especially relevant in determining the supply of agricultural land, and, since they vary tremendously not only in different regions of the world but also within given regions, there may be little correlation between the land area of a continent and its supply of agricultural land. The largest continent, Africa, for example, consists overwhelmingly of tropic savanna climate, desert, and tropic forest climate—all generally unsuited for agriculture, except of the most primitive kind.

Only a fairly small part of the land area of the earth is presently suitable for agricultural cultivation. Moreover, the productive possibilities of agricultural land are widely divergent. Wheat cultivation, for example, requires a combination of temperature, moisture, and topographic and soil conditions which restrict it largely to the temperate zone, though it is fairly well distributed among temperate-zone countries.

The supply of any one type of agricultural land is not absolutely fixed. Drainage, irrigation, and fertilization can enlarge the amount of land usable for specific crops. Some essential elements, however, are virtually fixed—such as climate and topography—so that there are limits on the degree to which the supply can be varied.

Land, when defined to include all natural resources, has other important uses besides agricultural production, of course. One of the most significant of the economic properties of land is its reserve of mineral and energy resources. A given area may be worthless as crop land but immensely valuable as a source of coal, iron, petroleum, bauxite, or other useful minerals. Just as the earth's climate, topography, and soil conditions are unevenly distributed, so, too, are its reserves of mineral and energy resources. It is impossible within the compass of a few pages even to summarize the available (but very incomplete) data on the distribution of all the important mineral and energy resources of the world. It may be useful, however, briefly to indicate the distribution of the three resources which are most fundamental to modern industry—coal, iron, and petroleum.

Coal, which is the principal source of energy and is indispensable, in the form of metallurgical coke, in the smelting of iron ore, is found mostly north of the equator. The United States and Canada possess 40–50 percent of the world's estimated reserves.[9] Iron ore is more widely distributed. Africa is the richest area in reserves, although they have been exploited to date very little. The United

---

[9] These estimates and those given below for iron ore and petroleum are found in Howard F. Gregor, *Environment and Economic Life* (Princeton, N.J.: D. Van Nostrand Co., Inc., 1963) , pp. 325–40.

States and the Soviet Union, together with the major industrial countries of Western Europe, produce 75 percent of the world's output of iron ore, but they possess less than half the world's reserves. In addition to the above countries, Brazil and India have important reserves. The distribution of known petroleum reserves is highly concentrated geographically. Sixty-five percent or more of the reserves is located in the Middle East.

Three observations are worth making in connection with the above data. The first is that our information on the extent and distribution of mineral and power resources is very scanty. Notwithstanding perennial cries of alarm that natural resources are in danger of exhaustion, new discoveries are constantly being made and estimates of reserves are rising.

Second, for a mineral or power resource to be economically significant, it must be accessible. Accessibility refers not only to location but also to the presence of the equipment, know-how, and incentive required to exploit the resource. Coal seams located in the middle of Africa would not at present be economically significant, although, of course, they would have potential significance.

It follows from the above remarks that although the potential supplies of natural resources are limited, the effective supplies are exceedingly variable. Effective supplies in some areas may increase, as the requirements of exploitation are created, while in other areas they will decrease as the result of exploitation.

Finally, it is important to realize that the economic value of natural resources is in good part a function of the state of technology. Land that may be economically useless today may be extremely valuable tomorrow, as, for example, a source of minerals that new technical developments make valuable. A static, point-of-time survey of productive resources is very likely, therefore, to be outmoded before it is completed.

Capital

Capital, or the stock of reproducible instruments of production, is the product of past net income which has not been consumed. *Additions* to the supply of capital (or net *investment*) are created out of that portion of current net income which is not consumed.

Hence additions to the stock of capital require savings, or the abstention from consuming all of current income. There is a circular relationship here, however, for the volume of saving is in great part determined by the size of the per capita national income,

TABLE 4.3

Estimated Capital Supply of Selected Countries, 1935–38
(in billions of international units*)

United States	220.00	Poland	14.20
Great Britain and Northern			
Ireland	104.50	Australia	12.70
Germany-Austria	85.00	Czechoslovakia	9.90
India	82.00	Holland	9.80
U.S.S.R.	73.00	Belgium-Luxembourg	8.70
Central and South America, except		Sweden	7.58
Argentina and Uruguay	61.40	Switzerland	6.30
France	49.70	Hungary	5.30
Japan	36.00	Denmark	4.40
China	35.00	Portugal	3.99
Africa	32.00	Eire	3.29
Italy	25.00	New Zealand	3.00
Argentina and Uruguay	23.50	Norway	2.85
Balkan countries	20.20	Finland	2.52
Canada	18.30	Baltic States	2.50
Spain	18.00		

Source: Colin Clark, *The Economics of 1960* (London: Macmillan & Co., Ltd., 1942), p. 80.
* International units are defined as the amount of goods and services which could be purchased for $1 in the United States over the average of the decade 1925–34.

which in turn depends partly upon the stock of capital already accumulated. Once an economy has succeeded, through past savings, in building up a large supply of capital goods, the national income is likely to be sufficiently great easily to allow a part of it to be saved and thereby to permit a further addition to capital. On the other hand, if the per capita supply of capital goods is small, income and the ability to save are also small, so that it is difficult to improve the capital position.[10]

Apart from forcibly reducing consumption, the only means of increasing capital available to a country with a low per capita income is by long-term borrowing abroad. As we shall see in the next chapter, borrowing from abroad permits an increase in the supply of capital available to the domestic economy and may thereby increase the net national income and the ability to augment the stock of capital goods out of domestic production.

Estimates of the supply of capital, excluding land values, non-income-yielding personal possessions, such as furniture and personal cars, but including dwelling houses and useful publicly owned assets, have been made by a prominent economist, as shown in Table 4.3.

---

[10] It should not be concluded, however, that a rising national income is inevitably accompanied by an increasing proportion of income saved or that the proportion of income actually saved is always higher in the richer countries. Institutional factors and monetary and fiscal policies play an especially important role in determining the proportion of income which is actually saved.

The data in Table 4.3 should not be taken too seriously as accurate absolute measures of capital stock. Apart from certain theoretical difficulties of making international comparisons, there is a lack of detailed and accurate information on the capital supply of most countries.[11] But the data may be accepted as revealing in a rough fashion the order of magnitude of the *disparity* in the capital wealth of different countries.

THE RELATIVE DISTRIBUTION OF PRODUCTIVE FACTORS

It is clear from the data summarized in the preceding section that, in absolute terms, the world's productive resources are very unevenly distributed. We are more interested, however, in the *relative* supplies of factors of production possessed by different regions and countries, for this is the basis of trade.

Since there are, in fact, thousands of different factors of production, it is impossible to determine the relative abundance of each of them for each country.[12] It is necessary, therefore, to confine ourselves to broad categories of factors and to remember that conclusions are very general, admitting of many specific exceptions and qualifications.

Land-Labor Ratios

First, let us compare the factor category "land" with the factor category "labor." Ignoring the fact that there are variations in the proportion of national populations which work and in the kinds of labor of which the working population is composed, as well as the fact that "land" varies enormously in its usefulness, we must conclude that the supply of land, relative to that of labor, varies among countries by wide margins. From the calculations contained in Table 4.4, it will be noted that, for the countries listed, area per capita varies from 69.4 hectares (Australia) to about 0.3 hectares (Belgium, and the Netherlands), with the average for the world being 4.2 hectares.

If the fact that not all land area is utilizable for agricultural pursuits is taken into account, even greater disparity in the land-labor ratio is found. The last column of Table 4.4, in which agricultural

---

[11] See the comments in n. 13.

[12] The difficulty arises not only because of the lack of information but because the concept of relative supply loses meaning when the number of factors is large.

TABLE 4.4

RELATIVE LAND-LABOR DISTRIBUTION IN SELECTED COUNTRIES

Country	Total Area (In Millions of Hectares*)	Agricultural Area† (In Millions of Hectares*)	1964 Population (Millions)	Total Area per Capita (Hectares*)	Agricultural Area† per Capita (Hectares*)
Australia	770.4	383.5	11.1	69.4	34.5
Canada	996.1	61.2	19.2	51.8	3.2
Argentina	280.8	145.2	22.0	12.8	6.6
South America (excluding Argentina)	1,497.1	183.8	136.9	10.9	1.3
New Zealand	26.9	13.1	2.6	10.3	5.0
Africa	3,028.0	867.0	304.2	9.9	2.8
Soviet Union	2,227.0	349.0	227.7	9.8	1.5
United States	782.8	452.0	192.1	4.1	2.4
France	55.2	33.6	48.4	1.1	0.7
Denmark	4.3	3.2	4.7	0.9	0.7
India (including Kashmir)	328.1	131.3	471.6	0.7	0.3
Switzerland	4.1	2.2	5.9	0.7	0.4
Italy	30.1	21.8	51.1	0.6	0.4
Germany (Western)	24.4	14.1	58.3	0.4	0.2
United Kingdom	24.4	19.5	54.2	0.4	0.4
Japan	36.8	6.5	96.9	0.4	0.1
Belgium	3.1	1.8	9.4	0.3	0.2
Netherlands	3.5	2.4	12.1	0.3	0.2
World Total	13,540.0	3,619.0	3,220.0	4.2	1.1

SOURCE: Calculations made from data in Food and Agricultural Organization of the United Nations, *Yearbook of Food and Agricultural Statistics, 1965.*

   * One hectare = 2.47 acres.

   † "Agricultural" area is defined as crop land, orchards and gardens, temporary fallow land, and meadows and pastures.

land available per capita is calculated, reveals a range for the countries listed of from 34.5 hectares of agricultural land per capita (Australia) to 0.1 hectares per capita (Japan). Admitting that qualitative factors may considerably modify the relative positions indicated in the table, it is still safe to conclude that, in general, Japan, Belgium, the Netherlands, Western Germany, the United Kingdom, India, Italy, Switzerland are relatively land-scarce, while Australia, Argentina, New Zealand, Canada, Africa, the Soviet Union, and the United States are relatively land-abundant. Hence we would tentatively conclude that agricultural pursuits in the first group of countries would tend to emphasize intensive-cultivation products, while in the second group extensive-cultivation products would probably be more important.

    The criterion of abundance or scarcity so far employed is too narrow, however, for the supply of capital has been ignored. Relative to land supply, labor may be scarce or abundant; but relative to capital supply, it may be the opposite.

Capital-Labor Ratios

Table 4.5 contains estimates of the capital supply per head of *working population* of several countries. The estimates of total capital supply, upon which the supply per head is calculated, are the

TABLE 4.5

ESTIMATED CAPITAL SUPPLY PER HEAD OF WORKING POPULATION IN SELECTED COUNTRIES, 1935–38
(in international units*)

Great Britain and Northern Ireland.	5,020	Belgium-Luxembourg	2,470
New Zealand	4,760	Norway	2,370
Australia	4,370	Czechoslovakia	1,580
United States	4,360	Italy	1,460
Canada	4,240	Central and South America (excluding Argentina and Uruguay)	1,440
Argentina and Uruguay	3,760	Japan	1,350
Switzerland	3,350	Poland	1,200
Holland	2,910	U.S.S.R.	1,130
Denmark	2,740	India	580
Sweden	2,740	Africa	580
France	2,740	China	180
Germany-Austria	2,670		

SOURCE: Colin Clark, *The Economics of 1960* (London: Macmillan & Co., Ltd., 1942), p. 80.
* For the definition of international units see footnote to Table 5.

same as those presented in Table 4.3 and exclude land values and nonincome-yielding personal possessions but include dwelling houses and useful publicly owned assets.

The import of the data in Table 4.5 is emphasized by the fact that the lowest amount of capital per head of working population is in Asia and Africa, whose combined population—excluding Japan and the Soviet Union—is nearly 60 percent of the world total. At the other extreme, the five countries whose capital per head of working population is highest have a combined population of only slightly greater than 9 percent of world population.[13]

_____

[13] As observed in connection with the data given in Table 4.3, the estimates of capital supply in different countries should be interpreted as showing only rough degrees of disparity. It is very difficult to believe that the supply of capital per head of working population is less in the United States than in Great Britain, New Zealand, and Australia, or that Argentina and Uruguay are as close to the United States in this respect as Table 4.5 would lead us to believe. (See the comments of P. T. Ellsworth in his *The International Economy*, pp. 180–81, on earlier data by the same author.) Subsequent estimates of capital supply are given by Clark in the second edition of *The Conditions of Economic Progress* (London: Macmillan & Co., Ltd.,

Relative to labor supply, most countries of Asia and Africa are quite clearly capital-scarce, while Great Britain, New Zealand, Australia, the United States, Canada, and the chief countries of Western Europe are capital-abundant. This would suggest that Asian and African countries would not have a very high industrial development and that whatever industries do exist would be small scale and light, requiring relatively a great deal of labor and little capital. The capital-abundant countries, on the other hand, would tend to have heavier industries, requiring larger concentrations of capital and lesser amounts of labor.

The supply of capital relative to that of labor is especially relevant in determining the degree to which an economy is agricultural or industrial. Agricultural pursuits can be carried on with little capital compared to the capital requirements of industry, other than light, handicraft industries. If a country has a large per capita supply of both capital and land, some portion of its capital is likely to be applied in agriculture in the form of mechanical means of cultivation and harvesting, irrigation works, and so on. But it is also likely to develop industrially, for the scope for the profitable use of capital in industry is ordinarily much greater than in agriculture, at least after a certain amount of capital has been applied to agriculture.

Where both capital and land are scarce relative to labor supply, therefore, a country will tend to be predominantly agricultural. Similarly, where land is abundant compared to labor supply but capital scarce, agriculture will tend to be more important than industry. But where capital is abundant and land scarce, each in relation to labor supply, the economy will tend to be predominantly industrial, with agriculture largely of an intensive-cultivation type.

Types of Economy

There are, therefore, three broad types of economies, based on different relative factor endowments, that may be distinguished. The first type we may designate the *balanced economy*. It is characterized by an abundance of both capital and land, relative to labor supply, compared to other types of economy. Or, put in other terms, labor is comparatively scarce, relative to land and capital. Industries requiring a large amount of capital and small amounts of la-

1951), but they do not materially change the impression of the vast disparities revealed in Table 4.5.

bor, and agricultural production requiring large amounts of land and small amounts of labor, are both encouraged. Since labor is scarce in relation to both land and capital, labor productivity is high and per capita income large.

The second type of economy is *agricultural,* with both land and capital scarce relative to labor supply or with land abundant relative to labor and capital scarce relative to labor. The scarcity of capital precludes any significant industrial development, although the abundance of labor may encourage some light, handicraft industries, particularly if the necessary raw materials are locally available. Per capita productivity and income are low, except where land is relatively abundant.

In between the first two extremes are the *industrial* economies, abundantly supplied with both capital and labor but with relatively small amounts of land. Manufacturing is highly developed; agriculture tends to be of an intensive character. Per capita productivity and income are higher than in the agricultural countries but lower than in the balanced economies.

It is recognized, of course, that the above classification of economic types is, like all broad generalizations, subject to numerous qualifications and specific exceptions. Nevertheless, if its limitations are kept in mind, a useful picture of international specialization and trade can be gained on the basis of the classification adopted.

Referring to the data contained in the two preceding tables, we may classify the chief countries listed as follows:

Type I (*Balanced* *Economies*)	*Type II* (*Agricultural* *Economies*)	*Type III* (*Industrial* *Economies*)
United States	China	Great Britain
Canada	India	Switzerland
Australia	Other Asiatic countries,	Belgium
Argentina	excluding Japan*	Netherlands
New Zealand	Africa	Germany
	South America, exclud-	France
	ing Argentina	Italy
	Balkan countries*	Japan

* Data have not been given for other Asiatic countries and the Balkans, but it is certain that they fit into this category.

THE PATTERN OF SPECIALIZATION AND TRADE

We would expect the international trade of the balanced economies to be characterized by the export of either manufactured goods, or agricultural products requiring relatively large amounts of land, or both. Trade data indicate, in fact, that of the five balanced economies we have listed, only the United States and Canada export relatively large amounts of both manufactured goods and raw materials and foodstuffs. Australia, New Zealand, and Argentina are all primarily agricultural and raw material exporters. It is significant, however, that among the chief exports of these countries are products requiring relatively large amounts of land and little labor. Thus meat and meat products are important exports in all three countries; wheat and wheat products in the exports of Argentina and Australia; wool in the exports of all three; dairy products for New Zealand and Australia; and so on.

We would expect Type II (agricultural) economies to export primarily agricultural products and raw materials requiring relatively large amounts of labor and little land and capital and to import mostly manufactured articles. Trade statistics confirm this conclusion. All the countries we have listed as agricultural fall into the category of "less developed." Approximately 80 percent of the exports of less developed countries consist of primary products, and over two thirds of their imports are manufactured goods. The primary product exports of these countries typically are relatively labor-intensive: rice, sugar, tea, rubber, cocoa, coffee, cotton, peanuts, bananas, and minerals.

Finally, we would expect the composition of trade of the industrial economies (Type III) to be generally opposite to that of agricultural economies, with a predominance of manufactured goods exports and primary-product imports. Again, actual trade data confirm this expectation. The exports of Great Britain, continental Western Europe, and Japan consist overwhelmingly of manufactured goods, while the great bulk of their imports consists of foodstuffs and raw materials.

The sweeping generalizations drawn above conceal, of course, important differences in detail. Neither primary products nor manufactures are homogeneous categories. A country may be highly industrialized, with a relative scarcity of land in general and yet have a relative abundance of a particular *type* of land. Great Britain, for instance, is a prime example of an industrial country, but she has large coal reserves, with coal constituting until very recently one of her major exports. Temperate-zone countries, however well endowed with land, such as the United States, import *tropical*-land products. Manufactured products also vary greatly, as the large volume of trade among industrial countries in manufactures attests. In short, the opportunities for profitable international specialization and exchange are extensive, and not limited to manufactures against primary products.

The Multilateral Character of Trade

We learned earlier that there is no reason and, in a free world market, no necessity for trade to be balanced bilaterally between each pair of trading countries, unless, as in our earlier theoretical model, there are only two countries involved. Indeed, one of the most important aspects of international trade is its natural tendency to be multilateral in character

FIGURE 4.1

THE SYSTEM OF MULTILATERAL MERCHANDISE TRADE, 1928

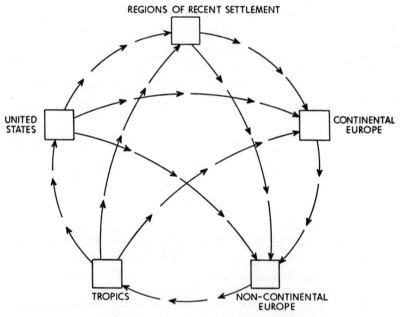

SOURCE: Based on Diagram 6, p. 78, *The Network of World Trade* (Geneva: League of Nations, 1942).

The prewar multilateral pattern of world trade can be shown in rough outline by dividing up the world into five broad trading regions: the "tropics"—including Central Africa, the tropical agricultural and mineral-producing countries of Latin America, and tropical Asia; the United States; other regions of recent settlement—South Africa, northern North America, Oceania, and the nontropical agricultural countries of Latin America; continental Europe; and noncontinental Europe. In 1928 the United States had a commodity export surplus with all regions except the tropics, from which there was an import surplus. Regions of recent settlement had export surpluses to continental and noncontinental Europe and import surpluses from the other two regions. Continental Europe had an export surplus to noncontinental Europe and import surpluses from all other regions. Noncontinental Europe had an export surplus to the tropics and import surpluses from all other regions. The tropics had an import surplus from noncontinental Europe and export surpluses to all other regions. The multilateral network of world trade thus composed is graphically shown in Figure 4.1. The direction of the arrows indicates the movement of merchandise export surpluses of regions from which the arrows emerge, and import surpluses of regions toward which the arrows point.

CONCLUSION

We have not "proved" the validity of the Heckscher-Ohlin theory of trade by the preceding survey of factor endowments and patterns of trade. Two points, however, seem to be justified. The first is the fact of wide disparity in relative factor endowments, which is the empirical basis for their exercising an important influence on trade. The second point is that observed broad patterns of trade at the least are not inconsistent with what the Heckscher-Ohlin theory would predict. It must be admitted, however, that the data are crude and the techniques used unsophisticated. Hence, the most we can say on the basis of such a survey is that it creates an impression in favor of the Heckscher-Ohlin theory which may or may not be supported by more rigorous tests.

RECOMMENDED READINGS

BHARADWAJ, R.   *Structural Basis for India's Foreign Trade.* Bombay, 1962.

————.   "Factor Proportions and the Structure of Indo–U.S. Trade," *Indian Economic Journal,* October, 1962.

CLARK, COLIN.   *The Economics of 1960,* chaps. ii, vi. London: Macmillan & Co., Ltd., 1942.

———. *The Conditions of Economic Progress,* chaps. iii, xi. 2d ed. London: Macmillan & Co., Ltd., 1951. See also 3d ed. (1957).

LEAGUE OF NATIONS. *The Network of World Trade.* Geneva, 1942.

STOLPER, W., and ROSKAMP, K. "Input-Output Table for East Germany with Applications to Foreign Trade," *Bulletin of the Oxford Institute of Statistics,* November, 1961.

TATEMOTO, M., and ICHIMURA, S. "Factor Proportions and Foreign Trade: The Case of Japan," *Review of Economics and Statistics,* November, 1959.

WAHL, D. F. "Capital and Labour Requirements for Canada's Foreign Trade," *Canadian Journal of Economics and Political Science,* August, 1961.

ZIMMERMAN, ERICH W. *World Resources and Industries.* Rev. ed. New York; Harper & Row, Publishers, 1951.

STUDY QUESTIONS

1. Indicate some of the major difficulties encountered in attempting to verify empirically theories of trade.

2. Review the results of empirical tests of the classical and Heckscher-Ohlin theories of trade. What conclusions can be reached on the basis of these tests?

3. In what sense are there thousands of different factors of production?

4. Describe some of the elements which determine the rate of population growth in a given area.

5. What qualitative differences would you expect to find in populations living in equatorial regions from those living in the northern temperate zones? What other kinds of influences account for qualitative differences in population?

6. In what respect can it be said that the supply of land is fixed? In what respects is it variable?

7. Define what, in the terminology of economics, is meant by "capital."

8. Why are the ratios of factor supplies possessed by a country more significant for international economics than are the absolute supplies?

9. If a country has only a very small per capita supply of capital, why is it likely to be predominantly agricultural, even though it has also very little land per capita?

10. The same cause that operates to make a country fall into the classification of an "agricultural" economy, as defined in the text, also

is responsible for the low standard of living which usually prevails in such a country. Explain.

11. What type of agricultural commodities would you expect an "industrial" economy like Belgium to produce for herself?

12. What differences would you expect to find between the type of manufactured goods in which Great Britain has a comparative advantage and the type of manufactured goods in which the United States has a comparative advantage?

13. Look up the statistics on the kind of foodstuffs which the United States imports. How do you explain the facts?

14. Other things being equal, why would a country with a high per capita income tend to import a larger quantity of goods per capita than poorer countries do?

15. Explain the low percentage which imports into the United States bear to national income, and contrast this with the situation of most European countries.

16. Industrialization of a country is likely to have more important effects on the pattern of its foreign trade than on the volume of its trade. Why?

17. What does Figure 4.1 in the text suggest to you would happen if world trade were forced into rigid bilateral channels?

Chapter 5

THE THEORY OF INTERNATIONAL FACTOR MOVEMENTS

The substantive content of international economic relations consists of (*a*) the exchange of goods and services among countries, and (*b*) the international movement of the factors of production. While (*a*) refers to the movement of the *products* of factors, (*b*) relates to the movement of the factors themselves.

The theory of trade addresses itself to the causes and effects of trade in goods and services, and was the subject of Chapters 2 and 3. The theory of trade is built on the assumption that productive factors are perfectly *immobile internationally, though perfectly mobile within each trading country.* The purpose of this assumption is not to describe the real world, where factors have some degree of mobility internationally and some degree of immobility intranationally, but rather to isolate for analytical study the pure theory of trade in a setting free of extraneous influences.

In the present chapter, our primary focus of interest is the causes and effects of international factor movements. As in the pure trade model, certain assumptions will be made for the purpose of distilling from the complicated set of real-world influences on factor movements the essential and central forces of an economic character. Chief among these assumptions are the absence of artificial barriers or restraints on factor movements, and the operation of strictly economic motives.

THE MEANING OF FACTOR MOVEMENTS

Before attempting to discover the reasons for and consequences of international factor movements, it is necessary to identify what they are. As far as the movement of labor is concerned, it is self-evident that reference is made to the migration of persons from one country to another as places of more or less permanent residence and of employment. Temporary changes in residence for tourist travel, study, and so on, are therefore not included.

The definition of international capital movements is not so simple. It is important to remember that capital, as a factor of production, refers to the stock of reproducible goods useful in helping to produce other goods and services. In concrete, physical terms, the capital stock of a country consists of its railroads, highways, harbor installations, power plants, dams, buildings, industrial and agricultural machinery and tools, inventory of raw materials, and so on. But an international capital movement does *not* consist of the transfer of specific capital goods from one country to another, though the transfer of capital goods may accompany a capital movement. Rather, an international capital movement means, in the first instance and as recorded statistically, the movement from one country to another—or, more accurately, from individuals, businesses, or institutions in one country to those in another country—of *money capital,* or loan funds. It is bonds, stocks, and other evidences of debt or ownership which are dealt with in domestic and international capital markets. Specific capital goods, like all other goods, are dealt with in the commodity markets and they are recorded in commodity trade statistics.

Our immediate interest at the moment, however, is the international allocation of *real* capital—that is, of concrete instruments of production. The question, then, is: What is the connection between international monetary capital movements and the distribution of the supply of real capital? The answer is to be found in the nature of the process of real capital accumulation.

In order for any country or region within a country to acquire a larger stock of capital goods, it must have available a current flow of goods and services in excess of its current consumption of goods and services. One method of accumulating capital, therefore, is to *save* (that is, not consume) some portion of the national income or current aggregate net production of goods and services. This is the normal and by far the more important source of real capital formation. But in countries that are meagerly endowed with capital and land per head of population, the ability to save is severely limited by the low level of per capita income and the desire to consume a very high proportion of all that is currently produced.

Fortunately, there is a second method by which a country may increase its domestic stock of real capital. With a given level of national income, the domestic stock of capital goods can be increased without further reducing current consumption, provided that an *import surplus* of goods and services from abroad can be developed. Moreover, the import surplus need not consist of capital goods. Even if only consumer goods are imported, the import surplus permits a diversion of domestic productive agents from consumer goods production to capital goods production.

But how can a country develop an import surplus—especially for a long enough period to allow a significant increase in its stock of real capital? In Chapters 2 and 3, we assumed that the only method of paying for imports was with exports. Now, however, we are dropping this artificial assumption and admitting the existence of international transactions in evidences of debt—that is, of international monetary capital movements. We must now also admit, therefore, that a country may develop an import surplus of goods and services, provided that individuals, businesses, or institutions (including governments) in other countries are willing to lend or give the means of paying for such a surplus. As far as private individuals and businesses are concerned, the willingness to lend abroad depends upon their expectation that the rate of financial return will be greater there than at home. More specifically, is the rate of interest obtainable abroad greater than that offered in the domestic market on securities of similar kinds and degree of risk? If so, there is an incentive to purchase foreign securities, or to make what is called a *portfolio* investment. Or is the rate of profits earned by concerns abroad higher than that earned in similar businesses at home? If so, there is an incentive to acquire ownership shares in the foreign concerns, or to form a company in that country—that is, to make a *direct investment*.[1] In either of these two cases—portfolio or direct foreign investments—the receiving country obtains the financial means of paying for an import surplus and increasing its domestic stock of capital.

Apart from private loans and investments from abroad, a country may be enabled to acquire an import surplus by receiving loans or

---

[1] Although, in general, "portfolio investments" refer to fixed-interest securities or bond capital, and "direct investments" to equity or share capital, the technical distinction is somewhat sharper than this. "Direct investments" refer to equity shares in foreign concerns in sufficient amount to give an important voice in their management, and the direct branches abroad of domestic companies. Once a foreign enterprise is defined as a direct-investment company, however, all private investments in the securities of that company by nationals of the investing country are considered to be part of the direct investment. Portfolio investments consist of holdings of foreign stocks, bonds, real estate, etc., which do not constitute an important voice in the management of an enterprise but are held primarily as a source of income.

grants from foreign governments or other public institutions. In this case, the *motives* for the capital transfer are likely to be different from those of private lenders and investors, but the result is the same as far as permitting an increase in the domestic stock of capital in the receiving country is concerned. In short, an international monetary capital movement provides the means by which the receiving country can increase its domestic stock of real capital.[2] In effect, a money capital movement constitutes a transfer of purchasing power, which, in turn, permits the receiving country to develop an import surplus. It is the latter which constitutes the *real* capital movement; indeed, as we shall see in a subsequent chapter, the net movement of goods and services is the only way in which a net monetary capital movement can in fact occur. The *mechanism* by which a monetary capital flow is transformed into a real capital movement is a difficult subject in itself and will be taken up in a later chapter.

Finally, there is one very important consideration entering into capital movements not found in the case of population movements. A monetary capital inflow into a country, except for grants or gifts, ordinarily carries with it an obligation of repayment at some later date and of interest payment in the interim.[3] Just as a real capital inflow can take place only in the form of a net import surplus of goods and services, so, also, capital *repayment* can be made only in the form of an *export* surplus of goods and services. This raises numerous problems, some of which we shall consider later in other contexts; but at the moment we are interested in its implications from the standpoint of capital supply. How can a capital inflow contribute to a permanent increase in the stock of domestic capital if, later on, an export surplus must be developed to repay the loans received or to liquidate the equity interests of foreigners?

The same question can be raised about the capital expansion of an individual business, financed by floating a loan or stock issue domestically, and essentially the same answer is applicable in both cases. Real capital contributes to the production of goods and services a *net* amount over and above its cost. More specifically, the use of capital involves a more roundabout and efficient method of production that raises output sufficiently not only to repay the cost

---

[2] As we shall learn later, however, there are several different kinds of monetary capital movements, not all of which are significant as means of allowing real capital transfers.

[3] In the case of investments in the form of equity shares, however, there is no problem of fixed principal or interest payments, but foreign holders expect to receive any profits due them.

of the capital but with a surplus left over. Just as an individual business concern may be able, therefore, to increase its *net* assets and income by borrowing, so a country as a whole may add to its net stock of capital and flow of real income by borrowing internationally.

ECONOMIC MOTIVES FOR FACTOR MOVEMENTS

In analyzing the reasons for international trade, we concluded that the immediate cause is differences in the money prices (costs) at a given rate of exchange of commodities produced at home and in foreign countries. In a similar fashion, the immediate economic reason for factor movements is differences in the international prices (calculated in a common unit of measurement) of the factors. Higher wage rates (the "price" of labor) for a given type of labor service in the United States than in Mexico provide an economic incentive for Mexicans to cross the border—sometimes even illegally. Higher returns on capital investment in Canada than in the United States attract American capital.

REASONS FOR FACTOR PRICE DIFFERENCES

But why do the prices of factor services differ from country to country? In competitive markets, the price of a factor service is equal to the value of the factor's marginal product. Higher real wages in the United States than in most other countries are a reflection of the greater marginal productivity of American labor.

Since international differences in factor prices are based on differences in their marginal productivities, we are led to inquire into the reasons for the latter. We find that a major reason may be *differences in relative factor endowments.* If country *A,* compared to country *B,* has a relatively large labor force and small stock of capital, there is a strong presumption that wages will be lower and the rental price of capital higher in *A* than in *B.* The principle involved here is that of variable proportions or diminishing returns: the greater the quantity of any factor working with given amounts of other factors, the lower tends to be the marginal productivity of the factor.

The reader will observe at once that the above is merely a restatement of the conditions underlying the Heckscher-Ohlin theory of trade. In that theory, relative factor abundance determines relative factor prices, which in turn determines relative costs of goods. We therefore reach the interesting conclusion that *international trade and international factor movements are the result of the same underlying cause*—differences in relative factor endowments.

A labor-scarce, capital-abundant country, such as the United States, tends not only to specialize in and export commodities requiring large amounts of capital and small amounts of labor but also to attract immigrants and to export capital. A capital-scarce, labor-abundant country, like India, tends not only to specialize in and export labor-intensive products but also, in the absence of artificial barriers and noneconomic considerations to the contrary, to "lose" labor through emigration and attract capital from abroad.[4] This statement must be qualified, however, to take into account the effects of transfer costs. We noted earlier that the costs of transporting commodities in many cases make trade in them uneconomic. So, too, costs of factor movements may outweigh in particular cases the advantages of movement. Transfer costs are likely to be especially important in the movement of labor. The money required merely for rail and ship fare can alone be a formidable obstacle to the emigration of a poor family to a distant land. Nevertheless, the tens of millions of persons who have emigrated to other lands in the course of history are witness to the fact that the opportunities for *net* gain (after deducting transfer costs) have not been lacking.

A word of caution is now in order. We earlier noted that for the Heckscher-Ohlin theory of trade to hold, the assumptions on which it is built must be valid. Similar caveats must be introduced for the theory of factor movements as stated above. In order for the cause of international factor price differences to be assigned to differences in relative factor endowments, a major assumption is necessary: that supply conditions are of dominating importance. Conceivably, the demand for a factor service in relatively abundant supply may be so great as to cause its price to be relatively high. This is equivalent to the conclusion reached in our discussion of the Heckscher-Ohlin theory of trade that relative factor abundance need not necessarily be associated with a relatively low price of the factor.

---

[4] The conclusion that India would tend in a free market to attract foreign capital must be modified additionally by the fact that relative scarcity is not the only determinant of the marginal productivity of a factor of production. The general social and political atmosphere and the economies of scale are, among others, elements that help determine the marginal productivity of any factor. Hence the return on capital in India might not be as attractive to foreigners as its relative scarcity alone would indicate. This does not, however, reduce the economic motive for Indians to emigrate.

A more general theory of factor price differences, therefore, is that they are caused by differences in relative factor supplies in relation to relative factor demands. The assignment of dominating influence to the supply side is a special case of the general theory, with the pattern of demand for goods—and thence the factors producing the goods—being not significantly different internationally.

THE ECONOMIC EFFECTS OF FACTOR MOVEMENTS

In Chapter 3 we investigated the effects of free international trade on the level of the world's and of each participating country's real income. A similar inquiry for factor movements is now in order.

The Level of World Income

Free international trade, we have concluded, increases the efficiency of world production and increases the level of real income. So, too, do free international factor movements induced by economic considerations. If labor and capital move from areas where the net value of their marginal products (and, therefore, their prices) are lower to where they are higher, more is added to world output than is destroyed. For example, suppose that a given type of labor service commands a wage of $15 per day in the United States and the equivalent of only $3 per day in Italy. Then, as one such laborer emigrates to the United States, output rises by $15 per day in the United States and falls by $3 per day in Italy; net gain in world output: $12 per day (ignoring transfer costs). Of course, as Italian labor continues to emigrate to the United States, its marginal productivity would tend to rise in Italy and fall in the United States. But, so long as the marginal productivity of labor remained greater in the United States than in Italy, there would continue to be both an economic motive for continued emigration and a net gain in world output. If the marginal productivity were to become equal in the two countries (a point to be considered shortly), then both the motive for further emigration and the possibility of further gain in world output would be eliminated.

The same analysis applies to capital. World output is increased if capital moves out of the United States, where its marginal productivity is relatively low, to capital-scarce countries, where its marginal productivity is higher.

The Level of National Income

We have shown that there is an unequivocal economic gain to the world as a whole realizable through both free international trade and free international factor movements. From a cosmopolitan point of view, then, the case for free and unimpeded international economic relations is unexceptional.

But all of us, even those sophisticates who regard themselves as "citizens of the world," are identified first as nationals of a particular country. International economic *policies* are formulated by each national state, for the most part with its own *national* interests in mind. In a world organized in this fashion, the effects of trade and factor movements on the national economy of each participating country have more relevance to attitudes and policies than do the effects on the world economy as a whole.

Now we have already shown, in Chapter 3, that free trade leads to a greater real national income for each participating country than it could produce in isolation. Can the same thing be said of international factor movements? Would free movement of labor from labor-abundant to labor-scarce countries and of capital from capital-abundant to capital-scarce countries enlarge the real national incomes of both the sending and the receiving countries?

Let us first consider labor movements and construct a case where the answer would clearly be affirmative. Suppose that there are two countries, one of which has a population below the optimum and the other with a population far above the optimum. As concrete contemporary examples, we might take Canada as the country with below-optimum population and India as the country with above-optimum population.

Now an increase in the labor supply of Canada—provided that it were not excessive for any given period of time—would in all probability increase the real national income of Canada by an amount *proportionately greater* than the increase in the number of workers. The economic reasons for expecting this result lie in the advantages to be gained from greater specialization and division of labor and perhaps also from the economies of scale permitted by a larger market. In this case, *all* factor owners—labor as well as property-holders—would tend to gain from the immigration.

At the same time, average per capita real income in India would tend to be higher after than before the emigration, since the per capita supply of land and capital would be raised. However, whether the remaining (nonemigrating) population would be better off depends upon circumstances. If there were unemployment or underemployed before the migration for lack of land or capital with which to work, or if the net marginal productivity of the emigrating workers were zero in India,[5] the population remaining after emigration would undoubtedly be better off on the average. However, emigration might leave the home population worse off than before. This would be the case, for example, if the emigrants were the higher-skilled or better-educated workers whose productivity was considerably above those remaining behind. A similar adverse effect on the remaining population would be produced if the emigrants owned a relatively large amount of wealth which they took along with them.

Now let us turn to a second kind of example. This time let England instead of Canada be the second country. In contrast to Canada, it is fairly clear that England is not underpopulated. Whether or not England is actually overpopulated is a debatable point, but let us assume for the sake of argument that her population is just about at the optimum. Hence any increase in England's population from the immigration of Indians would result in an above-optimum population. In other words, with the supply of land and capital and the state of technology remaining unchanged, the larger population in England would reduce *per capita* output, even though the aggregate national income would presumably be larger. How, then, can it be said that the movement of labor provides the basis for an improvement in the economic welfare of the immigrant country?

Assuming that competition prevails in the immigrant country, the immigrant workers (as well as native labor) will receive a wage equal to the value of their marginal product. Now it is clear that if the immigrants receive only the value of what they *add* to production (their marginal product), natives will have no less real income available to them than before the immigration took place. Indeed, actually the native population as a whole will have a *larger* per capita real income available, *provided that the immigrant labor is economically discriminated against.*[6] The reason for this result is as

---

[5] It has been observed that in some underdeveloped economies, agricultural workers may have a zero marginal product, indicating a redundant supply of labor. In such cases, the wage paid tends to be at or near a subsistence level but above, of course, the marginal product of the labor.

[6] See Abba P. Lerner, *The Economics of Control* (New York: Macmillan Co., 1944), pp. 364–65.

follows: as immigration continues to force down the marginal productivity of labor, the total wages received by the immigrants will be less than their total contribution to the national income, with a "surplus" thus being made available for distribution to the native population.

For example, suppose that the value of the marginal product of the first immigrant in his new home is $15 per day. The arrival of a second immigrant reduces the value of labor's marginal product to, say, $14, and the third immigrant reduces it to $13. After three immigrants have arrived, then, each receives a wage of $13 (the value of his marginal product), or a total of $39 in wages. But the national income of the country has increased by $15 plus $14 plus $13, or a total of $42. Hence there is $3 "surplus" available for distribution to the native population. In order, however, for native labor to be at least as well off as before, income received by it would have to be greater than the value of its marginal product—for its marginal product declines at the same time that the immigrants' marginal product declines. This is where discrimination between native and immigrant labor comes into the picture. Now, of course, the immigrants, even though receiving less income per head than the native population, would presumably still have a higher income than in their own country. Hence *everyone,* native as well as immigrants, could have his economic welfare improved through the population movement. On *social* grounds, however, there might be very strong objections to discriminating in this fashion, and this is perhaps the most important "practical" economic argument against immigration under the circumstances described.

Let us now briefly consider the national economic effects of capital movements. An inflow of capital into capital-poor countries will tend to increase the per capita productivity of the receiving country. It is true, of course, that the national wealth is not increased by the full amount of the capital inflow, for the country has at the same time acquired an external debt. But, as we have argued earlier, capital may produce a surplus over and above its costs, so that, after the loan is repaid, there remains a net gain in the capital wealth of the borrowing country. Presumably, then—barring the dissipation of the loan proceeds in added consumption or uneconomic investments—the capital-receiving country will have its real per capita income increased.

Turning to the lending country, the outflow of capital reduces the domestic supply of capital and therefore tends to reduce the per capita domestic productivity of the population. But note that the capital exported is not lost to the economy. Rather, the locus of its investment has changed—from lower-return to higher-return uses. Suppose, for example, that capital investments in the United States yield a marginal rate of return of 5 percent, while similar-risk investments in Mexico yield a marginal rate of return of 10 percent. The flow of capital from the United States to Mexico, then, will yield a larger return to the American economy (in the form of imports paid for with the interest earnings) than if the capital had been invested within the United States. The per capita output of the American economy—from domestic production and the return on investments abroad combined—will be larger as the result of the capital outflow.

In general, we conclude that the level of the real national income of participating countries is increased by free factor movements as well as by free trade, with some qualifications applicable in the case of labor movements into areas with above-optimum population.

Factor Prices

It was shown in Chapter 3 that trade tends to reduce international differences in factor prices, and can even theoretically completely eliminate them, although only under a rather stringent set of assumptions. However, it will be remembered that the tendency toward factor price equalization as the result of trade crucially depends upon the absence of factor-intensity reversal. With factor reversal occurring, factor price differences may either be narrowed or widened by trade, depending upon circumstances.

While trade may tend to reduce international differences in factor prices, a still stronger tendency in this direction is exerted by factor movements. Whereas trade affects factor prices indirectly through the repercussions produced by the reallocation of resources, factor movements affect factor prices directly through changing factor supplies. A movement of labor from low-wage areas to high-wage areas increases the supply of labor in the immigrant country and reduces it in the emigrant country; in a like manner, capital movements increase the supply of capital in the receiving countries and reduce it in the sending countries. To the extent that the marginal productivity and price of a factor depends upon its supply in relationship to the supplies of other factors, the result of factor movements is clearly in the direction of eliminating factor price differences. Even so, there are possible exceptions. One exception was cited earlier: an immigrant country with a suboptimum population. A similar exception applies if both labor and capital move jointly in the same direction toward a country abundantly supplied with land, as discussed below. Nevertheless, the presumption remains strong in the general case that factor movements reduce factor price differences.

The impact of factor movements on factor prices is naturally accompanied by redistribution of the national income. The share in the national income of the relatively highest-priced factor tends to be reduced, the share of the relatively lowest-priced factor increased. This tendency results, of course, from the effects of factor movements on relative factor supplies.

FACTOR MOVEMENTS AND TRADE AS SUBSTITUTES

From our survey of the many respects in which trade and factor movements are parallel in their causes and effects, it is reasonable to suppose that these two components of international economic relations are to some extent substitutes for each other. The greater the volume of trade under the conditions posited by the Heckscher-Ohlin theory, the lesser will be the differences in international factor prices and the motives for factor migration. The greater the movement of factors internationally, the smaller tend to be the differences in comparative costs and the reasons for trade.

Actually, however, neither factor movements nor trade can entirely eliminate the function of the other. To begin with, factors are not, and cannot be, perfectly mobile. The degree of mobility of resources varies tremendously. At one end of the scale, there are those resources which are inherently incapable of movement. Into this category fall land, including climate, mineral deposits, water power, and location. At the opposite extreme is the high sensitivity and mobility of money capital, at least when there is a well-organized international capital market and an appropriate atmosphere prevails. Indeed, capital in general, whether in its monetary form or in real terms, is capable of movement and historically has played a tremendously important role in the creation of a world economy.

The obstacles to the movement of capital are not inherent, therefore, but are rather of an institutional and psychological character. In a world divided into numerous independent national states, each of which has sovereign authority over its own peoples and territory, there is always an additional element of risk and uncertainty in investing capital in a foreign country. In the latter part of the 19th century, these risks and uncertainties were reduced to a minimum because of the institutional framework which then prevailed, and consequently large international movements of capital occurred. In later years and particularly since the early 1930's, however, political uncertainty and divergent and sometimes discriminatory national economic and financial controls have rendered foreign investment a risky business, not to be undertaken without the prospects of a very high return.

In between the complete immobility of land and the potentially great mobility of capital lie human productive agents. Physically, labor is, of course, easily capable of international migration. Even more than in the case of capital, however, the actual international movement of labor is restricted by institutional and psychological barriers. To consider the latter first, there are the ties that bind individuals and families to their homeland: language, customs, habits, friends and relatives, and the whole array of sentiments and emotions subsumed under the name of "nationalism." Nevertheless, the history of international migration demonstrates that while these factors may limit the movement of human beings, they do not prevent them. If the atmosphere is propitious and the motives strong, labor *will* move, although noneconomic motives may in some cases be more important than economic reasons.

Whatever might be the natural tendencies, institutional restrictions, as in recent years, can reduce migration to a mere trickle. Immigration laws, exclusion acts, work permits, and numerous other devices have been invented to reduce, or in some cases eliminate, the possibility of moving to another country.

Since movements of factors do not, in fact, eliminate differences in their relative scarcities in different countries, international trade has a continuing basis as a substitute for factor movements. The steamy jungles required for natural rubber production cannot be transferred to the temperate zones; nor can the soil and climate required for wheat be moved to tropical regions. But natural rubber and wheat can be exchanged for each other in international trade. Similarly, immigration laws may prevent Indian labor from moving into the United States, and the institutions and sociopolitical environment of India discourage American capital from flowing to India, but American tractors can be exchanged for Indian jute.

Just as, in practice, factor movements do not eliminate the function of international trade, neither does trade entirely remove the basis for factor movements. For this to happen, trade would have to result in factor price equalization. But, as we noted much earlier, the conditions necessary for such an effect are so stringent as to be virtually impossible of fulfillment in the real world.[7] Again, then, we reiterate that there is a continuing economic basis for both factor movements and trade.

COMPLEMENTARY ASPECTS OF TRADE AND FACTOR MOVEMENTS

We have concluded that trade and factor movements are substitutes for each other, but only partially so. Rather than regard trade and factor movements as mutually exclusive phenomena, each may be looked upon as performing functions not achievable, or not so easily achievable, by the other. Indeed, we may go further and indicate some important respects in which trade and factor movements are complementary rather than substitutive.

Factor movements, for example, even though they reduce the disparities in relative costs and thereby reduce the opportunities for profitable trade that existed before, themselves create new fields of trade. This is perhaps best seen in the case of long-term capital flows.

Take a capital-poor country that receives long-term loans from abroad which are used, for example, to aid in the industrialization of the country. Some manufactured goods (such as textiles) which were formerly imported may now be produced as cheaply at home as abroad and therefore no longer be imported. But, as per capita real income grows in the country, the volume and composition of consumption changes, creating new demands for a wide variety of goods and services, both domestic and imported. The *composition* of trade is likely to change and the volume of trade to grow. This has been, in fact, the experience of countries that have industrialized.

By an analogous line of reasoning, it is probably true that international trade actually encourages international capital movements, notwithstanding the fact that trade reduces inequalities in the re-

---

[7] One of the required conditions, for example, is that transport costs be zero, so that a given good has an identical price in all countries. Needless to say, zero transport costs do not exist.

turns received by capital in different countries. In the first place, it must be remembered that capital is capable of movement, in the final analysis, only in the form of goods and services. Trading relations are, then, a necessary accompaniment of international lending and borrowing. Beyond this, however, international trade, by broadening markets and stimulating more efficient use of resources, creates investment opportunities, attractive to foreign as well as domestic investors. Indeed, in the history of long-term capital movements it has most often been the presence, or potential development, of *international* markets that has stimulated foreign investments. Moreover, a high volume of trade is more likely to be accompanied by well-developed financial facilities and institutions and by some degree of stability in political and economic relations, which reduce the risks and uncertainties of foreign loans and investments and encourage a greater flow of capital.

THE COORDINATE MOVEMENT OF CAPITAL AND LABOR

Just as commodity trade and factor movements are, in practice, often complementary, so also may the movements of different factors be complementary under certain circumstances. Suppose, for example, that some countries are well supplied with both labor and capital, compared to others that have a great abundance of land but small amounts of labor and capital. Under such circumstances, there might be a tendency for both labor and capital to move to the relatively land-abundant region. This is well illustrated historically by the mass migrations of peoples from Europe to the Western Hemisphere in the 19th century and the accompanying flow of capital.

In such coordinate movements of capital and labor, each tends to reinforce and encourage the other. Immigration into a lightly populated area enlarges the market, creates additional demand, and opens up new opportunities for capital investment. Likewise, the inflow of capital creates new employment opportunities, raises real wages, and increases the attractiveness of the area to those living in land-scarce countries. Furthermore, capital cannot be separated from the knowledge and skills required to use it. The development of industries in young countries is often dependent, therefore, not only upon the inflow of capital from wealthier and more mature countries but upon the importation of know-how and technology as well. The combined movement of both capital and individuals to the United States in its earlier history and up to, roughly, World War I, for example, gave an incalculable impetus to the rapid growth in the income and wealth of the United States.

FACTOR MOVEMENTS AND WELFARE

In considering the welfare aspects of trade in Chapter 3, we observed that some segments of a population are likely to be harmed while others gain. The same holds for factor movements. As already noted, the income share of high-priced factors tends to shrink as the result of factor movements. The clearest-cut example is the share of labor in a high-wage country which is at or above the optimum level of population prior to immigration, as cited above.

In such cases of conflicts of interest, we may appeal to the welfare principle adduced earlier in connection with the welfare argument for trade. Since everyone *could* be made better off by factor movements, the potential welfare at least is advanced. In this connection two points deserve emphasis. The first is the tremendous magnitude of the potential economic benefits to the world as a whole and to each country realizable from unimpeded trade and factor movements. The second is that the problem of distributing the gains realized should not be exaggerated. As noted earlier, virtually all economic progress is accompanied by distributional effects. From a welfare point of view, it would not make good sense to forgo the advantages of trade and factor movements in order to avoid changes in income distribution, in view of the fact that machinery for controlling distribution exists and can be put into operation. This does not, of course, deny that there may be valid social, political, or other noneconomic values or objectives that, in cases of conflict with economic goals, may take precedence.

RECOMMENDED READING

BERRY, R. ALBERT, and SOLIGO, RONALD. "Some Welfare Aspects of International Migration," *Journal of Political Economy,* Vol. 77, No. 5 (September–October, 1969).

HECKSCHER, ELI. "The Effects of Foreign Trade on the Distribution of Income," *Ekonomist Tidskrift* (1919). Reprinted in American Economic Association, *Readings in the Theory of International Trade* (eds. HOWARD S. ELLIS and LLOYD A. METZLER), pp. 272–300. Homewood, Ill.: Richard D. Irwin, Inc., 1949.

MEADE, J. E. *Trade and Welfare,* Vol. II of *The Theory of International Economic Policy,* chaps. xix–xxiii, xxvii. London: Oxford University Press, 1955.

STOLPER, WOLFGANG F., and SAMUELSON, PAUL A. "Protection and Real Wages," *Review of Economic Studies* (1941). Reprinted in *Readings in the Theory of International Trade,* pp. 333–57.

THOMAS, BRINLEY. *Migration and Economic Growth.* Cambridge, England: Cambridge University Press, 1954.

STUDY QUESTIONS

1. Describe the two methods that are open to a country through which it may increase its stock of real capital.

2. Distinguish between an international money capital movement and an international real capital movement.

3. Show how an import surplus of consumer goods might permit a country to build up its stock of capital goods.

4. What fundamental situation leads to economic motives for international capital and population movements?

5. Prove that the world's real output and income would rise if factors of production were to move internationally in accordance with economic motives.

6. Describe the conditions under which a population movement would most favorably affect both the emigrant and immigrant countries. What modifications in the analysis are required under less favorable conditions?

7. Analyze the effects of factor movements on factor prices and the distribution of income.

8. In what sense and under what conditions are trade and factor movements substitutes for each other? Why, in fact, are they never complete substitutes?

9. Show the respects in which trade and factor movements may be complementary.

10. Describe a situation in which you might expect capital and labor to migrate jointly in the same direction.

11. What welfare questions and principles are raised by factor movements? How do these compare to those raised by trade?

Chapter 6

A SURVEY OF INTERNATIONAL CAPITAL AND POPULATION MOVEMENTS

From the analysis in the preceding chapter we have concluded that the unequal relative endowments of the means of production in different countries create the basis and incentive for both commodity trade and the movement of productive factors. Of the latter, only capital and labor are physically capable of movement. Theoretically, there would be economic motives which would operate to cause continued international capital and labor movements as long as unequal relative supplies and therefore differential rates of return in different parts of the world persisted. This theoretical expectation must be modified in practice, however, to take into account the extent to which (a) economic motives are not allowed by institutional and political conditions to work themselves out and (b) noneconomic considerations intervene.

It is the purpose of this chapter to review broadly the historical experience with international capital and population movements, with an eye to revealing their importance in various eras.

A BRIEF HISTORY OF INTERNATIONAL CAPITAL MOVEMENTS

It will be recalled from the discussion in the preceding chapter that only *real* capital movements are significant from the standpoint of the allocation of resources. While it is often monetary capital movements which allow real capital movements, not all monetary capital movements are significant from this point of view. More specifically, as we shall see later, it is only net *long-term* portfolio investments and direct investments which ordinarily give rise to the real capital movements that are important in the allocation of resources.[1] The data in this chapter on capital movements are confined, therefore, to long-term portfolio and direct investments.

---

[1] The dividing line between long- and short-term investments is usually arbitrarily set at one year.

Capital Movements before 1914

The 19th century and the first decade and a half of the 20th century were the "golden age" of private international investment activity. It is estimated that by 1914 the *gross* long-term foreign investments of the major creditor countries amounted to over $41,000 million—the accumulated result of decades of large-scale capital movements.[2] As we shall see, only recently have private long-term international capital flows reached their pre-1914 volume. Relative to the national incomes and volume of domestic investments of capital-exporting countries, however, international capital movements on private account have never recovered anything like their volume before World War I. What accounts for this historical fact?

The principal explanation lies in a combination of circumstances which made the era before 1914 an especially favorable one for the encouragement of private capital movements. We have observed that the prime motive for private investing abroad is the earning of higher rates of return than on comparable investments at home. We have also learned that higher returns on capital tend to be produced in those areas where capital is relatively more scarce than at home.

In the period under review, several European countries, with Great Britain in the lead, were rapidly accumulating large amounts of capital. This was the consequence of the Industrial Revolution and the accompanying increase in national income and savings. At the same time, there were vast areas in other parts of the world rich in land and natural resources but short of capital. Moreover, as Great Britain and certain other European countries became more and more highly industrialized, specializing in manufactured goods, their import demand for raw materials and foodstuffs grew. This increased prospective returns from investments in overseas countries whose economies were best suited to specialization in primary-type commodities. The economic conditions were present, therefore, for investors in the wealthier and more economically advanced countries to find attractive the investment prospects opening up in various less developed countries.

---

[2] Norman S. Buchanan and Friedrich A. Lutz, *Rebuilding the World Economy* (New York: Twentieth Century Fund, 1947), p. 156. Some indeterminate portion of the $41,000 million would have to be deducted to arrive at the *net* amount of investments, which represents the difference, for each country, between the amount its residents have invested abroad and the amount of foreign capital invested domestically.

But more than the immediate rate of return is involved in foreign investments. Political and economic institutions and attitudes must be conducive to taking those risks that are peculiar to investment activity in foreign lands. Is there governmental interference in making loans and investments or in transferring interest returns and profits? Is there danger that the capital-receiving country will unfairly tax or discriminate against foreign capital? How great is the risk of loss from changes in the rate of exchange or from political disturbances, including war? These are a few of the questions which investors must ask themselves before they can decide to place their capital abroad rather than at home. Generally, however, before 1914 the answers were favorable. The philosophy of laissez-faire was at its zenith, with its emphasis on individualism and governmental noninterference. Not only were trade and factor movements relatively free from artificial restraints and obstacles on the part of governments, but the prevalence of the international gold standard created what amounted to an international currency, minimizing the risk of loss from fluctuating exchange rates. No major international conflicts arose between the end of the Napoleonic Wars and 1914 to create economic maladjustments and political uncertainty.

Great Britain, France, and Germany were the largest international creditor countries before 1914, though a few smaller countries, such as the Netherlands and Switzerland, were not unimportant as sources of foreign capital. The United States remained a net debtor internationally—that is, foreign investments in the United States exceeded the latter's investments in other countries —until after World War I. But toward the end of the 19th century, concomitantly with its rapid economic growth and industrialization, the United States began to invest abroad in considerable volume. These investments are estimated to have reached about $3,500 million by 1914, compared to $7,200 million of foreign investments in the United States.[3]

Great Britain was by far the largest creditor country before World War I, accounting for nearly half the total long-term foreign investments outstanding in 1914. Britain's predominant position is not too difficult to explain. The Industrial Revolution came first to the British economy, increasing productivity and income and allowing the creation of exportable surpluses of manufactured

---

[3] Cleona Lewis, *America's Stake in International Investments* (Washington, D.C.: Brookings Institution, 1938) , p. 447.

goods. Although some British overseas investments were made early in the 19th century, the tempo increased rapidly in the last quarter of the century and reached a peak in the years immediately preceding the outbreak of the war. It is estimated that in 1913 British overseas investments increased by probably more than £200 million, or approximately $1,000 million.[4]

In the earlier years of the 19th century, Britain's overseas investments were oriented largely toward continental Europe, hastening thereby the spread of the Industrial Revolution. As the Continent developed industrially, it became relatively less attractive as an investment outlet. After about 1870 an increasingly larger share of British capital flowed toward the great agricultural and raw material-producing countries—especially the United States, Australia, Canada, Argentina, and New Zealand. The capital furnished these countries increased agricultural output and also aided in their developing industrialization.

France and Germany did not become important international lenders until near the end of the 19th century. In contrast to the bulk of British investments, French loans were strongly influenced by political considerations: loans to Russia, Turkey, and the Balkan States, in particular, appear to have been politically motivated. To some extent, the same thing was true of German foreign investments, especially in Central Europe, the Balkans, and Turkey, but in the main the economic motive of higher returns appears to have been predominant.

The nature of prewar international investment may be summed up in one sentence: apart from some loans for political and military purposes by France and Germany, the main body of investment was directed towards undeveloped primary producing countries, and the chief borrowers were those who could offer the highest returns.[5]

On the whole, we should have to agree that the long-term international capital movements which occurred before 1914 probably came as close to conforming to the expectations dictated by economic theory as conditions in the real world allow. The experience of the United States is eloquent evidence of the economic benefits to be derived from the inflow of capital from abroad for there can be no doubt that its development during the 19th century was

---

[4] Royal Institute of International Affairs, *The Problem of International Investment* (London: Oxford University Press, 1937), p. 129.

[5] *Ibid.*, p. 129.

thereby hastened. Even so, there were unfortunate aspects of the experience during this era which modified the full realization of the economic benefits predicated by theory. We have already noted that in some instances loans were dictated by noneconomic considerations. More serious than this, however, was the tendency for many direct investments in some areas to lead to ruthless exploitation of so-called "backward" peoples and the creation of economic and political rivalries. It may be seriously questioned, for example, whether either the native peoples of Africa or the general citizenry of the imperialist powers which fought over the territorial division of Africa gained any lasting economic benefits. A discussion of colonialism and imperialism falls outside the scope of this book, but it should be pointed out that in their worst manifestations they may destroy the benefits that would otherwise accrue from the international flow of capital.

The Interwar Years

World War I brought about tremendous changes in the international capital position of many countries and introduced a new era in the history of capital movements. The immediate impact of the war was to turn the United States from a net international debtor into a large-scale net creditor and greatly to diminish the foreign investments of most European countries—in the case of Germany to such an extent that she became a debtor country.

These important changes were the result of financing the war and postwar reconstruction. In order to finance their extraordinary wartime import surpluses, the Allied powers were forced to borrow and liquidate much of their investment in the United States. Until the entry of the United States into the war in April, 1917, Allied borrowing—chiefly by Great Britain and France—was from private sources. Subsequently, the U.S. government made direct advances to her belligerent partners, which constituted the war debts proper. These credits amounted to over $7,000 million. Post-Armistice loans by the United States added another $3,000 million to the Allied war debts, bringing the total to some $10,000 million. In addition to the private and governmental loans made by the United States, foreign investments in the United States were liquidated in an amount of approximately $2,000 million. As a result of the war financing, the United States was transformed from a net international debtor, to the extent of about $3,700 million in 1914, into a net international creditor in 1919 of roughly the same amount—excluding intergovernmental debts.

Great Britain and France, on the other hand, as a result of large-scale borrowing, liquidation of foreign assets, and depreciation of investments in enemy countries, found themselves at the war's end with greatly reduced creditor positions. In the case of Germany, liquidation of investments to finance the war, seizure of her investments in Allied countries, and depreciation of the value of investments elsewhere all combined to convert her from a net creditor to a net debtor country, even apart from reparations obligations of nearly $32,000 million which the victorious powers imposed upon her.

The Postwar Decade

The war not only abruptly changed the international capital positions of the belligerent countries but also profoundly affected future international capital movements. The capacity to lend abroad was redistributed as the result of the war, the chief source of new long-term capital shifting from Great Britain to the United States, More than that, the type of loans made and their effects on the world economy were vastly different from those of the prewar period.

The foreign long-term lending of the United States in the decade following World War I included two major types of loans. The first consisted of large loans to countries which were normally international creditors (almost exclusively European countries) for the purpose of relief and rehabilitation. The capital shortage in these countries was of a temporary nature, and in many cases they did not require long-term loans but rather supplies of foreign exchange to tide them over the few critical years immediately following the war.[6]

The second and more important type of loans was specifically for the purpose of long-term capital investment. These loans were made to countries which, with the exception of Germany, had been debtor countries.

Table 6.1 shows the *net* movement of long-term capital from the United States during the first 12 years of the postwar period.

---

[6] The analysis in this section concerning American lending experience is largely taken from the excellent study by Hal B. Lary and Associates in U.S. Department of Commerce, *The United States in the World Economy* (Washington, D.C.: U.S. Government Printing Office, 1943), pp. 90 ff.

In the early postwar years, foreign borrowing from the United States was mostly for rehabilitation. The largest part of the capital outflow in 1919 represented loans from the U.S. government for this purpose. By 1922, however, the U.S. government was out of the foreign-loan business, and the capital movements that occurred thereafter were on private account.

The heaviest private borrowings occurred in the years from 1924 to 1928. The reasons for this are numerous: economic activity was booming in nearly all countries, the gold standard had been re-

TABLE 6.1

Net Long-Term Capital Outflow from the
United States, 1919–30
(in millions of dollars)

1919	$2,712
1920	1,007
1921	562
1922	784
1923	−46*
1924	672
1925	543
1926	696
1927	991
1928	798
1929	240
1930	221
Total	$9,180

Source: U.S. Department of Commerce, *The Balance of International Payments of the United States, 1946–1948* (Washington, D.C., 1950), Table XXIII, pp. 272–73.
 * Net capital inflow.

stored and currencies stabilized, long-term interest rates fell in the United States, and high-pressure bond salesmen of American investment banks engaged in a competitive race of selling foreign issues to the public. After 1928, however, new foreign issues dropped sharply. Probably the chief explanation for this decline was the hectic domestic stock market boom which occurred in 1928 and 1929 and depressed the market for new fixed-return securities. In addition, evidence of economic recession abroad, especially in Germany, began to appear in 1928, making foreign lending less attractive.

United States direct investments abroad increased steadily in the postwar years until 1930, although they were not nearly so important as new foreign issues. The general prosperity and economic expansion which characterized these years were primarily responsible for the exodus of American capital and its investment in public utility, mining, railroads, automobile, and similar undertakings abroad.

Notwithstanding the fact that Great Britain suffered some reduction in her creditor status during World War I, and despite the heavy foreign investments by the United States during the 1920's, Great Britain in 1930 was still the world's largest long-term international creditor country. Several factors combined to limit Britain's overseas investments compared to the prewar era: the increased internal need for capital, the rise of New York as a competing international financial center, the lower rates of interest prevailing in the United States, and the overvaluation of sterling on the exchange market between 1925 and 1931.

Nevertheless, a considerable volume of new capital issues on foreign account were placed in London in the postwar years, mostly for British dominions and colonies. Indeed, there is some evidence that Britain's long-term loans in the postwar years were excessive and were in some measure accompanied by her borrowing short term abroad. Although some long-term international loans were made during the 1920's by other countries (notably France, the Netherlands, Switzerland, and Belgium), these were comparatively minor and do not justify more than passing mention in this survey.

We may now summarize the long-term international investment position of the world in 1930. The *gross* external long-term investment of the three principal creditor countries in 1930 are estimated to have been about $18,500 million (Great Britain), $15,200 million (the United States), and $3,500 million (France). The long-term investments of all other countries probably totaled more than $10,000 million, making a grand total of more than $47,000 million of long-term international debts outstanding in 1930, exclusive of war debts.

Nearly every country in the world was a long-term international borrower in 1930, but a relatively few countries accounted for most of the borrowing. Canada, Australia, and Argentina were the principal long-term debtor countries, but China, India, Germany, and Brazil were also important borrowers.

The Depression Decade

The student of international economics cannot avoid being impressed by the tremendous impact on the world economy of war and depression. We have seen that World War I caused rather abrupt changes in the international economic position of the major powers; in later pages we shall see that even greater changes were wrought by World War II.

In the meantime, during the decade preceding World War II, a worldwide economic depression made its contributions to the unbalancing of economic relations and to the setting of the stage for the coming war. The postwar period of net long-term international capital movements reached its end in 1930. The next few years were marked by a severe drop in output and employment, deflation, a sharp decline in the volume of international trade, the disorganization of the international monetary mechanism, the introduction of trade and exchange controls, the intensification of tariffs and other trade impediments, and political instability. In some measure as a cause, as well as a result, of these developments, new long-term international investments virtually ceased, and outstanding loans were widely defaulted.

TABLE 6.2

NET LONG-TERM CAPITAL INFLOW INTO THE
UNITED STATES, 1931–39
(in millions of dollars)

1931....... $194	1934....... $200	1937....... $521
1932....... 225	1935....... 436	1938....... 97
1933....... 77	1936....... 777	1939....... 27

Average annual net long-term capital *outflow* from the United States, 1919–30 = $765 million.

SOURCE: U.S. Department of Commerce, *The Balance of Payments of the United States, 1919–1953*, p. 4.

Indeed, in the case of the United States, the flow of long-term capital reversed direction after 1930. New dollar issues for foreign account and U.S. direct investments abroad decreased to an insignificant volume during most of the 1930's and were exceeded in amount by the amortization of past loans and net sales of outstanding securities to foreigners. Thus, compared to an average annual net long-term capital outflow of $765 million in the preceding 12 years, there was an average net long-term capital *inflow* into the United States of nearly $290 million per year in the 9-year period 1931–39, as shown in Table 6.2.

The decade of the 1930's was also marked by extensive defaults on interest and amortization payments due from foreign borrowers, both private and governmental. By 1933 some $3,000 million of foreign dollar bonds were in default, representing 37 percent of total issues outstanding, and in 1938, 40 percent of the issues were in default.[7] Defaults resulted in a general and sharp drop in bond prices, which encouraged large repurchases by foreigners of their own bonds, accounting for the substantial reduction in the foreign portfolio held by American investors which occurred after 1930.

The net result of 12 years of long-term capital outflow from the United States, followed by several years of a reverse movement during the depression years, is shown in Table 6.3.

TABLE 6.3

PRIVATE LONG-TERM INTERNATIONAL INVESTMENT POSITION OF THE UNITED
STATES IN THE YEARS 1919, 1930, AND 1939
(in millions of dollars)

	1919	1930	1939
U.S. investments abroad:			
Direct	$3,900	$ 8,000	$ 7,000
Portfolio	2,600	7,200	3,800
Total	$6,500	$15,200	$10,800
Foreign investments in the United States:			
Direct	$ 900	$ 1,400	$ 2,000
Portfolio	2,300	4,300	4,300
Total	$3,200	$ 5,700	$ 6,300
Net long-term creditor position of the United States	$3,300	$ 9,500	$ 4,500

SOURCE: U.S. Department of Commerce, *Survey of Current Business*, August, 1956, p. 15.

Viewing the interwar period in its entirety, the student will be impressed especially with two outstanding aspects of America's foreign-investment experience: (*a*) the very large amount of defaults on foreign dollar bonds which occurred during the 1930's and (*b*) the abrupt cessation of U.S. long-term investing abroad beginning in 1931. Neither of these events is consistent with the worldwide economic allocation of capital resources which is prescribed by our theoretical analysis and which in fact occurred during the 19th century and in the prewar years of the 20th century.

Two major elements go far in explaining the rather unfortunate foreign-lending and -investment experience of the United States in the interwar years. The first was the fundamental structural changes in the world economy which the rapid industrialization of

---

[7] Institute of International Finance of New York University, Bulletin No. 110 (May 13, 1940), pp. 14–15.

the United States and World War I combined to bring about. Around 1870, the merchandise trade of the United States with Europe was approximately balanced, and imports into the United States consisted mainly of manufactured goods. After 1870, the commodity exports of the United States to Europe steadily increased relative to imports from Europe, and the composition of imports shifted from manufactures to primary products. In other words, America's trade, which was earlier in balance with and complementary to Europe's, changed before World War I to an export surplus and competitive position. The war hastened this shift in structural relationships by increasing the tempo of industrialization in the United States and enlarging its export surplus to Europe.

Just as net loans can be made only in the form of a net export surplus of goods and services, so net repayment of loans can be received only if the creditor country develops an *import* surplus of goods and services. A net reduction of European debts to the United States, therefore, would have required a net export surplus from Europe, either directly to the United States or to other countries which in turn had a net export surplus vis-à-vis the United States. Whether or not the structural changes required to allow debt repayments would ultimately have been made, had a long period of adjustment ensued, is a moot question. In any event, new American loans rather abruptly disappeared, as we have seen, thereby foreclosing any long-period adjustments.

This brings us to the second major element which contributed to the unsatisfactory investment experience of the interwar years— the worldwide depression of the 1930's, which was especially severe in the United States. Even before the depression hit the United States, the volume of foreign lending by the latter had begun to decline. Nevertheless, it is quite certain that the cessation of lending and the reverse flow of long-term capital was the direct result of the economic and financial crisis which descended upon the United States and other countries.

The cessation of American lending removed the props that had supported the large volume of world trade during the 1920's. In addition, it rendered virtually impossible the repayment of loans. Even if the structural maladjustments previously described had not existed, the sharp decline in American demand for imports, resulting from the fall of income and aggravated by the imposition of higher tariffs, would have made the creation of an import surplus into the United States virtually impossible.

World War II and the Early Postwar Years

As during World War I, except on a much larger scale, the United States was the arsenal of the Allied nations during World War II. In contrast to the method of financing the export surplus of the United States in the earlier conflict, the largest part of America's aid to her allies in World War II was in the form of government gifts, which did not increase the indebtedness of foreign countries.[8] In any event, however, the huge export surplus on government account during the war did not represent a normal real capital movement, significant in the long-term allocation of productive resources, for the goods and services thus provided were rapidly consumed in the prosecution of the war.

The war left the net debtor-creditor position of the United States relatively unchanged, but net long-term investments abroad increased. Notwithstanding the considerable liquidation of British investments in the United States before Lend-Lease came into operation, foreign long-term investments in the United States remained practically unchanged because of the increase in the market value of American securities. United States private long-term foreign investments increased by about $2,500 million between 1940 and 1945, reflecting a rise in the market value of foreign securities, reinvested earnings by American direct-investment enterprises, and a net capital outflow of a relatively small amount.[9] In addition, government long-term loans to foreigners increased during the war years by $1,200 million.

The war resulted in the destruction of wealth in virtually all belligerent countries, except the United States. Not only were plant and equipment and stocks of raw material and other working capital destroyed, damaged, or depreciated, but foreign investments, especially of Great Britain, were reduced through liquidations early in the war, while huge short-term overseas liabilities were created.

In order for Europe to restore its productive capacity and prewar standard of living, its capital resources had to be replenished and expanded. The only source which could provide the capital was the United States, whose productive capacity not only was untouched by the war but was actually greatly expanded.

---

[8] Net gifts, mainly through Lend-Lease arrangements, from 1940 to June, 1945, amounted to nearly $41,000 million. See U.S. Department of Commerce, *Foreign Aid by the United States Government, 1940–1951* (Washington, D.C., 1952), p. 10.

[9] U.S. Department of Commerce, *International Transactions of the United States during the War*, p. 110.

It was recognized, however, that there was little possibility of Europe's being able to repay all the vast amount of dollar loans which she required. A considerable part of the loans, especially in the early part of the postwar period, would have to be used primarily for relief purposes rather than for capital reconstruction. Both because of the large amount of capital required and because much of it would have to be on a grant or gift basis, the postwar capital exports of the United States were to a large extent on an intergovernmental basis.

The net outflow of U.S. private long-term capital after the end of World War II did not reach, in real terms, the volume attained in the previous peak year of 1928 until 1956. That year marks the turning point of postwar private long-term capital movements from the United States, bringing the volume well above the highest level reached at any time in the past.[10]

Private foreign investment activity by the United States has now reached approximately the same position, relative to other sectors in the economy, as it had in the 1920's. However, the character of the investments has changed considerably. Some 60 percent of U.S. foreign investments during the 1920's were of the portfolio type— foreign dollar bonds purchased by American investors. By contrast, since the end of the war, direct investments, representing active ownership of business concerns abroad, have constituted the great bulk of American foreign investments (see Table 6.4).

Moreover, while the foreign investments made by American residents during the 1920's were held by a large number of individuals and businesses, the direct investments that have recently become so much more relatively important are heavily concentrated in the hands of a few American companies with foreign branches and subsidiaries. According to one estimate, only one half of 1 percent of U.S. corporations have overseas investments.[11]

Finally, postwar private foreign investments by American busi-

---

[10] Actually, the data given in Table 6.4 on the outflow of capital from the United States considerably underestimate the volume of foreign-investment expenditures. Especially important in this connection is the large amount of expenditures by foreign branch plants and subsidiaries for plant and equipment, exploration and development, etc. that are charged to depreciation allowances or accounted for as operating costs and therefore do not appear as part of the increase in the book values of the investments—see U.S. Department of Commerce, *Survey of Current Business*, August, 1957, p. 22.

[11] American Enterprise Association, Inc., *American Private Enterprise, Foreign Economic Development, and the Aid Programs* (U.S. Senate Special Committee to Study the Foreign Aid Program, committee print [Washington, D.C.: U.S. Government Printing Office, 1957]), p. 2.

nesses have been highly concentrated geographically and by industry, though this tendency has been weakening recently. Until the mid-1950's, Canada and a few Latin American countries (especially Venezuela) received the lion's share of American private capital. In the last few years, however, investments in Europe have risen sharply, while Canadian and Latin American investments have become relatively less important.

TABLE 6.4

NET OUTFLOW OF U.S. PRIVATE LONG-TERM CAPITAL, SELECTED YEARS
(in millions of dollars)

	Annual Average 1946–55	1956	1958	1960	1964	1968
Direct investments:						
New....................	652	1,838	1,181	1,694	2,416	3,025
Reinvested earnings.......	613	974	945	1,266	1,431	2,142
Total..............	1,265	2,812	2,126	2,960	3,847	5,167
Portfolio investments (net)...	163	634	1,444	850	1,961	1,267
Total..............	1,428	3,446	3,570	3,810	5,808	6,434

SOURCE: U.S. Department of Commerce, *Survey of Current Business*, various issues.

There has been a similar concentration of U.S. direct foreign investments by industry, with petroleum the leading attractor of funds. Again, however, the recent trend has been in the direction of a larger flow of capital into manufacturing industries, especially in Europe.

Whatever the qualitative changes that have occurred, the accumulated total of private long-term U.S. foreign investments by the end of 1969 reached nearly $94,000 million. When account is also taken of U.S. government long-term foreign claims of some $31,000 million, the total long-term foreign assets of the United States totals $125,000 million. However, since foreigners have been investing in the United States over the years, the long-term *net* creditor position of the United States at the end of 1969 was about $78,000 million (Table 6.5). (If *short-term* foreign claims and liabilities are included, the net creditor position of the United States is reduced to around $52,000 million.)

The United States is not, of course, the only source of international long-term capital funds. It will be remembered that, before World War II, Great Britain was still the world's largest international investor, though she was rapidly losing her leading position. World War II finished the switch, begun by World War I, in the international investment positions of the United States and Great Britain. Just as World War I converted the United States from a net debtor to a net creditor country, the second war had the reverse result for Great Britain. Between 1938 and 1948 the nominal value of British overseas investments is estimated to have fallen from £3,545 million to about £1,960 million, while, over the same period, sterling overseas liabilities increased by considerably more than the value of remaining British foreign investments.[12]

TABLE 6.5

Long-Term International Investment Position of
the United States in Selected Years
(in millions of dollars)

	1939	1946	1960	1969
U.S. foreign long-term claims:				
Private...............................	11,000	12,000	44,000	94,000
Government.........................	—	5,000	17,000	31,000
Total........................	11,000	17,000	61,000	125,000
Foreign long-term claims against the				
United States........................	6,000	7,000	19,000	47,000
U.S. net long-term creditor position........	5,000	10,000	42,000	78,000

Source: U.S. Department of Commerce, *Survey of Current Business*, various issues.

Basic structural changes, plus the effects of two wars, resulted, over a period of about a third of a century, in the substitution of the United States for the United Kingdom as the world's leading industrial and trading country and source of international capital. (Needless to say, this has had far-reaching implications not only for the world economy but also for international politics.) This does not mean, however, that the United Kingdom and other advanced countries have ceased to be sources of international capital. On the contrary, as their economies recovered from the war and then entered into a period of very rapid growth, the United Kingdom and other European countries, as well as Canada and Japan, have become significant sources of international capital, with an increasing participation in the future highly probable.

We may conclude with some general observations on the role of international capital movements in the middle of the 20th century,

[12] Bank of England, *United Kingdom Overseas Investments, 1938 to 1948* (London: Bank of England, 1950).

compared with their role in the heyday of the 19th and early 20th centuries. First, there is the contrast in relative magnitudes. During the half century preceding 1914, Great Britain invested overseas an amount equal to about 4 percent of her national income, and in the latter part of the period this ratio was as high as 7 percent.[13] This compares with the private foreign investments by the United States today of 1 percent or less of the national income.

Second, the bulk of British foreign investments in the 19th century went to the "regions of recent settlement"—Canada, the United States, Argentina, Australia, etc.—that were land-abundant and both labor- and capital-poor. As a consequence, *both* labor and capital moved together in the complementary fashion described in theoretical terms in the preceding chapter. Today there are no longer many such areas available. The countries that are the most capital-poor are also unfortunately the most labor-abundant. Capital movements, to the extent that they take place, are now in the nature of *substitutes* for labor movements rather than complements to them.

And, finally, except for the relatively small amount of British 19th-century investments that went to colonies, capital moved chiefly in the form of subscriptions to securities with a fixed return, issued by public authorities and public utilities. Today, as we have seen, American foreign investments tend to be primarily of the direct type and attracted to the so-called "colonial" pattern—that is, for the purpose of developing raw materials for exports—though there appears to be a recent tendency for a wider variety of investment patterns to develop.

That these differences in investment experience should have developed ought not be surprising: the 20th century is not the 19th. Institutional conditions and, above all, the focus of attention and interest have drastically changed. It is primarily the role of capital flows in promoting the development of so-called backward areas that now commands the most attention and interest. We shall, however, defer our consideration of this problem to a later chapter.

INTERNATIONAL POPULATION MOVEMENTS

Just as capital tends, under free conditions, to flow from capital-abundant to capital-poor regions, so labor tends to migrate from

---

[13] Ragnar Nurkse, "International Investment Today in the Light of Nineteenth-century Experience," *Economic Journal*, Vol. 64 (1954), p. 745,

areas where it is in relative abundance to areas where it is relatively scarce. To a considerably greater degree than in the case of capital movements, however, immigration is significantly affected by other than economic motives. Immigration, after all, involves human beings and is subject, therefore, to cultural and social influences which are largely absent in the impersonal calculation of relative returns available to capital.

Flight from domestic tyranny or, more positively, the search for political and religious freedom; escape from personal maladjustments to family and community life; and broader military and national considerations have all at various times entered into the determination to seek a new life in other lands. Nevertheless, it is a fairly safe generalization that by far the predominant motive behind the vast international migrations of the past was economic— the desire of the immigrant to improve his standard of living.[14]

A cursory glance at the tremendous disparities in the standards of living in different parts of the world today would indicate that a large part of the world's population has strong economic reasons for migrating. Per capita incomes in North America, industrial Europe, Australia and New Zealand, and a few countries of South America are several times higher than in most other countries of the world. Yet immigration into the higher-income countries has been in recent years a mere trickle. Why is this? There are many reasons, but one is overwhelmingly the most important: nearly every country today has strict limitations on the number of immigrants it will admit, and some countries are just as strict in controlling emigration from their homelands. The economic motive has, therefore, little opportunity to express itself. It is characteristic of the present era that mass movements of population are largely confined to political and religious refugees from totalitarian countries or to religious and national groups seeking to establish new communities (such as in Israel, India, and Pakistan) .

As in the case of international capital movements, the conditions postulated by economic theory as favoring immigration were more nearly fulfilled during the 19th century and up until 1914 than in any other period of history. First, there were numerous regions of the world rich in natural resources and equable in climate but with sparse populations. Second, knowledge of the economic opportuni-

---

[14] This is the conclusion reached by the noted population authority, Warren S. Thompson. See his *Population Problems* (4th ed.; New York: McGraw-Hill Book Co., 1953) , p. 274.

ties in the new lands was widespread, and the costs of moving were relatively low. Third, for the most part, individuals were free to move across national boundaries with a minimum of artificial restrictions.

It is not surprising that the United States was by far the most popular area of immigration or that Canada, Argentina, Brazil, Australia, and New Zealand were the other major countries of immigration. Between 1820, when the United States first began to keep accurate records, and 1950, over 39 million immigrants entered the country, of which some 32 million remained permanently.[15] If immigrants into other parts of America are added, a total of approximately 60 million persons have migrated into the Western Hemisphere since the beginning of the 19th century.

Overwhelmingly the largest number of immigrants arrived before the introduction of strict controls shortly after World War I. Before 1880, immigration into the United States was left to the different states; thereafter, jurisdiction was assumed by the federal government. For the next 30 to 40 years, American controls were selective rather than restrictive—that is, they were concerned chiefly with what sort of immigrants should be admitted rather than with how many. Generally, the requirements for admittance were in terms of such criteria as the state of health, morals, and finances of the immigrants. But, in addition, some racial groups, chiefly Oriental, were excluded, with certain exempt classes. Exclusion of the Chinese began in 1882, of the Japanese in 1907, and of East Indians and other Asiatics in 1917. In 1943 the ban on Chinese was lifted, and in 1946 the ban on East Indians, but the numbers admissible under the quota system (see below) were very limited.

Other immigrant countries followed roughly the same type of selective controls as the United States, though Argentina and Brazil interposed no formal restrictions because of racial origin. In all countries, however, there was increasing insistence upon more severe immigration controls, and, after World War I, national policies generally shifted from a selectivity basis to a restrictive basis. In this movement the United States took the lead.

After 1922, and until the enactment of new legislation in 1965, the basic method of restriction was the quota system. Under this system, except for immigrants from the Western Hemisphere, there was an absolute limit on the total number of immigrants admitted

---

[15] Thompson, *op. cit.,* p. 277.

each year, with an allocation of quotas among different countries according to the proportion of U.S. population already composed of the different national stocks. Since by far the largest part of the population of the United States consists of Caucasians having their national origins in countries of northern and western Europe, the effect of the quota system was to limit severely immigration from other areas.

The national origins quota system was eliminated by a new immigration law signed in 1965. Under the new legislation, immigrants are to be selected on the basis of special labor skills, family relations with U.S. citizens and residents, or need for political asylum. The country of origin is considered only to the extent that no more than 20,000 immigrants are to be admitted per year from any one country.

However, severe limits on the number of immigrants continues in effect. The previous policy of allowing unlimited immigration from the Western Hemisphere (with minor exceptions) is replaced by a maximum annual inflow of 120,000 from that area. For the rest of the world, a maximum of 170,000 is set. Additional immigrants, numbering perhaps 30,000–40,000, may be admitted on the basis of special considerations, mainly family ties with U.S. citizens.

The Economic Effects of Immigration

We concluded in the preceding chapter that, theoretically, population movements in response to economic motives tend to raise the level of the world's real income and to benefit economically both the country of emigration and that of immigration. We found it necessary to modify this conclusion, however, according to specific circumstances. In brief, the benefits of population movements are clearest when they permanently increase the per capita supply of capital and land in the emigrant country and when the receiving country is economically young and undeveloped, with sparse population. The benefits are much more doubtful, however, if the country of emigration has both a high birthrate and a high death rate and if the receiving country has already reached its optimum-size population.

It is impossible to reach any firm conclusions on the precise economic effects of historical migrations. It would seem fairly certain that the large population movements of the 19th century took place under conditions which were generally favorable for the realization of economic benefits. There can be little doubt that the United States and the other major countries of immigration benefited from the increased supply of labor. Not only did the increased supply of labor in these countries tend to raise per capita productivity by allowing a greater division of labor but it also greatly encouraged industrial development. We noted before that in economically young countries, with unexploited land and natural resources, both labor and capital are attracted from abroad, each reinforcing the other. Indeed, under such circumstances the addition to the labor supply and the development of new industries may be so closely related that neither would occur without the other.[16] Thus a study by the United States Immigration Commission indicates that the great industrial expansion in the United States between 1907 and 1911 would have been impossible without the new immigrants.[17]

The economic effects on the countries of emigration during the 19th century are a good deal less certain; but if the per capita supply of land and capital was not permanently increased by emigration, neither was it probably decreased.

The possibilities of realizing in the future the kind of benefits derived from past migrations are limited. In particular, there appears to be little hope of any appreciable contribution to raising the standard of living in overpopulated, impoverished areas through emigration. The basic reason for this is the absence of many areas in the world where a large influx of labor would raise rather than lower the productivity of the native population, unless immigrants were discriminated against. The probability of the current numerous artificial restrictions on population movements being removed is, therefore, rather remote.

RECOMMENDED READING

AMERICAN ENTERPRISE ASSOCIATION, INC. *American Private Enterprise, Foreign Economic Development, and the Aid Programs.* A Study Prepared for the Special Committee to Study the Foreign Aid Program, U.S. Senate. Committee print. Washington, D.C.: U.S. Government Printing Office, 1957.

---

[16] See J. Isaac, *Economics of Migration* (New York: Oxford University Press, Inc., 1947), pp. 214–17.

[17] See National Committee on Immigration Policy, *Economic Aspects of Immigration* (New York, 1947), p. 11.

Feis, Herbert. *Europe, the World's Banker.* New Haven, Conn.: Yale University Press, 1930.

Isaac, J. *Economics of Migration.* New York: Oxford University Press, Inc., 1947.

Lary, Hal B., and Associates. *The United States in the World Economy,* chap. iii. U.S. Department of Commerce. Washington, D.C.: U.S. Government Printing Office, 1943.

Lewis, Cleona. *America's Stake in International Investment.* Washington, D.C.: Brookings Institution, 1938.

———. *The United States and Foreign Investment Problems.* Washington, D.C.: Brookings Institution, 1948.

Nurkse, Ragnar. "International Investment Today in the Light of Nineteenth-Century Experience," *Economic Journal,* Vol. 64, pp. 744–58.

Royal Institute of International Affairs. *The Problem of International Investment.* London: Oxford University Press, 1937.

Salter, Sir Arthur. *Foreign Investment.* Essays in International Finance, No. 12. Princeton, N.J.: Princeton University Press, 1951.

Thompson, Warren S. *Population Problems.* 4th ed. New York: McGraw-Hill Book Co., 1953.

U.S. Department of Commerce. *Survey of Current Business,* August issues of each year.

———. *The Balance of Payments of the United States, 1919–1953.* Washington, D.C.: U.S. Government Printing Office, 1954.

———. *Factors Limiting U.S. Investment Abroad,* Part I: *1953.* Part II: *1954.* Washington, D.C.: U.S. Government Printing Office.

———. *United States Business Investments in Foreign Countries.* Washington, D.C.: U.S. Government Printing Office, 1960.

STUDY QUESTIONS

1. What were the conditions prevailing during the 19th century which made it the "golden age" of long-term private international capital flows?

2. Why was Great Britain the leading international investor before 1914?

3. Investigate the role which foreign capital played in the economic development of the United States during the 19th century. (Refer to any good text on the history of the United States.)

4. How did Great Britain's pre-1914 international investments promote her specialization in manufactured goods?

5. Define what is meant by an "international debtor country" and by an "international creditor country."

6. Summarize the effects of World War I on the international capital position of Great Britain, Germany, and the United States.

7. What were the effects of the world depression during the 1930's on (a) the volume of international investment and (b) the servicing and repayment of past foreign loans?

8. Contrast the nature of America's financial assistance to her Allies during the two world wars.

9. Investigate the type and geographic distribution of post–World War II private foreign investments by the United States. (Regular articles on this subject appear in the U.S. Department of Commerce publication *Survey of Current Business*.)

10. List the chief motives, economic and other, for international population movements. Which motive do you think is the most important?

11. If all artificial barriers to international migration were lifted, what would you guess would be the effects on the volume and direction of immigration?

12. What fundamental difference is there in the natural opportunities for large-scale international migration now as compared to earlier times?

13. Trace the historic development of American immigration policies.

14. What part did immigration play in the economic development of the United States?

15. Argue for, and against, the lifting or reduction of the immigration barriers currently in effect in the United States.

PART II

Public and Private Barriers to Trade

In Part I the pure theory of international trade and factor movements was described. We call it the "pure" theory in the sense that it is based on a highly abstract model of how the international economy would be structured under purely competitive market conditions and in the absence of artificial barriers to the free flow of goods and services. It is a realistic and useful model in that it identifies the fundamental causes and effects of trade and factor movements. But it is unrealistic to the extent that it ignores the presence in the real world of various conditions and policies which interfere with the operations of the system. The chief sources of interference are twofold: (a) restrictive governmental policies and (b) imperfect market structures. Each of these will be considered in the next few chapters.

Chapter 7

THE THEORY OF TARIFFS AND OTHER TRADE RESTRICTIONS

Three broad types of artificial interference with international trade may be distinguished. The first type is associated with problems in international monetary relations which lead to policies that restrain free trade in goods and services. For instance, because of balance-of-payments problems a country may impose exchange controls under which its foreign trade is restricted or diverted into channels different from those based on comparative cost relationships. Consideration of this type of interference with free trade will be delayed until we discuss international monetary relations.

The second type of artificial impediments to free trade has its origins in the desire of national governments to change in some fashion the volume and pattern of trade produced by free market forces. Whereas in the first type restrictions on trade are a by-product of monetary policies, in the second type they are direct instruments of governmental commercial policy.

The third category of trade restrictions is of a different variety from the others, being the result of imperfectly competitive market structures, rather than of governmental policies as in the first two cases.

The distinctions we have drawn between types of interference with free trade are blurred in practice. Import quotas, for example, are frequently employed for balance-of-payments purposes as well as for commercial policy ends, and in a particular case it may be difficult to disentangle the motivations involved. Analytically, however, it is possible and useful to make the distinction.

In this and the following three chapters, we shall concern ourselves with commercial policies, after which private restrictions due to imperfect competition will be considered.

THE NATURE OF TARIFFS AND OTHER COMMERCIAL RESTRICTIONS

Tariffs

A tariff is a tax, or "duty," levied on a commodity when it crosses the boundary of a customs area. Usually a customs area coincides with national political boundaries, but often it also includes colonies and territories of the country and, in exceptional cases, embraces two or more national states. The customs area of the United States includes not only continental United States but all the territory under its sovereignty, with a few minor exceptions. A customs area is extended beyond national boundaries when a *customs union* or a *common market* is formed by two or more countries. The distinction between a customs union and a common market will be explored in a later chapter (see Chapter 10), but a characteristic they have in common of relevance to our present discussion is the creation of a single customs area for member countries. Thus, the Netherlands, Belgium, and Luxemburg—"Benelux"—have constituted a customs union for several years, with a common external tariff. More recently, a much larger customs area has been created through the formation of the European Common Market, embracing the Benelux countries, plus France, Italy, and West Germany.

Tariffs may be levied on goods passing through a customs area en route to a third country—*transit duties;* on commodities leaving a country—*export duties;* or on merchandise entering a country—*import duties.* Generally speaking, the last-named type of tariff is the most common and important, and we shall concentrate our attention on it.

Import duties may be either *specific, ad valorem,* or, a combination of the two, *compound* duties. Specific duties are levied according to the physical quantity of the import (so much per pound, per yard, etc.), while ad valorem duties are calculated as a percentage of the value of the import. Hence the real burden of ad valorem duties remains constant as the prices of imports vary, while the real burden of specific duties varies inversely with changes in the prices of imports.

A list of all the existing import duties levied by a country is called its *tariff schedule.* The schedule may have one or more "columns"; in a single-columned tariff, the rate is the same for a particular good from whatever country it is imported; a double- or multicolumned tariff discriminates according to the country of origin of the import. For example, imports from countries with which there are tariff agreements may be subject to lower duties than are those from other countries.

Protective tariffs are designed to reduce or eliminate the import of the goods on which the tariffs are levied; *revenue* tariffs are for the purpose of obtaining revenue for the government. Hence protective tariffs are ordinarily higher than revenue tariffs, and the latter are usually confined to imports of wide consumption for which the demand is inelastic.[1]

A brief warning must be given here concerning the measurement of the height of a tariff wall. There is, in fact, no completely satisfactory method of doing this, but some methods commonly employed may be utterly misleading. One of these methods, for example, is to take the ratio which total duty collections bear to the total value of imports. But suppose that on a large list of commodities the tariff is so high that the import of these commodities is very small, while other commodities are on the "free" list (no duties) or are subject to low duties and therefore are imported in relatively large volume. Since the volume of imports of the highly protected articles is low, obviously the amount of duties collected will also be low; hence the ratio of duties collected to total imports may be small, even though some or most tariff rates are very high.

Perhaps the least unsatisfactory method of measuring the height of tariffs is converting all tariffs to an ad valorem basis and calculating the average. Theoretically, a *weighted* average would be more significant than an unweighted one. But there are serious statistical and conceptual difficulties in choosing the proper weights to be assigned. If duties are weighted by the amount of each commodity imported, we are back to the misleading results described above, with high duties given little weight and low duties high weights. For these reasons, an *unweighted* average, notwithstanding its limitations, may be the most meaningful.

Finally, there is an important distinction to be drawn between the *nominal* rate of a tariff and the *effective* rate of protection. This distinction becomes necessary whenever a tariff is levied on a finished good which contains imported raw materials or intermediate products on which tariffs are applied at a different rate from that on the finished good.

For example, suppose that woolen fabrics are subject to a 30 per-

---

[1] When the imported article, or close substitute, is also manufactured at home, the protective aspect of a duty can be eliminated by imposing an excise tax on the domestically produced output, equal to the import duty.

cent import duty, while wool is duty-free. The effective rate of protection for the domestic fabric industry is then greater than indicated by the tariff. The difference between the nominal and the effective rates depends upon the proportion of the final value of the fabric contributed by the wool component. For instance, assume that the wool input contributes half the value of the finished fabric. This means that the *value added* by the wool fabric industry is the remaining half the value of the finished product. Hence, the 30 percent tariff on the fabric is in reality a *60 percent* tariff on the value added by the domestic fabric industry!

Should a tariff be imposed on wool greater than that on finished fabric, the effective rate of the fabric tariff would be *less* than the nominal rate. For instance, a 50 percent tariff on wool would place domestic producers of fabrics at a disadvantage compared to foreign producers by 25 percent of the final value of the fabric (continuing to assume that wool contributes half the value of fabric). Subtracting this from the 30 percent duty on fabric leaves a net protection of 5 percent of the value of the fabric, or 10 percent of value added by fabric manufacturers. Thus the effective rate of protection for the fabric industry would be only 10 percent, compared to the nominal rate of 30 percent. Only when the same rate of duty is levied on a final product and all its imported components are the nominal and effective rates of protection the same.

Quotas

Quotas are limits on the amount of a good which may be imported (import quotas) or exported (export quotas) during a given period of time. The limits may be set in physical terms or in value terms. The quota may be on a country basis—that is, varying limits set according to the country of origin—or on a global basis, wherein the total limit is specified without reference to the countries of origin. A "tariff quota" is distinguished from an absolute quota, in that the former does not set a fixed limit on imports but rather the amount beyond which a higher rate of duty is imposed. A tariff quota is often a device for keeping tariffs lower than otherwise would be the case, by allowing at least a specified quantity of imports to enter free of duty or subject to lower rates than ordinarily applicable.

The administration of quotas usually necessitates the use of a licensing system. This in itself raises serious practical problems, especially as to how the limited number of licenses is to be distributed among various applicants. Since the volume of imports is specifically limited, the domestic selling price of the good may be far in excess of its import cost, and the profit realized from obtaining a license may be very high. These windfall profits can, however, be eliminated through a system of auctioning import licenses to the highest bidders.

From the point of view of the country desiring to restrict the volume of imports, quotas are obviously a much more certain and precise instrument than are tariffs. In addition to this, quotas differ fundamentally from tariffs in their effects on international trade. Apart from tariffs so high that they make imports entirely prohibitive, an import duty does not set an arbitrary limit on the volume of the good that can be imported. Anyone may import as much as he wants of the dutiable good, provided that he pays the import tax. Therefore, the price system of the importing country is not divorced from that of other countries, even though its relationship to other price systems is changed by the tariff. In the case of an import quota, however, the price mechanism is allowed to operate only until the quota is filled; beyond that point, price considerations are irrelevant.

Miscellaneous Restrictions

Besides tariffs and quotas, there are numerous other less important devices that often add to the restrictiveness of the protective system.

Mixing and milling regulations require the mixture or use of some percentage of domestic product with the imported good, thus restricting, of course, the import market. An example is the requirement that flour contain a minimum percentage of domestic grain.

Marks-of-origin laws require the country of origin to be stamped on imported goods, thereby serving to restrict imports in two ways: (a) by encouraging and making effective nationalistic sentiments in the form of boycotts of foreign goods or "buy-at-home" campaigns and (b) by raising the costs of production to the foreign producer.

Sanitary regulations, theoretically designed to protect the public health, are quite often used in fact as an excuse for refusing to permit the importation of certain commodities or for making their importation cumbersome and expensive. Sumptuary laws often have the same effect.

Administrative protection is the term applied to a miscellany of procedures and regulations which make importing more difficult and expensive. The procedure for clearing imports through customs, for example, may be made an expensive and time-consuming affair if the regulations are detailed and if customs officials are inclined to be overly meticulous.

THE ECONOMIC EFFECTS OF TRADE RESTRICTIONS

The economic effect of tariffs and quotas are multiple and impinge not only upon the tariff- or quota-levying country but upon other countries as well.

Price-Cost Effects

The immediate impact of tariffs and quotas is on the prices and costs of the commodities affected. There are other, more fundamental, consequences, but they are brought about, in a market price system, through the mechanism of changing price and cost relationships, so that it is the latter that we shall consider first.

The most general price effect of tariffs and quotas is to create a *differential* in the international price (and cost) of the affected commodity. Without tariffs or quotas, assuming pure competition and ignoring transportation costs, we know that the price (and cost) of any traded commodity will tend to be the same in all countries. Now introduce a tariff or quota on a particular commodity, and its price will become different in that country from its price in the supplying country or countries. In the case of a tariff, the price differential will be equal to the amount of the tariff (expressed as a specific duty). In the case of a quota, the price differential may be any amount, depending upon considerations to be examined shortly.

The reason that a tariff creates an international price and cost differential equal in amount to the amount of the tariff can be easily shown. Suppose that the United States imposes a specific duty of 25 cents per pound on Danish blue cheese. Then, under competitive conditions, the equilibrium price of the cheese is 25 cents higher in the United States than in Denmark. For if the price in the United States, after the tariff is paid, were less than

25 cents higher than in Denmark, importers would lose on cheese imports—the cheese costing the Danish export price *plus* 25 cents per pound. Hence the import of cheese would be reduced, and its price in the United States would rise. On the other hand, if the cheese commanded a price in the United States higher than in Denmark by more than the 25 cent duty, the profits realized by importers would stimulate greater imports until the price fell.

Now it will be noted that the equilibrium condition just described can be fulfilled in any one of three ways: (*a*) the price of the commodity may *rise in the importing country* by the full amount of the tariff; (*b*) the price of the commodity may *fall in the exporting country* by the full amount of the tariff; or (*c*) the price may rise in the importing country by less than the full amount of the tariff and fall in the exporting country by less than the full amount of the tariff. From the standpoint of fulfilling the equilibrium condition that the price differential equal the amount of the duty, it makes no difference which of these three possible reactions occurs. But, on other grounds, it makes a great deal of difference, as we shall presently see. It is important, therefore, to investigate what determines the kind of price reaction to be expected from a tariff.

The effect of a tariff on the price of a good depends upon the volume and elasticities of demand and supply, in both the importing (tariff-levying) country and the exporting country. A complete analysis of these forces would become too detailed and involved to present here.[2] But the essence of the analysis can be briefly indicated by concentrating on what is probably the most common case in practice—that where, as the result of the tariff, the price falls in the exporting country and rises in the importing country.

Suppose that a country produces at home some part of its domestic consumption of a commodity and imports the remainder from another country. This implies, as we learned early in the book, that the commodity is produced under increasing-cost conditions, with the supply curves in both countries rising from left to right on the conventional diagram. In competitive equilibrium and ignoring transportation costs, the price (and costs) of the

---

[2] For a discussion of the relevance of the *volume* of demand and supply to the price effects of tariffs—a point that is largely ignored in what follows—see Gottfried von Haberler, *The Theory of International Trade* (New York: Macmillan Co., 1937), pp. 227 ff.

commodity are the same in both countries. Now let the importing country impose a tariff on the commodity. Several reactions will follow.

First, as an immediate reaction, the price of the commodity in the importing country will tend to rise, and the quantity demanded to fall. Second, domestic producers of the good in the importing country will be induced by the higher market price to expand their output. Third, producers in the exporting country will find that the export market has shrunk—both because of the greater domestic output in the importing country and because of the smaller quantity demanded in the importing country. Therefore, the output in the exporting country will tend to fall. Fourth, the costs (average and marginal) of production will rise in the importing country with its increased output and fall in the exporting country with its decreased output. Hence, in the new equilibrium position, the price of the commodity will be higher in the importing country and lower in the exporting country.

The foregoing analysis can be easily presented and sharpened through a diagrammatic illustration. Since we know that, ignoring transportation costs, the competitive equilibrium price of a commodity subject to an import tariff is higher in the importing country than in the exporting country by the full amount of the tariff, we need to investigate the price effect of the tariff in only one of the countries concerned. If we know, for example, that the price of the commodity in the exporting country falls by an amount equal to one third of the amount of the tariff in the importing country, then we also know that the new equilibrium price in the importing country is higher than formerly by two thirds of the amount of the tariff.

Let us, then, analyze diagrammatically the price effect of an import tariff from the standpoint of the exporting country. In Figure 7.1, S_x is the supply curve of the commodity in the exporting country, D_m is the demand curve of the importing country for the product of the exporting country. To simplify the analysis, we shall assume that the exporting country does not consume at home any of its export product, so that D_m represents the total demand in the absence of any tariff imposed by the importing country. On the other hand, let us assume that the importing country also produces the commodity, so that D_m represents only the excess of the importing country's demand over domestic output.

Originally, the international equilibrium price of the commod-

ity is *P,* for at this price the demand in the importing country is
just equal to the combined supply from domestic and foreign
production. Now let the importing country impose a tariff of, say,
10 cents per unit of the commodity. The effect is to cause the de-

FIGURE 7.1

PRICE EFFECTS OF A TARIFF, EXPORTING COUNTRY

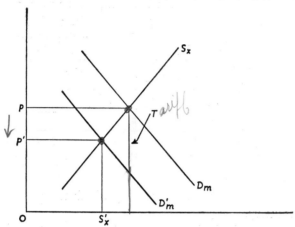

mand curve for the exporting country's output to fall by the
amount of the tariff, in Figure 7.1 from D_m to D'_m. The reason for
this can be seen from the following example.

Let the following be a portion of the importing country's import demand schedule, based on the exporting country's *export*
prices:

Export Price	Quantity of Imports Demanded
$1.10	900
1.00	1,100
0.90	1,300
0.80	1,500

After the import duty of 10 cents is imposed, an export price of $1
is the same as an import price, with duty, of $1.10. Hence, before
the tariff, at an export price of $1, the exporting country could sell
1,100 units of the commodity to the importing country; with the
tariff, at an export price of $1 (and therefore an import price of

$1.10), only 900 units of imports are demanded. In order to export 1,100 units, with the tariff, the export price would have to be $0.90; to export 1,300 units, the export price would have to be $0.80, etc. These changes in demand are diagrammatically represented by the shifting of the curve in Figure 7.1 from D_m to D'_m.

Because the demand for the exporting country's output has fallen to D'_m, the equilibrium export price falls to P'. Accordingly, the amount produced and offered for export decreases. In the importing country, the price of the good must be such that the excess of the quantity domestically demanded over the quantity domestically produced is equal to the reduced amount produced in the exporting country. This clearly implies that the price of the good will rise in the importing country, since otherwise import demand would exceed the smaller supply offered by the exporting country. Moreover, we know by how much the price in the importing country will rise as a result of the tariff. It is obvious from inspection of Figure 7.1 that the fall in the export price from P to P' is less than the tariff, T. The amount by which the decrease in export price is less than the tariff is also the amount by which the price rises in the importing country.

In the case described, then, part of the tariff is "paid by the foreigner," in the sense that the foreign export price is lowered, and part is paid by the consumers of the importing country in the form of a higher price for the good. (It should be noted, however, that the government of the importing country collects import duties totaling $OS'_x \cdot T$, possibly relieving thereby the taxpayer of that much other tax burden.)

The influence of elasticity conditions on the price reactions to a tariff can now be shown in terms of the case outlined above and illustrated in Figure 7.1. First, it is to be noted that if the supply curve of the commodity in the exporting country had been less elastic, the fall in export price would have been greater, and therefore the rise in price in the importing country would have been smaller. At the other extreme, had the supply curve in the exporting country been infinitely elastic (horizontal), the export price would not have fallen at all, and therefore the price in the importing country would have risen by the full amount of the tariff. We may conclude in general, then, that, other things being equal, the less elastic the foreign supply of a commodity, the smaller will be the price effect of a tariff in the importing country.

The elasticity of supply in the importing country is also relevant in determining the price effect of a tariff. The more domestic production increases in the tariff-levying country in response to the duty, the less will the price rise in that country because of reduced imports.

On the demand side, elasticities have an effect similar to that stemming from the supply side. If the exporting country were also a consumer of the export commodity, the decrease in price caused by the tariff would ordinarily lead not only to reduced domestic production but also to increased domestic consumption. This means that the export supply would be less and therefore the price in the importing country would be higher. The less elastic the home demand in the exporting country is, however, the smaller will this effect be. If the demand for the commodity in the importing country were more elastic, the price in the importing country would not rise as much, and the price in the exporting country would fall by a greater amount.

In the above example, we assumed that one country was the only export market for the exporting country's output of the commodity. More realistically, the exporting country may export the commodity to many countries. In this event, the total demand in the exporting country for the commodity is less likely to be significantly affected by an import duty levied in only one of the importing countries. Correspondingly, the export price would be less affected by the tariff, and a larger portion of the price effect of the tariff would be borne in the tariff-levying country. In practice, any country whose import demand for a commodity is only a small fraction of total world trade in that commodity will not be able significantly to influence the world price through a tariff. In effect, the import supply curve is virtually infinitely elastic, and any tariff will result in an increase in the domestic price approximately equal to the amount of the tariff.

The situation is different, of course, if the tariff-levying country's import demand for a commodity is a significantly large proportion of total world import demand—for example, the import demand of the United States for coffee. In such instances, the effect of an import tariff on the export price is very likely to be much more pronounced, with the foreigners "paying" a large portion of the tariff.

Quotas. The price-cost effect of quotas can be much more drastic than in the case of tariffs. As indicated earlier, a quota may virtually sever international price-cost connecting links, since the market mechanism for relating prices in different countries is artificially stopped from functioning.

One result of quotas is nearly universal: the domestic price in the country imposing the quota is raised above the world price of the commodity. This, of course, is similar to the usual result of a tariff. But there is one important difference: there is no limit on the amount by which the price of the commodity subject to a quota may be raised above the world price. How much the domestic price is raised above the world price as the result of a quota depends, given the elasticities of demand and supply, upon how restrictive the quota is. Other things being equal, the lower the quota is set, the higher will the domestic price be forced upward. As in the case of tariffs, however, quotas may force export prices downward—depending on the elasticities of demand and supply in the exporting country or countries. But if the export price of a commodity is pushed downward because of a quota in the importing country, this does not mean, with a quota of given size, that the price of the commodity in the importing country will be raised by a lesser amount. Rather, it means that the international price and cost differential will be made greater than it otherwise would be.

The above conclusion leads to another important difference between tariffs and quotas. In the case of a tariff, the difference between the export price and the domestic price with the tariff is collected by the government in the form of customs duties. In the case of a straight quota, the difference between the export price and the domestic price goes as a windfall gain to those fortunate enough to be able to import under the quota—meaning, usually, those who have received import licenses. This explains the scramble for import licenses that ordinarily takes place when there is a quota on an import.

The windfall gain to importers could, of course, be taxed by the government. One indirect way of doing this is through the auctioning of licenses to import the quota commodity. Competitive bidding would tend to push the price of licenses up to the point of eliminating expected windfall gains, the government, instead of private importers, receiving the profits.

The Volume and Benefits of Trade

From our preceding analysis it is clear that one of the major effects of tariffs and quotas is to reduce the volume of international trade. In the case of tariffs, this effect follows from the fact that, except in very unusual circumstances, the price of a commodity subject to a tariff is raised in the importing country, thereby reducing the total quantity demanded and, ordinarily, increasing the quantity produced domestically. In the case of quotas, the reduction in the volume of imports is directly brought about by quantitative limits on the volume of imports permitted.

Since international trade yields benefits to the world in the form of higher real income, tariffs and trade restrictions, by reducing the volume of trade, presumably lower the world's real income. The loss involved derives not simply from the quantitative reduction in trade but also from the misallocation of resources. This conclusion may be pointed up by comparing the effect of tariffs and quantitative trade restrictions with that of overall measures, such as exchange depreciation, designed to correct balance-of-payments disequilibrium.

The Allocation of Resources

Effective exchange depreciation also reduces the volume of imports, but it is a reduction that is compelled by the requirements of equilibrium. In contrast to tariffs and trade restrictions, exchange depreciation does not distort cost-price relationships but rather brings them into new alignment. By generally rendering imports more expensive to the depreciating country and by causing the prices of its exports to become cheaper to foreign buyers, exchange depreciation tends to contract the volume of imports and to increase the volume of exports. But internationally traded goods have the same price at the new equilibrium rate of exchange the world over, and resources have been reallocated in accordance with the principle of comparative advantage.

Contrast this situation with the impact of protective tariffs and other trade restrictions. Again resources are redirected, but this time to the production of goods the relative costs of which are *higher* than abroad; otherwise there would be no need to impose a protective tariff. Not only are imports reduced, but exports also tend, in the long run, to be reduced. This is so because of reduced income and import demand in foreign countries, the exports of which are contracted by the tariffs (though this will be negligible if the goods on which the tariffs are imposed constitute only a very small portion of other countries' exports), and because of the tendency for other countries to retaliate by raising their import duties.

In other words, resources are reallocated from more efficient export industries to less efficient domestic goods industries.

The distortion of optimum resource use caused by trade restrictions is brought about through the reactions of the latter on international price-cost relationships. As we learned in Chapter 2, the inequality of cost-price ratios in different countries is the condition making international trade mutually beneficial. The *result* of free and unrestricted international trade is to eliminate (except for transport costs) international differences in the price and cost of traded goods and services. But now we have seen that tariffs and quotas *artificially reimpose* international price-cost differences. This creates a situation similar to, though not so extreme as, that which would prevail if countries refused to take advantage of comparative cost differences and insisted upon producing at home all the goods and services consumed at home. In other words, international comparative cost differences create the opportunity for beneficial international trade; tariffs and quotas "freeze" this opportunity, not allowing it fully to be taken advantage of.

The uneconomic effects of tariffs on resource allocation are especially serious when, as is usually the case, the rates vary among different commodities. A still greater distortion of resource allocation results when there are superimposed upon differential rates according to commodities preferential or discriminatory rates on the same commodities according to the country of origin.

Preferential tariff rates are commonly found on trade between the "mother" countries and the colonial possessions or members of an empire. The best-known example is the "Ottawa" preference system between the United Kingdom and her dependent colonies and the various members of the British Commonwealth, negotiated at Ottawa in 1932. It has also been common practice for other countries to impose different import duties according to the country of origin, usually on the basis of bilateral agreements. Running counter to this practice is the adoption of the doctrine of "most-favored-nation" treatment, concerning which we shall have something to say in the next chapter.

The uneconomic effects of quantitative limitations on trade are even more severe than in the case of tariffs. When, because of an import quota, the quantity of goods imported is less than the demand for imports at current prices, the link between the price abroad and that at home is entirely severed. The extensive employment of quantitative controls results, then, in a virtual breakdown of the price mechanism as a guide in the international allocation of resources.

Consumption Effects

The effects of trade restrictions are not confined to distorting the allocation of resources and the accompanying loss of some of the specialization benefits of trade. Consumption is also distorted, and the full exchange benefits of trade are prevented from being realized.

Just as the loss from inefficient allocation as the result of trade restrictions is the counterpart of the gain from specialization under free trade, so the loss to consumers as the result of trade restrictions is the counterpart of the exchange benefits of free trade. (On the specialization and exchange benefits of trade, see Chapter 3.) From the point of view of the individual consumer, the loss shows up directly in the form of higher prices and reduced consumption of imported products. More generally regarded, the creation of artificial price differences through tariffs and quotas forces consumption into patterns which yield less total utility than is yielded by given expenditure when prices are equalized internationally. Tariffs and quotas divide consumers in different countries into separate sets, each set subject to different price relationships. Consequently, they are denied the opportunity of maximizing utility through equalizing the marginal utility ratios of each pair of goods.[3]

Effects on the Balance of Payments

Apart from the effects of tariffs, quotas, and related policies on the allocation of resources and on consumption, they may also be a source of balance-of-payments disequilibrium and an impediment to the adjustment mechanism. Starting from a position of equilibrium, an increase in tariffs by one major country or group of countries reduces the exports of other countries, causing a balance-of-

---

[3] For consumer sets A and B each to realize maximum total utility from the consumption of X and Y, the ratio of the marginal utility of X to the marginal utility of Y must be the *same* for A and B. Otherwise, both could gain utility by trading, each exchanging the good the marginal utility of which is relatively smaller for him for the good the marginal utility of which is relatively greater. When each set of consumers is confronted with a common set of prices, the maximum utility condition is satisfied, since each consumer seeks to equate the ratio of the marginal utilities of X and Y to a common price ratio. Different prices for different consumers interfere with this process.

payments deficit and necessitating readjustments of a structural character. Or, to take another example, a major creditor country may, by raising a high tariff wall, make it virtually impossible for its debtors to develop the export surplus which repayment of their debts demands. This is one, though not the only, reason why, for example, there were such widespread defaults in the 1930's on the foreign loans of the United States. At the beginning of that decade, the United States raised its tariffs to the highest level in its history, thereby adding to the effects of the depression in reducing American import demand.

THE ORIGINS OF TRADE IMPEDIMENTS[4]

In view of the indisputable distortions in the structure of world production and trade and the loss of real income that are caused by tariffs, quotas, and related measures, it may be a source of some wonderment to the student that mankind has devoted so much of its energy to creating such devices. Upon closer examination, however, the apparent paradox disappears. As in other social sciences, so in international economics we must always clearly distinguish between the general and the particular, the impact on society as a whole and that on individuals or groups within the society. With respect to the problem under discussion, it is necessary to examine possible *conflicting interests* on three different levels: (*a*) the national economy versus the world as a whole, (*b*) the national economy versus those productive factors within the economy that are in relatively scarce supply, and (*c*) the national economy versus domestic producers that compete with foreign producers.

THE NATIONAL ECONOMY VERSUS THE WORLD ECONOMY

The arguments in favor of free trade and against all forms of artificial impediments to trade up to this point have had as their base of reference the world as a whole. In the application of theoretical principles to the actual world, we must take account of the fact that an overall, world point of view can seldom be expected to be taken by each of the numerous individual national states which are the component parts of the world economy.

---

[4] The discussion which follows relates to *protectionist* measures. So-called "revenue" tariffs are no longer very important except in underdeveloped areas where the fiscal machinery is inadequate to finance government expenditure from other sources.

Improve the Terms of Trade

While free trade can be proved on rational grounds to be the best policy for the world as a whole, it is more difficult to reach a similar conclusion from the point of view of the individual national economy. Our earlier analysis proved only that *some* trade is more desirable, from the national standpoint, than no trade at all; but it has not proved that a *free-trade* policy is always preferable to a policy which includes tariffs, quotas, or other trade restrictions short of complete stoppage of trade.

Indeed, it can be theoretically demonstrated that, *under certain conditions,* an individual country can realize a net gain by imposing tariffs.[5] This can be done, on the analogy of an individual firm, by the country acting monopolistically. A monopolistic firm raises the price at which its product sells (i.e., improves its "terms of trade") by restricting output below the competitive level. A country's terms of trade are improved, and its share of the gain from trade therefore increased, if import prices are lowered relative to its export prices. Now we have already seen in the discussion above of the price effects of tariffs and quotas that the foreign export price of a commodity may be lowered as the result of a tariff or quota in an importing country. Particularly is this the case if (*a*) the country imposing the tariff or quota imports a significant proportion of total world imports of the commodity and (*b*) the supply of the commodity is relatively inelastic in the exporting country or countries. Under such conditions, a country may lower the price it pays for its imports, improving its terms of trade, by, analogously to the monopolistic firm, artificially restricting import demand through tariffs or quotas.[6] *This means, however, that the gain realized by the country imposing the tariff (or quota) is at the expense of other countries;* that is, the distribution of world income is altered in favor of the tariff- or quota-levying country.

---

[5] See the analysis, which has been heavily drawn upon in this section, of Tibor Scitovsky, "A Reconsideration of the Theory of Tariffs," *Review of Economic Studies,* Vol. 9 (1942) ; reprinted in American Economic Association, *Readings in the Theory of International Trade* (eds. Howard S. Ellis and Lloyd A. Metzler, Homewood, Ill.: Richard D. Irwin, Inc., 1949) , pp. 358 ff.

[6] A distinction must be drawn between the effects of the tariff or quota on the price paid by private importers (and consumers) and the *social cost* of imports to the economy. If the foreign export price falls, the social cost falls to the importing country, even though private importers pay a higher price, with the duty, than before. Similarly in the case of quotas, the domestic consumer ordinarily pays a higher price because of the quota, but the social cost of the good is less if the foreign export price falls.

The possibility of a country's increasing its gains from trade by raising tariffs is contingent upon the absence of retaliatory action by other countries. In fact, however, other countries would be able to reduce the loss imposed upon them by foreign tariffs through increasing their own tariffs. As Scitovsky has shown, there is, therefore, a strong natural tendency for tariffs to be raised, in a series of retaliations and counterretaliations, until the volume of trade shrinks to a fraction of its former level and any initial gains realized by individual countries are wiped out. Even though, then, there is sometimes the possibility of gain by a national economy through raising its tariffs and improving its terms of trade, such a policy, besides being unneighborly, runs the risk of being self-defeating in the end.

Reduce Unemployment

There are three other arguments for protective tariffs based on the interests of an individual national economy as a whole which, under certain conditions, have a limited validity. The first is that tariffs or other import restrictions may, in times of unemployment, increase employment and national income. As we shall see later, import expenditures, like savings, constitute a leakage in the domestic income stream, while exports add to the domestic income stream. If, therefore, imports can be reduced while exports are maintained, the foreign-trade multiplier will operate to increase national income by a multiple of the reduced import expenditures.

Again, however, the practical consideration arises that this can be an effective means of reducing unemployment only if it is not adopted by all or a large number of countries. Clearly, all countries cannot simultaneous'y reduce imports and maintain exports. If just one small country is plagued with unemployment, it may be successful in combating it by decreasing its imports. In fact, however, unemployment in a major country tends to spread internationally, and the attempt of such a country to "export" its unemployment through restricting imports results in accelerating the spread.

Apart from its practical limitations, tariffs as a device for mitigating unemployment have the unfortunate effects on the efficiency of resource use described previously. Moreover, alternative policies are possible which would relieve unemployment at home while encouraging greater employment abroad and a larger volume of international trade.

Encourage Industrialization

Another "national" basis for protective tariffs is that a free-trade policy may prevent an agricultural country or an underdeveloped economy from realizing the industrialization upon which, in the modern world, a higher standard of living depends. This is one of the primary arguments for protection and goes back to the early period of economic expansion accompanying the Industrial Revolution.

The Infant-Industry Argument. The "infant-industry" argument is the most famous and widely invoked variation of the general thesis. Alexander Hamilton, in his *Report on Manufactures* (1791), was one of the first to state it clearly. The broader thesis, involving quasi-political and sociological elements as well as economic aspects, was developed on the European Continent, especially by Friedrich List in *The National System of Political Economy* (1840). The argument runs that certain individual industries in a country may not have the opportunity to develop because of the competition from already established industries in more highly developed countries, even though, once developed, they would have a comparative advantage. If these industries are protected from foreign competition during their early development, or "infancy," later they will be able to stand on their own feet and survive foreign competition.

Theoretically, the infant-industry argument has a considerable degree of validity. The economic development of countries has not proceeded simultaneously, and historical accident in the location of industries has played a not unimportant role. Even on a theoretical basis, though, the argument can be, and often has been, carried too far. Organizing an industry always requires an interim period before it is firmly established and able to operate efficiently. This has not prevented the rapid development of new industries in competition with older ones *within* countries, and there is no fundamental reason why competition from established industries in other countries should always constitute a much more serious barrier.

Whatever its theoretical merits, the infant-industry argument runs into serious difficulties in practical application. How can it be determined which particular potential industries would, under a protective cover, develop a comparative advantage and be able to withstand foreign competition without continued protection? It is certain that many would clamor for protection, and it is equally certain that the claims of most would not be economically justifiable. Moreover, in the numerous instances where protection turns out to have been a mistake, it becomes extremely difficult to remove the protection and thereby seal the fate of inefficient firms. Lastly, unless the protective tariff is placed on a definite timetable, which is firmly adhered to, the incentive to develop increasing efficiency is weakened, and the basic idea of the program is subverted. Historical experience demonstrates that, in fact, it is much easier for infant industries to obtain protection than it is to remove protection.

General Industrialization. Broader than the infant-industry argument, but in a similar vein, is the proposition, stated at the beginning of this section, that not only particular industries but general industrialization must be developed if a country is to enjoy a high standard of living. This argument is of especial current interest in connection with the efforts of underdeveloped areas to improve their economic situation.

There are good reasons for believing that a considerable degree of industrialization is indeed necessary for raising the standard of living of many of the underdeveloped areas of the world to a level approaching that of, say, Western Europe. It is also clear, on the other hand, as we shall show later, that the fundamental barrier to industrialization in such areas is not competition from abroad but rather the paucity of capital and technological knowledge and the absence of other conditions favorable to development.

It may be granted that underdeveloped areas have little chance of creating heavy industries, such as steel, for example, in open competition with the highly developed industries of the United States and Western Europe. It may also be true that, in some instances at least, general industrial development carries with it economic by-products which are not realized in the case of the limited and partial industrialization accomplished by the creation of a few infant industries.

The great danger of protective tariffs and quantitative import controls as devices for encouraging overall industrialization, however, is that the wrong kind of industries will be created. There is nothing in the theory of comparative advantage that requires a division of the world into primary producing countries and industrial countries. But it is contrary to economic principles for all countries to attempt to develop the *same* industries. The types of industry which the underdeveloped areas can economically create and maintain are generally those which do not require protection on any large scale, for they are based on natural advantages. Although generalizations are often misleading, we may conclude that, with some possible exceptions, any country that requires general protection in order to industrialize is probably developing an uneconomic structure which is inconsistent with the future realization of its full potentialities.

Military and Political Security

Protective tariffs and similar measures are sometimes defended as a means of safeguarding the military or political security of the state. Untrammeled international trade leads to the economic interdependence of national states. Hence, it is argued, the more important foreign sources of supply are in the functioning of an economy, the more susceptible it is to pressure resulting from military or naval blockade in time of war. Protective tariffs levied on strategic raw materials encourage the home production of these materials, or of substitutes, and in this manner lessen the dependence on external sources of supply. In particular instances there may be merit to this argument, but there are cogent reasons for believing that it is invalid if applied indiscriminately.

In some cases, the argument to the effect that tariffs lessen dependence on foreign supplies in time of war is false. Take, for example, the case of nonreproducible strategic materials the natural domestic reserves of which are limited and for which satisfactory substitutes cannot be developed. Protective tariffs result in a more rapid exhaustion of the available domestic resources in peacetime and thereby *increase* the dependence upon foreign supplies in wartime. As the President's Materials Policy Commission report has shown, this must be a matter of concern for even the resource-rich United States. Hence, for example, the quotas placed on oil imports into the United States, avowedly for the purpose of sustaining the domestic oil industry as essential to national defense, may in the long run have exactly opposite results.

More generally, the effects of protective tariffs on military security must take into account the close relationship between overall economic strength and military power. Any weakening of the economy is bound to have adverse repercussions on military potential. This holds not only for individual national economies but also for the group of countries which are politically and militarily allied. In other words, economic interdependence among countries which are politically and militarily interdependent is a source of strength rather than weakness. A report by a Senate committee has concluded: "National security depends upon many factors, not the least of which is a community of economically healthy nations devoted to living in harmony and tied together by mutually beneficial trade."[7]

THE NATIONAL INTEREST VERSUS THE INTEREST OF OWNERS OF SCARCE FACTORS

In Chapter 3 it was shown that participation in international trade inevitably results in the functional redistribution of income within each trading country. Although trade increases the aggregate real national income and therefore allows the real income of all groups within the economy to benefit, the income of one group of factor owners may actually be reduced unless deliberate measures are taken to assure the general distribution of the gains from trade.

It follows from this that protective tariffs or other import restrictions may be of benefit to one segment of the economy, even though they are deleterious to the economy as a whole. This may help to explain, in fact, many of the bitter historical tariff controversies: between landlords and manufacturers in England over the effects of the Corn Laws on agricultural rents and real wages; between the advocates of protective tariffs in the industrial North and the free-trade agricultural South in the United States; and the arguments for tariffs in Australia on the grounds of protecting the share of workers in the national income.

Whether or not this argument for protective tariffs is acceptable depends upon value judgment comparisons of the welfare of one group within the economy and the welfare of the society as a whole. Such conflicts of interest cannot be solved by objective standards, but one point should be emphasized: free trade, by increasing real national income, makes it *possible* for *everyone's* economic welfare to be advanced; tariffs for the benefit of one particular group of productive agents lower real national income below its free-trade level and therefore reduce the economic well-being of other factor groups. (Exceptions have already been noted in those cases where the national economy as a whole benefits from tariffs.)

---

[7] *Defense Essentiality and Foreign Economic Policy* (Senate Report No. 2629, 84th Cong., 2d sess. [Washington, D.C.: U.S. Government Printing Office, 1956]), p. 28.

Prevent the Pauperization of Labor

One of the most common arguments used in the United States in favor of protective tariffs is that free trade would tend to "pauperize" American labor. The logical basis for this assertion is usually put in something like the following terms: (*a*) wage rates in the United States are far higher than in most other countries of the world; (*b*) therefore, costs of production tend to be lower in other countries; (*c*) hence, under free trade, foreign goods would flood the American markets; and (*d*) American producers would thereby be forced to lower wage rates to a level approximating foreign wage rates.

The critical defect in the above line of reasoning lies at stage (*b*), rendering the remainder of the argument and the conclusion reached invalid. It is not true to say that low money wages necessarily mean low *wage costs per unit of output*. The latter is a function of two elements—money wage rates *and* the *productivity* of labor. Suppose that the wages of workers in the shoe industry are the equivalent of 25 cents per hour in Italy and $2 per hour in the United States. Suppose, further, that the average output of shoes per man-hour is 1 pair in Italy and 10 pairs in the United States. Then the wage costs per pair of shoes is 25 cents in Italy and 20 cents in the United States.

But, it might be objected, the above example is unfairly "loaded" with the assumption that labor productivity in the United States is so much greater than in Italy. The objection is overcome by the principles of wage determination: real wages are the *fruits* of per capita productivity. Wages in the United States are higher than in Italy because the American worker is more productive than the Italian worker—not, let it be emphasized, because of an inherent superiority, but because of the larger supply of capital, more advanced technology, (possibly) the advantages of large-scale production, and so on. The only way, then, that real wages could be lowered would be through decreases in labor productivity. On the basis of this principle, a grain of truth hidden in the pauper labor argument can be detected. As our earlier theoretical discussion of the effects of trade on income distribution showed, free trade tends to lower the marginal productivity—and therefore market income share—of a country's relatively most scarce factor of production. Labor's income share in the United States might therefore be higher with protective tariffs than under free trade. However, to the extent that free trade results in an aggregate national income greater than would be produced under restricted trade, any adverse effect of free trade on the income share of a particular group could be compensated for and still leave the remainder of the population better off than they would be under restricted trade.

THE NATIONAL INTEREST VERSUS SPECIAL-INTEREST GROUPS

Protective tariffs affect not only the functional distribution of income within a country, but, like most taxes, also affect the *personal* distribution of income.[8] Besides the owners of the relatively scarce factors of production who may benefit from protective tariffs in general, there are numerous individuals and firms who ordinarily stand to gain from nearly every specific tariff. As we have seen, an import duty tends to reduce the volume of import and to raise the domestic price of the commodity on which the tariff is levied. This is bound to be of immediate benefit to domestic producers of the good, or of close substitutes for it, and to those factors of production, if any, which are specific to the protected industry.

On the other hand, as consumers, the public is forced to pay higher prices for the protected commodity. There appears, therefore to be a conflict of interest between the particular producers who benefit from the tariff and the general public, which suffers higher consumer prices.

The special-interest advocates of tariffs deny that there is such a conflict of interests. In support of this contention, a large battery of arguments has been built up, the chief of which we shall now state and critically evaluate.

Expand Production and Enlarge the Market

The argument that protective tariffs are in the general interest of a country because they expand production and enlarge the market has a beguiling appeal. The interests of various producer groups are closely woven together, so that direct benefits accruing to one group will indirectly redound to the profit of others. Hence, if manufacturing industries are given the benefits of protective tariffs,

---

[8] Personal income distribution refers to the distribution of income among families or individuals, rather than according to the productive functions performed by the income receiver (functional distribution of income).

thereby increasing wages and profits, the market for agricultural and other goods will expand, and the farmers and other producing groups will have reflected upon them the prosperity which only appears to be confined to the protected industries.

Moreover, if it is true, as we have said, that an individual industry may benefit from a protective tariff, is it not true that all producers could be benefited by extending the tariff to protect them?

There are two serious flaws in the above argument. The first is that, with fully employed resources,[9] aggregate domestic production cannot be expanded by protective tariffs, for any expansion in one field of economic activity must necessarily be at the expense of reduced output in other fields. The main effect of tariffs in this event is to draw resources away from previous employments into the protected industries.

The second flaw in the argument ties in with the statement made in the last-preceding sentence. Some of the resources reallocated by the effects of protective tariffs are very likely to be drawn away from the production of export goods. There is, in fact, a probability that export industries would undergo a considerable contraction; for, by leading to a reduction in the volume of imports, protective tariffs tend to reduce the foreign demand for the country's exports. While it may very well be true, therefore, that the *domestic* market would be expanded, any such expansion would tend to be at the expense of the export market. In the final analysis, then, protective tariffs tend to result in a reallocation of resources from the relatively efficient export industries to the relatively inefficient protected industries. This can hardly be said to be of benefit to the economy as a whole.

Equalize the Costs of Production at Home and Abroad

This argument is designed to appeal to the sense of fair play in eliminating "unfair" and "cutthroat" competition from abroad. Some foreign producers, it is said, are able, because of special advantages, to undersell domestic producers. The advantages enjoyed by the foreign producers might be lower wage costs, more favorable climatic conditions, or any of the other numerous factors which help determine costs of production. In order to equalize the position of domestic and foreign producers in these instances, tariffs

---

[9] If there is unemployment, the argument reduces to that already described and evaluated above.

equivalent to the differences in the costs of production should be levied.

We may agree with everything in this proposition, except the conclusion. There are indeed special advantages enjoyed by the foreign producers of certain products; precisely for this reason international trade is advantageous. Artificially to eliminate the advantages is tantamount to eliminating the gains from trade. As a matter of fact, carried to its logical conclusion, a policy of equalizing foreign and domestic costs through tariffs would totally eliminate trade and would produce the conditions of an isolated and self-sufficient economy with the lower standard of living that inevitably would accompany it.

May there not, however, be a danger that foreigners will be able to produce *everything* cheaper than at home? The answer is emphatically negative. International trade is based on *comparative* advantages, and, as demonstrated in the second and third chapters of this book, it is inherently impossible for a country to have a comparative disadvantage in *all* products.[10] Confusion on this point usually derives from the belief that since wages or some other element of costs are generally lower abroad than domestically, all foreign goods must have lower costs of production. Lower wages do not, however, mean lower *wage costs,* which are a function of labor productivity as well as wages. Low real wages normally are the *result* of low productivity, and high real wages are the result of great productivity. Hence it is quite possible for high wages to be accompanied by low *wage costs* per unit of output.

Since low wages and a relatively abundant labor supply ordinarily go hand in hand, it is generally true, of course, that low-wage countries do have an advantage in the production of those goods requiring in their production a relatively large quantity of labor. The *proportion* of labor to other factors of production varies, on the other hand, among different goods, so that the advantages thus realized are limited to only certain commodities.

Keep Money at Home

Imports, as we shall see, reduce the domestically held supply of money. Do not imports, therefore, have undesirable repercussions on the economy?

---

[10] For a comparative disadvantage in one product necessarily implies a comparative advantage in another. Thus a comparative disadvantage in wheat compared to cloth *means* a comparative advantage in cloth compared to wheat.

In its crudest form, this argument is based on the most elementary type of fallacious thinking. First, it is based on a mercantilist identity of money and wealth. Even if it were true that tariffs, by reducing imports, keep the domestic supply of money at a higher volume, this would make no direct contribution to the real income and wealth of the country.

Moreover, even though imports, per se, tend to reduce the domestic supply of money, exports tend equally to increase it. If, as we have concluded, a reduction in imports tends to have the ultimate effect of also reducing exports, no net addition to the supply of money is realized. To put it in commonsense terms, any money that is "exported" to pay for commodity imports will ultimately tend to seek its way back to the country of issue, in the exercise of its only real basis of value—the purchase of goods and services or payment of debts.

It must be granted, however, that in a more sophisticated form the argument is not wholly devoid of meaning. If a country is suffering from unemployment and deflation, an increase in the supply of money may well have beneficial effects, especially through lowered interest rates. Particularly if a country is on the gold standard and has rigid limitations on the ratio between the gold reserve and the supply of money, protective tariffs, if they are successful in promoting an export surplus, may have beneficial repercussions on employment and income, not only directly via the foreign-trade multiplier, but indirectly via easier money conditions. This is a variation of the full-employment argument, considered earlier, and is subject to the limitations noted at that time.

In any event, in most contemporary economies, the supply of money is no longer mainly or even significantly dependent upon the balance of payments. Central bank and fiscal policies are much more potent weapons of monetary control within a country than is manipulation of the trade balance, and they have the additional advantage of not interfering with the most efficient allocation of resources.

Retaliation or Increased Bargaining Power

Retaliation may be appropriately labeled the "small-boy" argument: if you are punched in the nose, hit back, even if you lose your front teeth in the process.

If foreign countries raise their tariffs, a given country will lose some of the benefits of trade formerly received. Retaliation does not, however, recoup the loss but, on the contrary, only aggravates it by still further reducing the volume of trade. As noted earlier, retaliation may yield immediate benefits in the form of improved terms of trade, but the probability is that this will prove ephemeral by leading to counterretaliation.

The bargaining-power argument also involves an increase in tariffs in response to foreign tariff increases. In this case, though, the intent, at least, is honorable, for the avowed purpose is to use offers of rescinding the retaliatory action as a weapon for obtaining reciprocal treatment.

In some instances, there may be validity in this line of reasoning. The danger, however, is that the expected agreement on reciprocal reduction of tariffs will not materialize, in which case it is highly unlikely that the tariffs will be brought back to their original level by unilateral action. Moreover, we may suspect that opposition to lowering tariffs, on the grounds that this would weaken the country's bargaining position, as well as advocacy of higher tariffs to strengthen bargaining power, are both often used as cover for ulterior and less generous motives.

CONCLUSION

With one or two possible exceptions of a very limited kind, none of the arguments for protective tariffs can withstand searching analysis. Some have a degree of theoretical validity under certain assumptions, but in practice they are, more often than not, self-defeating.

The truth is that most specific tariffs are put on the books through the efforts of special-interest groups. We have examined some of the arguments with which these efforts have been rationalized and have found them to be misleading, at least, and often based on crudely fallacious reasoning.

One of the real difficulties in combating tariffs is the failure on the part of the consuming public to realize how its interests are affected. In effect, a tariff amounts to a subsidy to the domestic producers of the dutiable article, paid by the consumers of that article in the form of a higher price. It is rare for a tariff to be levied for that specific and avowed purpose. But, if it is deemed desirable to subsidize certain producers, it would be much more in the public's interest to do so directly; for in that case, the subsidy would have to withstand the scrutiny of the taxpayer.

RECOMMENDED READING

CORDEN, W. M. "The Structure of a Tariff System and the Effective Protective Rate," *Journal of Political Economy*, June, 1966.

MEADE, JAMES. *Trade and Welfare*, chaps. iv, ix, xxvi. London: Oxford University Press, 1955.

SCITOVSKY, TIBOR. "A Reconsideration of the Theory of Tariffs," *Review of Economic Studies*, Vol. 9 (1942); reprinted in American Economic Association, *Readings in the Theory of International Trade* (eds. HOWARD S. ELLIS and LLOYD A. METZLER), pp. 358–89. Homewood, Ill.: Richard D. Irwin, Inc., 1949.

TOWLE, LAWRENCE W. *International Trade and Commercial Policy*, chaps. xvii–xxii, xxiv. 2d ed. New York: Harper & Row, Publishers, 1956.

VON HABERLER, GOTTFRIED. *The Theory of International Trade*, chaps. xv–xvii. New York: Macmillan Co., 1937.

VERNON, RAYMOND. "Foreign Trade and National Defense," *Foreign Affairs*, Vol. 34 (October, 1955), pp. 77–88.

YEAGER, LELAND B., and TUERCK, DAVID G. *Trade Policy and the Price System*. Scranton, Pa.: International Textbook Co., 1966.

STUDY QUESTIONS

1. Define each of the following: import duty, export duty, transit duty, specific rate, ad valorem rate, compound rate, tariff schedule, single-columned tariff, multicolumned tariff, import quota, and administrative protection.

2. Why would a successful protective tariff be a poor revenue tariff?

3. Describe a tariff system that is highly protective even though the amount of import duties collected constitutes a very low percentage of the total value of imports.

4. Compare the restrictive effects on international trade of tariffs and quotas.

5. Describe the exact reason why import duties ordinarily cause the volume of imports to be less than under free trade.

6. Ignoring transportation costs and assuming that there are no quantitative restrictions on trade, why will the price of a good on which an import duty is levied tend to be higher in the importing country than it is abroad by the full amount of the duty?

7. Explain the statement that the effect of free international trade is to eliminate the inequality of price ratios in different countries, whereas the effect of tariffs is artificially to re-create relative price

differences. Which of these two effects is the more desirable from the standpoint of the optimum allocation of the world's productive resources?

8. Why would the extensive use of import quotas tend to destroy the function of the price mechanism as a guide in the international allocation of resources?

9. Under what circumstances may a country obtain a larger share of the gain from international trade by raising its tariffs? Why cannot all countries play this game at the same time? Why is any gain realized by a country through this method likely to prove temporary?

10. An increase in tariffs for the purpose of reducing unemployment is more likely to redistribute the unemployed than to cause a net reduction in the total number unemployed. Explain.

11. State and critically evaluate the "infant-industry" argument for tariffs. In what countries of the world today would you expect to find the infant-industry argument most commonly invoked?

12. Evaluate the argument that tariffs on some commodities are required for the purpose of increasing the military security of the state.

13. On what theoretical grounds might labor in the United States justify opposition to lowering tariffs? Would the same argument be applicable in India, for example?

14. Do high American wages imply high labor costs per unit of output in all American industries? Why not?

15. What is wrong with the proposition that protective tariffs expand production and enlarge the market?

16. Why is it impossible for a given country to be able to sell *all* goods and services at lower prices than other countries?

17. What are the logical implications of the proposal to levy tariffs in an amount that would equalize foreign and domestic costs of production?

18. Granted that imports do tend to reduce the supply of domestically held money, why is this not a valid argument in favor of reducing imports through protective tariffs?

19. Explain in what manner a protective tariff amounts in effect to a subsidy to the domestic producers of the commidity.

| Chapter | COMMERCIAL POLICIES OF |
| 8 | THE UNITED STATES |

The world has never experienced international trade completely free of artificially erected barriers of one kind or another. But the nature and extent of trade barriers have varied greatly in different periods of history, the pendulum swinging from eras marked by exceedingly detailed and stringent controls over trade to eras during which a free-trade philosophy was more or less closely carried out in practice, and back again to a resurgence of timeworn restrictionism. These vacillating commercial-policy movements have not, of course, taken place in a vacuum: they have been part and parcel of broader historical developments—political, social, and ideological, as well as economic.

It is manifestly impossible within the space of one chapter to give a detailed historical review of the commercial policies of all major countries. In this chapter we shall concentrate, therefore, on the commercial policies of the United States, with special emphasis on the period since 1934. Before embarking upon this, however, it might be useful to have in mind the perspective afforded by a résumé of the main currents of commercial-policy development in the major trading countries in modern times.

A BIRD'S-EYE VIEW OF COMMERCIAL-POLICY HISTORY

Mercantilism

The mercantilist era, which may be roughly dated from about 1500 to 1750, was characterized by a mass of detailed regulations and controls over international trade. England, France, Spain, and Portugal were the chief powers that followed the policies associated with mercantilism. The other great power during this period—Holland—pursued a much less restrictive course with respect to trade, except for that with her colonies.

The main underlying objective of commercial policy was to develop an export *surplus*—a so-called "favorable" balance of trade. In pursuit of this objective, exports were pushed to the utmost—through export subsidies, prohibition of the export of raw materials necessary in the domestic production of more valuable exports, "drawbacks" of excise and import duties, and so on.[1] At the same time, imports were severely restricted, except for raw materials needed for domestic production and except for the precious metals. The devices employed to restrict imports ranged from outright prohibition to high protective tariffs.

The immediate function of an export surplus was to acquire the precious metals. The reasons advanced for considering this to be a prime objective of economic policy varied greatly among mercantilist writers: the crude identification of gold and silver with wealth; the desirability of creating an emergency reserve for the state; as a means of exercising thrift and storing wealth; in order to stimulate domestic economic activity. From the point of view of modern economic theory, many, though not all, of these arguments appear to be based on fallacious reasoning. But such a pervasive doctrine can hardly be explained as simply the consequence of errant logic.

Mercantilism can be explained only in terms of the historical setting out of which it grew; the rise of national states, the almost continuous series of civil wars and international conflicts, the growing power of the commercial class, and the beginnings of scientific thought.

The Free-Trade Movement

As the historical circumstances which produced mercantilism gradually changed, the balance-of-trade theory and the restrictionist policies which were appropriate thereto became anachronistic and hostile to the spirit and requirements of the time. Of outstanding importance were the economic and technological developments described as the Industrial Revolution and the accompanying growth of power and influence on the part of the business class. Detailed regulations and controls by the state over both internal and external trade were antagonistic to the developing notions of industrial venture and opportunity for profit after about the middle of the

---

[1] "Drawbacks" are rebates to exporters of duties which have been paid on materials used in the manufacture of exported commodities.

eighteenth century. At the same time, the intellectual and philosophic basis for rejecing the mercantilist theories was brilliantly provided by a series of writers, culminating in the classic work of Adam Smith. The virtues of free and unhampered private enterprise, both at home and in international trade, and the identification of the public interest with the pursuit of private gain by individuals were rationalized by Smith and the succession of classical economic theorists who followed him.

The long and unaccustomed period of peace which followed the Napoleonic Wars provided the atmosphere congenial to the practical implementation of the philosophy of laissez-faire. Gradually the mass of detailed regulations on internal commerce was swept away, and the free-trade movement gained momentum. After a long struggle between the landed aristocracy and the manufacturing interests, the culmination of the free-trade policy in England was reached in 1846 with the repeal of the Corn Laws.

For several decades in the middle part of the 19th century, the free-trade philosophy was in the saddle in the most important trading countries, though at no time were artificial restrictions completely eliminated.

The Revival of Protectionism

The era of laissez-faire and of the companion doctrine of free trade was not destined to continue unchallenged. Toward the last quarter of the 19th century, protectionist sentiment got the upper hand in most of the important trading countries, with the exception of Great Britain and Holland.

The explanation of this trend lies, for the most part, in the efforts of other countries to promote the kind of industrial development which had already come to England; the growing strength of nationalism and imperialism as a political and economic force; and the clamor of powerful special-interest groups for protection against the competition of foreign producers. The "intellectual" basis for protectionism has already been described in the preceding chapter.

The dislocations and maladjustments in the world economy caused by World War I, the rapid growth of competing industries and agriculture which a period of war naturally encourages, and the increasing economic instability which characterizes the highly complex modern industrial economies caused a further weakening of the laissez-faire and free-trade philosophy during the 1920's,

Notwithstanding the rising height of tariff walls, commercial policy in most countries never approached the extremes of mercantilism until the onset of worldwide depression at the beginning of the 1930's. Then, in a desperate attempt to stem the tide of unemployment and deflation, one country after another, with the United States in the vanguard, pushed tariffs to unprecedented heights, subsidized exports, introduced quantitative restrictions, practiced discrimination, and in other ways so emulated mercantilist policies as to evoke the description "neomercantilist." This appellation was especially apposite to Germany after 1933, when her commercial policy became simply a weapon of economic warfare, an integral part of the Nazi ultranationalistic, militaristic program of conquest. But, in a less extreme form, many other countries besides Germany revived mercantilist notions in their attempts to "export" unemployment and to relieve deflationary pressures by developing an export surplus.

Although, as previously indicated, the United States was one of the first major countries to resort to the highly restrictive commercial policies which characterized the depression decade, a few years later American policy underwent an apparently drastic change in outlook. Beginning in 1934 and continuing down to the present, the United States has become the leading official protagonist, as Great Britain was in the 19th century, for freer world trade. The nature and results of this movement can best be understood in the context of American commercial policy, so that we shall defer our discussion of it until the later pages of this chapter and the next chapter.

U.S. TARIFFS, 1789–1934

From the very beginnings of the United States as an independent nation and continuously since then, tariffs have been one of the major aspects of her foreign economic policy. Periodic increases and decreases of import duties have characterized the tariff history of the United States, but at no time has the doctrine of free trade been put to practice.

Tariffs for Revenue

Perhaps the primary origin of tariffs in the United States was the convenience which they offered in the early years of the Repub-

lic as a source of government revenue. Until the last decade of the
19th century, customs receipts provided half or more of the total
ordinary revenue of the federal government. The political pro-
ponents of lower tariffs have nearly always, until recent decades, defended a minimum level of tariffs as a source of government revenue. Strange as it may seem to this generation, at times the strongest reason for reducing tariffs was to avoid an embarrassing redun-
dance of revenue! This was the chief reason for reducing rates in
1857 and again in 1872. The basis of the revenue argument has,
however, progressively weakened with the growth in government
expenditure and the development of alternative sources of revenue,
especially the income tax. By 1929 customs receipts constituted less
than 15 percent, and by 1938 less than 6 percent, of ordinary government revenue; since then they have yielded a negligible percentage, currently less than 1 percent, of total federal revenue.

Tariffs for Protection

The weakening of the revenue argument for tariffs was accompanied by the growing strength of protectionist arguments. Indeed,
there has probably been no tariff in American history which has
not had some protectionist elements. According to its preamble,
even the first tariff bill (1789), though imposing low rates, had as
its purpose not only the provision of revenue but also "the encouragement and protection of manufactures."

The Napoleonic Wars and the War of 1812 greatly reduced the
import of manufactured goods into the United States and stimulated domestic manufactures. Upon the conclusion of peace with
England in 1814, a flood of imports from that country flowed into
the United States, threatening to ruin the recently established domestic manufacturing concerns. Agreement was general, therefore,
even among those who were fundamentally low-tariff in principle,
that tariffs should be high enough to protect American industry.
The Tariff of 1816 reflected these sentiments; compared to the rates
in 1789, which averaged about 8 percent ad valorem, rates on various imports were doubled, trebled, or quadrupled.[2]

---

[2] The percentage figures on the average height of the U.S. tariff, given here and
elsewhere in this chapter, are subject to the weaknesses discussed earlier. The reader
is warned, therefore, against accepting the figures as accurate measures of the absolute height of tariffs or as indicative of the degree of protection afforded thereby.
However, there is evidence that *comparison* of the average rates for different periods

While import duties were generally increased still further in the following years, increasing opposition was expressed to high rates, especially in the South. The Tariff Act of 1828 represented the extreme of protective legislation before the Civil War, earning the derisive epithets of the "Black Tariff" and the "Tariff of Abominations."[3] Its extremist character is indicated by the fact that it resulted in average ad valorem rates on dutiable imports of nearly 49 percent and on free and dutiable imports together of over 45 percent.[4] Such violent opposition was provoked in the South by these rates that there were threats of "nullification" and secession. As a consequence, the "compromise" Tariff of 1833 provided for the gradual reduction of all the higher rates and the enlargement of the free list. Although higher rates were restored in 1842, they were again cut in 1846 and 1857, bringing them, in general, to the lowest level since 1816.

Just before the outbreak of the Civil War, the tariff cuts of 1857 were eliminated. As war-financing requirements increased, higher duties were imposed; and in 1864, rates were raised to an average of 47 percent on dutiable goods. This high level of protection constituted the basis of tariff policy until 1883, when popular demand for reform led to minor downward revisions.

The election of Cleveland in 1884 put the Democratic party in power for the first time since the Civil War. Cleveland put his party on record for tariff reform, but his efforts to reduce rates failed. The Republicans returned to power with Harrison in 1888 on a platform that included as a major plank the protection of American labor against foreign "pauper" labor. The McKinley Tariff of 1890 raised the level of tariffs to close to 50 percent on dutiable articles and embodied the principle of protection as a permanent policy.

Although the Democratic administration which returned to office in 1892 attempted a general revision and reduction of the high duties imposed under the McKinley Tariff, Congress prevented any fundamental changes, except the abolition of the duty on wool.

---

of time gives a roughly accurate index of the *changes* in the height of the tariff, and it is only for this purpose that use of the figures is justified.

[3] The bill was apparently never intended to become law but was designed as a political strategem to weaken the position of protectionist presidential candidates to the advantage of Jackson by including extremely high duties on raw materials. This was supposed to incur the wrath of northern manufacturing interests and result in its defeat; but the plan backfired when the bill was passed.

[4] U.S. Tariff Commission, *The Tariff and Its History* (Washington, D.C.: U.S. Government Printing Office, 1934), p. 73. Most of the factual material in this section is based on this study.

The election of McKinley in 1896 and the ensuing enactment of the Dingley Tariff of 1897 restored the duty on wool and raised the general level of tariffs to a thoroughly protectionist plane. Although some minor downward revision was effected by the Payne-Aldrich Tariff of 1909, no major changes were made until the administration of Woodrow Wilson.

The Underwood Tariff of 1913 threatened the first successful breach of the high protectionist wall which had been built up since the Civil War. Over one hundred items were added to the free list, and hundreds of rates were reduced on other items. The average rate was lowered from over 40 percent to less than 30 percent.

The war prevented the implementation of the Underwood Tariff; and, following the election of a Republican administration in 1920, the previous protectionist trend was firmly reestablished. In response to the postwar plight of the farmer, an emergency act in 1921 added many agricultural products to the protected list. The Fordney-McCumber Tariff of 1922 contained agricultural protection, raised other rates, and gave the President the power to raise or lower rates by as much as 50 percent to "equalize" foreign and domestic costs of production.

The culmination of the protectionist trend in the United States, which, as we have seen, suffered few interruptions from the time of the Civil War, was reached in 1930 with the passage of the notorious Hawley-Smoot Tariff. Probably no other piece of legislation in history has ever aroused as much furor and international ill will as this bill. Notwithstanding the protests of 24 countries, the export markets of which were in many cases seriously threatened, nor the more than 1,000 prominent American economists who petitioned President Hoover to veto the bill, tariffs were raised to the highest level (an average rate of over 52 percent on dutiable imports) in American history.

The unreasonable and frenetic character of the Hawley-Smoot Tariff is demonstrated by the fact that it covered many articles which were in no sense competitive with domestic products. Although many articles were on the free list, a number of them were not produced at all in the United States, while others appear to have been added for purposes of padding.[5]

The foreign retaliation which followed the Hawley-Smoot Tar-

---

[5] Among others on the free list were: broken bells, bread, dried blood, bones, bird eggs, unmanufactured hoofs, ice, ivory tusks, leeches, lava, sheep dip, skeletons, natural teeth, turtles, and worm gut.

iff is an excellent historical illustration of the probable reaction to the attempt on the part of any major importing country to raise its tariffs, especially during a period of general economic and financial crisis. Partly as an independent policy but also partly in retaliation against the American tariff increases, tariffs in many foreign countries were raised very soon after the enactment of the Hawley-Smoot bill.

Although the decline in income and employment in the United States and other industrial countries was undoubtedly the main factor responsible, the network of tariffs, quotas, and other trade restrictions, which the American tariff of 1930 contributed to and encouraged, constituted an important independent cause of the drastic contraction in world trade which occurred beginning in 1930. The volume of world trade declined by one third between 1929 and the third quarter of 1932, while the gold value of world trade fell by nearly two thirds over the same period.[6] It is also interesting to observe that not only did the volume of U.S. imports fall during the years 1930–33 more than that of any other major industrial country, but the volume of her exports also fell by the greatest amount.[7] It is reasonably safe to conclude that the net effect of tariffs and other trade restrictions during the Great Depression was in the direction of contracting the total market, income, and employment of each country rather than in the direction posited by tariff advocates.

Major Tariff Issues before 1934

The United States won its independence during a period of transition in Europe from mercantilism to laissez-faire and free trade. The prevailing opinion in the United States was also favorable at this time to freedom in trade relations, in part as a reaction against the restrictions and controls to which the colonies had been subjected. Although the theory of protectionism had early been advanced by Hamilton, American tariffs before the Civil War were, generally speaking, based more on the need for revenue than on the desire for protection. Major exceptions to this were the Tariff of 1816—which was designed to protect domestic industries that had

---

[6] League of Nations, *World Economic Survey, 1933–34* (Geneva, 1934), p. 187.

[7] In 1932 the volume of U.S. exports was only 53 percent of 1929, while that of the United Kingdom was 63 percent; France, 59 percent; Germany, 59 percent; Italy, 77 percent; and Japan, 94 percent (*ibid.*, p. 196).

developed during the war with Great Britain—and the Act of 1828, which, as we have seen, contained excessively high rates because of a political maneuver that went awry. Concurrently with the free-trade policy of Britain after the removal of the Corn Laws, the United States, in the Acts of 1846 and 1857, also moved toward a low-tariff system.

After the Civil War, although the revenue aspects of tariffs continued to exert an important influence, the principle of protection grew progressively stronger, culminating in the McKinley and Dingley tariffs of 1890 and 1897, respectively. By this time, tariffs had unfortunately become a matter of partisan politics.

The party of Jefferson and Jackson, purporting to represent the interests of the farmer and the "mechanic" against the manufacturing and "monied" interests of the North and East, generally stood for low tariffs for revenue purposes, though certainly not for free trade in any strict sense. The party of Hamilton, the father of the "infant-industry" argument, consistently emphasized the dangers of competition from cheap foreign labor and the virtues of a protected domestic market. The platforms of the two major parties became increasingly bitter and denunciatory with respect to tariffs after the Civil War.

Conflict between Agricultural and Industrial Interests. At the risk of oversimplification, we may say with a good deal of truth that the conflict over protective tariffs in the United States up until roughly World War I was the product of a clash between agricultural interests, mainly in the South, and manufacturing interests, mainly in the North.[8] This was a reflection of the basic position of the United States in the 19th century as an importer of manufactured goods and an exporter of agricultural products. It was natural for the planters of the South and West to object to the higher prices for manufactured goods which they had to pay because of tariffs, and for the manufacturers of the North to desire protection against competition from abroad.

Over the period from the Civil War to World War I, the economy of the United States underwent profound changes in structure, with a tremendous increase in the relative importance of manufacturing industry. Correspondingly, the comparative advantage of the United States shifted from primary products to manufactured

---

[8] Some agricultural interests, such as woolgrowers, were protectionist; but the producers of the main staples of American agriculture—especially cotton and tobacco, supplemented by corn and wheat—depended on export markets and were free trade.

goods. Thus, whereas earlier the United States was an importer of manufactured goods and an exporter of raw materials and food-stuffs, it later became an exporter of manufactured goods and an importer of raw materials and foodstuffs. As pointed out in Chapter 5, however, the United States now has a "balanced" economy, under which it continues to have a comparative advantage in certain agricultural goods as well as heavy manufactures.

This change in America's international economic position tended somewhat to blur the division of tariff sentiments. Those manufacturing interests which rely upon raw material imports and finished exports generally became low-tariff protagonists, while producers of foodstuffs and raw materials in competition with the growing volume of primary-products imports joined the ranks of the protectionists. In this connection it should be noted that the Emergency Tariff of 1921 and the Fordney-McCumber Tariff of the following year imposed high import duties on major agricultural products in response to the demands of farmers for protection. These measures were in large part the reaction to the plight of the farmers caused by a war-induced overexpansion of production and a subsequent sharp decline in farm prices. But large segments of American agriculture have since continued to be protectionist.

It would be misleading, however, to believe that the American tariff is the product solely of selfish interests, even though many individual duties have been enacted through the collective influence of small, but mutually supporting, local interests. At one time or another, nearly every one of the theoretical arguments in favor of tariffs examined in the preceding chapter has been invoked. Of these arguments, two of the stronger ones have had considerable influence in the development of the American tariff and thus deserve special mention.

Protection of Infant Industries. The first is the infant-industry argument, which constituted the chief theoretical or intellectual basis for the American tariff during the 19th century and the early part of the 20th. As we observed earlier, this argument is not without merit for a country that is in the early stages of economic development and is faced with the competition of other countries already industrialized. But American history also illustrates its weakness, for high protective tariffs were kept on the books long after industries had lost their "infant" status.

Military Security. The second intellectual basis for American tariffs—to preserve military security—has been applied in more recent decades. This, too, is an argument which may in some circumstances have merit. But we may question its general applicability in a period when American military security is so intimately bound up with the economic and military strength of other free nations, the economies of which are dependent upon the ability to find a market in the United States.

AMERICAN COMMERCIAL POLICY, 1934–62

The highest protective tariff in American history was followed, four years later (1934), by the inauguration of the most ambitious tariff-reducing program in the country's history. Within a quarter of a century, the average level of import duties was reduced by over three quarters, from a level of 53 percent in 1930–33 under the Hawley-Smoot Tariff to approximately 12 percent under the Reciprocal Trade Agreements program.

The Reciprocal Trade Agreements Program

The first, and basic, step in the new tariff program was the adoption in June, 1934, of the Reciprocal Trade Agreements Act. By this act, the President was empowered to negotiate treaties with foreign countries for the purpose of reciprocally reducing tariff barriers and without the necessity of ratification by the Senate. The "teeth" in the power to negotiate mutual trade concessions was the authority granted the President to lower or raise duties by as much as 50 percent of the existing level. Later, the base to which the 50 percent limit applied was changed to the duties prevailing on January 1, 1945. The provisions of the act were to extend three years, but extensions were successively made, although with important amendments, which will be discussed later.

Before the conclusion of the General Agreement on Tariffs and Trade in Geneva, Switzerland, in 1947, trade agreements were negotiated by the United States separately with 29 different countries. The general procedure followed in these negotiations may be briefly described.

Negotiating Procedures. Upon a tentative understanding with another country that the basis for reciprocal tariff concessions exists, the Trade Agreements Committee of the U.S. government —consisting of representatives from various departments of the government designated for the purpose of giving information and advice to the President on trade agreements—appoints a "country" committee to make a detailed examination of all factors pertinent to the negotiation. If, on the basis of these investigations, it appears that an agreement is feasible and desirable, the Trade Agreements Committee recommends to the President that formal negotiations be undertaken, and it accompanies the recommendation with tentative lists of items on which tariff concessions might be granted and on which concessions by the other country might be asked.

If the other country involved is willing to negotiate, a tentative list of articles subject to concessions is agreed upon, and formal negotiations are ready to begin. Before actual negotiations are entered into, however, public notice is given of the government's intentions, and a list of the import articles which the United States proposes to consider for concessions is circulated. The public is invited to supply any information which might be useful in the negotiations, including briefs on the part of domestic producers who are fearful that their interests would be jeopardized by tariff concessions.

Most of the agreements concluded before 1947 provide that they shall remain in force for an initial period of three years, after which they are automatically extended for an indefinite period but are subject to termination by one or the other of the contracting parties on giving six months' notice.

Negotiating Principles. Two major principles are embodied in the trade agreements of the United States. The first is the so-called "unconditional most-favored-nation" treatment. Under this principle, adopted by the United States as a general policy in 1923, any benefits or concessions granted to a given country automatically extend, without specific concessions in return, to all other countries. Hence any trade concession which the United States now extends to any foreign country (except for the Philippines, for which preferences are authorized in all trade agreements) it extends to any country with which it makes an agreement, unconditionally and without restriction.[9] Similarly, any concession granted by the other contracting party to any third country, but often with specified exceptions, must be extended unconditionally to the

---

[9] There is an exception, however: the President is authorized to withhold trade concessions from countries which either discriminate against American commerce or pursue policies which tend to defeat the purposes of the Trade Agreements Act.

Tariff concessions granted under U.S. trade agreements are not currently applied to imports from Communist-controlled countries or areas.

United States. In effect, therefore, even though trade agreements are bilateral, the concessions are "multilateralized."

The second principle followed in negotiating trade agreements is informal and is designed to avoid the weakening of bargaining power in obtaining concessions from other countries through the operation of most-favored-nation treatment. The principle is that of confining concessions to "chief suppliers." That is, the general policy, in an agreement with any given country, is not to grant a concession unless that country has been, or is likely to become, the principal, or at least a major, source of import of the commodity.

Although the principal objective of trade agreements is to provide for specific tariff concessions on listed articles, they also include certain general provisions concerning trade relations, apart from tariffs, between the signatories. Included in the general provisions are such commitments as the prohibition or limitation on the use of quantitative restrictions (quotas) and trade discriminations. The fullest and most general nontariff provisions, however, are contained in the General Agreement on Trade and Tariffs negotiated in Geneva in 1947, which will be discussed in a later section.

The Proposed International Trade Organization (ITO)

During the last war, the U.S. government began to do preliminary work on postwar economic problems and took the initiative, in consultation with her allies, in proposing various forms of international economic cooperation after the war's end. Some of the major concrete results of these proposals will be described in Parts III and IV. Those dealing mainly with commercial policy can most appropriately be discussed now, however.

In very general terms, U.S. government policy in the postwar years in the field of commercial relations has been directed toward two main objectives: (*a*) an international agreement on a code of trading relations and (*b*) the reduction or elimination of various specific trade barriers through international negotiation.

The most ambitious attempt at developing a code of commercial conduct is the Charter for an International Trade Organization (ITO). The Charter was the product of nearly five years of preparatory work during the war and over two years of laborious negotiations after the war. Agreement on the Charter was finally reached by the representatives of 54 countries at the end of the Havana Conference in March, 1948. As we shall see, however, the

Havana agreement has never been ratified. Nevertheless, the ITO Charter is of interest as the first attempt on an international scale to draw up a code of commercial relations, and in revealing some of the obstacles to freeing world trade from restrictive practices.

Objectives of the ITO. Under the Charter, signatories would become members of an International Trade Organization and would pledge themselves to work co-operatively in the promotion of the following major objectives:

Reduction of tariffs and other barriers to trade, and the elimination of discriminatory treatment in international commerce;

The access by all countries, on equal terms, to markets, products, and productive facilities;

A large and steadily expanding volume of real income and an increase in the production, consumption, and exchange of goods;

The economic development of economically backward areas, and the encouragement of the international flow of capital for productive investment;

The promotion of mutual understanding, consultation, and co-operation to facilitate the solution of problems relating to international trade in the fields of employment, economic development, commercial policy, business practices, and commodity policy.

The operating provisions of the Charter as it was finally agreed upon at Havana were the product of compromises between the broad, general principles set forth above and the demands of various countries for allowable exceptions to meet particular problems, especially of a temporary or transitional character. This may be illustrated by reference to the provisions relating to commercial policy.

General Obligations. The most general and basic rule of the charter concerning commercial policy is the obligation laid upon the members to negotiate, upon the request of any other member, for the reduction of tariffs and other barriers to trade and for the elimination of discriminatory treatment. The effectiveness of this general obligation was greatly reduced, however, by an "escape" clause. This provided that if, as a result of carrying out its obligations under the Charter, a member should find that such increased quantities of imports caused or threatened serious injury to domestic producers, the member had the right to withdraw or modify the concessions it had negotiated to the extent necessary to prevent or remedy the injury to its producers. Although provision was made for consultation between the affected members before such action should be taken, if agreement is not reached the members are free to take unilateral action. The U.S. representatives at Havana supported the escape clause, which is not surprising in view of the similar provision in the trade agreements of the United States (see page 196) and the probable refusal of Congress to ratify any agreement not including such a clause.

Though the Charter obliges members to negotiate on tariffs and other trade barriers, members are free to maintain or raise any particular rate not bound in an agreement with other members. *Quantitative* restrictions, mainly quotas and import and export licenses, however, are prohibited. The outlawing of quantitative restrictions was in recognition of their greater potentiality as a restrictive barrier to trade and as an obstacle to free-market forces than is true of tariffs. Here, too, however, exceptions were made. The most important of the exceptions relate to the use of quantitative restrictions for balance-of-payments purposes, for the development of economically backward countries, and for the purpose of enforcing domestic governmental measures, especially agricultural support programs. In general, the smaller, industrially underdeveloped countries insisted at Havana on the right to use quantitative restrictions to aid in the development of their indusries; European countries faced with serious balance-of-payments disequilibrium insisted on the right to use import restrictions, even in a discriminatory manner if necessary, to improve their balance-of-payments position; and the United States, among others, argued for the agricultural exception in order to reconcile the Charter's obligations with farm-support policies.

Without attempting to describe in detail other provisions in the Charter relating to commercial policy, we may briefly mention the following: the obligation to accord unconditional most-favored-nation treatment to all other members; the application of any permitted trade restrictions in a nondiscriminatory manner; the simplification and standardization of customs practices and formalities; the assimilation of state-trading practices with those of private trading; the provision for intergovernmental commodity agreements with respect to primary commodities, under certain conditions and for the purpose of alleviating the special problems faced by primary-commodity producers; and the adoption of appropriate measures to prevent restrictive business practices affecting international trade.

Results of the Havana Conference. Sixty-five countries were invited by the United Nations to the Havana Conference; seven, including the Soviet Union, did not accept; and, of those which did accept, two did not send representatives. Of the 56 countries represented, all but Argentina and Poland signed the Final Act of the Conference. After years of preparatory work and negotiation, the stage was set for ratification of the Charter. The other signatories at Havana awaited action by the United States, since its participation was indispensable for the success of the ITO. But the United States never ratified the Charter, the efforts of the administration to secure congressional authorization being formally given up in 1950.

The failure of U.S. ratification was caused by widespread opposition to the Charter by business and other groups. Some opposed it on the grounds that it represented a codification of malpractices and sanctioned exceptions to liberal trade principles, such as the right to impose quantitative restrictions to safeguard balance-of-payments positions. Many felt that the allowable exceptions to general obligations under the Charter would have the effect of committing the United States to liberal commercial policies while permitting other countries to follow discriminatory and restrictive policies. Another charge against the Charter was that it represented a victory for "economic planning" in recognizing the right of members, and even encouraging them, to maintain full employment through governmental action and, if necessary, to insulate the domestic economy from disrupting external forces through direct controls.

We shall not attempt to evaluate these and other numerous arguments against adoption of the Charter, except to say that some were misleading and indefensible, while others were not without validity, even if often exaggerated. In any event, in view of the fact that it was the United States which took the initiative and leadership in promoting the proposed ITO, its end may seem anomalous and strange. Undoubtedly it is so regarded by foreigners, friend and foe alike.

In fact, however, not all the work on the Charter was in vain. First of all, it must not be forgotten that, for the first time in history, representatives of nearly all important trading countries in the world assembled to discuss, and reached agreement on, a set of

principles on the conduct of international trade, based on cooperative action to expand world production, trade, and investment.
While it is true that practical considerations forced compromises
on many of the principles, these were generally surrounded with
safeguards from abuse and represented a great advance over previous unilateral action. Second, and most important, many of the
provisions of the ITO Charter concerning commercial policy are
embodied in another international agreement in effective operation—the General Agreement on Trade and Tariffs.

The General Agreement on Trade and Tariffs

While a United Nations committee to draft a charter for the
ITO was at work, the second principle of U.S. international commercial policy—negotiation of specific trade-barrier reductions—
was being implemented. Upon the proposal of the United States,
23 countries began negotiations for the mutual reduction of tariffs
in the summer of 1947 at Geneva, Switzerland. The General Agreement on Trade and Tariffs (GATT) concluded at Geneva was regarded as an interim and provisional measure, pending the adoption of the ITO Charter, which was to supersede those provisions
of GATT covered in the Charter. Since, however, the Charter has
not been ratified, GATT, as amended in subsequent conferences,
continues in force as an independent agreement. As far as the
United States is concerned, no special authority was needed to participate in the Geneva Agreement, since the negotiations were carried out under the Reciprocal Trade Agreements program.

General Provisions of GATT. The General Agreement reached
at Geneva included not only a schedule of specific tariff concessions
but, in addition, certain general provisions which, as indicated before, were similar to the principles of commercial policy which
were .contained in the Havana Charter, though narrower in scope.
In later sessions of the contracting parties to GATT, amendments
were adopted to bring the general commercial provisions more
closely in line with those contained in the Havana Charter.

The major general provisions of GATT include unconditional
most-favored-nation treatment; elimination of quantitative restrictions, but with exceptions similar to those in the Havana Charter;
obligation to negotiate for the reduction of tariffs upon the request
of another contracting party; nondiscrimination in the application of allowable restrictions, with certain exceptions; freedom of

transit; simplification of customs formalities; liberalization of marks-of-origin requirements; adaptation of state trading practices to the same general principles of nondiscriminatory treatment applicable to private traders; and, finally, a general escape clause similar to that in the Havana Charter and described previously.

Multilateral Tariff Negotiations. In the Geneva negotiations and subsequent sessions, specific tariff concessions were negotiated. The type of negotiations, though falling within the scope of the Reciprocal Trade Agreements Act of the United States, represented a considerable departure from previous practices. Before Geneva, as we have seen, the United States negotiated its trade agreements separately with each country on a strictly bilateral basis. After Geneva, the negotiations were also conducted bilaterally, on a product-by-product basis, each country usually negotiating as to its treatment of each particular import commodity with its principal past or anticipated supplier of that commodity. However, the understandings reached in the bilateral negotiations were combined to form the schedules of concessions of the several countries set forth in the Agreement and the Protocols. The close contacts among the negotiating teams, the ability of each country to observe how its position was affected not only by its own bilateral negotiations but also by the simultaneous negotiations among other countries, together with most-favored-nation treatment, rendered the proceedings, in effect, *multilateral.*

The two most significant characteristics of GATT, therefore, are, first, its general provisions, which constitute a code of commercial policy, and, second, the essentially multilateral approach to negotiations which it embodies.

The Accomplishments of GATT. No doubt the greatest contribution of GATT consists of the acceptance by the major trading countries of the world of the principle of free international exchange of goods and services, without discrimination or quantitative restrictions, and the commitment to negotiate multilaterally to reduce existing tariffs and other artificial trade barriers. In the hundreds of individual negotiations that have been carried on under GATT, covering tens of thousands of commodities, tariff concessions have been made applying to products constituting more than two thirds of the total import trade of the participating countries and considerably more than half of the total import trade of the world. The most tangible accomplishment of GATT lies in the significant reduction (and "binding")[10] of tariffs that the multilateral negotiations it has sponsored have effected.

Less tangible, but perhaps of equal value in the long run, is GATT's role as an international forum for the discussion of the commercial policies of its members and for the adjustment of disputes arising out of the implementation of the general principles of GATT and the obligations assumed in specific tariff negotiations. The necessity for frequent consultation and discussion is especially great because of the numerous allowable exceptions to the general principles embodied in GATT and the danger that such exceptions, if not controlled, would "take over." For example, one of the basic principles of GATT is that members refrain from quantitative restrictions (quotas) on its imports from other members. An exception is permitted in case a member can demonstrate that import quotas are necessary for balance-of-payments reasons. There are no clear-cut criteria for determining when quotas are necessary to protect the balance of payments. Hence it is provided that members of GATT resorting to quotas for this purpose must consult with other members regarding the nature and extent of the restrictions and their justification. Members resorting to quota restrictions are thus put on the defensive and encouraged to create conditions that will allow the quotas to be removed. Essentially the same procedure helps safeguard against abuses of allowable quotas for promoting the industrialization of underdeveloped members and for the carrying-out of domestic price-support programs.

The Provisional Status of GATT. The vitality of GATT is especially remarkable in view of its provisional status. Intended to be only on interim measure pending establishment of the ITO, GATT has continued to function as an independent institution, but one without permanent administrative machinery or even the definitive sanction of all its members. The United States is a member of and participates in GATT on the basis of executive agreements, without the express approval of the Congress. Indeed, an amendment to the Trade Agreements Act of 1951 provided specifically that the act shall not be construed to indicate the approval (or disapproval) by the Congress of GATT.

In 1955 an agreement was reached to renegotiate GATT and create a permanent institution to be known as the Organization for

---

[10] A tariff rate is "bound" when a country agrees not to raise it.

Trade Cooperation (OTC). The chief purpose of OTC would be to provide a permanent administrative machinery for carrying out the substantive provisions of GATT. However, President Eisenhower's efforts to obtain congressional approval of U.S. membership in OTC failed, and since the participation of the United States is required for its creation, OTC, like ITO before it, has been relegated to the archives, though presumably revivable should the sentiments of the Congress change.

Tariff Reductions under the Reciprocal Trade Agreements Program

As a result of the numerous trade agreements negotiated under the Reciprocal Trade Agreements program, the height of the U.S. tariff wall has been significantly reduced. Remembering the weaknesses of the measure used, we may still get an approximate picture of changes in the level of U.S. tariffs from the following data. In the period 1930–33, before the trade agreements program began, the average ad valorem equivalent of duties on total dutiable U.S. imports was about 53 percent. By the time the Trade Agreement Act came up for its last renewal, in 1958, the average level of duties had fallen to around 12 percent. Except for important negotiations concluded in 1962 with the European Common Market and 18 other countries, providing for tariff reductions averaging 20 percent on more than 1,000 items, the last several years of the Reciprocal Trade Agreement Act's life witnessed no further significant progress in reducing tariffs.

The decrease in U.S. tariffs of by more than three quarters between the inception of the Reciprocal Trade Agreements Act in 1934 and its final expiration in 1962 was by no means all attributable, however, to trade agreement negotiations; a large part of the reduction was attributable to inflation. When prices rise, the ad valorem equivalents of specific duties fall. Since a large proportion of dutiable imports into the United States is subject to specific duties, inflation is one of the most effective "automatic" reducers of the tariff wall. Indeed, the honors for the decrease since 1934 in the average level of U.S. tariffs are about equally divided between the trade agreements program and inflation, with approximately half the decrease attributable to each.

It is difficult to obtain a quantitative measure of the concessions received by the United States from other countries under the trade agreements program, since there are many countries involved with varying tariff structures and rates. The problem of meaningful measurement of the tariff wall is compounded when comparisons among different countries are attempted. Nevertheless, it cannot be doubted that reciprocal concessions from other countries have substantially lowered foreign barriers to the import of United States goods.

Between 1937 and 1956, the average tariff was reduced in Great Britain by 44 percent; France, 68 percent; Germany, 70 percent; Italy, 28 percent; and Sweden, 73 percent.[11] According to a study made in late 1961, the average level of tariffs of the United States on industrial products is lower than for some countries but higher than for others, as shown by the following comparisons:[12]

Country	*Percent*
Japan	19
Austria	19
United Kingdom	17
Italy	16
Canada	16
France	15
United States	11
Norway	11
Benelux	11
Germany	9
Sweden	8
Switzerland	8
Denmark	6

Until fairly recently, however, tariffs were not nearly so important as a barrier to U.S. exports as were exchange controls and quantitative import restrictions. Although members of GATT have a general obligation to avoid quantitative trade restrictions, and members of the International Monetary Fund a similar obligation with respect to quantitative payments restrictions, relief from both obligations may be provided a member with balance-of-payments difficulties. During the first years after the war, most of the major trading partners of the United States maintained strict quantitative trade and payments restrictions on these grounds. Con-

[11] Testimony of U.S. Secretary of Commerce before House Ways and Means Committee in 1958, cited in Don D. Humphrey, *The United States and the Common Market* (New York: Frederick A. Praeger, Inc., 1962), p. 38.

[12] Congress of the United States, Joint Economic Committee, *Trade Restraints in the Western Community* (Washington, D.C.: U.S. Government Printing Office, 1961), p. 6.

sequently, negotiated reductions in their tariffs had a limited significance. But concurrently with improvement in their economic situation and balance of payments, quantitative restrictions were reduced. Beginning with the general return to currency convertibility in late 1958, the movement toward trade and payments free of quantitative controls gained momentum, so that by 1962 the leading importers of U.S. goods had virtually eliminated quantitative limits on the import of industrial products. With this development, tariff reductions—past as well as future—assumed greater significance.

Weakening of the Trade Agreements Program

The Trade Agreements Act of 1934 was never a permanent part of American law, but required a periodic renewal of authority. Until the act finally expired in 1962 and was replaced by new legislation—the Trade Expansion Act—it had been renewed 11 times. As each renewal act expired, further extensions were subject, of course, to congressional amendments. The last several renewal acts, beginning with the one in 1951, included amendments greatly reducing the effectiveness of the program. The chief weakening amendments related to the "escape," "peril-point," and national security clauses, and to the President's authority to negotiate tariff reductions.

The Escape Clause. In the trade agreement concluded with Mexico in December, 1942, an escape clause was included, providing that a concession on any article might be withdrawn, in whole or in part, whenever, as a result of the concession and from "unforeseen" developments, the import of the article increased in such quantity as to cause or threaten "serious injury" to domestic producers of like or similar articles. In 1947 the President issued an executive order requiring the insertion of a similar escape clause in all future trade agreements. The Trade Agreements Extension Act of 1951 made it mandatory for an escape clause to be included not only in all future trade agreements but, as soon as practicable, in all existing trade agreements currently in force.

The procedure and criteria to be followed in escape-clause action were spelled out in the Extension Act of 1951, as modified by amendments in 1953, 1955, and 1958. The Tariff Commission was charged with the responsibility of promptly conducting an escape-clause investigation upon the request of the President, resolution of either house of Congress, resolution of either the Senate Committee on Finance or the House Committee on Ways and Means, upon its own motion, or upon application of any interested party. As part of an investigation, the Tariff Commission held public hearings at which interested parties were afforded an opportunity to testify. Should the Commission find the existence or the threat of serious injury attributable to increased imports of articles on which trade agreement concessions have been made, it recommended to the President withdrawal or modification of the concession or the imposition of an import quota. The President was not obliged to follow the recommendations of the Tariff Commission, but if he failed to do so he had to submit a report to the Congress stating his reasons. Further, an amendment in 1958 provided the President could be overruled by a two-thirds vote of Congress.

The criteria to be employed in defining "serious injury" under the escape clause were successively expanded to enable producers more easily to obtain relief. The 1951 act directed the Tariff Commission to take into consideration, without excluding other factors, "a downward trend of production, employment, prices, profits, or wages in the domestic industry concerned, or a decline in sales, an increase in imports, either actual or relative to domestic production, a higher or growing inventory, or a decline in the proportion of the domestic market supplied by domestic producers." The Trade Agreements Extension At of 1955 greatly broadened the base for escape-clause action by defining the term "domestic industry" to embrace each single product of multiproduct firms, and by allowing a finding of injury even when increased imports were not the primary cause of the injury.

As it turned out in practice, the escape clause was not extensively used to revoke trade agreement concessions. Out of several dozen investigations by the Tariff Commission, injury was found in only about one quarter of the cases, and only about one half of these was accepted for action by the President. Moreover, with the exception of lead and zinc (on which import quotas were levied), the articles affected were of minor importance—such things as clothespins, dried figs, hatters' fur, bicycles, alsike-clover seed, and so on. However, the *indirect* effects of the escape clause as a restrictive device may be considerable, since it subjects foreign exporters to the risk of having their American market suddenly circumscribed. We shall have more to say on this point in the next chapter.

The Peril Point. Increasing opposition to reduced tariffs by affected American producers led to the "peril-point" provisions in the Trade Agreement Extension Act of 1948. The Extension Act of the next year eliminated the peril-point provision (primarily because of the pressure put on Congress by the administration, who at that time was vigorously opposed to it), but that of 1951 reinstated the provision, with some changes. Thereafter, it remained in force in subsequent extention acts.

Under the peril-point provision, the President was required, before entering into any trade agreement negotiation, to transmit to the Tariff Commission a list of the commodities to be considered for concessions in forthcoming negotiations. The Commission was then required to make an investigation and report on (*a*) the maximum decrease in duty, if any, that can be made on each listed commodity without causing or threatening serious injury to domestic industries producing like or directly competitive products or (*b*) the minimum *increase* in duty or additional import restriction that may be necessary to avoid serious injury or threat of injury.

The President could not conclude a trade agreement until the Commission's peril-point report was made or until after the lapse of 120 days from the date the list of articles proposed for negotiation was transmitted to the Tariff Commission. The President was not bound, however, to follow the conclusions of the Tariff Commission; but if he failed to do so, he had to transmit to the Congress a copy of the trade agreement in question, identifying the articles on which concessions had been made inconsistently with the Commission's report and stating his reasons for not carrying out the Commission's recommendations. Thus, in the GATT tariff negotiations in 1956 at Geneva, the United States failed to provide increased import duties on tungsten alloys and violins and violas, as specified in the Commission's peril-point report, and this failure was reported by the President to the Congress as required.

It is quite obvious that the escape-clause and peril-point provisions were closely related. The former was designed primarily to take care of injuries caused by concessions already made in trade agreements, and the latter was designed primarily to prevent concessions from being made in new negotiations that might cause injury in the future.

Before the 1960–62 tariff negotiations between the United States and the European Economic Community (EEC) and other GATT members, the peril-point clause had no great impact on U.S. trade negotiations. But in the last negotiations conducted under the Reciprocal Trade Agreements Act—1960–62—the peril-point restriction proved nearly fatal.[13] While the EEC offered to reduce its common external tariff by 20 percent on about 60 percent of the products requested by the United States, reciprocal concessions offered by the United States included only about one quarter of the products requested by the EEC. This unbalanced offer by the United States was the result of elimination of negotiable items under peril-point determinations. The ensuing deadlock in the negotiations was broken only when the United States offered new concessions at rates below peril-point findings.

The National Security Provision.   In the 1955 renewal of the trade agreements program, a provision was inserted allowing the imposition of trade restrictions on imports that threaten the national security, whether or not the products affected were subject to trade agreement concessions. The determination of whether the import of a product threatened the national security was to be made in the first instance by the Office of Civil and Defense Mobilization, but the final decision rested with the President. The basis for action was greatly extended by an amendment in 1958 providing that restrictions might be applied to nondefense industries if it was determined that imports were weakening the internal economy and thus impairing national security.

Many industries took advantage of the national security provisions as a basis for advancing their claims to protection against imports, including, among others, producers of wool felts, dental burs, wire cloth, textiles, watches, stencil silk, electrical equipment, and petroleum. Few, however, were successful in convincing the Office of Civilian and Defense Mobilization of the legitimacy of their cases. The most important exception was petroleum. In 1959 the United States imposed import quotas on crude oil and petroleum products under the national security provision, on the grounds that imports were discouraging the domestic exploration necessary to assure an adequate supply of oil in the event of a national emergency.

Authority to Reduce Tariffs.   The last, and perhaps most serious, weakening of the Reciprocal Trade Agreements Act came from limiting the President's authority to reduce tariffs. The original act authorized reductions in tariffs up to 50 percent of the rates in effect in 1934. Later, the base on which 50 percent reductions were permitted was changed to the rates prevailing on January 1, 1945.

---

[13] See Don D. Humphrey, *op. cit.,* pp. 156–57.

The President's authority remained thus until the Trade Agreements Extension Act of 1955. Thereafter, only a small margin of further reductions was permitted, as evidenced by the fact that nearly all the reduction in tariffs accomplished under the program until its expiration in June, 1962, had been achieved by 1953.

The 1955 Extension Act provided for a 15 percent reduction of prevailing rates, spread over three years, and also for a reduction to 50 percent of all rates higher than 50 percent. The last renewal, in 1958, permitted reductions under three alternative methods: by 20 percent, or by 2 percentage points, or to 50 percent, reductions in any event to be effected in no more than four annual stages.

It should be noted that the formal authority to reduce tariffs could never be fully utilized in practice. Apart from the constraint imposed by the necessity to receive reciprocal concession in bargaining negotiations, the President was subject to the pressures exerted by the escape and peril-point clauses and the national security provision described above. As we observed earlier, much of the significant reduction in the average tariff level accomplished during the life of the Reciprocal Trade Agreements Act was the fortuitous by-product of inflation rather than the result of negotiated actions.

Other Aspects of U.S. Commercial Policy

So far we have been concerned in this chapter primarily with tariff policies. Though these are certainly, in general, the most important part of the commercial policies of the United States, they are by no means the whole story. There are other restrictions on imports into the United States too numerous to spell out in detail, but brief mention must be made of some of the more important of them.

Import Quotas. We have noted previously that quotas are generally much more restrictive of trade than tariffs, for they set absolute limits on the import volume of affected commodities. Under Section 22 of the Agricultural Adjustment Act, as amended, import quotas have been imposed on various commodities by the United States since 1939. In carrying out Section 22, special import "fees," as well as absolute quotas, are employed, such fees being additional to the regular duties provided for by the tariff act.

Section 22 of the Agricultural Adjustment Act authorizes the President to restrict the importation of commodities, either by fees or by quotas (within specified limits), whenever such imports render or tend to render ineffective, or materially interfere with, programs of the U.S. Department of Agriculture relating to agricultural commodities. The Trade Agreements Extension Act of 1951 provided, further, that no trade agreement or other internaional agreemtent entered into at any time by the United States may be applied in a manner inconsistent with the requirements of Section 22.

Cotton, wheat and wheat flour, certain dairy products, peanuts, oats, rye, and barley have all been subject to quantitative import restrictions by the United States under Section 22.

In addition to Section 22, the President was directed by an amendment to the Defense Production Act of 1950 to control imports unnecessarily burdening any domestic farm program. Under this provision, known as the "Cheese Amendment," cheese and a number of other products were placed under quotas, and butter, rice, fats, and oils were embargoed. Quotas imposed under this authority seriously affected the export markets of some foreign countries and evoked grave protests from them, including retaliatory action against American goods.[14] Criticism was particularly aroused by the fact that the quotas violated American commitments under GATT.

To resolve the differences between the policies on agricultural imports forced by Section 22 and the provisions of GATT, the United States requested a waiver of its commitments under GATT, insofar as such commitments might be regarded as inconsistent with action required to be taken under Section 22. The waiver was granted, but the United States is obliged to follow certain rules of procedure and consultation with respect to its quota practices and to report annually on its actions under the waiver.

As noted above, the employment of import quotas by the United States has not been limited to agricultural commodities. Under the national security provision, quotas may be imposed for defense purposes, as in the case of oil and petroleum products since 1959. Another device is the "voluntary" limitation of exports to the United States by other countries. The best example is cotton textiles. Under the threat that import quotas would otherwise be imposed by the United States, Japan agreed, beginning in 1956, to limit her export of various categories of cotton textiles. This system was later

---

[14] For some of the political implications of the "Cheese Amendment," see Hans Landsberg, "The Role of Cheese in Our Foreign Policy," *The Reporter,* May 27, 1952, pp. 32–34.

extended to other textile exporting and importing countries under an international textile agreement.

"Buy-American" Restrictions. In 1933 the "Buy American" Act was passed, providing that, unless it is deemed inconsistent with the public interest or is unreasonably more costly, only American-made goods shall be acquired for public use—i.e., bought by the federal government or any of its agencies. Frequently, similar buy-American provisions have been included in particular acts of Congress. For example, an amendment to the 1953 defense appropriation act provided that no part of the appropriation be used for the purchase of clothing made out of cotton or twill fiber not grown in the United States, except to the extent that satisfactory quantities or qualities could not be produced at home when needed and at reasonable prices.

By administrative order, the Buy American Act was interpreted in its early years to mean that foreign goods might be purchased by the government when comparable domestic goods were more than 25 percent higher in price. This rule was not always strictly adhered to, and on occasion even ignored. Recently, foreign producers have been severely discriminated against in government purchases, primarily for balance of payments reasons. However, domestic producers may be given preference regardless of the price differential for any of the following reasons: (*a*) to safeguard security, (*b*) to relieve domestic unemployment, (*c*) to assist small business firms, or (*d*) to promote the national or public interest. In practice, only the national security and unemployment exceptions have been significant.

THE TRADE EXPANSION ACT OF 1962

On the expiration in June, 1962, of the 11th renewal of the Reciprocal Trade Agreements Act inaugurated 28 years earlier, the United States was confronted with a critical decision on its future commercial policy. It was hardly conceivable that the reciprocal trade agreements program should be allowed to expire, but a choice had to be made between continuation of the program as it had evolved over the past years or its replacement with a rejuvenated and expanded program. At least two major considerations led to the second alternative.

The first was the exhaustion of the program as an effective instrument of commercial policy. Little scope for further reciprocal trade negotiations remained; indeed, no significant reduction in the level of U.S. tariffs had been made for a decade or more. The President's authority to pursue a positive commercial policy had progressively been so surrounded with restrictions that he barely had left the power merely to "hold the line" on past accomplishments, let alone to advance further.

In itself, this situation was not especially novel, and probably would not have led to any large change in program had it not been for a second development—the formation of the European Common Market. The Common Market, to be fully discussed in Chapter 10, presented a sharp challenge to the United States. The reaction to it could consist either of rebuff and defensive withdrawal into possibly bitter and divisive trade bloc discrimination or of efforts to shape it into a unifying and expansionary force in free-world economic relations. The United States chose the latter option, both because she had long supported the movement toward Western European economic and political unification, and because her own export position would otherwise have been seriously threatened.

The principal requirement for turning the Common Market into a force for positive benefit to the world economy lay in its establishment of a low-level common tariff wall on the goods and services of nonmember countries. But for this to be possible, the United States, as a main competing country in the world economy, had to be willing reciprocally to reduce its trade barriers. The Trade Expansion Act of 1962 was largely designed with this situation in mind. Indeed, some provisions of the act are specifically directed toward relations with the Common Market.

Let us now see what the major provisions of the Trade Expansion Act were.

Authority to Reduce Tariffs

As we noted earlier, the President's authority to reduce tariffs had been greatly restricted during the last years of the Reciprocal Trade Agreements Act. The Trade Expansion Act reinstituted and expanded this authority.

The general authority extended to the President allowed him to negotiate reductions in U.S. tariffs by as much as 50 percent of the rate existing on July 1, 1962. Provision for even greater reductions under certain conditions was made but did not in fact become significantly operative. The President's authority to negotiate tariff reductions was limited to the five-year period ending July 1, 1967.

A major change in negotiating procedures was provided by the act. Instead of being restricted, as in the past, to negotiating article by article, the President was authorized to negotiate by broad categories of goods.

Escape Clause

The Trade Expansion Act eliminated the former peril-point clause and significantly modified escape-clause procedures. As before, the President was authorized to increase or impose any duty or import restriction necessary to remedy or prevent serious injury to a domestic industry by reason of increased imports due to trade agreement concessions. However, the concept of "serious injury," which in previous legislation had been interpreted very liberally, was considerably narrowed. Moreover, the increase in imports responsible for injury had to be the result in "major part" of trade agreement concessions and such increase in imports must have been the "*major* factor" in causing or threatening injury. The net effect of these changes was greatly to reduce the scope for escape-clause action.

Adjustment Assistance

The tightening of the escape clause was made more palatable by a major innovation which introduced an alternative to increased trade barriers as a remedy for any injuries sustained as the result of tariff concessions. The alternative consists of "adjustment assistance" to firms and workers.

Both business firm and workers may apply for adjustment assistance whenever, upon application of an interested party, it is determined that the applicant is eligible for assistance. The criteria for eligibility are virtually the same as those used in deciding whether escape-clause action is called for. A firm is eligible for assistance whenever, as a result in major part of trade agreement concessions, an article competitive with an article produced by the firm is imported in such increased quantities as to cause or threaten serious injury to the firm. Among other criteria to be applied, idling of productive facilities, inability to operate at a reasonable level of profit, and unemployment are to be taken into account in determining whether injury has been sustained. A group of workers is eligible for assistance if, because of the same circumstances applicable to the firm, unemployment or underemployment of a significant number or proportion of workers occurs. In both cases, increased imports must be the *major* factor causing injury.

Adjustment assistance to firms takes the form of technical assistance, financial assistance, and tax assistance, furnished singly or in combination. Technical assistance is for such purposes as helping an injured firm to become more efficient or to shift into other product lines. Financial assistance may consist of loans or loan guaranties, to enable the firm to modernize, expand, or convert its productive facilities. Tax assistance is given in the form of allowing an injured firm operating loss carrybacks for a longer period than normally permitted, thus reducing the firm's net tax liabilities.

Adjustment assistance to workers include training, unemployment compensation ("readjustment allowances"), and relocation allowances. Primary emphasis is to be placed on retraining displaced workers to prepare them for new jobs. During training periods, and thereafter if employment is not secured, unemployment compensation may be paid for up to 52 weeks, or longer if necessary to allow completion of training or if the worker is 60 years or older. Finally, an unemployed worker, head of a familly, may obtain an allowance for meeting the expenses of moving to another area where employment or an offer of employment has been received.

Results of the Kennedy Round

Negotiations under the Trade Expansion Act—known as the "Kennedy Round"—were finally concluded by 53 countries after four years of fruitless effort in May, 1967, only a month and a half before the act expired. Negotiation proved extremely difficult. One of the principal reasons was the problems the European Common Market was having in settling upon agricultural policies and the conflict between its intent to protect agriculture and the desire of the United States to keep its agricultural export markets open. A second reason was the French government's policy of fostering Europe's independence from U.S. political and economic influence, which created political tensions unfavorable for trade negotiations.

Nevertheless, the Kennedy Round succeeded in producing the most extensive tariff reductions ever negotiated in the 20-year history of GATT. The reduction in tariffs on industrial goods by the leading countries averaged 35 percent, and on a large number of articles the reduction reached 50 percent. In all, 60,000 items, representing an estimated $40 billion of trade, were affected. Less success was achieved in removing quotas and other nontariff barriers to trade, and restraints on trade in agricultural products were not significantly lowered.

In general, the Kennedy Round must be regarded as a resounding victory for freer trade. Perhaps its chief significance lay in its warding off the threat posed by the formation of the European Common Market of the division of the Western world into rival trade blocs sheltered from each other's markets and vulnerable to economic warfare.

It would be fatuous to suppose, however, that the Kennedy Round at last finished the task of creating an international economy free of artificial impediments. Tariffs of varying degrees of restrictiveness continue to exist; quota restrictions, especially on agricultural products, are widely practiced; and a long and varied list of other nontariff barriers remain as serious obstacles to trade. Moreover, trade negotiations have affected chiefly the trade of developed countries. The trade of the less-developed countries remains encumbered by the policies of the leading developed countries, in what manner and with what implications we shall investigate in a later chapter.

Finally, it must not be forgotten that the results of trade negotiations are not irreversible. The United States participated in the Kennedy Round under the authority granted by the Congress in the Trade Expansion Act. That act expired in 1967, and three years later had not yet been extended or replaced by a new authorization. In the meanwhile, a resurgence of protectionist sentiment in the United States had become manifest, with the threat of a reversion in trade policies. The issues thereby raised are important enough to justify separate treatment in the next chapter.

RECOMMENDED READING

BROWN, WILLIAM ADAMS, JR. *The United States and the Restoration of World Trade.* Washington, D.C.: Brookings Institution, 1950.
> A thorough analysis and appraisal of the ITO Charter and GATT.

DIEBOLD, WILLIAM, JR. *The End of the ITO.* Essays in International Finance No. 16. Princeton University, International Finance Section, October, 1952.

ELLSWORTH, P. T. *The International Economy,* chaps. ii, iii, xii–xv. New York: 4th ed.; Macmillan Co., 1969.

An excellent brief survey of trade-policy history, which ties in commercial policies with both broader historical forces and the development of international trade theory.

HUMPHREY, DON D. *The United States and the Common Market,* chaps, ii, vii, viii, x, xi, and xii. New York: Frederick A. Praeger, Inc., 1962.

ISAACS, ASHER. *International Trade: Tariff and Commercial Policies.* Chicago, Ill.: Richard D. Irwin, Inc., 1948.

An exhaustive history of the commercial policies of the United States and other countries.

PIQUET, HOWARD S. *The Trade Agreements Act and the National Interest.* Washington, D.C.: Bookings Institution, 1958.

UNITED STATES CONGRESS. *Public Law 87–794.* The text of the Trade Expansion Act of 1962.

U.S. TARIFF COMMISSION. *The Tariff and Its History.* Washington, D.C.: U.S. Government Printing Office, 1934.

———. *Operation of the Trade Agreements Program.* Issued periodically.

Official reports on the history, operation, and effects of the trade-agreements program.

STUDY QUESTIONS

1. The term "favorable" balance of trade is still used in its original meaning as developed during the mercantilist era. What is its meaning, and how do you explain its origins?

2. Describe the general economic and political changes, dating from about the middle of the 18th century, which finally led to the abandonment of mercantilism and the victory of a laissez-faire, free-trade philosophy.

3. Why were the policies pursued by many countries during the 1930's often described as "neomercantilist"?

4. From the history of American tariffs, what influence would you say wars ordinarily have on tariff policies? Why?

5. What was the general trend of United States tariff policies from the Civil War to 1934?

6. Which of the protariff arguments described in Chapter 7 would you suppose were the most influential in the passage of the Hawley-Smoot Tariff? Did experience with this tariff strengthen or weaken these arguments?

7. How did the comparative-advantage position of the United States in the 19th century help explain her tariff policies? The free-trade outlook of the South?

8. Describe briefly the procedure through which U.S. tariffs were lowered by agreements made under the Reciprocal Trade Agreements program.

9. What is the significance of the principle of "most-favored-nation" treatment? Why has it not appreciably weakened the bargaining position of the United States in its tariff negotiations with other counries?

10. What was the major aim of the proposed International Trade Organization? Do you feel that the Havana Charter made any contribution to the cause of freer international trade?

11. How have tariff negotiations under GATT differed from those previously conducted?

12. Describe the major general provisions of GATT which constitute a "code of commercial conduct."

13. In what way has the increase in the level of prices since 1934 contributed to a lowering of the average tariff rate of the United States?

14. Explain how the "escape" clause and the "peril-point" provisions in the amended versions of the Trade Agreements Act operated.

15. How do government price-support programs tend to conflict with tariff-reducing programs? Name some specific examples of this conflict in the United States.

16. Describe some of the other artificial obstacles to U.S. imports currently in force.

17. What major considerations led to the adoption of the Trade Expansion Act of 1962?

18. Summarize the chief provisions of the Trade Expansion Act. To what extent does the act represent a continuation of past policies, and to what extent does it break new paths?

Chapter 9   THE PAST AND FUTURE OF
U.S. COMMERCIAL POLICY

Judged in the light of the protectionist trend that had prevailed with only short-lived deviations since the Civil War period, the commerial policies of the United States since 1934 might appear to be the epitome of liberalism. And indeed it is true that notable progress has been achieved in moving toward free trade.

However, it would be a serious miscalculation to conclude that a liberal commercial policy has become firmly established in the United States. Protectionist sentiment, overt or latent, has always been strong in this country, with the ever-present threat of a weakening of liberal policies. Such a weakening of the Reciprocal Trade Agreements program occurred during the 1950's, as shown in the preceding chapter. As these words are being written (in July, 1970), a strong resurgence of protectionism is threatening to destroy some of the gains achieved in the Kennedy Round of negotiations. Soon after these negotiations had been concluded in 1967, several major U.S. industries—led by steel, chemicals, textiles, and oil—started a campaign for protective legislation. During the year following, several hundred bills were introduced in Congress calling for import quotas on products ranging from steel, meat, shoes, and textiles to strawberries and baseball gloves. This early drive was fended off by the Johnson administration, but it was revived in 1970 with the approval by the House Ways and Means Committee of a bill setting quotas on textiles and apparel and giving the President an open-ended authority to place quotas on any import the volume of which reaches certain minimum levels.

The history of U.S. commercial policies is characterized by periods of protectionism or retrenchment following upon periods of liberalism. As we have seen, this is what happened during the 1950's when the liberal thrust of the Reciprocal Trade Agreements program was deadened by escape-clause and peril-point amendments. The possibility of a similar sequence has arisen since the expiration of the Trade Expansion Act in 1967. In 1968 Congress refused to act on the President's proposal to extend and revise the act. The succeeding administration submitted a new trade proposal to the Congress in late 1969. The proposal (which has not been acted upon to the date of this writing) authorizes the Executive to make further modest reductions in tariffs through June 30, 1973, but the provision of especial interest concerns the escape clause. It is proposed to permit invoking escape-clause procedures whenever increased imports are the "primary cause" of actual or potential serious injury to a domestic industry, *whether or not caused by prior tariff reductions*. This represents a major loosening of the criteria for escape-clause action under the Trade Expansion Act, and is in the spirit of the 1968 Republican party platform, which proposed "fair" trade instead of free trade. The guide as to what constitutes "fair" trade is that imports should not be allowed to capture "excessive portions" of the U.S. domestic market.

The idea that the government should protect domestic industries against "injury" from imports is widely held as part of a general set of attitudes responsible for the tenuous status of liberal commercial policies and the perennial threat of reversion to restrictive practices. In the following pages, the economics and politics of protection of domestic industries against "injury" and of related notions will be critically examined.

PROTECTION AGAINST INJURY

Carried to its logical conclusion, the implementation of a policy to prevent "injury" to domestic industries as the result of foreign trade would preclude the lowering of most existing trade barriers, and indeed in many cases would lead to raising new or additional barriers.

Most protective tariffs and quotas are, by the nature of the case, applied to products the supplies of which are furnished to a large extent by domestic firms. Import restrictions tend to be low or nonexistent on those commodities not produced at home. If tariffs are reduced or import quotas enlarged, the normal consequence is an increase in the volume of the affected goods imported. Competing domestic producers can then claim injury, in the sense either of suffering an absolute loss in sales or of being deprived of a full share of expanding sales. The same kind of claim can be advanced whenever the volume of imports increases for whatever reasons, such as a decrease in the price competitiveness of domestic industries.

What is involved here, of course, is the proposition discussed earlier that trade nearly inevitably adversely affects some groups within an economy even though the national economy as a whole benefits. The issue, therefore, is whether the interests of particular groups should be allowed to outweigh the national interests. There is no objective way of deciding this question, but there is a way of mitigating it—through direct assistance to genuinely injured parties, as first provided for in the Trade Expansion Act of 1962. The great advantage of what the latter termed "adjustment assistance" as an alternative to escape-clause procedures is that it can provide relief to injured parties without impairing liberal commercial policies. It can be sensibly argued that a country can well afford to bear the cost of compensating particular groups for injuries incurred as the result of policies of general benefit. The difficulty with adjustment assistance is in defining and identifying genuine injury meriting assistance. The criteria first established under the Trade Expansion Act were so stringent that no assistance was actually granted. (The trade proposal made by President Nixon in 1969 referred to earlier includes a relaxation of the former eligibility requirements for assistance.) Too easy access to assistance, on the other hand, could be equally unsatisfactory or more so. In any event, assuming that a reasonable and practical solution to these problems can be found, adjustment assistance would seem to offer the most promising escape from the threat of protectionist measures posed by the injury concept.

THE EXPORT ORIENTATION OF U.S. COMMERCIAL POLICIES

The counterpart of the concern to prevent injury from trade is the common belief that the principal advantage to be gained from trade is in the export markets it provides. This attitude distorts the classical conception of international trade, in which exports are only the means (and the social cost) of achieving the ultimate end, namely, imports. Rare indeed is the policy maker who acts fully in the spirit of the classical approach. On the contrary, it would be a more accurate generalization to say that policy makers are more often moved by the mercantilist spirit, that reverses the classical ends-means relationship, putting exports as the end and imports as perhaps a necessary, but generally unfortunate, means.

The mercantilist slant of the Reciprocal Trade Agreements program was present at the latter's very inception. The "father" of the program was the then Secretary of State, Cordell Hull, who, in presenting the case for the program before Congress, argued in terms of the need to reduce domestic unemployment and to expand exports. "The primary objective of this new proposal," Hull stated before a congressional committee, "is both to reopen the old and seek new outlets for our surplus products."[1] A similar emphasis was placed on the program by President Roosevelt, and there can be little doubt that the Congress was persuaded to accept the program only because this was the emphasis.

The deep depression in which the United States found itself at the time the Reciprocal Trade Agreements Act was formulated and accepted was certainly an extenuating reason for the export orientation of the arguments advanced in favor of it. Indeed, from a strictly nationalistic point of view, the mercantilist approach to international trade ceases to be nonsense in periods of widespread unemployment.

But let us now shift the scene to 1955 and listen to the Secretary of Commerce testifying before a congressional committee on the Trade Agreements Extension Act of 1955: ". . . We should continue the trade-agreements legislation for the same reason as it was started in the first place, *as an important export-promotion measure.*"[2] Similar reasons were expressed for supporting the Trade Agreements program each time it came up for renewal. Apparently it made little difference whether the economy was in deep depression or suffering from shortages and inflation; in order to get congressional approval of the Trade Agreements program, it was necessary to characterize it as an export-creating measure. From this general attitude stemmed most of the weaknesses of American commercial policies, as seen from a "liberal" or "classical" viewpoint.

The Trade Expansion Act of 1962 was considered and adopted in a considerably broader context than had prevailed in previous trade policy acts. The economic and political strength of the free-

---

[1] Ways and Means Committee, *Hearings on H.J. Resolution 407,* 76th Cong., 3d sess. (1940), pp. 7–8, quoted in Don D. Humphrey, *American Imports* (New York: Twentieth Century Fund, 1955), p. 111.

[2] Committee on Ways and Means, House of Representatives, *Hearing on H.R. 1, Part I, 84th Cong., 1st sess.,* p. 151. (Italics not in original.)

world economy, the need for new markets for the products of the underdeveloped countries, and the benefits to the American consumer, were all important reasons advanced by the President to the Congress for passage of the act.[3] Nevertheless, there can be little doubt that the *primary* stimulus back of the act was the threat to U.S. exports posed by the formation of the European Common Market. Without the negotiation of reduced tariffs by the Common Market countries, American exporters would stand to lose a large and growing outlet for their products.

It is a safe guess that whatever policy finally emerges as a successor to the expired Trade Expansion Act will be defended, as in the past, on the grounds of export promotion. (The disappearing of the balance-of-trade surplus of the United States, accompanied by the continuing balance-of-payments deficit, can only serve to reenforce the export orientation of policy makers.) It is also safe to predict that unless and until the public and its elected representatives come to understand that the fundamental source of gain from trade is to be found on the *import* side of the ledger, liberal commercial policies will not rest easy.

THE ATTITUDE OF THE CONGRESS

The commercial policy of the United States is determined by the President, within limits established, and subject to conditions laid down, by the Congress. One of the great advances in the tariff-making process introduced by the Reciprocal Trade Agreements Act was the delegation to the President by the Congress of tariff-setting authority (within specified limits) for a number of years, subject to periodic renewal. The Trade Expansion Act of 1962 continued this procedure, strengthened by a five-year grant of power, as compared to the one- to four-year grants under the Reciprocal Trade Agreements Act.

Because the ultimate authority to determine commercial policy rests with the Congress, the long-run character of policy depends upon the attitudes and pressures in the Congress. Since the members of Congress are elected by, and responsible to, their respective constituencies, special-interest groups opposed to free trade have no difficulty in obtaining a hearing in the halls of the legislature. It is not therefore surprising to find that the executive branch of the

---

[3] See the President's message to the Congress in House Committee on Ways and Means, *Hearings on the Trade Expansion Act of 1962, Part I,* pp. 1–9.

government, under the leadership of the President, has generally taken a more liberal stance on commercial policy than has the Congress. During the last years of the Reciprocal Trade Agreements Act, there was nearly a continuous battle between the relatively liberal outlook of the President and the strongly protectionist attitude of the Congress. The result was that the President had to act gingerly in trade agreement negotiations for fear of having his authority taken away by congressional reaction. Even so, as we have seen, the President's power effectively to pursue liberal policies was progressively eaten away by restrictive amendments.

A prime example of congressional reluctance to go along with liberal commercial policies has been its position with respect to GATT and the proposed Organization for Trade Cooperation. The United States is a contracting party to GATT without the blessings of the Congress. The agreement was entered into under the authority granted to the President by the Reciprocal Trade Agreements Act. But the legality of having done this has been openly challenged on several occasions in the Congress, and the latter has always taken great pains to make clear that approval (or disapproval) of GATT has not been implied by renewing the trade agreements program.

Apart from the uncertainty thus injected into the official policy of the United States with respect to GATT, it has created the more immediate problem of stymying the establishment of the Organization for Trade Cooperation (OTC), discussed in the preceding chapter. Despite the fact that OTC would involve the United States in no additional policy commitments but would serve only to facilitate the work of GATT, the Congress has refused to approve U.S. participation, necessary to its establishment. The reason for this attitude apparently lies in the strong opposition to GATT, for to approve OTC would in effect constitute an *indirect* approval of GATT. The U.S. government is thus put in the anomalous position of officially supporting and participating in an international organization that its own legislative branch officially refuses to approve and unofficially criticizes.

More than this, the Congress has forced the executive branch, constitutionally responsible for conducting foreign relations, to violate the international commitments of the United States under GATT and to seek therefor a waiver of its commitments, as described in the preceding chapter.

The presumption is that the Congress reflects the opinion of the public. The public's attitude in turn depends upon how well the economics and politics of commercial policy are understood. At the moment, we may hazard the judgment that this understanding leaves much to be desired. Some of the major areas of confusion and uncertainty deserve discussion.

THE ECONOMICS AND POLITICS OF TRADE-BARRIER REDUCTIONS

Large segments of American opinion are apparently convinced either that further liberalization of commercial policy offers little of value, or that whatever value it might hold is not worth the cost.

The Beneficial Effects of Further Liberalization

The effects of U.S. commercial policy are multiple: they are political as well as economic, international as well as domestic. Let us start with the narrowest focus—the domestic economic effects.

It is not necessary to repeat the economic case for freer trade, but a few comments on its relevance to current and future U.S. policy are in order. From a selfish national point of view, there cannot be the slightest doubt that the American economy as a whole would benefit from a relaxation of the barriers that now exist to the import of foreign goods and services. The classical gains to be realized from allocating resources to where their productivity is greatest are as available to rich countries like the United States as they are to impoverished underdeveloped economies. But perhaps even more important for the United States than the direct economic benefits flowing from specialization according to comparative costs are the indirect benefits produced by freer trade in enlarging the area of free consumer choice, and in increasing the competitiveness of domestic market structures.

Notwithstanding the great advances made since 1934 in reducing the artificial restrictions on imports into the United States, they still remain at a formidable level. The measure of the American tariff wall given by the ratio of import duties collected to the total value of imports conceals the actual degree of protection afforded to domestic producers. There are many duties far above the 12 percent ratio of duties collected to dutiable imports; moreover, for some products a relatively low tariff can be more protective in its effects than are high tariffs for other products.

It is especially important to distinguish between the *nominal* and the *effective* rate of protection, as discussed in Chapter 7. In a study of tariffs for the year 1962, Professor Bela Balassa found sharp differences between nominal and effective rates for many commodities. Overall, compared to a nominal average rate of 11.6 percent, the effective rate for the United States is estimated at 20 percent.[4]

From a broader point of view, a liberal trade policy by the United States is an integral and essential ingredient of an enlightened foreign policy. In this connection the drive of the less-developed countries of the world for growth is importantly affected by the extent to which the markets of the United States and Western Europe are open to the products of these countries, as we shall see in a later chapter. A policy of assisting less developed countries in their search for improved living standards is not consistent with restrictive trade policies of the United States and other developed countries.

The "Cost" of Further Trade Barrier Reductions

Except for extreme protectionists, most persons would agree that the case for a liberal commercial policy is strong. But for a large middle group in between the extreme protectionists and the doctrinaire free traders, the admitted benefits of liberal commercial policy are not obtainable without paying a price. For many, the alleged price is regarded as too high in comparison to the benefits received in return.

It is indeed true that any reduction in trade barriers is bound to cause some disturbance in certain sectors of the domestic economy. The very essence of the economic case for freer trade lies in the benefits obtainable from the reallocation of resources away from less efficient employments. Previously protected firms and industries can be expected therefore to find the demand for their products reduced (or less rapidly increasing) as competing imports rise in response to lowered barriers.

Moreover, generally speaking, the sectors of the economy likely to be hardest hit by lowered tariffs are among those already suffering from difficulties. It is the relatively *stagnant* industries in the United States in which foreign producers have the greatest compar-

---

[4] See Bela Balassa, "Tariff Protection in Industrial Countries: An Evaluation," *Journal of Political Economy*, Vol. 73 (December, 1965).

ative advantage—such as pottery, chinaware and glassware, and leather goods. But relatively stagnant industries are precisely the ones least able to adjust to greater import competition. Industries with a rapidly growing demand for their products would generally be able to maintain, or even to continue to increase, their sales, notwithstanding the loss of part of their market to foreign producers. Other industries might find that increased imports would reduce not only the relative market share of domestic producers but their absolute volume of sales as well.

The "classical" answer to this kind of problem—that resources released from industries unable freely to compete with foreign producers should be reallocated to the more efficient export industries—is not always satisfactory to those immediately affected. Resource reallocation is rarely in fact as smooth and easy as theory postulates. What about the workers who have spent a lifetime acquiring special skills not useful in other industries? Investors in the plant and equipment rendered idle by import competition? Those who have built their homes and made their friends in communities where the declining industries are located? Is it fair that these particular groups should bear the brunt of the burden of adjustment to increased imports? Here is where the practical politics of commercial policy liberalization become very important. The list of those who testify in congressional hearings against freer trade reads like the obituaries of declining American industries.

These are, within their own frame of reference, valid complaints deserving consideration. But there are reasonable answers, too, demanding "equal time" before it is concluded that liberal policies should be scuttled to avoid injury to domestic groups.

First, it is worth noting that *not* to lower trade barriers also causes injury. Export industries—domestic and foreign—and consumers generally are injured in just as real, though less obvious and direct, a sense by tariffs and quotas as import-competing industries are injured by the reduction of tariffs and quotas.

The injuries ascribed to reduced trade barriers have been vastly exaggerated in the minds of the American public. From statements commonly made by the more alarmist protectionist groups one gathers the impression that lower tariffs would result in mass unemployment and business failure. Objective analysis fails completely to lend credence to such conclusions.

Although many of the heavily protected, least efficient domestic industries would no doubt be unable to withstand the competition of freer imports, many others could adjust without too much difficulty, through shifts in product lines, improved management, more advanced techniques, and so on. For most U.S. industries, imports are only a small fraction of total domestic sales. As long as there is a generally buoyant economy, increases in imports are easily absorbed by expanding total sales with a margin left for increased sales by domestic producers.

In a careful study made by economists associated with The Brookings Institution, it was concluded that the median net effect on employment of increased imports into the United States because of lower tariffs would be a decrease of 86 employees per million-dollar increase in imports.[5] This is admitted to be a very generous estimate, probably exaggerating somewhat the true picture.

Compared to decreases in employment caused by cylical fluctuations in output, the employment effect of increased imports is seen to be very minor. For example, a net decrease of 86,000 employees caused by an increase in imports of $1,000 million would have amounted to only one eighth of 1 percent of civilian employment in 1959, whereas decreases in employment between the peaks and troughs in the first three postwar recessions varied between 3.0 and 3.5 percent of the respective employment peaks.[6] In short, the average net decrease in employment expected from a $1 billion increase in imports is less than *one twentieth* of the smallest cyclical decrease in employment during recent recessions.

The relatively minor adjustment problem created by increased imports under liberalized trade policies can be shown in another way. In order to maintain full employment in the American economy, beginning with a full-employment level of the gross national product, in each succeeding year the GNP must rise enough to offset the effects of (a) increased labor productivity and (b) increases in the working force. It is estimated that increases in average labor productivity reduce the number of workers required to produce a given GNP by approximately 1.5 million per year. Adding to this number annual increases in the labor force of about 1.0 million workers gives a total of 2.5 million workers who would be without employment opportunity were the GNP to fail to increase in any year over the preceding year's full-employment level. Compared to the 2.5 million new job opportunities required each year because of

---

[5] Walter S. Salant and Beatrice N. Vacarra, *Import Liberalization and Employment* (Washington, D.C.: Brookings Institution, 1961), pp. 213 ff.

[6] *Ibid.*, p. 263.

changes in productivity and the size of the labor force, the added employment problem caused by increased imports is seen to be only marginally significant. Thus, a $1 billion increase in imports would raise the number of new job opportunities required for full employment from 2.5 million to less than 2.6 million.[7]

In summary, the alleged "high cost" of more liberal commercial policies turns out on inspection to be something of a myth. All economic progress involves disturbance to existing relationships. In the case of more liberal commercial policies, the additional disturbances created become lost in the dynamics of a continuously changing economy.

RECOMMENDED READING

KENEN, PETER B. *United States Commercial Policy, A Program for the 1960's.* Joint Economic Committee, Congress of the United States, 87th Cong., 1st sess. Washington, D.C.: U.S. Government Printing Office, 1961.

KREININ, MORDECHAI E. *Alternative Commercial Policies—Their Effect on the American Economy.* East Lansing, Mich.: Michigan State University, 1967.

MACKENZIE, KENNETH C. *Tariff-Making and Trade Policy in the U.S. and Canada.* New York: Frederick A. Praeger, Inc., 1968.

REISCHER, OTTO R. *Trade Adjustment in Theory and Practice.* Joint Economic Committee, Congress of the United States, 87th Cong., 1st sess. Washington, D.C.: U.S. Government Printing Office, 1961.

SALANT, WALTER S., and VACCARA, BEATRICE V. *Import Liberalization and Employment.* Washington, D.C.: Brookings Institution, 1961.

STUDY QUESTIONS

1. If carried to its logical conclusion, why would the doctrine of protection against "injury" as the result of trade preclude the lowering of trade barriers?

2. In what sense does a lowering of tariffs cause "injury" to certain domestic producers?

3. What is the main argument in favor of "adjustment assistance"?

4. Contrast the classical and the mercantilist concepts of the benefits from trade.

5. What is meant by the "export orientation" of U.S. trade policies?

---

[7] *Ibid.,* pp. 265–66.

6. How do you account for the frequent conflict between the executive and legislative branches of the government with respect to commercial policies?

7. Why are nominal tariff rates a poor indicator of the protective effect of tariffs?

8. Why would those sectors of the economy already in relative decline be most adversely affected by lower tariffs?

9. What group would be injured by the *failure* to lower tariffs?

10. Assess the magnitude and significance of the internal adjustment problems lower trade barriers would create for the United States.

11. What is the connection between commerical policy and foreign policy in general?

Chapter	REGIONAL ECONOMIC
10	INTEGRATION

The classical model of international trade envisages the exchange of goods and services among independent national economies without the interposition of artificial barriers. The model has never been fully implemented in practice. However strong the economic case for unfettered trading relations, opposition to the removal of national barriers has successfully resisted all attempts to make the world conform to the classical prescription.

Nevertheless, the idea of free trade is persistent, displaying a vitality unusual in the realm of economic doctrine. It reaches its full expression *within* each national state as the latter develops into its modern form. But, beyond this, it also finds full expression when two or more national states remove all tariffs and quantitative restrictions on the flow of goods and services between them.

Regional free-trade areas, embracing the national economies of two or more countries, are sometimes feasible, where worldwide free trade has little chance of being adopted in the foreseeable future. Regional groupings for the purpose of freeing trade between them have a considerable historical background,[1] but the greatest interest in them has developed in recent years, especially in connection with the most ambitious regional project, the European Common Market.

In this chapter we shall explore the economics of what may be broadly called regional *integration*.

---

[1] For a brief history of projects of this nature proposed during the interwar years, see United Nations, Department of Economic Affairs, *Customs Unions* (New York, Lake Success, 1947) .

221

THE FORMS AND DEGREE OF ECONOMIC INTEGRATION

There are various forms and degrees of economic integration.[2] The historical prototype is the *customs union,* but both less and more intensive degrees of integration are possible, and in fact currently in operation or projected.

The Free-Trade Area

The loosest and least intensive form of integration is the *free-trade area.* In a free-trade area, all artificial restrictions on the movement of goods and services among the participating countries are removed, but each country may retain its own tariffs, quotas, or other restrictive devices on its trade with nonparticipating countries.

The best known current movement for the establishment of a free-trade area is the European Free Trade Association (EFTA), embracing Great Britain, Norway, Sweden, Denmark, Switzerland, Austria, and Portugal (Finland joined as an "associate member" in 1961). When EFTA came into existence in 1960, its seven members (also known as the "outer seven") agreed to eliminate gradually tariffs and quotas among themselves and to promote economic cooperation.

The movement toward free-trade areas extends beyond Europe. In 1960 Argentina, Brazil, Chile, Paraguay, Peru, Uruguay, and Mexico formed the Latin American Free Trade Association. In addition, proposals for economic integration are under active consideration by various Asian and African countries.

The Customs Union

The customs union is one degree further along the scale of economic integration than a free-trade area. In addition to the complete elimination of tariffs and quotas on intraunion trade, a *common external tariff* is established on goods entering the union from outside. And, implied by the latter, is the apportionment of customs revenue between the members of the union according to an agreed formula.

The best-known recent example of a customs union is Benelux

---

[2] The following discussion leans heavily on the excellent treatise of Bela Balassa, *The Theory of Economic Integration* (Homewood, Illinois: Richard D. Irwin, Inc., 1961).

—Belgium, Luxemburg, and the Netherlands. Belgium and Luxemburg had established a customs union as far back as 1921. During World War II, they agreed to join the Netherlands in an expanded union. Today, Benelux embraces a single market with a common external tariff and free internal trade. (Indeed, Benelux is now closer to being a common market than just a customs union, for there is virtually free intraunion movement of labor and capital as well as of goods and services.)

Again, as in the case of free-trade associations, the movement toward customs union has not been confined to Western Europe. For example, the formation of a union is in progress in the West Indies, and it is possible that the Latin American Free Trade Association will eventually evolve into a union.

The Common Market

A common market represents the next higher degree of economic integration beyond customs union. Besides (*a*) eliminating trade barriers among member countries and (*b*) establishing a common external tariff, a common market involves the important further integrating step of (*c*) removing national restrictions on the movement of labor and capital among participating countries.

By far the most significant current example of a common market is the European Economic Community (EEC), established by the Treaty of Rome of 1957.[3] Popularly known as the European Common Market (and also as the "Inner Six," as distinguished from the "Outer Seven" of the European Free Trade Association), the EEC embraces West Germany, France, Italy, and the three Benelux countries. The possibility of its area being greatly expanded eventually to include Great Britain and other continental countries is rather great, even though enlargement of the market was retarded, at least temporarily, by the French veto of Britain's first application for membership. The EEC is more or less an extension of the European Coal and Steel Community (ECSC), created in 1953 among the same six countries later forming the EEC. In a real sense, the Coal and Steel Community was an experiment on a limited scale with the common market concept, and even with still more highly integrated operations. Tariff and quota restrictions on coal and steel were abolished, discriminatory transport rates removed, a

---

[3] Several other regional blocs of countries, in Latin America and Africa, are considering, or are already in process of establishing, customs unions or common markets.

common pool of labor and capital funds created, and supervisory institutions with supranational powers formed. The great success of the Coal and Steel Community, together with the invaluable experience gained from it, contributed mightily to the extension of its principles to all goods and services.

The chief provisions of the Treaty of Rome establishing the EEC may be briefly summarized as follows:

1. The gradual elimination of tariffs, quotas, and other barriers to trade among members, to be accomplished within 12 to 15 years starting from 1958. (The target date has been shortened by several years through an accelerated rate of tariff reductions and quota removals.)

2. The creation of a uniform tariff schedule applicable to imports from the rest of the world. The common tariff is to be based on the unweighted average level of duties prevailing on January 1, 1957, in the six-member countries. However, in 1960 it was decided to use this average, *minus 20 percent,* provided a reciprocal reduction in tariffs is agreed to by other members of GATT.[4]

3. The removal of restrictions on the movement among members of labor, capital, and business enterprises.

4. The prohibition of cartels and similar restrictive devices, unless they contribute to improvements in production or to technical and economic progress.

5. The pursuit of common agricultural policies.

6. The creation of two investment funds, one to operate in Europe and the other in associated overseas territories, to channel capital from the more advanced to the less developed regions of the Community.

7. The creation of a Social Fund to help relieve economic injuries to workers resulting from the movement toward integration.

It should be noted that lying behind the European Common Market and inspiring its development is a powerful movement looking toward the eventual political unification of Europe. In addition to creating the economic base for political integration, the Common Market provides a set of administering and implementing institutions—including a Commission, a Council of Ministers, an

---

[4] The 20 percent reduction does not apply in the case of members whose tariffs are lowered in the process of reaching a common tariff schedule.

Assembly, and a Court of Justice—constituting a nucleus from which a European government could someday evolve.

The possibility that the EEC may eventually lead to some form of political integration is accompanied—or perhaps preceded—by the likelihood of a still greater degree of economic integration than the Common Market, as now constituted, entails. Indeed, the door to greater integration is left open in the Treaty of Rome by the general provision for the coordination of the members' economic and social policies.

The formation of a common market inevitably increases the interdependence of its members' national economies. In renouncing the use of tariffs, quotas, payments restrictions, immigration and emigration barriers, and control over capital movements, as instruments of national policy, the members of a common market remove the chief insulators protecting their national economies from the full impact of external economic developments. The coordination of—or at least the avoidance of inconsistent—national economic and monetary policies is therefore implicit in a common market. However, this does not necessarily require full-scale economic integration, with supranational institutions having binding powers over the policies of member states.

THE ECONOMIC EFFECTS OF REGIONAL ECONOMIC INTEGRATION

The formation of the European Common Market has aroused intense interest all over the world. Economically, it poses the prospect of creating the largest aggregation of productive power and wealth in the world, next to the United States. Politically and socially it is being advanced as a "third force" in the East-West bipolar power complex.

Our primary interest now is in the economic effects that can be expected to flow from regional economic integration, especially integration of the kind represented by the European Common Market.

To its most enthusiastic protagonists, a common market offers the potentiality of a virtual economic revolution. The free movement of goods, persons, and capital is conceived as the means of releasing vast sources of productive energy hitherto held in check by artificial barriers erected at national boundaries. A favorite appeal to historical support for this sanguine prognostication is to cite the tremendous economic fruits produced by the vast single market of the United States.

The professional economist has been put in the unenviable position of having to throw a little cold water on the burning enthusiasm of the most ardent advocate of regional economic integration. In view of the economist's predilection for condemning artificial hindrances to free trade and factor movements, this may be somewhat surprising. But not really, for it must be remembered that there is another side to the coin of integration when pursued on a regional basis: namely, *regional discrimination. Part and parcel of the process of creating a single regional market is the erection of a wall around the region separating it to a greater or lesser degree from the outside world.* Whether, therefore, regional integration results in a net economic gain depends upon the adverse effects of this substituted barrier to free-world trade as compared to the beneficial effects of tearing down previous barriers. (A second, and related, question is *whose* net economic gain one is referring to—that of the members of the region, or of the outside world, or of the world as a whole?) The only kind of economic integration the unreconstructed "liberal" economist would support without qualification is one that would embrace the world.

This does not mean, however, that there is necessarily an economic case against regional integration; it only means that one should proceed with caution and not overlook the negative as well as the positive effects to be expected. Generalizations are dangerous in this connection, for what might be true in one particular case may not be in another. For instance, conceivably the European Common Market may turn out to be a tremendous success, while the Latin American Common Market may have indifferent or harmful effects. It all depends on circumstances and policies.

We shall now consider more specifically some of the major economic effects of regional integration.

Trade Creation versus Trade Diversion

One of the chief potential economic benefits of economic integration—applicable to free-trade association, customs unions, and common markets alike—is brought about by the substitution of lower-cost foreign supplies of a good for higher-cost domestic production. The source of the gain here is precisely the same as that which we earlier concluded follows from the removal of protective tariffs.

Suppose, for example, that prior to the formation of the European Common Market, both Italy and France produced sewing machines, but that Italy had a marked comparative cost advantage, so that France's domestic production was carried on only by reason of a highly protective tariff. On removal of the French tariff, resources in France would be shifted out of the sewing machine industry into more efficient areas, and the French consumer would obtain the benefit of lower-priced Italian sewing machines.

Whenever integration has the happy effect of replacing higher-cost domestic production with lower-cost foreign production, a net economic gain is undeniable, and the gain has aptly been labeled "trade creation."[5]

Unfortunately, however, the removal of tariffs on a regional basis accompanied by the erection of a common external tariff wall may lead to *trade diversion* instead of trade creation. Trade diversion occurs when higher-cost sources of supply are substituted for lower-cost sources.

For example, suppose that even though Italy has a cost advantage in sewing machines compared to France, the United States has a still greater comparative cost advantage. Assume further that before France and Italy become members of a regional integration arrangement, France has a low tariff, or no tariff, on sewing machines and therefore imports them from the United States, while Italy produces them at home under the cover of a protective tariff. Now France and Italy join in a customs union or common market and impose a common tariff on sewing machines high enough to make American machines more expensive to France, with tariff, than the Italian product without tariff. As a consequence, the source of supply to France is shifted from the lower-cost American producers to the higher-cost Italian producers. In this case, there is clearly a net economic loss incurred because of the customs union or common market.

There are obviously many other possible combinations of situations in addition to the two preceding illustrations. In some, integration leads to trade creation, in others to trade diversion, and in

---

[5] The term was coined, as was also its opposite "trade diversion"—described in the following paragraphs—by Jacob Viner. See his *The Customs Union Issue* (New York: Carnegie Endowment for International Peace, 1950), pp. 41 ff.

still others there is no effect (as, for example, when no members of the union or common market produce the commodity under tariff protection either before or after integration). Theoretically, and in general, *a net gain* will be realized if the sum of cost savings through trade creation exceeds the sum of cost increments through trade diversion, and *a net loss* incurred if the reverse balance prevails. But it is more difficult to predict which way the balance will fall in any particular integration scheme.

In the case of the European Common Market, judgments on the relative magnitudes of trade creation and trade diversion vary from the expectation of negligible differences between the two effects to the expectation of a significant net balance in favor of trade creation.[6]

One of the important determinants of what the net effect will be is the level of tariffs ultimately established by the Common Market. The lower the common tariff wall is, the less will be the diversion from lower-cost outside sources to higher-cost inside sources. This, in turn, will probably depend to a large extent upon the commercial policies pursued by other countries, and especially by the United States. If the United States were to react to the Common Market in a protectionist fashion, the danger of the world's being divided into warring and strongly discriminatory economic blocs, leading to a net loss from trade diversion, would be great. But if the United States vigorously pursues a policy of cooperation with the Common Market in reciprocal tariff reductions, the chances of trade creation being predominant are much increased.

The Economic Effects of Free Factor Movements

We recall that a common market not only frees trade among the member countries but also frees the movement of labor, capital, and entrepreneurship. (This does not hold for customs unions and free-trade associations, however, so that the present discussion is not applicable to the latter two types of regional integration.) What benefits, or disadvantages, can be expected to flow from free factor movements?

Recalling our much earlier discussion of factor movements (see

---

[6] For the pessimistic view of the net gain to be realized see Tibor Scitovsky, *Economic Theory and Western European Integration* (Stanford, Calif.: Stanford University Press, 1958), pp. 64–67. For an optimistic view, see Franz Gehrels and B. F. Johnston, "The Economic Gains of European Integration," *Journal of Political Economy*, August, 1955.

Chapter 5), we would presume that their freedom from artificial hindrances would contribute to the welfare of the common market as a whole. The theoretical reason for this conclusion is easily stated: the total output of the community is increased, with the same volume of inputs, when labor and capital move from areas of lower marginal productivity to areas of higher marginal productivity. Likewise, total production is increased if entrepreneurial skills can be freely transferred from areas of relative plentifulness to areas of relative scarcity. The potentiality for further gain from the movement of factors is exhausted only after their marginal productivities have become equalized in different areas.

Moreover, the chances of integration having a negative effect from factor movements, comparable to the possible negative allocation effects described previously, are small. Theoretically, an adverse effect could be produced by diverting factor movements from third countries. But in practice this is not likely to be very significant, especially for labor movements. Because of strict national immigration controls, very little movement of labor occurs across national boundaries to be diverted by regional integration. National restrictions on international capital movements are much less severe, but it is doubtful that any great diversion of the flow from third countries would be caused by the formation of a common market.

In addition to the potentialities for net gains realizable from reducing the national disparities in the marginal productivity of resources, a related and very important, though less measurable, gain may be forthcoming from free factor movements within an integrated region. It is the advantages stemming from the closer communication among the peoples of the region. New ideas, techniques, and skills can be expected to flourish under the impact of closer contact and the removal of national discriminatory policies and attitudes.

While the potentiality for significant gain from free factor movements can hardly be denied, there is one troublesome question to be raised. The gain we have identified is that accruing to the integrated *region as a whole*. Unfortunately, however, there is no assurance that this gain will be equally distributed among the member countries, nor even that some members or sectors may not actually suffer a loss of welfare. This possibility recalls the analogous problem we earlier discussed in connection with the internal distribution within a country of the national gain produced by free trade (see pages 64–65). Not surprisingly, the most reasonable solution may also be similar: a greater emphasis on capital movements, rather than labor movements, and redistributive measures by the regional organization.

Dynamic Effects of Integration

So far we have been considering the economic effects of regional integration on the assumption of given and unchanging factor supplies, state of technology, and economic structure. It is quite probable, however, that potentially the greatest advantages to be gained from integration stem from essentially *dynamic* forces that may be released by integration. Especially important is the extent to which integration will stimulate an accelerated rate of economic growth. Not only is this an extremely relevant consideration from the standpoint of the countries integrating their economies but it is also of prime importance from the standpoint of the outside world, as we shall see later.

We shall now investigate the major forces released or created by integration that may contribute to an accelerated rate of economic growth.

Internal Economies of Scale. Let us begin with a phenomenon that has been the subject of a considerable amount of controversy among economists: economies of scale.

There are two types of economies of scale: internal and external. Internal economies are those realized by an individual firm as a consequence of expanding its scale of operations. External economies are realized by individual firms, not as the result of their own actions, but as a consequence of expansion in the industry or economy as a whole.

There is doubt in the minds of some economists about the extensiveness and significance of either kind of economies of scale, especially of the external variety. However, several empirical studies in recent years indicate that *in some industries,* though by no means in all, there definitely are marked internal economies realizable as the size of firms expands.[7]

When large internal economies of scale are present in an industry, the ability fully to appropriate them depends upon the size of the market. If the demand for the product is not large enough to

---

[7] See, for example, Joe S. Bain, *Barriers to New Competition* (Cambridge, Mass.: Harvard University Press, 1956), chap. iii.

absorb the output of firms in the industry operating at optimum scale, economies of large-scale production cannot be fully exploited. In some cases, the market may not be large enough to support even *one* firm operating at optimum scale. For example, it has been estimated that in the manufacturing of rayon yarn, the optimal operation is at an output of approximately 20,000–25,000 tons per year per plant, with costs of production about 8 percent higher for a plant half this size and 25 percent higher for a plant with one quarter the optimum output. Yet a few years ago the entire annual output was only about 10,000 tons in Belgium, 30,000 tons in the Netherlands, 14,000 tons in Argentina, 13,000 tons in Mexico, 1,000 tons in Peru and Uruguay, and so on.[8]

In those industries where the appropriation of significant economies of scale requires a total output in excess of the absorptive capacity of the national economy, the integration of several national economies obviously may permit the achievement of lower costs of production.[9] There is evidence that such might be the case in the European Common Market for such industries as atomic energy; steel; the smelting and refining of copper, zinc, tin, and lead; metal engineering; electrical engineering; automobiles; synthetic fibers; paper and allied products; chinaware and glass; furniture; leather; and footwear.[10] There likewise appears to be considerable scope for capturing economies of scale through the integration of Latin American economies.[11]

A related advantage that may be yielded by a larger market is increased competition. Even if a national market is large enough to allow the exploitation of large-scale economies, it may not be large enough to support more than one or a very few optimum-sized firms. Enlargement of the market through regional integration would then permit a larger number of optimum-sized firms to survive and reduce the degree of monopolistic control in the industry. We shall return to this aspect of integration shortly.

External Economies of Scale. As indicated earlier, the reality of external economies of scale is seriously questioned by some economists (Professor Frank Knight being the leading sceptic). Others

---

[8] See Bela Balassa, *op. cit.,* pp. 135 and 139 and references cited therein.

[9] International trade among nonintegrated countries may also permit the reaping of economies of scale through the presence of large export markets. However, artificial barriers to trade clearly reduce the scope of this possibility.

[10] See Balassa, *op. cit.,* pp. 132–35.

[11] *Ibid.,* 138–42.

are convinced that external economies are not only genuine but may be of the first order of importance. The weight of the evidence, both theoretical and empirical, seems to be on the side of the latter. Let us briefly explore some of the possible sources of external economies.[12]

In general, the source of external economies lies in the interaction of the various sectors of an economy, with developments in each sector having favorable repercussions on the others. The expansion of one industry may lead to the creation of certain skills of labor, techniques of management, or technological developments, which then become part of the economy's "pool" of resources, available to be drawn upon by other industries. A technological improvement in industry X, supplying intermediate products to industry Y, lowers costs in Y. An innovation in industry A, supplying industry B, may lead to an expansion in the output of B that in turn allows the capture of economies of scale by the latter. There may be a circular "feedback" effect—for example, the expansion of coal production may lower the cost of steel, in turn lowering the cost of mining equipment and of coal.

An expansion in the size of markets through regional integration widens the scope for the gains originating in the interplay of sectoral developments. As the situation of underdeveloped economies clearly indicates, the absence of a large enough market frequently stymies the development of particular industries whose absence in turn hinders the development of other industries. Moreover, the larger the market the greater are the opportunities to realize economies through further specialization. For instance, whereas in the United States automobile parts and accessories are produced by a large number of independent firms, in some European countries, because of the limited output of each firm, manufacturers produce component parts themselves.

Increased Competition. One of the less tangible and unmeasurable, but still potentially very significant, benefits of economic integration lies in the more efficient market structures it may encourage. A well-established proposition in economics is that, other things being equal, the more competitive a market is, the more efficient it will be in the sense that the resulting allocation of resources will more nearly approach the social optimum.

It is not inevitable that regional integration will lead to more

---

[12] A good summary of the evidence is to be found in Balassa, *op. cit.*, pp. 144–62, on which the following discussion draws freely.

competitive market structures. Indeed, some observers are of the opinion that integration will result in the formation of cartels and other forms of oligopolistic coordination among the firms of member countries, decreasing economic efficiency.[13]

Others expect a greater degree of competition to evolve because of integration.[14] By a "greater degree" of competition is certainly not meant in this context the theoretical model of *pure* competition. More realistically, it means a decrease in the degree and extent of oligopolistic uncertainty and coordination, brought about by a dilution of the influence of each firm. For instance, suppose that within each of several national economies there are only a few firms operating in a given industry, with each national industry protected by tariffs from the effective competition of the firms in other countries. Very likely the firms in the industry in each country will reach an understanding, tacit or overt, not to "rock the boat" by price competition. Inefficient firms are likely to be protected from the competition of efficient firms by agreement to share the market and "live and let live."

Now assume that national barriers to trade and investment are removed through integration of the countries. The vulnerability of each firm in the industry to the actions and reactions of other firms is reduced, for each firm's share of the larger regional market is less than it was of its smaller national market. The oligopolistic interdependence of firms is lessened and the possibility of effective collusion among firms reduced. Inefficient firms lose the protection afforded by the absence in nationally separated markets of competition from foreign producers.

Moreover, the wider markets offered by integration may open the door to the entry into some industries of a larger number of optimum-sized firms. As noted earlier, to the extent that marked internal economies of scale are responsible for oligopolistic concentration of output in the hands of a few firms, integration reduces this barrier to a larger number of firms and more effective competition.

Whether or not the advantages of greater competition are in fact reaped from integration depends in large measure upon the policies adopted by the participating countries. In the case of the European Common Market, it is not yet clear what these policies will be. The treaty establishing EEC forbids, in principle, the formation of car-

[13] See, for example, K. Rothschild, "The Small Nation and World Trade," *Economic Journal*, April, 1944, pp. 26–40.

[14] See especially Scitovsky, *op. cit.*, pp. 123–30.

tels and the abuse of dominant market positions. But an exception is allowed for agreements among firms which "contribute to improvements in the production and distribution of goods or to the promotion of technical and economic progress, while reserving a fair part of the resulting profit to the users." Moreover, industrial concentration is not prohibited, and it remains to be seen whether or not various forms of tacit collusion will develop.

Nevertheless, in comparison to the widespread previous practice of many European producers, often with the approval or even outright support of their governments, to engage in restrictive agreements, the Common Market Treaty outlawing cartels and abuses of oligopolistic power represents a significant step in the direction of greater competition. Provided that the spirit of this approach is not too badly violated in practice, the forces operating in the wider market to increase competition will probably predominate over any tendencies toward extending national interfirm coordination to regional industries.

REGIONS VERSUS THE OUTSIDE WORLD

Up to this point we have concentrated our analysis on the effects of regional integration on the participating countries. There remains for discussion the impact of regionalism on the world economy as a whole, and on nonparticipating countries in particular.

Generally speaking, we would expect any effects of regional integration beneficial to the participating countries also to be beneficial to the world as a whole, and regionally harmful effects likewise to be detrimental to the whole world. Such, for example, is the case with respect to trade creation and trade diversion. If regional integration leads to trade creation, member countries benefit, while other countries are certainly not harmed. But if it leads to trade diversion, both member countries and other countries whose export markets are diverted suffer economic loss.

Quite conceivably, however, integration could benefit member countries while harming third countries. A distinct possibility of this occurring lies in the *terms-of-trade effect* of integration. If the terms of trade of countries integrating their economies are improved, their share of the gain from trade with the outside world is increased at the expense of the latter.

The terms of trade of a regional group may be more favorable than prior to integration for at least two reasons. First, to the extent that trade diversion occurs, the demand for the export products of third countries is reduced, and this may have the effect of depressing their export prices. Second, the bargaining power of a regional bloc in tariff negotiations with other countries is likely to be much greater than that of each of the participating countries negotiating separately. (This would not apply to integration arrangements not involving a common external tariff, such as free-trade association.)

That some third countries may lose from the trade-diverting and/or terms-of-trade effects of regional integration cannot be gainsaid. Certain industries in the United States—such, for example, as automobiles—will undoubtedly find their markets in Europe contracted because of the diversion of demands to within the EEC; tropical countries will probably lose markets in Europe because of the diversion of demand for such products as coffee, cocoa, and bananas to the associated overseas countries and territories of EEC, and so on.

It would be a serious mistake, however, to concentrate attention on these probable static, short-run effects of integration to the neglect of the dynamic, long-run effects. If, as we have generally concluded, integration promotes the more rapid economic growth of participating countries, its *income* effect may overwhelm its allocative effects. Prosperity, as we have frequently observed, is internationally contagious. As per capita real income rises in a region, it becomes a larger customer for the products of other countries, and a supplier of cheaper and better products to other countries.

The extent to which the potential advantages to the outside world of regional integration are realized depends in large measure upon the commercial policies adopted by both groups of countries. Regionalism can deteriorate into the formation of discriminatory trade blocs and bitter economic warfare, or it can be a step in the direction of freer world trade on a multilateral and nondiscriminatory basis.

It is precisely in this connection that the response of the United States to the formation of the European Common Market is so critical for the future of the free-world economy. Reciprocal tariff reductions and continued economic cooperation through such institutions as the Organization for Economic Cooperation and Development (OECD) would open the way for a great expansion in international specialization and trade; reversion to a protectionist stance would suppress the potential sources of mutual benefit and unleash the potential negative forces dormant in regionalism.

RECOMMENDED READING

BALASSA, BELA. *The Theory of Economic Integration.* Homewood, Ill.: Richard D. Irwin, Inc., 1961.

HUMPHREY, DON D. *The United States and the Common Market.* New York: Frederick A. Praeger, Inc., 1962.

SCITOVSKY, TIBOR. *Economic Theory and Western European Integration.* Stanford, Calif.: Stanford University Press, 1958.

UNITED NATIONS, DEPARTMENT OF ECONOMIC AFFAIRS. *Customs Unions.* Lake Success, N.Y., 1947.

VINER, JACOB. *The Customs Union Issue.* New York: Carnegie Endowment for International Peace, 1950.

STUDY QUESTIONS

1. Distinguish between a free-trade area, a customs union, and a common market.

2. Describe the chief provisions of the Treaty of Rome establishing the European Economic Community.

3. Why does the establishment of a common market strongly imply the close coordination of member countries' national economic, monetary, and social policies?

4. Regional economic integration necessarily involves trade discrimination. Explain.

5. Show how the formation of a regional economic bloc may lead either to trade creation or trade diversion. Illustrate with examples.

6. What relevance does U.S. commercial policy have for the question of whether the European Common Market will eventually promote or retard nondiscriminatory international trade?

7. Demonstrate the economic advantages likely to accrue to members of the European Common Market as a result of the freeing of factor movements.

8. Define *internal economies of scale.* Why can economic integration be expected to lead to a greater realization of such economies?

9. Define *external economies of scale,* and show how the European Common Market may promote their development.

10. What benefits may economic integration confer with respect to market structures?

11. Under what circumstances are nonmember countries harmed by regional economic integration?

12. What is meant by the "income effects" of economic integration? Are these effects harmful or beneficial to other countries?

Chapter 11

MONOPOLY AND
INTERNATIONAL TRADE

The pure theory of international trade is based on the assumption of pure competition in the commodity markets within each country and in buying and selling internationally. With a single international commodity market, a given good commands the same price, except for transportation costs, the world over. A second assumption underlying the pure theory is that productive resources are perfectly mobile and competitively priced *within* each country, but imperfectly mobile internationally. Hence, in the *factor* markets, one price for any given productive service is assumed to exist within each country but with different prices prevailing in different countries (although, since international commodity trade is a substitute for international factor movements, differences in factor returns tend to be reduced as a result of trade).

We have shown that, under these assumptions, free international trade leads to the optimum allocation of the world's resources and the maximization of the world's real income. A corollary proposition is that anything that prevents these assumptions from being fulfilled in practice reduces the gains derived from international trade. We already know that one very important deviation in practice from the basic assumption is the widespread creation of artificial barriers to trade in the form of tariffs, quantitative restrictions, exchange controls, and similar devices.

We must now admit the existence of another set of circumstances which interferes with the optimum worldwide allocation of resources that a completely free and competitive price mechanism would otherwise bring about. Reference is made to the absence, in fact, of pure competition in both factor markets, internally, and commodity markets, internally and internationally.

Pure competition requires that the production and exchange of a given commodity or service be carried on by such a large number of individual sellers and buyers that no one or group of them is able significantly to influence supply, demand, or price. Whenever any one seller or buyer, or group of sellers or buyers acting in collaboration, is in a position to exercise an influence on price, monopoly in some form is present.

Historically, the bulk of international trade has consisted of staple primary commodities—foodstuffs and raw materials—produced under highly competitive conditions. But the traditional assumption of pure competition has tended to become increasingly less realistic. In what forms monopolistic tendencies have manifested themselves we shall presently see, after having first examined some of the general economic effects of monopoly.

THE DOMESTIC ECONOMIC EFFECTS OF MONOPOLY[1]

On the Allocation of Resources

In a perfectly free and competitive market, resources tend to be allocated in response to consumer demand and to be combined in the productive process in the most economical manner. These results are brought about automatically by the price mechanism. In long-run equilibrium, the price of each commodity is such as to equate aggregate demand and supply and is equal to marginal and lowest average costs of production. Marginal costs of production are in turn equal to the sum of the prices paid for the services of the various factors which, in combination, are required to produce a unit of the commodity and which command the same price in alternative employments. Thus, if the equilibrium price of commodity X is $1 and of commodity Y is $2, this is an indication that two additional units of X can be produced, at the margin, with the productive factors employed in producing one unit of Y. Moreover, it is a further indication that consumers value, at the margin, two units of X and one unit of Y equally, so that resources are allocated in accordance with consumer preferences.

Conditions of Ideal Resource Allocation. In order for these ideal results to be achieved, several conditions are required, among which two are critically important. First, the equality of marginal costs and price is assured if there are so many firms in the industry, each producing the same standardized product, that no one firm or group acting in collaboration influences the sale price. In this event,

---

[1] For a fuller discussion of the meaning and effects of monopoly, the student is referred to any good text on the principles of economics.

each firm will maximize its profits by producing that output at which marginal cost equals the market price of the commodity. The general rule for maximizing profits is to produce that output at which marginal costs equal marginal revenue, marginal costs being defined as the addition to total costs caused by the production of one additional unit of the commodity, and marginal revenue being defined as the addition to total revenue from the sale of one additional unit of the commodity. Under pure competition, each firm can sell any amount of its output at the prevailing market price, so that sales price per unit and marginal revenue are equal; and, since the latter is brought into equality with marginal costs, it follows that sales price and marginal costs are also equated.

Moreover, provided that there is free entry of new firms into the industry, the long-run sales price of the commodity will tend also to equal the lowest average costs of production—which is the criterion of optimum productive efficiency. The equality of sales price and average costs under free-entry conditions is effected by the tendency for additional firms to enter any industry in which sales price exceeds average costs—for this is an indication of profit opportunities in that industry. Alternatively, if average costs are above sales price, losses are incurred and firms will drop out of the industry. In either case, the total market supply is either increased or decreased until price equals average costs. Further, average costs equal marginal costs only at the lowest point on the average-cost curve of the firm. Hence the equality between marginal and average costs occurs at the optimum efficiency output of the firm.

Second, provided that there is perfect mobility of resources, every firm must pay each factor of production the same price that other firms in the same and other industries are willing to pay; and if no one firm or group of firms is able to influence this price, it will be equal to the value of the factor's marginal product. For if the value of the additional output produced by adding another unit of the factor (the value of the marginal product of the factor) is greater or less than the price of the factor, the firm can increase its profits, or reduce its losses, by employing more or less units of that factor.

The Distorting Influence of Monopoly. Now let us see how monopoly in any form interferes with the above process. First of all, suppose that there are so few producers that each can influence the sales price of the commodity by changing his output. In order to sell a larger quantity of output, then, the unit price must be lowered. Since, however, any lowering of price must apply to *all* the

units sold (except under discriminating monopoly, discussed below) , and not just the last, the additional, or marginal, revenue derived from the sale of an extra unit of output is *less* than the sales
price, a loss of revenue being incurred on the other units which
previously sold at a higher price and now sell at a lower price.
Hence, whereas under pure competition, price, marginal revenue,
and marginal costs are all brought into equality, under monopoly,
marginal costs and marginal revenue are equated at an output at
which price is *above* marginal revenue and marginal costs. This is
shown graphically in Figure 11.1.

FIGURE 11.1

OUTPUT AND PRICE OF COMPETITIVE FIRM AND MONOPOLISTIC FIRM

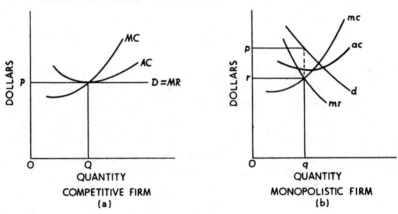

In Figure 11.1 (*a*) the competitive firm is confronted with an infinitely elastic demand curve, *D*, indicating that it can sell all it desires at the prevailing market price, *P*. The firm's demand curve is
equivalent, therefore, to its marginal revenue (*MR*) and the sales
price (*P*). Free entry also keeps average costs (*AC*) equal to the
market price, and, since average costs and marginal costs are equal
only at the lowest point on the average-cost curve, *OQ* represents
the firm's most efficient output.

In Figure 11.1 (*b*) the demand curve for the monopolistic firm
(*d*) falls from left to right, indicating that, in order to sell a larger
quantity of its product, the firm must lower its price. Hence the
firm's marginal-revenue curve (*mr*) lies below the demand curve.
The output *oq* maximizes the firm's profits (equalizes marginal
costs and marginal revenue) , and sells at price *p*, which is *rp* greater
than the marginal revenue and marginal costs. Furthermore, since
the marginal-revenue curve cuts the average-cost curve to the left of

its lowest point, the firm is not using its plant and equipment at maximum efficiency. (And since there is not free entry into the industry, price can continue to exceed average costs, and excessive profits can be realized.)

The results described tend to follow from any monopolistic element—whether on the producers' or buyers' side and whether because of natural advantages enjoyed or because of a special position acquired through producer or buyer collaboration or legal protection.[2] By preventing the equalization of price and marginal costs, monopoly leads to an uneconomic allocation of resources. Suppose, for example, that the marginal costs of producing X are $1 and of Y $2 but that, on account of monopoly in producing it, Y sells for $3. Consumers will tend to adjust their purchases of X and Y so that, at the margin, one unit of Y contributes to their satisfaction as much as three units of X. But in terms of resources used to produce the two commodities, an extra unit of Y could be obtained by giving up only two units of X. In other words, total satisfaction would be increased with the use of the same amount of resources if more of Y and less of X were produced. Maximum satisfaction would be yielded when the marginal rate of substitution between X and Y in the eyes of consumers equaled the ratio of the marginal costs of producing X and Y. This is automatically brought about under perfect competition but is prevented whenever monopoly is present.

MONOPOLY AND INTERNATIONAL TRADE

How is international trade affected by monopolistic markets? How are monopolistic market structures affected by international trade? In view of the widespread existence of imperfectly competitive market structures, these are vital questions. Of especial interest is the question of whether the origins and benefits of trade are fundamentally changed when the assumption of pure competition is relaxed.

Effects on the World Economy

Let us begin the discussion with a basic proposition: Other things being equal, international trade conducted within the framework

---

[2] A monopoly on the buyers' side—usually called "monopsony"—prevents the equalization of marginal costs and price and the optimum utilization of plant through its effects on the cost curve rather than the revenue curve of the firm.

of monopolistic markets will tend to result in a suboptimum allocation of the world's resources and the realization of less than potential maximum benefits to the world economy. We have learned that
international trade is beneficial wherever relative costs of production are not the same in different countries and that benefits continue to be gained until, as a *result* of trade, cost differentials are
eliminated. The immediate determinants of trade in a free market,
however, are *price* differentials; and if within the trading countries
the costs and price of each commodity are not the same, the international equalization of commodity prices ordinarily will not be
accompanied by the equalization of costs.[3] Conversely, international
equalization of costs may be prevented, even if within each country
costs and price of each article are equal, if prices are prevented
from being equalized internationally on account of artificial barriers to trade, including monopoly in international buying and selling.[4] In either event, the persistence of international cost differences
is evidence that the potential advantages of international trade are
not fully realized. To put it another way, the elimination of monopolistic elements would have the same kind of beneficial economic effects as those produced by the opening of an isolated economy to international trading relations—and for the same reasons.

The above is a statement in capsule form of the case for trade
free of artificial restraints and the distorting influence of imperfectly competitive markets. Free trade and price competition are
the twin ideal conditions for the world's capturing the full benefits
of international trade. However, ideal conditions are seldom found
in the real world. We have seen how tariffs, quotas, and similar
public restrictions on trade represent one type of deviation from the
ideal. Monopolistic practices are another type. But all deviations
from ideal conditions do not stand on the same footing, either theoretically or in practice. A distinction should be drawn between (*a*)

---

[3] A possible theoretical exception, of little practical applicability, is if the *same
degree* of monopoly (spread between costs and price) existed in each industry in
all trading countries—that is, if the *ratio* of price to costs were the same for all commodities in all countries.

[4] Generally speaking, commercial and payments restrictions interfere with the
international equalization of cost-price ratios by preventing single prices from being
established internationally, while monopolies interfere by preventing the equality of
price and costs within the trading countries. Some monopolies also, however, result
in different prices being charged in different markets—as, for example, under discriminating monopoly (see pages 248–49). In practice, of course, both commercial and
payments restrictions and monopolistic practices are often found to coexist, so that
the obstacle to international equalization of cost-price ratios is double-barreled.

those that are either unavoidable or have some compensating advantages and (*b*) those that are contrived and are without any compensating advantages.

Into the first category fall those monopolistic elements arising out of unavoidable product differentiation; those arising out of desirable, even if avoidable, product differentiation; and those based on genuine economies of scale. The second category embraces those monopolistic elements derived from avoidable and undesirable product differentiations and those based on contrived market power positions. Examples drawn from each of these categories in turn will serve to illuminate the distinction between them.

Consider first unavoidable and/or desirable product differentiation. There are many products which by their nature cannot be standardized, as required for pure competition. This is true for national economies, and even more so for the international economy. For example, whenever location is an element entering into the value of a product, its standardization is normally precluded, simply because of spatial differences. The services sold by retail stores, gasoline stations, hotels, and so on, are of this nature. In other cases, standardization is ruled out because of the personal nature of the product, as exemplified by most personal services—those of the doctor, dentist, barber, and the like. An important class of international transaction—the wide variety of services included in tourism —obviously is not susceptible to competitive standardization.

Next consider avoidable but conceivably desirable product differentiation. Articles of clothing could each be standardized, with shoes, suits, dresses, shirts, and similar items each produced by many firms in standardized form. If this were done, costs of production would tend to be less, both through the saving from standardization and through avoiding the excess capacity associated with monopolistic competition. But would the social welfare be greater? Not if the extra benefits of the wider variety of choice made available by product differentiation are at least as great as the extra costs entailed by the latter. Only individual consumers can say whether this is the case, but at least the virtues of pure competition as compared to monopolistic competition are called in question.

Finally, the economies of large-scale production may in some instances justify the absence of pure competition. If in order to obtain the lowest average costs of production each firm's output in a given industry must be so large that the market can absorb the total output of only one or of a few firms, pure competition is not feasible.

The tendency for pure monopoly (one firm) or oligopoly (a few firms) in such cases cannot rationally be objected to, although abuse of the resulting monopolistic or oligopolistic position, of course, can be rationally resisted through appropriate public policies.

In contrast to the above cases stand imperfectly competitive markets without any kind of social justification. The clearest case here is where one or a few firms succeed in establishing a monopolistic position through power maneuvers—such as mergers and combines, the organization of cartels, and collusion to control output and price, and where economies of scale do not preclude feasible competition. Falling into the same category are imperfections in the market due to product differentiation that is artificially contrived and without a genuine basis. Admittedly it may be difficult in practice to separate artificial and genuine differentiation, but conceptually the distinction is important.

The Effects of Imperfect Competition on Trade

With some exceptions to be considered shortly, the presence of monopolistic market elements does not prevent international trade nor eliminate its social benefits. Indeed, in some cases it can be argued that the volume and benefits of trade are greater under imperfect competition than they would be under pure competition.

That imperfect competition does not prevent international trade is clear enough from the observation of the great amount of trade actually occurring under such conditions. This is in conformity with what we would expect theoretically. Unless monopolistic restraints extend across national lines, as under international cartels discussed later, the relative price differences underlying trade can be expected to be as manifest under imperfect competition as under pure competition. The question, however, is whether the trade proximately caused by such price differences is socially beneficial.

Under perfect competition, since price is equal to marginal cost, the international equalization of prices as a result of trade carries with it the international equalization of marginal costs. The latter is the condition signifying the exhaustion of all the potential benefits of trade—in other words, it represents the optimum pattern and volume of trade. But, as we have noted, prices tend to be higher than marginal costs under imperfect competition, so that the price-equalizing effects of trade may be accompanied by a continuing disparity in marginal costs. Hence, imperfectly competitive markets prevent trade from reaching its optimum pattern and volume.

It is important now to avoid a confusion. To say that trade under imperfect competition will be less beneficial, other things being equal, than under perfect competition is not to say that trade yields no benefits unless perfect competition prevails. Suboptimal resource allocation is caused by imperfect competition, not by trade, and generally the deviations from the optimum is less with trade than without it. The basis for believing that ordinarily the optimum is more closely approximated under imperfect competition with trade is as follows. Monopolistic elements are socially harmful in restricting output below the optimum level at which the marginal value of each good, as measured by its price, is equal to its marginal social cost. If a good is imported, it must be because it is lower priced (in relation to its marginal worth) abroad than at home. This means that the effect of restricted domestic output is partially counteracted by the greater availability of the product through importation. Moreover, as will be pointed out later, if domestic firms continue to produce the good, its importation may, paradoxically, induce firms to expand domestic output. In sum, trade tends to alleviate monopolistic scarcity.

There is a second point to be made on the trade effects of imperfect competition. While, on the one hand, by restricting output and raising prices imperfect competition reduces the volume of trade that would occur under pure competition, on the other hand, by expanding the variety of products available to consumers, it increases the volume of trade. A great deal of trade occurs, especially in consumer goods and services, because of the genuine differentiation between foreign and domestic products. The welfare effects of the greater choice afforded to the consumer by trade are difficult to measure, but the presumption is strong that they are very significant.

Finally, in those industries where imperfect competition is due to economies of large-scale production, trade may well be greater and socially more beneficial than if pure competition were to prevail. Of course, there are contrary forces at work in such cases. Monopolistic output and pricing policies discourage trade, while the lower costs associated with economies of scale are favorable to trade. But price may be lower under oligopoly than under pure competition because the effect of lower costs outweighs the effect of oligopolistic output restriction.

Monopolistic Restrictions of Trade

In the foregoing discussion we have identified various circumstances in which imperfect competition does not destroy the benefits of international trade and even in some instances exerts a favorable influence. It is time now to examine quite different results produced under other circumstances by monopolistic markets.

Cartels. The most serious adverse effects of imperfect competition on trade are produced when monopolistic practices extend across national boundaries, as exemplified by international cartels. Because of their importance as potential destroyers of socially beneficial trade, cartels will be separately discussed in some detail in the next chapter.

Commodity Agreements. Private restrictive practices through international cartels have their counterpart on the public side in intergovernmental commodity agreements, although the latter are usually infused with a greater degree of social responsibility.

The chief objective of intergovernmental commodity agreements is to stabilize the prices of the primary commodities involved. Because of structural maladjustments and the combination of inelastic demand and supply functions, many primary commodities (raw materials and foodstuffs) tend to fluctuate sharply in price. To achieve greater price stability, commodity agreements typically provide for export quotas—that is, allotting to the participant countries certain percentages of the world market—in order to restrict output and prevent a competitive scramble for markets.

Production limitations, quotas, and price-maintenance agreements have many of the same unfortunate effects as tariffs and private monopolies: inefficient producers are protected, adjustment of supply to changing demand is discouraged, and shifts in resource allocation in response to changing bases of specialization are interfered with.

On the other hand, it must be granted that primary producers face special difficulties in an unregulated market. Whether control measures can be devised which would eliminate excessive price fluctuations without incurring the undesirable by-products associated in the past with commodity agreements is a moot question, which only further experimentation may illuminate.

State Trading. The tendency in recent years has been more and more in the direction of international trade conducted by governments or their agencies in place of private importers and exporters. The extent of state trading varies enormously, of course, among different countries: at one end of the scale is the Soviet Union and its satellites, the foreign trade of which is exclusively in the hands of state monopolies; at the other extreme are those countries, like the United States, where only a small fraction of foreign trade is directly handled by the state; in between are countries, like the United Kingdom, which, through arrangements such as bulk-purchase agreements, import all or most of certain types of products through an agency of the state, but with the largest part of trade remaining in private hands.

Theoretically, state-conducted trade could be just as advantageous and conformable to the principle of comparative advantage as private trade. In practice, however, it usually departs considerably from the pattern of private trade.

In the first place, noneconomic considerations are prone to enter more importantly into state than into private trade. This is especially the case when the state has a complete monopoly on imports and exports and may arbitrarily decide to shift its sources of foreign supplies or its export markets. The postwar trade of Eastern Europe, for example, has been redirected toward the Soviet Union, presumably for political reasons.

Apart from political considerations, however, state trading on a large scale necessarily means the introduction of monopoly elements, though of a public rather than private character. From a national point of view, it may be possible for a particular country to obtain a larger share of the gains from trade by pursuing in its international economic relations the same policies that a monopolistic firm follows within the national economy (compare this with the use of tariffs as a means of getting a larger share of the gains from trade, pages 161–62). That is, by channeling exports and imports through state agencies, higher prices for exports and lower prices for imports may be obtained, improving thereby the terms of trade. It should be observed, however, that if other countries also engage in state trading, bargaining replaces price comparisons as the guiding force of trade; and the ability of any one country to get the lion's share becomes uncertain and dependent upon its relative bargaining strength. In other words, in this case we enter the no-man's-land of bilateral monopoly or oligopoly.

The effects of state trading on the volume and efficiency of international trade depend not only upon the degree of monopoly or monopsony in exporting or importing but perhaps even more importantly upon internal marketing policies. If, as often happens, state-imported goods are sold below or above world market prices, then, of course, relative cost comparisons lose their function of guiding international specialization. If, on the other hand, the state-trading monopoly acts simply as an intermediary, furnishing the domestic market all the imports freely demanded at world market prices, no serious compromise of free-market forces is as likely to result. This appears, however, to be more of an ideal than a reality.

Discriminating Monopoly. Another monopolistic practice which interferes with optimum trade is the charging of different prices for the same good in different markets.

FIGURE 11.2

INTERNATIONAL PRICE DISCRIMINATION

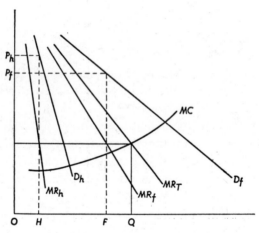

Theoretically, a monopolist could realize the greatest possible amount of profits from a given output by charging each individual buyer the highest price he was willing to pay rather than go without. Fortunately, this type of price discrimination cannot easily be practiced on a large scale within a national economy. In combination with tariffs, quotas, or other types of obstacles to reimportation, however, a monopolist may find it much easier to discriminate in price between the home market and foreign markets.

It will increase monopoly profits to pursue this policy if the elasticity of demand for the commodity is different in the home and foreign markets, for, at any given price, the more elastic the demand, the greater is marginal revenue—that is, the more total revenue will increase as a result of selling an additional unit of the commodity. Suppose, then, that the domestic demand is less elastic than the foreign demand. The monopolist will tend to produce that output at which marginal costs equal total marginal revenue, which is the sum of marginal revenue at home and abroad. But a higher price is charged domestic buyers than foreign buyers in order to equalize the marginal revenue in the two markets. This is shown graphically in Figure 11.2: let D_h be the home demand; D_f the foreign demand; MR_h and MR_f the corresponding marginal-revenue curves; and MC the marginal-cost curve. MR_T is the total marginal-revenue curve, equal to MR_h and MR_f summed horizontally. Total output is OQ, at which marginal costs and total marginal revenue are equal, but the output is sold in the home and foreign markets in the proportions OH and OF, respectively; for, with this distribution of sales, the marginal revenue is the same in both markets. But OH supply on the home market commands a price P_h, which is higher than the price P_f commanded in the foreign market by OF supply.

The practice of charging a higher price at home than abroad, apart from transportation costs, is called "dumping" in the foreign market. While foreigners may gain from the lower price charged them, domestic consumers are exploited by the higher price which they must pay. And, in any event, the allocating function of the free price mechanism is subverted and resources are misdirected.

THE EFFECTS OF TRADE ON MONOPOLY

We have examined the impact of imperfect competition on trade; now let us look at the reverse relationship: how trade affects imperfect competition. The chief question of interest here is whether trade, carried on within the framework of imperfectly competitive national markets, reinforces or resists the tendency of the latter to produce suboptimum allocation of resources. Our conclusion shall be that trade nearly always tends to narrow the deviations from the optimum caused by imperfect competition. If this conclusion is valid, it signifies that international trade yields important social benefits that extend well beyond those earlier identified.

The general basis for concluding that international trade improves the social efficiency of imperfectly competitive markets lies in the extra competitive elements which trade normally injects into national market structures. The opening of the economy to imported goods and services increases the number of firms in competition with each other in serving the domestic market. This holds both for imported products that are identical with those also produced in the importing country and for imports that are differentiated from domestic products, but are more or less close substitutes for them.

The greater competitiveness introduced by trade manifests itself most importantly in the increased elasticity of the demand curves confronting monopolistic domestic firms. We recall that in the case of pure competition the firm's demand curve (average revenue curve) is infinitely elastic (horizontal), signifying the absence of any control by the firm over the market price of its product. Under imperfect competition, the firm's demand curve falls from left to right, indicating that price is determined by the firm when it decides on its output. The greater the degree of competition, the more elastic is the firm's demand curve and the more closely is approximated the competitive social optimum.

Consider the case of domestic firms enjoying some degree of monopoly power when the national economy is insulated from the world economy, and then being exposed to a going world market in the *identical* product, with a single world price below the domestic price. Assuming the absence of trade barriers and transportation costs, the domestic price of the good becomes the same as the world price, and the position of the domestic firms is transformed from imperfectly competitive to virtually purely competitive. The reason for this transformation, of course, is that the one previously missing requirement for pure competition under the assumption of a standardized product—namely, the presence of a large number of firms—is supplied by enlargement of the market to include the outside world. From the standpoint of the individual firm, the demand curve is therefore tilted to a horizontal position at the world price, from its previous shape of falling from left to right (compare Figure 11.2). Following the maximum-profit rule of equating marginal revenue and marginal cost, domestic firms now expand their output until marginal cost is equal to the world price. This is the same as the purely competitive equilibrium output, monopolistic restriction having been exorcised by free trade.

A second case, of no doubt wider applicability, relates to imperfect competition with product differentiation. As long as the products of the firms in an industry are differentiated from firm to firm there cannot be pure competition, with or without international trade. However, the degree of monopoly present can vary widely, depending upon (*a*) the number of firms in the industry, (*b*) the ease of entry of new firms into the industry, and (*c*) the number and closeness of substitute products available. If there are only a few firms in the industry (oligopoly), the restriction of output below optimum levels, and the divergence between price and marginal cost, are likely to be greater than if many firms are in the industry (monopolistic competition). The influence of large numbers of firms (with presumed ease of entry into the industry), combined with a wide variety of close substitute products, is in the direction of a lower demand curve (smaller market share) and a more elastic demand curve for the average firm. This means a lower degree of control over price and a closer approximation to the position of a purely competitive firm.

The opening up of free trade relations with the outside world in effect increases the number of firms and substitute commodities included in the markets, thereby diluting the monopolistic elements present. If close substitutes for the products of a domestic oligopolistic industry can be freely imported, at prices comparable to or lower than those charged by the home firms, the effect may be the same as if the industry were transformed from oligopoly (a few firms) to monopolistic competition (many firms). In the case of home markets monopolistically competitive even without trade, the impact of the latter is not so strong, although presumably it is in the direction of reducing the level and increasing the elasticity of the demand curves facing home firms.

Our general conclusion is that free trade tends to increase the competitiveness of markets in participating countries. This must be counted among the important social benefits of free trade. It also explains why tariffs and quotas foster and protect monopolies and why large oligopolistic firms have a strong motive to form international cartels.

RECOMMENDED READING

KINDLEBERGER, CHARLES P. *International Economics,* chap. ix. 4th ed. Homewood, Ill.: Richard D. Irwin, Inc., 1968.

LOVASY, GERTRUD. "International Trade under Imperfect Competition," *Quarterly Journal of Economics,* Vol. 55 (1941), pp. 567–83.

MARSH, D. B. *World Trade and Investment,* chap. xxi. New York: Harcourt, Brace & World, Inc., 1951.

STUDY QUESTIONS

1. Define "pure competition." What condition with respect to the number of buyers and sellers would create a monopolistic element?

2. Why, in competitive equilibrium, is the price of each commodity equal to its marginal costs of production? Why is this not true under monopolistic conditions?

3. Show how monopoly, through preventing the equalization of price and marginal costs, leads to an uneconomic allocation of resources, both internally and internationally.

4. The elimination of monopolistic elements would have the same kind of beneficial economic effect, and for the same reason, as that produced by the opening of an isolated economy to international trading relations. Explain.

5. Distinguish between unavoidable and/or desirable imperfect competition and avoidable and socially undesirable imperfect competition.

6. What is the basis for believing that optimum resource allocation is more closely approximated under imperfect competition with free international trade than in isolation?

7. In what respects may imperfect competition increase the volume of trade?

8. List the chief monopolistic practices and devices that prevent realizing the benefits of international trade.

9. What is the economic basis for international monopolistic price discrimination?

10. Show how international trade increases the competitiveness of national market structures.

Chapter 12 INTERNATIONAL CARTELS

International cartels should not be conceived of as a specific form of business organization; the term, rather, is loosely applicable to a wide variety of arrangements among producers of the same, or similar, commodities in different countries. One authority has distinguished three major forms which international cartels assume: (*a*) the *association*—which resembles the well-known national trade association that engages in restrictive practices and which is expressed in a more or less formal agreement or adhesion to common rules and regulations; (*b*) the *patent-license agreement*—which is a market-sharing arrangement based upon patents or patent licenses held by the participants; and (*c*) the *combine*—which unites competitors in different countries under a common ownership or management.[1]

THE EXTENT OF CARTELIZATION

It is difficult to assess the quantitative significance of international cartels for international trade, for there is no way of determining what the volume or direction of trade would be in their absence. The extent of cartelization in the international field has been variously estimated. "According to League of Nations and other official statistics, at least thirty-two per cent of all international trade was under some form of 'marketing control' in 1937."[2] Other estimates of the total volume of world trade subject to some

---

[1] See the monograph of Corwin D. Edwards, *Economic and Political Aspects of International Cartels* (Washington, D.C., 1946; prepared for the Kilgore Committee of the U.S. Senate on War Mobilization, 78th Cong., 2d sess.) , pp. 2–7. Unless otherwise specified, all examples in the text are drawn from this monograph.

[2] Fritz Machlup, "The Nature of the International Cartel Problem," in Corwin D. Edwards and Others, *A Cartel Policy for the United Nations* (New York: Columbia University Press, 1945) , p. 11.

degree of cartel control range from 40 to 50 percent; one author considers 42 percent as a "minimum" for the period between 1924 and 1937.[3] On the basis of very incomplete data, the U.S. Department of Justice enumerated 179 international cartels which were in effect in 1939, of which 109 included American enterprises.[4]

The list of commodities which have been affected by international cartel arrangements is too long to be included here. But it should be mentioned that nearly all branches of industry and all stages of production are represented. Among raw materials affected are important industrial metals, such as steel, copper, zinc, lead, tin, aluminum, mercury, magnesite, and platinum, and nonmetallic minerals, such as petroleum, phosphates, potash, nitrates, sulfur, and cement. Cartelized manufactured products have included chemicals and pharmaceuticals, dyestuffs, electrical appliances, machines, surgical instruments, wagons and locomotives, plastics, explosives, and even such items as felt hats, safety pins, and children's toys. (Important foodstuffs—coffee, tea, sugar, meat, and so on—have also been subject to some form of international marketing control, but often the control has been more in the nature of a commodity agreement than a cartel proper.)

Official international recognition of restrictive private international business arrangements as one of the chief barriers to an expansion of world trade was granted by the Havana Charter, which included an article on "Restrictive Business Practices." The first paragraph of this article stated:

> Each Member of the ITO shall take appropriate measures and shall cooperate with the Organization to prevent, on the part of private or public commercial enterprises, business practices affecting international trade which restrain competition, limit access to markets, or foster monopolistic control, whenever such practices have harmful effects on the expansion of production or trade. . . .

Later in this chapter we shall see how the Havana Charter proposed to deal with the cartel problem.

While international cartels are probably not so significant as tariffs, quotas, and exchange controls, nonetheless they must be counted as one of the major obstacles to free international trade.

---

[3] Edward S. Mason, *Controlling World Trade* (New York: McGraw-Hill Book Co., 1946), p. 26, footnote.

[4] Corwin D. Edwards, "International Cartels as Obstacles to International Trade," *American Economic Review,* Supplement (March, 1944), p. 330.

WHY ARE CARTELS FORMED?

Each cartel has its own background and history, which makes it impossible to state reasons for the formation of cartels which are equally applicable to all. In many cases, especially of raw material cartels, agreed-upon production, marketing, and price policies were the outgrowth during the interwar years of difficulties caused by war-created excess capacity.[5] Cartels have also been attributed to eras of depression. Indeed, it is safe to say that any maladjustments which threaten existing producers with contracting markets and unstable prices encourage cooperative efforts to protect vested positions. Other factors could be mentioned which create a favorable atmosphere or incentive for the development of cartels—for example, protective tariffs, which make it easier for producers to divide up the world market and pursue differential price policies; the economies of mass production, which keep the number of producers small and make entry into the industries difficult; and patent laws, which give exclusive rights to the use of new processes and open the way to control over other firms through patent-license agreements.

Reduce Competition and Increase Profits

Whatever the background out of which particular cartels develop, however, there is one central feature which they all have in common: they all seek to reduce, control, or avoid the forces of free-market competition. We may go still further and say that all cartels have essentially the same ultimate objective: to procure a higher rate of profits for their members than would otherwise be realized. In some cases it might be more accurate to qualify this by saying that the objective is to assure *more stable* profits and markets, though in the last analysis it is difficult to distinguish, over the long run, between a more stable and a higher average rate of net return.

All business enterprises attempt to maximize their profits; this is not to be condemned, for it is an essential part of a free-market mechanism for allocating resources. But international cartels, like domestic monopolies, seek to obtain profits which in a free and competitive market would be reduced by the entry of new firms and

---

[5] This is given as the "main reason" for the formation of raw-material cartels in *International Cartels: A League of Nations Memorandum* (United Nations, Department of Economic Affairs, 1947), p. 5.

the expansion of output. The ability of a cartel to achieve its prime objective depends, therefore, upon the degree of control which it exercises over total output and its success in keeping outside competition to a minimum. It is for this reason that an international cartel must necessarily control the internal market for the product in each of the participants' countries. In the event that there is effective competition from producers in other countries, it is not unusual for such competition to be reduced or eliminated with the help of the members' governments in the form of tariffs, quotas, or other public import restrictions. In many countries, such, until recently, as Germany and Great Britain, cartels not only are legal but have been encouraged and protected by the state.

The problem of controlling competition is a serious one for cartels. The more successful the cartel is in reaping higher-than-competitive profits, the greater is the incentive for "outsiders" to break into the market. Some of the techniques employed to forestall this contingency will be described later. Less easy to meet is the constant threat of competition from other products which are more or less close substitutes for the cartelized article. As in the case of any monopoly, domestic or international, the ability to exploit the market is greater, the more inelastic is the demand for the product. But the larger the number of substitutes produced outside the control of the cartel, the more elastic will tend to be the demand for the cartel's product.

CARTEL TECHNIQUES

We are now ready to consider the major devices employed by international cartels to overcome the obstacles mentioned and to achieve their central objective of cashing in on monopoly profits.

Price Policies

Profits per unit of output are the difference between average costs of production—including the "normal" or average rate of return on the factors owned by the firm and on any management services rendered by the owners—and sales price. Theoretically, therefore, the rate of profits can be increased either by lowering costs of production through greater efficiency or by raising the sales price. The great social virtue of competition is that only the first method is open to the firm, sales price being a parameter, or constant, which each firm must accept, since it is unable to change it. Cartels are not excluded from the possibility of enlarging profits by reducing costs, and it would be inaccurate to deny that in some instances this has been done—through, for example, the pooling of research facilities and the exchange of technological information.

Monopoly Prices. The history of cartel practices, however, would seem to justify the conclusion that price raising has generally been preferred to cost reducing, not out of any nefarious delight in being antisocial, but rather because of its greater simplicity and expediency. Although the price policies pursued by cartels have greatly varied, one authority concludes that "the typical purpose and effect of cartelization is to set prices higher than would prevail under competition, to reduce them as seldom as possible and to raise them further whenever opportunity permits."[6]

It is difficult to measure precisely the effects of cartels upon prices, but there are some clear-cut cases where the evidence is unmistakable. One of these, though perhaps extreme, concerns tungsten carbide, a hard-metal composition extensively used in machine tools requiring wear-resistant surfaces. In 1927–28, an American company, under an agreement with its German competitor, was given control of the sale price of tungsten carbide in the United States. Before this agreement, the price in the United States was $50 per pound; afterward, the price ranged, during the 1930's, from $225 to $453 per pound, and in 1940 it was still at a minimum of $205. After an indictment under the antitrust laws in April, 1942, the price of tungsten carbide fell to a range of from $25 to $45 per pound.

Price Discrimination. Besides maintaining higher-than-competitive prices, cartels often result in different prices being charged in different markets. This type of price discrimination is most likely to develop when sales territories are allotted among the cartel members (see pages 261–63 for a description of territorial allotments). Thus, under the Incandescent Electric Lamp Cartel, which provided for the division of markets and the fixing of prices in home territories by the quota participants, the retail prices of 25-, 45-, and 60-watt bulbs in 1938 were, respectively, 32, 59, and 70 cents in Holland; 30, 36, and 48 cents in Germany; 23, 27, and 33 cents in Sweden; and 15 cents for all three types in the United States.[7] The

---

[6] Edwards, *Economic and Political Aspects of International Cartels,* p. 12.

[7] U.S. Tariff Commission, Report No. 133, Ser. II, *Incandescent Electric Lamps* (Washington, D.C., 1939), p. 49.

mutual protection of markets by the members of the first international steel cartel made it possible for prices of steel products to be kept about twice as high in Germany as the Belgian export price. An example of domestic price discrimination made possible by control over the home market granted under an international cartel arrangement is in dental plastics. At one time the latter sold in the United States for 85 cents per pound to the price-elastic commercial molders' market and for $45 per pound to the price-inelastic dental market.

Price Wars. Finally, cartel practices also include the temporary reduction of prices as a means of preventing or destroying outside competition. The attempt in 1925 of a German explosives company to encroach upon the powder monopoly enjoyed by American companies in Mexico was met by the threat of a price war. In a similar fashion, the plans of an Argentine concern to obtain a larger share of the sulfuric acid market in 1936 were forcefully opposed by the Argentine joint subsidiary of the leading American and British producers. Besides promising that its existing share of the market would be maintained, "quite irrespective of the level to which prices might decline during the ensuing period of competition," the entrenched company further indicated its resolve "to bring about a reduction in acid prices by progressive stages to the point where that business would no longer provide a constant invitation to others to enter the same field."[8]

In their efforts to raise prices to the level which yields the highest net return and to foreclose the possibility of price competition among their members, cartels sometimes resort to direct price-fixing agreements. Implicit in all attempts at price-fixing, however, is control over output—for, given the demand for a commodity, the price at which it can be sold depends upon the quantity offered for sale. Instead of direct price-fixing agreements, therefore, cartels are usually more concerned with *indirectly* supporting higher prices through limiting production and offerings on the market. The most usual methods of accomplishing this end will be described in the sections which follow.

Restriction of Output

Output and Sales Quotas. The most direct way of limiting output is to set quotas or limits on the amounts which each of the

---

[8] Quoted from Edwards, *Economic and Political Aspects of International Cartels,* p. 11.

members of the cartel may produce or sell. To be effective, this requires that the cartel have the power to enforce output regulations by imposing sanctions or penalties of one kind or another upon fractious members. (It also presupposes that the members of the cartel as a group account for a large enough percentage of total output to preclude effective outside competition.) Thus the attempt in 1929 of a private association of tin producers to curtail production failed because of policy disagreements and lack of adequate authority to enforce regulations. As a result, an International Tin Committee was formed in 1931 under the sponsorship of several interested governments, and restriction of output was made compulsory by law.

One of the best-known examples of cartel output restrictions is provided by the international steel cartel. The first such cartel was formed in 1926 among the iron and steel producers of Germany, Luxembourg, Belgium, the Saar, and France. The total amount of crude steel to be produced was agreed upon periodically and was then distributed among the countries according to predetermined quotas. To insure compliance with the production quotas thus established, a system of penalties and compensations was devised, under which a $4 fine was levied on each ton of steel produced in excess of the quota, while $2 was paid by the cartel for every ton below the quota, up to 10 percent of the permissible production.[9]

The first steel cartel ultimately broke down, partly because of outside competition, notably from British and American producers, who were not members of the cartel, but mainly because of the great contraction in the market brought on by the world depression. A second cartel was formed in 1933, with the subsequent adhesion of other national groups, including Great Britain in 1935 and the United States in 1938. About 90 percent of world trade in iron and steel was brought under the cartel's jurisdiction in 1937. As in the previous agreement, production quotas were established; but as market conditions improved, limitations on crude-steel production were eliminated. The outbreak of war ended the cartel.

Restriction of Productive Capacity. Besides setting output and sales quotas, cartels sometimes restrict output by artificially limiting the capacity to produce. The American capability to produce magnesium—a very light metal, in many uses substitutable for aluminum—was limited before the last war by cartel arrangements. In 1927 the Aluminum Company of America (Alcoa) reached an

---

[9] George W. Stocking and Myron W. Watkins, *Cartels in Action* (New York: Twentieth Century Fund, 1946), pp. 183–84.

agreement with the Dow Chemical Company that Alcoa's subsidiary, the American Magnesium Corporation, would cease to produce, purchasing all its requirements from Dow. Later, to prevent the chief German producer, I. G. Farben, from establishing magnesium plants in the United States, Alcoa and I. G. Farben pooled their magnesium patents in the Magnesium Development Corporation. Under this agreement, U.S. production was limited to a maximum of 4,000 tons yearly. Subsequently, Dow agreed to furnish the requirements of the American Magnesium Corporation at less than market prices, in return for which the patent pool abandoned plans to construct a magnesium plant. "The effect of the series of contracts was to close the existing plant which had been competing with Dow and to prevent the development of new capacity operating under the I. G. Farben patents."[10]

Patent-License Restrictions. Patents, by giving an exclusive right to manufacture a given product to the patent-holder, obviously make it possible in many instances to limit output through provisions included in patent licenses. A study by the Office of the Alien Property Custodian of a sample of 333 international patent contracts in effect at the outbreak of the last war revealed that 43 percent contained restrictions on the fields of use.

In the patent-license agreement between the Texas Company and Ruhrchemie A.G., the American concern was limited in its annual aggregate production to not more than 1 million tons of primary petroleum products in any or all of its plants. By the terms of another contract, the Texas Company was granted the right to produce $166,666\frac{2}{3}$ tons per annum of primary products by hydrocarbon synthesis under the synthesis patent rights of Ruhrchemie.

In an agreement between Rohm and Haas of Philadelphia and I. G. Farben, the former was forbidden to use the chemical products covered by the license to make photographic articles, dyestuffs, artificial rubber, pharmaceutical articles, abrasives, and celluloid-like masses or products made therefrom, but received patent protection in certain other fields.

Buying-Up of Patents. One of the common devices practiced by cartels to prevent the development of competing products is the buying-up of patents. This is illustrated in a patent agreement between International General Electric Company and Allgemeine Elektrizitaets Gesellschaft, relating to electrical apparatus. The agreement provided, in part, that

---

[10] Edwards, *Economic and Political Aspects of International Cartels,* p. 31.

when an invention relating to such fields is offered to either party with due notice from the other party that such invention is of particular value to the party offering the same, the party to whom it is offered agrees to use its best endeavors to obtain such patent or patents in all countries of its exclusive territory, so that, as far as the patenting of such inventions is concerned, third parties may be restrained from manufacturing within its exclusive territory for export into the nonexclusive territory.[11]

A similar example is provided by Du Pont's application for a patent on the use of chlorisopropyl benzines. Apparently Du Pont discovered that these materials, provided that they became available at sufficiently low cost, constituted a competitive threat in their use as dielectrics. Hence the patent application was filed "as an insurance application to secure what protection might be available but without expectation of future commercial use."[12]

Allocation of Markets

One of the most common techniques of cartels to maintain prices and avoid competition is the division of the market among the participating members. Market allotments may be made on either a product or a geographic base, or both. There is perhaps no clearer example of how international cartels may subvert the foundations of international trade than through such arrangements.

The underlying philosophy of the market allocation technique was well expressed in a report to the executive committee of a leading American company in 1925:

It is sound business procedure to restrict ourselves to a certain degree to those markets in which we have advantage over foreign competitors so long as those competitors restrict themselves to other markets in which they have economic advantages.[13]

The logical end result of this philosophy, if extensively carried out in practice, would be the breaking-down of the world economy into virtually isolated economic blocs.

The world chemical cartel offers one of the best examples of territorial allocation of markets. In an agreement in 1933 between Bayer Company, of Leverkusen, Germany, and Winthrop Chemi-

---

[11] Quoted by Edwards, *ibid.*, p. 31.

[12] *Ibid.*, p. 32.

[13] *Ibid.*, p. 19.

cal Company, the market in the United States and Canada for certain pharmaceutical and chemical products was reserved to the American company, in return for the latter's promise to stay out of all other markets. Similar arrangements were made between Imperial Chemical Industries (British) and Du Pont involving the allocation of markets for 20 or more different types of products. With certain exceptions, Du Pont obtained exclusive rights in the United States and Central America, Imperial in the British Empire, except Canada, while the Canadian, Brazilian, and Argentine markets were to be exploited through jointly owned subsidiaries. Under the alkali cartel agreement, the Belgian Solvay Company and I. G. Farben held exclusive rights to the European Continent, the American Alkali Export Association and a California association obtained rights to North America, and Imperial Chemicals held rights to most British possessions. South America and certain other areas were shared, in agreed-upon proportions, between the British and American producers.

The markets for motion-picture recording and reproducing instruments were divided by an agreement in 1930 among the principal American film producers and distributors, subsidiaries of American Telephone and Telegraph and the Radio Corporation of America, three German electrical manufacturing companies, and a Dutch company. The German companies were designated exclusive agents to make, use, sell, and lease such equipment and to license recording apparatus in Germany, Austria, Hungary, Switzerland, Czechoslovakia, the Scandinavian countries, Yugoslavia, Romania, Bulgaria, Holland, and the Dutch East Indies; the American companies in the United States and Canada, Australia, New Zealand, India, the Straits Settlements, and Russia.

In a series of contracts between the International Business Machines Corporation and manufacturers in other countries, territorial restrictions were imposed on the manufacture of business machines. For example, under a contract in 1934 between IBM and a French concern, the latter agreed that it would not

operate or do business directly or indirectly outside the territory herein designated . . . and [would] make and use every proper and lawful effort to enforce the condition that none of the said products [should] be taken out or used outside of its own territory without the written consent of IBM.[14]

---

[14] *Ibid.*, p. 22.

A reciprocal promise was made by IBM to keep out of the French company's territory.

Summary

Without attempting a complete cataloging, we have listed and briefly illustrated the major devices used by international cartels to achieve their central purpose of reducing competition and increasing profits. It should be fairly obvious that in their efforts to restrict output, raise prices, allocate territories, and suppress competition, international cartels undermine the functioning of the free price mechanism in allocating the world's scarce productive resources and reduce the adaptability of national economies to changing conditions. More specifically, cartels reduce the volume of international trade, distort its pattern, and obstruct its responsiveness to changes in relative costs and demand.

PUBLIC POLICY TOWARD CARTELS

There are two extreme attitudes regarding international cartels. The first, adopted, needless to say, by most cartel members, is that cartels perform a useful social function in leading to more stable markets, averting "ruinous" price wars and "cutthroat" competition. The other attitude is an uncompromising condemnation of cartels and all they stand for, accompanied by a call for their outright prohibition. In between these two extremes is the more moderate point of view that, while indeed cartels generally have undesirable effects on public welfare which justify some measure of control and regulation, it is neither possible nor desirable to attempt their complete abolition. Let us examine in more detail each of these attitudes.

Preserve Cartels

The defense of cartels has been cogently stated by Lord McGowan of Imperial Chemical Industries. In remarks made before the House of Lords in 1944, McGowan said, in part:

The purpose of those [international cartel] agreements is, in the main, to regulate but not to abolish competition. They can help to stabilize prices at a reasonable level. . . . They can lead to a rapid improvement in technique and a reduction in costs, which in turn, with enlightened administration of industry, can provide the basis of lower prices to consumers. They can spread the benefits of inventions from one country to another by exchanging research results, by the cross-licensing of patents and by the provision of the important know-how in the working of these patents. They can provide a medium for the orderly expansion of world trade and can make a substantial contribution —and this is important—to the difficult problems of the postwar readjustment of production in countries greatly affected by the war. They can also assist in providing much greater stability of employment.[15]

This is obviously an idealized statement of the benefits which international cartels can provide. The history of cartels does not, however, support the conclusion that these benefits are, in fact, provided. For example, two of the chief claims on behalf of cartels are that they exert a stabilizing influence on prices and that they facilitate adjustment to structural imbalance. But if past experience is any guide, neither of these alleged benefits is in fact generally realized through cartel arrangements.

It is nearly inevitable that an organization which represents producers will, if it attempts to stabilize prices, set prices high enough to keep marginal, high-cost members in business. The likely consequence is to induce existing low-cost producers to try to obtain a larger share of the market and to encourage "outsiders" to break into the market, followed by a later sharp fall in price.

The efforts of cartels to solve the problem of excess capacity have also rarely been successful. Excess capacity, instead of being reduced by elimination of high-cost producers, is more often preserved indefinitely; and protection of the least efficient members of the cartel is achieved at the cost of the general efficiency of the industry. In fact, it has not been uncommon for the high-price policy of the cartel to stimulate new investment in the industry and thereby to increase surplus capacity still further.

Abolish Cartels

The argument here is simple and straightforward: since cartels, as we have shown, have the effect of restricting output, raising prices artificially, destroying or muffling competition, isolating markets, and otherwise interfering with the optimum use of resources, their prohibition is justified. The counterargument that cartels prevent cutthroat competition is regarded as a euphemism for main-

---

[15] Quoted in Mason, *op. cit.,* footnote, pp. 19–20.

taining higher prices than free competition would bring about. The price "stability" which cartels allegedly promote is in reality limited to the products of members and has the general effect of reducing employment opportunities and of shifting the burdens of cyclical fluctuations to the more competitive sectors of the economy. The notion that cartels facilitate adjustment in the case of overexpanded or depressed industries through temporary restrictive arrangements is more often than not belied in practice; restrictions of output tend to become permanent, and inefficient producers are permitted to remain in operation. The exchange of technological knowledge and processes and patent-license agreements, far from encouraging new and better products at lower costs, more usually serve as weapons in the drive to forestall innovations and suppress potential competition.

Even if the indictment of cartels as presented above is accepted, however, the conclusion that they should be abolished outright does not necessarily follow. It would be overly optimistic to assume that the outlawing of cartels would be equivalent to replacing them with free, competitive markets. In many industries no more than a few firms can exist if the economies of large-scale production are to be realized. Outlawing cartels would not change the basic reason for the absence of pure competition in such industries. Similarly, if the stimulus which patents give to technological advance is not to be sacrificed, some firms will continue to be in a monopolistic position whether or not there are cartels.

Moreover, cartels have been in part a natural market response to very real problems, such as excess capacity following unusual expansion during wars, severe fluctuations in prices, especially of primary products, and cyclical fluctuations in demand. Until something is done publicly to alleviate the problems which producers have tried to meet through private arrangements, the case for abolishing cartels is weaker than it otherwise would be.

Regulate Cartels

If neither the continuance of cartels as they have operated in the past nor their outright abolition is accepted as public policy, there remains only their public regulation or control in some fashion.

There are also difficulties encountered here. What kind, and how severe, should the controls be? How are they to be enforced, especially in view of different national legal and administrative concepts? It is safe to predict that no completely satisfactory answer, generally agreed to, will be found to these and similar questions. It is significant, however, that one possible answer was included in the Havana Charter of the ITO, even though it has never been implemented.

Briefly, this is how the Havana Charter proposed to meet the problem of international cartels. The following restrictive business practices are specified (Paragraph 3, Article 46) :

a) Fixing prices, terms or conditions to be observed in dealing with others in the purchase, sale or lease of any product;

b) Excluding enterprises from, or allocating or dividing, any territorial market or field of business activity, or allocating customers, or fixing sales quotas or purchase quotas;

c) Discriminating against particular enterprises;

d) Limiting production or fixing production quotas;

e) Preventing by agreement the development or application of technology or invention whether patented or unpatented;

f) Extending the use of rights under patents, trade marks or copyrights granted by any Member to matters which, according to its laws and regulations, are not within the scope of such grants, or to products or conditions of production, use or sale which are likewise not the subject of such grants;

g) Any similar practices which the Organization may declare, by a majority of two-thirds of the Members present and voting, to be restrictive business practices.

Each member of the ITO would be obligated to insure that private and public commercial enterprises do not engage in the above practices. In addition, every member would have the right to present a complaint to the ITO that in a particular instance a prohibited practice exists. The ITO would then investigate the complaint, and, if it were found justified, would request each member concerned to take remedial action.

The Havana Charter includes an entirely separate chapter providing for intergovernmental commodity agreements to meet the special difficulties which arise in the production and international marketing of primary products.

Whether ultimately some such scheme for controlling international cartels as envisaged in the Havana Charter will come into force is impossible to foretell. (Considerable opposition was expressed in some quarters to the Charter proposals, especially those concerning intergovernmental commodity agreements, which, it was charged, amounted to the promotion of international cartels under government auspices. This much, however, can be said: international recognition has been given to the fact that international cartels, like public barriers to trade, prevent the full realization of the benefits of international trade and warrant public regulation or control.

THE INTERNATIONAL CARTEL POLICY OF THE UNITED STATES

Monopolies and other forms of restraint of trade have been illegal in the United States ever since the enactment of the Sherman Antitrust law in 1890. An exception, however, was provided in the Webb-Pomerene Act (1918), which permits an association of exporters to limit, or even eliminate, competition among themselves *in the export trade.* Presumably the purpose of the Webb-Pomerene Act is to put American exporters on an equal footing with foreign monopolies in exploiting export markets. The act does not, however, legalize the participation of American companies or associations in international cartels, which are still subject, so far as they affect the foreign commerce of the United States, to the Sherman Act.

It is, nevertheless, somewhat anomalous that the Webb-Pomerene law permits American companies to engage in activities for export purposes which they are forbidden by the Sherman Act to practice in domestic trade. The philosophy of the Webb-Pomerene Act appears to be defensive protection against foreign monopolies, which are in many countries either tolerated or legalized. On the other hand, there can be little doubt that permitting export associations to be formed facilitates participation in international cartels.[16] Notwithstanding its illegality under American law, the fact is that American firms have participated in international cartels and have exerted perhaps as much influence in the latter as those of any other country.[17] High tariff barriers, a patent system which encourages monopolistic practices, and lax corporate charter laws in some states are, in conjunction with only limited success in enforcing the pro-

---

[16] See "Consensus Report on the Webb-Pomerene Law" by a committee of the American Economic Association, *American Economic Review,* Vol. 37 (December, 1947), p. 852.

[17] Theodore J. Kreps, "Experience with Unilateral Action toward International Cartels," in Edwards and Others, *A Cartel Policy for the United Nations.*

visions of the Sherman Antitrust law, responsible for this situation.

It may be, as has been argued, that, so long as foreign monopolies are allowed and even encouraged, the United States has no recourse other than defensive protection against their abuses. There may be merit in this view if one accepts the premise that international cartels are here to stay. This attitude is not, however, in harmony with the notion that there should be a positive approach by the United States as a world leader in the reduction of barriers to trade and in the promotion of an expanding volume of international trade and investment.

By a more vigorous enforcement of the Sherman Act as it applies in both domestic and international trade, by a reduction in tariffs, and by repeal of the Webb-Pomerene Act, the United States undoubtedly could go a long way by unilateral action in reducing restrictive cartel practices. As in so many other fields, however, the best hope for successfully combating international cartels lies in coordinated international efforts. This was recognized by the United States government when it included in its draft proposal for an international trade organization provisions for eliminating restrictive business practices.

RECOMMENDED READING

EDWARDS, CORWIN D. *Economic and Political Aspects of International Cartels.* U.S. Senate, Subcommittee on War Mobilization of the Committee on Military Affairs, 78th Cong., 2d sess. Washington, D.C.: U.S. Government Printing Office, 1946.

——— AND OTHERS. *A Cartel Policy for the United Nations.* New York: Columbia University Press, 1945.

HEXNER, ERWIN. *International Cartels.* Chapel Hill: University of North Carolina Press, 1946.

A more or less sympathetic approach to cartels. Includes numerous case studies.

MASON, EDWARD S. *Controlling World Trade.* New York: McGraw-Hill Book Co., 1946.

STOCKING, GEORGE W., and WATKINS, MYRON W. *Cartels in Action.* New York: Twentieth Century Fund, 1946.

Case studies of some important cartels.

UNITED NATIONS, DEPARTMENT OF ECONOMIC AFFAIRS. *International Cartels.* Lake Success, N.Y., 1947.

STUDY QUESTIONS

1. Define what is meant by an "international cartel." How does an international cartel differ from a domestic monopolistic arrangement?

2. Mention some of the conditions which favor the formation of international cartels.

3. What common characteristic is shared by all international cartels?

4. Show the relationship which exists between international cartels and domestic monopolies.

5. Why are competitive producers under greater pressure to increase their efficiency than ordinarily is the case with producers participating in a cartel?

6. How would you describe in general terms the price policies typically followed by the members of international cartels?

7. What is meant by "international price discrimination"? Why cannot competitive producers in a free market practice international price discrimination?

8. Name some of the devices employed by cartels to limit the total output of cartelized commodities. In this connection, compare the socially desirable aspects of international patents and their use for restrictive purposes.

9. Compare the results of international trade under cartel arrangements providing for the territorial allocation of markets with those produced by competitive trading.

10. Does historical experience with international cartels justify the assertion of their protagonists that they tend to stabilize prices? In any event, do you regard the stabilization of individual commodity prices as a desirable objective?

11. In your opinion, do international cartel policies facilitate, or hinder, balance-of-payments adjustments? Give your reasons.

12. What are the arguments for and against the outright abolition of cartels? What possible middle ground is there with respect to cartel policy?

13. Describe the legal status of international cartels under United States law.

14. What is the apparent purpose of the Webb-Pomerene Act?

15. How would you suggest that the problem in international cartels be approached?

PART III

International Monetary Relations

The chapters in this part describe the problems arising from the existence of separate national monetary systems. These problems were ignored in the preceding chapters by the device of postulating freely fluctuating exchange rates and the assumption of continuous monetary equilibrium automatically produced by market forces. However, international monetary relations are a prolific source of problems and demand thorough exploration.

| Chapter | INTERNATIONAL PAYMENTS |
| 13 | |

Up to this point, very little attention has been paid to the monetary aspects of international relations. In discussing the pure theory of trade, we assumed away the problems connected with monetary relations in order to concentrate on the real (substantive) content and effects of trade and factor movements. In the long run, these real aspects of international economic relations have the greatest significance.

However, the international as well as the domestic exchange of goods and services and movement of capital take place within the context of a monetary framework. How efficiently the system works in real terms heavily depends upon the efficiency of the monetary system. A smoothly functioning and stable monetary system performs a tremendously important facilitative role, creating the framework indispensable for attainment of the optimum volume and pattern of trade and capital movements. A malfunctioning and unstable monetary system inevitably interposes obstacles to realizing the maximum potentials of trade and capital movements. Unstable monetary relations raise problems of their own and, indeed, are the source of most of the short-run concerns of countries in their international economic relations.

Preparatory to an exploration of the international monetary system and the problems it raises, this chapter considers the elementary nature of international payments.

THE MEANS OF MAKING PAYMENT: FOREIGN EXCHANGE

The most obvious difference between domestic and international monetary relations is the presence of a single monetary unit in the former and a multiplicity of monetary units in the latter. The world today is divided into well over one hundred independent national states; there are very nearly as many national monetary systems. Yet, despite this great diversity of systems, superimposed upon them is an international monetary system, consisting of the institutions, arrangements, and practices through which international payments are made. As we shall see later, an international monetary system may take a variety of forms. However, they all have in common the basic purpose of transferring purchasing power from one currency[1] to another. The problem of transferring purchasing power internationally arises out of the presence of different national monetary systems. If there were a world-unified monetary system, similar to the system in effect in each national economy, making international payments would not involve problems any different from those relating to making payments from one region to another within the same country.

Since the same currency unit is used in different parts of a given country, domestic payments pose no difficulty. If a New Yorker purchases beef from Texas or an automobile from Detroit he pays in dollars, which is what the seller wants. But if he buys beef from Argentina or an automobile from France, two different currency units enters into the transaction—that of the buyer (dollars) and that of the seller (Argentine pesos or French francs).

How is payment made when different currencies are involved? The various instruments devised for this purpose are known collectively as "foreign exchange." It is not necessary to describe here the technical aspects of these instruments, such as cable and mail transfers and bills of exchange.[2] Suffice it to say that they constitute means of making payments across national currency boundaries. Thus, for example, if you had to remit 10 pounds sterling to England to purchase books, you would acquire sterling foreign exchange in this amount, probably in the form of a bank draft which you would mail to the British publisher.

Foreign exchange is bought and sold in organized markets through dealers. Foreign exchange dealers—in the United States, special departments of certain large banks—sell foreign exchange in any currency desired by a customer and purchase any foreign exchange offered to them. Purchases and sales are, of course, at specified prices known as rates of exchange. In the United States, rates

---

[1] "Currency" is used in this discussion as a shorthand expression for "national monetary unit."

[2] The interested reader may consult Morris T. Rosenthal, *Techniques of International Trade.* New York: McGraw-Hill Book Co., 1950.

of exchange are quoted in terms of cents or dollars per unit of foreign currency. For example, the rate of exchange on the pound at the time you pay for your British books may be $2.395. A £10 draft would therefore cost $23.95 (plus a small commission charge). How exchange rates are determined is considered later.

SOURCES OF FOREIGN EXCHANGE

The presence of a foreign exchange market where means of making payments from one currency into another are available for purchase and sale relieves individuals and business firms of the most immediate problems connected with foreign payments. Except for the special problems arising out of the possibility of variations in foreign exchange rates, making or receiving foreign payments is no more complicated for individual transactions than are domestic monetary settlements.

Even though the question of how foreign payments are made and received has been answered for the individual buyer and seller, it certainly has not been answered yet for the market as a whole. An individual buys foreign exchange from a dealer—but where has the dealer acquired it to sell? Another individual sells foreign exchange to a dealer—but what does the dealer do with it? These questions are clearly interconnected and the answers to them as well.

Let us first consider the sources of the foreign exchange that are dealers' stock-in-trade. Initially we will assume that the international economic relations of each country are confined exclusively to commodity trade, an assumption that later will be relaxed. In this case, there is only one source of foreign exchange: The foreign currency proceeds from commodity exports. Suppose that during some given period U.S. exports consist of the sale to France of machinery for 500,000 French francs. The U.S. exporter wishes to obtain dollars because his costs, taxes, and profits are all expressed in dollars. The exporter therefore sells the franc proceeds[3] of his export to a New York bank foreign exchange dealer. How many dollars are received for the francs depends upon the rate of exchange, which we will assume is $0.20 per franc. Hence, the exporter is paid $100,000 for the 500,000 francs. The exporter is now

---

[3] The francs should not be thought of literally as franc currency but rather as some kind of foreign exchange instrument, such as a bank draft. If the latter is used, the French importer purchases a franc draft from his bank, the draft being an order to pay a specified amount of money (in the case at hand, 500,000 francs) to the U.S. exporter or his order.

out of the picture, having finally received payment in his own currency. (The French importer at no time had a foreign exchange problem, since he paid for the machinery in his own currency, francs.) The French franc proceeds of the export are in the possession of the New York bank. What does the bank do with the francs? In the first instance, the bank merely adds the francs to its deposits held in a French correspondent bank. Before explaining this action, let us summarize what has occurred so far by referring to changes in the T accounts of the French importer's bank and the U.S. exporter's bank:

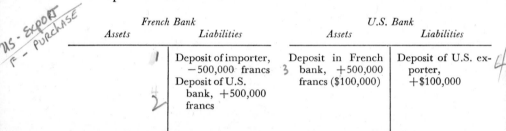

French Bank		U.S. Bank	
Assets	Liabilities	Assets	Liabilities
	Deposit of importer, −500,000 francs	Deposit in French bank, +500,000 francs ($100,000)	Deposit of U.S. exporter, +$100,000
	Deposit of U.S. bank, +500,000 francs		

For simplicity, it is assumed that the French importer's bank is also the correspondent of the U.S. exporter's bank. Observing first the French bank, we see that the importer's account has been drawn down in making payment for the machinery, while the franc deposit account of the American exporter's bank has been increased by the same amount. On the American side, the dollar deposit account of the exporter has been increased from the sale to the bank of French francs, while the franc deposit of the bank with its French correspondent has increased by the same amount.

An important effect of the transactions, the full significance of which is examined in a subsequent discussion, is a change in each country's domestically held stock of money in the form of bank deposits. The total stock of money in France has not changed, but there has been a switch in ownership from a domestic resident, the importer, to a nonresident, the U.S. bank. In the United States, the export has resulted in an increase in the total stock of domestic money, there having been an exchange between the exporter and his bank of francs for dollars.

Now we return to the question of why the U.S. bank was willing to purchase francs from the exporter. The reason is rather obvious: The bank is in the foreign exchange business, and foreign bank balances are its stock-in-trade. One principal way to acquire the "commodity" in which it deals is through purchasing it from exporters, who in turn have received it in payment from foreign importers. The bank needs foreign exchange balances to have available to sell, for an exchange dealer's profits are derived from the services rendered in providing a market for both buyers and sellers.

We have identified what is nearly always the largest source of foreign exchange to a country, namely, the export of commodities. Falling in the same category is the export of services. The sale to nonresidents of the services of transportation, tourism, insurance, capital funds (the services of which are measured in terms of interest and dividend receipts), and other so-called "invisible" items contributes in the same manner as commodity exports to the foreign exchange receipts of a country.

Besides the export of goods and services, there are other sources of foreign exchange receipts to a country. One of the more important of these is the inflow of foreign capital in the form of loans and investments. For example, when U.S. residents or the government loans or invests money in Canada, the Canadian economy receives U.S. dollars which, from its point of view, constitute foreign exchange.

Closely related to ordinary capital flows between countries is the special form of capital movement known as unilateral transfers. These differ from ordinary capital movements in that no interest payments or recovery of principal are involved. In short, they are in the nature of gifts or grants. Like capital receipts, a unilateral transfer into a country from abroad provides foreign exchange, unless it is directly in the form of commodities.

Finally, a country may acquire foreign exchange by selling special assets for which there is an established world market. The most important example of such special assets is monetary gold. Most countries have in their possession a certain amount of gold reserves which may be drawn upon if necessary to export in return for foreign exchange. The special role of gold in international monetary relations becomes clear later on. At the moment, we need only note that the sale of gold to other countries is one possible source of foreign exchange.

USES OF FOREIGN EXCHANGE

We have examined the various sources of foreign exchange that enter into a country's foreign exchange market. It is time now to look at the other side of the picture: the uses to which foreign exchange is put. Not surprisingly, we shall find that these are the exact counterparts of the sources.

Let us begin with the individual foreign exchange dealer, the New York bank in our previous example. The bank acquired 500,-000 French franc balances through purchasing them from a U.S. exporter of machinery to France. The bank is interested in foreign exchange balances for only one reason: to have them available to sell. Who, then, are its potential customers?

One clear possibility is importers of French goods. Suppose that an American firm wishes to purchase 500,000 francs worth of French perfume. To pay for the perfume, the firm must acquire this sum of franc foreign exchange, in the form, say, of a franc bank draft ordering a French bank to pay the sum to the French exporter. The draft may be purchased from the U.S. bank which had previously acquired francs from the exporter of machinery. At an exchange rate of $0.20 per franc, the American firm pays the bank $100,000 for 500,000 francs, and the bank's French correspondent pays the francs to the perfume exporter. The monetary results of these transactions are summarized below in terms of the T accounts of the two banks:

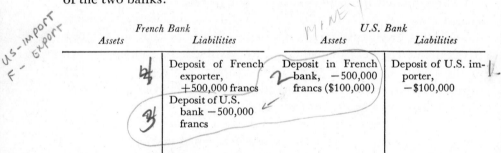

	French Bank			U.S. Bank	
Assets		*Liabilities*	*Assets*		*Liabilities*
		Deposit of French exporter, +500,000 francs	Deposit in French bank, −500,000 francs ($100,000)		Deposit of U.S. importer, −$100,000
		Deposit of U.S. bank −500,000 francs			

We note that these results are precisely the same as those produced in connection with the export of machinery from the United States, *except for the reversal of entries.* As in the earlier transaction, the export has led to an increase in the domestically held stock of money in the exporting country and a decrease in the stock of money in the importing country. The two transactions together canceled each other in both their foreign exchange and domestic monetary effects. Whereas the export of machinery from the United States increased the foreign exchange balances of the U.S. bank and the U.S. domestic money supply, the import of perfume used up the foreign balances and decreased the domestic supply of money. In France, the import of machinery decreased the domestically held supply of money and increased the foreign liabilities of the French bank, while the export of perfume increased the domestically held supply of money and decreased the bank's foreign liabilities.

It is clear from the above examples that the foreign exchange dealers—the American and French banks—served only as financial intermediaries, facilitating, but not basically altering, the transactions in goods. Conceivably, the foreign exchange market might have been circumvented entirely. The U.S. exporter of machinery could have been paid $100,000 by the importer of perfume, and the French exporter of perfume could have been paid 500,000 francs by the importer of machinery. Even though such procedures often would not be practical, they illustrate the fundamental nature of the more roundabout, and more efficient, methods of payment through organized foreign exchange markets.

While commodity imports are ordinarily the largest absorber of foreign exchange (just as commodity exports are the largest provider), foreign exchange is needed to make a variety of other foreign payments. The other transactions using foreign exchange are the precise counterparts of those providing it, discussed previously. A country uses foreign exchange to pay for the import of services (foreign travel, foreign transportation, and so on), to finance loans and investments in other lands, to make unilateral transfers to other countries, and to pay for any monetary gold acquired from foreigners.

RECOMMENDED READING

CRUMP, NORMAN. *The ABC of the Foreign Exchanges.* Rev. ed. London: Macmillan & Co., Ltd., 1957.

HOLMES, ALAN R., AND SCHOTT, FRANCIS H. *The New York Foreign Exchange Market.* New York: Federal Reserve Bank of New York, 1965.

SNIDER, DELBERT A. *International Monetary Relations,* chap. i. New York: Random House, Inc., 1966.

STUDY QUESTIONS

1. `Define the basic purpose of an international monetary system.
2. Compare the problem of making domestic payments with that of making foreign payments.
3. Define "foreign exchange."

4. Check the financial pages of a newspaper for the day's quotation of foreign exchange rates.

5. When the dollar rate of exchange on a foreign currency rises, what happens to the rate of exchange on the dollar in the foreign country?

6. Describe the nature of the business of foreign exchange dealers.

7. Describe several different kinds of transactions that provide foreign exchange in the market.

8. How does an import affect the domestically held supply of money? How does an export affect it?

9. If a U.S. resident were to purchase shares of stock from a resident of Switzerland, what kind of transaction in the foreign exchange market would this give rise to?

10. Show how if a country's imports just equal its exports the domestic monetary and foreign exchange effects of the trade cancel each other out.

Chapter 14 : THE BALANCE OF PAYMENTS

We have learned that in order to make international payments a country needs foreign exchange. Foreign exchange is provided by a variety of transactions, the main categories of which are the export of goods and services, an inflow of capital from abroad, unilateral transfer receipts, and gold exports. Foreign exchange is needed to pay for imported goods and services, to finance capital outflows and unilateral payments, and to pay for any gold imports. International monetary problems arise out of the relationship between these sources and uses of foreign exchange and their interconnection with domestic economic and monetary affairs.

The starting point for an analysis of these problems is the balance of payments. The balance of payments of a country is a summary record of all the international economic and financial transactions of the country during a specified period of time. A partial balance of payments includes the transactions between one country and a given number of other countries (one or more, but not all).

It is important to note that the balance of payments records transactions that take place over a particular period of time. If we want an instantaneous or "still" picture of a country's international economic position, the appropriate measure is not the balance of payments but rather the balance of international indebtedness. The latter is a balance sheet type of statement, showing, as of a given date, claims held by domestic residents against foreigners and vice versa. If claims against foreigners exceed obligations to foreigners, a country is said to be a net international creditor; in the opposite case, it is a net international debtor. In other words, the balance of international indebtedness shows the net results of past transactions on a country's international capital position. We are already familiar with this from our discussion in a previous chapter. By contrast, the balance of payments summarizes international transactions over a given period of time.

A balance of payments can be drawn up for any economic entity if relevant data are known: for an individual, household, community, region, or national economy. The *principles* of a balance of payments are the same in all these cases, although, of course, the content would vary considerably from one to the other. What these principles are we shall examine after having first given a more specific description of the makeup of an international balance of payments.

STRUCTURE OF THE BALANCE OF PAYMENTS

The major purpose of a balance of payments is to provide a summary statistical statement of the sources and uses of foreign exchange. Another way of putting it is to say that a balance of payments summarizes, on the one hand, the transactions of a country which create payment obligations to foreigners (i.e., nonresidents) and, on the other hand, the transactions which provide the means of settling these obligations. Clearly, a distinction between these kinds of transactions is called for.

Debit and Credit Entries

Any transaction of a country that requires a foreign payment or creates an obligation to make such payment is entered in the balance of payments as a *debit* or *payments* item. ("Payments" and "debits" are used interchangeably. A third designation is simply a negative sign.) Any transaction that provides foreign exchange to a country, or that discharges a foreign obligation of the country, is entered as a *credit* or *receipts* item. ("Receipts" and "credits" are used interchangeably. A third designation is a plus sign.) There are some transactions which do not involve an actual international payment or receipt but are included in the balance of payments for the sake of completeness. We shall refer to these at the appropriate time and indicate how they are identified as either debit or credit items.

A few examples will serve to clarify the distinction between debit and credit items in the balance of payments.

The import of goods and services is ordinarily the largest debit item and the export of goods and services the largest credit item in balances of payments. An import is a debit item, for it requires payment to the foreign exporter or creates an obligation to make

such payment. An export is a credit item, for it either leads to the
receipt of foreign exchange from the importing country or to the
creation of a claim for payment against the importing country.

Capital movements are a second source of international payments and receipts. Capital inflows into a country are credit items;
capital outflows are debit items. A capital inflow into a country
occurs if it receives loans or investments from abroad or if it liqui-
dates foreign assets. Thus, a loan by the U.S. government to the
British government constitutes a capital inflow into Britain and is
entered in the British balance of payments as a credit item since it
provides dollar foreign exchange. From the viewpoint of the
United States, the loan represents an outflow of capital and is entered as a debit item. The purchase and sale between residents and
nonresidents of evidences of debt or ownership are another form
capital movements may take. If U.S. residents purchase securities
from Canadian residents, this constitutes a capital movement from
the United States to Canada—a debit transaction for the United
States and a credit transaction for Canada. Still another form of
capital movements occurs when assets held in one country but
owned by the residents of another are acquired or liquidated. If
General Motors establishes a branch plant in Germany, this is a
foreign "direct" investment and appears as a capital outflow from
the United States, a debit entry in her balance of payments. On the
other hand, if a previously acquired foreign asset is sold to a nonresident, the capital flow is into the seller's country and is a credit
entry in her balance of payments.

A final category of capital movements that plays a special role in
the international monetary system includes changes in bank balances owned by nonresidents. An increase in foreign balances held
by the residents of a country represents a short-term capital outflow and therefore a debit in the country's balances of payments.
It is a debit transaction, for in acquiring or adding to bank balances held abroad the country is purchasing an asset which has to
be paid for. On the other hand, if a country draws down foreign
balances, a capital inflow (credit entry) occurs, for in this case the
country is in effect selling an asset which the foreign purchaser
must pay for. The same principles apply in identifying increases in
domestic balances owned by nonresidents as capital inflows, credit
items, and decreases in such balances as capital outflows, debit
items.

Other debit and credit entries in the balance of payments are created by unilateral transfers and gold movements. Unilateral transfers into a country are credit items; out of a country, they are debit items. If such transfers are made in kind, such as a gift of wheat by the United States to India, no money payment or claim for payment is involved, but they are still included in the balance of payments to keep the record complete.

Gold is no different from other commodities so far as debit and credit entries are concerned: exports are credits; imports are debits.

Total Debits Equal Total Credits

If balance-of-payments data are accurate and complete, the sum of all debits must equal the sum of all credits. In practice, this is rarely the case, since information on the thousands of individual international transactions of a country's residents is bound to be lacking in completeness and accuracy to the last dollar. Since we know, however, that in fact total debits equal total credits, any discrepancy between the two is attributable to "errors and omissions," which is entered in the balance of payments as a debit or credit, as required to bring the totals to equality.

How do we know that in fact total debits equal total credits? Because balance-of-payments accounting methods have this built-in result. Every international transaction has a dual aspect, each of which is entered separately in the balance of payments, one as a credit item, the other as a debit item. This double-entry bookkeeping assures the equality of debits and credits. One or two examples will illustrate the double-entry nature of balance-of-payments accounting.

Suppose an American firm exports $100,000 worth of equipment to Brazil. This is the first part of the transaction and is entered in the balance of payments of the United States as a credit item. But the export must be settled in some fashion, giving rise to the second aspect of the transaction. In whatever fashion settlement for the export is made, it will be a debit entry in the U.S. balance of payments of $100,000. Consider some of the various possible ways of settlement. A common method would be for the Brazilian importer to purchase dollar exchange from his bank. In this case, the dollar balances of the Brazilian bank held in its correspondent American bank is drawn down by $100,000 upon payment to the exporter. But as we have seen, a decrease in foreign-held balances represents a capital outflow from the country in which the balances are held and a debit entry in that country's balance of payments. If payment for the equipment were made by the importer in his own currency (Brazilian cruzeiros), the debit entry would be the increase in cruzeiro balances held by the exporter or the American bank to whom the foreign exchange was sold. Or perhaps the settlement is in the form of a trade credit extended to the importer. Again, this is a capital outflow from the United States and a debit entry. Another possibility is that the equipment is sent to Brazil as a gift under the foreign aid program, in which case the debit entry is for a unilateral transfer out of the country.

A second example is where the originating transaction is a capital movement. Assume that a California bank makes a loan to a Mexican firm of $1 million. This is a capital outflow from the United States, entered as a debit item in its balance of payments. What is the corresponding credit entry? If the Mexican firm uses the dollars to purchase U.S. exports, these would be the credit entry. If, on the other hand, the Mexican firm sells the dollar proceeds of the loan to its bank for Mexican pesos, and the bank in turn adds the dollars to its balances held in a U.S. bank—a not improbable transaction— a capital inflow from Mexico to the United States occurs, a credit entry in the U.S. balance of payments. In other words, the original capital outflow from the United States is accompanied by a reverse capital inflow into the United States, no *net* movement of capital having occurred.[1]

Double-entry accounting assures the equality of total debits and credits. There is, however, a more illuminating way of seeing the necessity for overall balance in the balance of payments. A country, like an individual or any economic entity, cannot pay out more than it currently receives except by drawing on its cash reserves, by selling some of its assets, by borrowing, or by receiving gifts—all credit items; nor can it currently receive more than it pays out without accumulating cash reserves or other assets, reducing its liabilities, lending, or making gifts—all debit items.

Balance-of-Payments Accounts

Identifying each balance-of-payments transaction as a debit or credit gives a "vertical" classification, separating entries according to which side of the balance sheet they fall on. Such classification is

---

[1] This is an illustration of the principle discussed earlier that net capital movements can only occur in the form of net movements of goods and services.

essential for making sense out of balance-of-payments data and is based on the obvious need for distinguishing the direction of movement of claims and counterclaims for payment between one country and the rest of the world. A second "horizontal" classification of international transactions is required to make the balance of payments a useful analytical tool. This second classification is based on the proposition that different kinds of transactions, even though they are all debit or credit items, have different significance and implication. We have already implied that such is the case by distinguishing between trade in goods and services, capital movements, unilateral transfers, and monetary gold movements. These we shall now formally designate as the four major accounts in the balance of payments and briefly recall what each encompasses.

The goods and services account—commonly called the Current Account—includes all commodity and service exports and imports. For several reasons the Current Account may be looked upon as the most basic of all payments categories. First, it is always the largest account. Second, the import and export of goods and services constitute the "real" substance of international economic relations, the fundamental economic basis for the existence of a world economy. As we shall see, many transactions in the other payments accounts perform largely auxiliary and supportive functions, facilitating the flow of goods and services but making no independent contribution. Even long-term capital movements, which do have an important autonomous role, can be effectuated only through the movement of goods and services—that is, through Current Account transactions. Third, the Current Account represents the international component of a country's national income. Exports are a component— along with domestic consumption, investment, and government purchases—of the gross national product. Imports represent that part of the national income spent on nondomestically produced goods and services. A full discussion of the relationship between the Current Account and the national income is presented in Chapter 16.

In contrast to the Current Account, the Capital Account embraces transactions consisting not of real commodities and services, but rather of paper claims and debts. The Capital Account has a strategic position in the balance of payments. Long-term capital movements—loans and investments with a maturity exceeding one year—provide the means of financing a new flow of goods and services from the lending or investing country to recipient countries.

Short-term capital movements serve mainly as the financial means of temporarily filling in the gaps between international payments and receipts on other transactions. For example, if a country's imports are greater than its exports, the difference may be made up through drawing upon accumulated foreign exchange balances or through an increase in domestic balances held by foreigners or through foreign short-term loans to the country. Each of these is an example of a short-term capital inflow into the country.

The Unilateral Transfer Account includes transactions that are a species of capital movement. They differ from ordinary capital movements in that they do not involve reciprocal obligations or claims. Thus, if the United States makes a foreign aid loan, eventual repayment of which is expected (together with interest), it is included in the Capital Account. But if a foreign aid *grant* is made, with no obligation on the part of the recipient for principal repayment or interest, it is included in the Unilateral Transfer Account. Other examples are indemnities, reparations, and immigrant remittances.

The Gold Account contains a record of the international flow of gold out of and into national official monetary reserves. The special interest in gold lies in its long-time status as a generally accepted means of international payment, as well as—for many countries—a national monetary reserve. Like short-term capital movements, gold is used primarily to fill in gaps in other accounts. A country with an excess of imports over exports, for example, may cover the deficit through exporting gold instead of through a capital inflow.

A BALANCE-OF-PAYMENTS MODEL

We are now in a position to set up a balance-of-payments model (Table 14.1) with a dual classification of all the major items which normally comprise a country's international accounts (*a*) as debit or credit and (*b*) as current, capital, unilateral transfer, or gold accounts.

PLANNED VERSUS REALIZED TRANSACTIONS

The balance of payments is an ex post statement—that is, it is an historical record of the international economic and financial transactions of a country during some *past period*. The record shows the various sources providing means of making foreign payments and the various uses to which the means thus provided were put. And we have learned that the sum total of these means cannot differ from the sum total of their uses.

The information contained in a balance of payments is ex-

TABLE 14.1

MODEL BALANCE OF PAYMENTS

	Debit	Credit
I. Current account:		
A. Merchandise trade:		
1. Merchandise imports.	X	
2. Merchandise exports.		X
B. Service transactions:		
1. Transportation:		
a) Rendered by foreign vessels, airlines, etc.	X	
b) Rendered by domestic vessels, airlines, etc.		X
2. Travel expenditures:		
a) In foreign countries.	X	
b) By foreigners in home country.		X
3. Interest and dividends:		
a) Paid to foreigners.	X	
b) Received from abroad.		X
4. Banking and insurance services:		
a) Rendered by foreign institutions.	X	
b) Rendered to foreigners by domestic institutions.		X
5. Government expenditures:		
a) By home government abroad.	X	
b) By foreign government in home country.		X
II. Capital account:		
A. Long-term:		
1. Purchase of securities from foreigners *.	X	
2. Sale of securities to foreigners *.		X
B. Short-term: †		
1. Increase of bank and brokerage balances abroad.	X	
2. Decrease of foreign-held bank and brokerage balances		
in home country.	X	
3. Increase of foreign-held bank and brokerage balances		
in home country.		X
4. Decrease of bank and brokerage balances abroad.		X
III. Unilateral transfers:		
A. Private:		
1. Personal and institutional remittances to non-		
residents.	X	
2. Remittances received from abroad.		X
B. Governmental:		
1. Grants, indemnities, and reparations made to other		
countries.	X	
2. Grants, indemnities, and reparations received from		
other countries.		X
IV. Gold account:		
A. Import of gold and increase of earmarked gold abroad ‡.	X	
B. Export of gold and increase of earmarked gold for foreign		
account ‡.		X

* Includes new issues, transactions in outstanding issues, and transfers resulting from redemption and sinking-fund operations.

† Also includes currency holdings, acceptances, and other short-term claims not listed.

‡ "Earmarked" gold is gold physically held in one country for the account of another.

tremely useful, but only if it is subjected to analysis to draw out significant implications. The fact that the balance of payments must balance is of no analytical interest but is only the consequence of the (very useful) method of accounting employed. The analytically interesting question that follows upon this accounting balance is in what manner and through what processes the balance is brought about. The question arouses curiosity especially in view of the thousands of individual decisions which are ordinarily involved in the international relations of a country, the results of which are summarized in the balance of payments. There is no basis for expecting the independent decisions of so many different individuals, business firms, and government bodies—both at home and abroad—to dovetail into an internally consistent set of relationships.

On the basis of such factors as consumer preferences, the level and distribution of income, the prices of goods and services at home and abroad, interest rates, and foreign exchange rates, a country will wish to import a certain volume of goods and services from the rest of the world, to lend and invest a certain amount of money capital in other countries, and perhaps to make some foreign gifts. In addition, as part of its foreign policy, the government of the country may want to make foreign expenditures and foreign loans and grants for economic and military purposes. All these are payment, or debit, items in the country's balance of payments. On the other side, similar forces operate in each of the other countries of the world to determine the international receipts, or credits, of the country from its exports, capital inflow, and inward unilateral transfers. How, then, could one expect the sum of debits to come out equal to the sum of credits? The answer, of course, is that one would not, except by accident.

Alongside the statement that the balance of payments must balance ex post we have set the improbability that it will balance ex ante. To put it another way, even though *realized* debits and credits must be equal (an ex post statement, referring to the past), *planned* debits and credits are not likely to be equal (an ex ante statement, referring to a forthcoming period).

In the likely event that the planned debit transactions of a country are not matched by planned credit transactions, what happens to bring them into actual realized equality? One of two things happens.

The first possibility is that the attempt to carry out plans which are inconsistent with each other may lead to changes in the underlying variables upon which the plans were originally based, thereby causing the plans to be revised. For instance, the attempt of a country to import more goods and services than it can pay for may cause exchange rates on foreign currencies to rise, which in turn would tend to cause a downward revision in import plans and upward revision in export plans. Exchange rates might continue to rise until planned foreign exchange expenditure is brought into equality with planned foreign exchange receipts.

The second possibility is of a quite different nature. Instead of inconsistent plans being forced to undergo revision, they may be allowed consummation through some sort of compensatory action. For example, a country may carry out planned international debit transactions in excess of planned credit transactions by drawing upon accumulated gold or foreign exchange reserves or obtaining a foreign loan for this purpose. Such transactions, undertaken in response to balance-of-payments considerations, are known as *accommodating* transactions. They are to be distinguished from *autonomous* transactions, which are undertaken for reasons independent of the balance of payments. Thus, while a country normally exports monetary gold only when this is necessary to fill a deficiency in foreign exchange earnings from other credit transactions, ordinary commodity exports are autonomous, for they are in response to forces independent of the balance of payments, such as the relationship between demand and supply at home and abroad.

EQUILIBRIUM AND DISEQUILIBRIUM

Equilibrium means a state of balance among opposing forces; disequilibrium means the absence of such a state of balance. Equilibrium is self-sustaining in the sense that, unless and until an external disturbance intrudes, no tendency arises for change in the relationship among the forces internal to the system. Disequilibrium, on the other hand, is inherently incapable of continuing, for imbalance among opposing forces generates change.

Applied to the sphere of economic relationships, equilibrium prevails when the autonomous decisions of various economic entities are consistent with each other. A familiar example is an equilibrium price, which equates the quantity of a good offered for sale with the quantity demanded. If at a given price the quantity supplied differs from the quantity demanded, disequilibrium prevails and the price will tend to change.

The same principles apply to a balance of payments. Equilibrium prevails when planned autonomous debit transactions equal planned autonomous credit transactions in total value. For in this case the intentions of those who wish to engage in transactions requiring foreign payments or creating foreign obligations can be carried out with the means provided by the planned credit transactions of other groups, with no residual payments or receipts balances requiring unplanned settlement. If, however, planned autonomous debits and credits are not equal, the balance of payments is in disequilibrium. An excess of such debits over credits constitutes a *deficit* disequilibrium—or simply a deficit (or adverse) balance of payments. An excess of planned autonomous credits constitutes a *surplus* disequilibrium—or simply a surplus (or so-called "favorable") balance of payments.

It follows from the above that disequilibrium in the balance of payments may manifest itself in either of the ways of reconciling differences between ex ante and ex post relationships previously identified. That is, disequilibrium either shows up in changes in one or more of the variables determining planned decisions, or else the differences in planned debits and credits is reconciled through accommodating transactions. The next several chapters will be devoted to exploring the implications of this statement.

RECOMMENDED READING

International Monetary Fund. *Balance of Payments Yearbook.* Washington, D.C. Issued annually. A comprehensive collection of balance-of-payments data for different countries and regions.

Snider, Delbert A. *International Monetary Relations,* chap. ii. New York: Random House, Inc., 1966.

STUDY QUESTIONS

1. Define, and contrast, an international balance of payments and an international balance of indebtedness.
2. In what sense do American tourist expenditures abroad constitute an "import" into the United States?
3. Justify the practice of regarding interest and dividend payments as a "service" transaction in the balance of payments.
4. Is the "import" or purchase from abroad of evidences of debt or ownership a capital inflow or outflow? A debit or credit entry in the balance of payments?
5. Suppose you purchase a foreign bond during 1964 and hold it until

its maturity in 1974, at which time it is redeemed by the foreign issuer.

a) During what year or years will this give rise to entries in your country's balance-of-payments capital account?

b) Assuming that regular annual interest payments are received on the bond, in what years will entries be made in the balance of payments for interest receipts? In what account will the entries be made?

c) Identify each of the entries made in (a) and (b) above as debit or credit.

6. So far as the balance of payments is concerned, in what respect is an increase in foreign bank balances held by U.S. residents equivalent to a decrease in U.S. bank balances held by foreigners?

7. In what sense is an increase in foreign-held bank balances in the United States equivalent to a short-term loan to the United States? (In answering this, first of all identify on which side of the bank's balance sheet a deposit appears.)

8. If the Ford Motor Company builds a branch factory in England, how is the transaction entered in the balance of payments of the United States? How does this differ from the purchase of bonds issued by a foreign-owned automobile company?

9. Compare a unilateral transfer receipt from abroad with a long-term capital inflow, from the standpoint of (a) debit or credit entry in the balance of payments, (b) subsequent entries in the balance of payments to which they give rise, and (c) effect on the balance of international indebtedness.

10. Suppose a Brazilian exporter ships $100,000 worth of coffee to the United States and receives payment in the form of a dollar deposit account in his name in a New York bank. Describe the entries, appropriately classified, in both the Brazilian and the U.S. balance of payments.

11. If there is a net positive or negative balance in any one of the accounts of the balance of payments, why must there be a net balance, of opposite sign, in one or more of the remaining accounts?

12. Test your understanding of the nature and content of a balance of payments by examining the latest data on the U.S. balance of payments, given in the *Survey of Current Business.*

13. Why are international gold movements recorded in the balance of payments only on a net basis?

14. The "Errors and omissions" entry in a balance of payments is an indication that the theoretical principle of equality between total debits and total credits is of doubtful validity. True or false? Why?

15. Name two other ways commonly used to indicate debit and credit entries in the balance of payments.

16. What is meant by the statement that the balance of payments is an ex post record?

17. Why are autonomous debits and credits not likely to be equal?

18. If planned balance-of-payments transactions are not consistent with each other, what kind of reactions may bring them into consistency?

19. Define and illustrate "accommodating" transactions.

20. Define balance-of-payments equilibrium. What are the various signs of disequilibrium?

	# THE BALANCE OF
Chapter	# PAYMENTS AND THE
15	# FOREIGN EXCHANGE
	# MARKET

The forces that shape a country's balance of payments are numerous and varied. Over the long run, such basic "real" factors as resource endowment, the state of technology, and consumer preference—in each case, both at home and abroad— exert a decisive influence. Most of the problems associated with balance of payments relations, however, arise out of shorter-run influences of a monetary or cyclical character. Among the most important of these are exchange rates, price levels, and income levels. In this chapter we shall concentrate our attention on the key role of exchange rates.

THE MEANING AND IMPORTANCE OF EXCHANGE RATES

If everything influencing the balance of payments, except for exchange rates, were to remain unchanged, a significant variation in exchange rates could be expected to have pronounced balance-of-payments effects. This is simply a way of saying that at least some of the major transactions entering into the balance of payments are a function of exchange rates.

Exchange rates are the links connecting different national currencies and making international cost and price comparisons possible. To a potential U.S. importer, a price quotation of 100 Greek drachmas means nothing until the exchange rate between the dollar and the drachma is known. Suppose that the American firm concludes that at an f.o.b. cost of $10 or less a certain Greek product could profitably be imported, but that at a higher price it would not be profitable to do so. If the Greek export price is 100 drachmas, the good would be imported if the exchange rate is 10 cents or less, for correspondingly the dollar equivalent of 100 drachmas would then be $10 or less. (Reminder: an exchange rate is the price in domestic currency per unit of foreign currency.)

By the same token, whether a given U.S. good is exported to Greece depends in part on the rate of exchange. Suppose that a Greek firm is interested in importing an article from the United States if its f.o.b. cost is 100 drachmas or less, but not if the cost is higher. Assume that the dollar price of the good is $10. Then the good will be exported if the drachma rate of exchange in the United States is 10 cents *or more*. At a 10-cent exchange rate, the equivalent of $10 is 100 drachmas. At a lower exchange rate, the drachma equivalent of $10 is greater. For example, at an exchange rate of 9 cents on the drachma, it costs somewhat more than 110 drachmas to acquire $10 on the foreign exchange market. If the drachma rate of exchange in the United States were, say, 11 cents, then the equivalent of $10 would be approximately 90 drachmas.

This simple example illustrates an important point. Other things being equal, the higher exchange rates are in your country the more costly to you are imported goods and services and the cheaper are your country's export goods and services to foreigners. It is well to keep in mind that exchange rates in different exchange market centers are reciprocals of each other. For instance, a rate of 10 cents per drachma in New York is exactly the same as a rate of 10 drachmas per dollar in Athens. Hence, a higher rate in New York means a lower rate in Athens. As long as exchange transactions are conducted in free and competitive markets, this reciprocal relationship will be assured through arbitrage operations.[1]

THE DEMAND FOR FOREIGN EXCHANGE

Implicit in the preceding example is the existence of a functional relationship between the quantity of foreign exchange demanded and the rate of exchange. (We shall also note shortly the functional relationship between the quantity of foreign exchange supplied and the rate of exchange.) Somewhat more loosely, this in turn implies a parallel functional relationship between the debit side of the balance of payments and the rate of exchange. It is true that not all balance-of-payments debit transactions give rise to a demand for foreign exchange—for example, unilateral transfers in kind—but it generally is true that all sources of demand for foreign exchange are debit transactions in the balance of payments.

---

[1] Arbitrage merely involves buying cheap and selling dear. For example, if the New York rate is 9 cents per drachma, and the Athens rate 10 drachmas per dollar, 90 cents will purchase in New York drachmas worth $1 in Athens. As a result of such purchases and sales, the rate is brought into reciprocal relationship in the two markets.

The functional relationship between the quantity of foreign exchange demanded and the rate of exchange is expressed in the *demand schedule* for foreign exchange. This schedule specifies the various quantities of exchange demanded at various rates of exchange and is constructed on the assumption that all influences on the demand for exchange other than the rate of exchange remain constant. A change in one or more of these other influences on demand results in a shift of the entire schedule.

FIGURE 15.1

THE DEMAND FOR FOREIGN EXCHANGE

What are the usual properties of the demand schedule for foreign exchange? An *inverse relationship* between the rate of exchange and the quantity demanded is the most important. We have already noted the chief reason for this inverse relationship: higher rates of exchange make imports more expensive, and lower rates make them cheaper. Hence, ordinarily the volume of imports demanded—and the quantity of foreign exchange necessary to pay for them—move in a direction opposite to the rate of exchange. When the demand schedule for foreign exchange on commodity and service account is expressed in graphical terms, the resulting demand curve falls from left to right in the conventional diagram, with the price (rate of exchange) measured on the vertical axis and the quantity of foreign exchange measured on the horizontal axis (see Figure 15.1).

In technical language, the fall of the demand curve from left to right reflects its having an *elasticity* with respect to the exchange rate that is less than infinite and greater than zero. The elasticity of demand refers to the degree of responsiveness in quantity demanded to a (small) change in price. The coefficient of elasticity is calculated by dividing the percentage change in quantity demanded associated with a change in price by the percentage change in price. If the coefficient is one, the demand is unit elastic; if it is greater than one, the demand is relatively elastic; if it is less than one, the demand is relatively inelastic.[2]

The demand for foreign exchange arising out of commodity and service imports has the same elasticity with respect to the exchange rate as the elasticity of demand for the imported goods and services has with respect to their prices in domestic currency. Suppose that the exchange rate falls by 10 perecnt. Other things being equal, import prices therefore decline by 10 percent. If as a consequence the quantity demanded of imported goods and services rises by, say, 20 percent, the quantity of foreign exchange demanded to pay for imports also rises by 20 percent. Hence, the elasticity of demand for foreign exchange is precisely the same as the elasticity of demand for imported goods and services. Since over usual price ranges the elasticity of demand for goods and services is greater than zero and less than infinity, the same holds for the demand for foreign exchange on goods and services account.

So far we have confined our attention to the demand for foreign exchange arising out of the demand for imported goods and services. Although normally this is by far the greatest component of the aggregate demand for exchange, it is by no means the only one. Foreign loans and investments and outward unilateral transfers are also possible sources of autonomous demand for foreign exchange. However, apart from speculative operations based on anticipated changes in exchange rates, ordinary foreign loans and investments and unilateral transfers are not influenced by the level of exchange rates. Autonomous capital outflows are induced by higher rates of return abroad than at home on comparable loans and investments. While exchange rates affect the foreign currency equivalent of a given loan or investment expressed in home currency, interest and dividend returns are affected in the same manner and to the same extent, leaving the *rate* of return unaffected. This is equivalent to saying that the elasticity of demand for foreign exchange to finance capital outflows is zero. Thus, the effect of capital outflows on the aggregate demand for foreign exchange is to increase it—that is, to

---

[2] Since price and quantity vary in opposite directions, the coefficient of elasticity is negative. However, the sign is conventionally ignored.

move the demand curve to the right—but to leave its shape un-affected.

Unilateral transfers have a similar effect on the demand for for-eign exchange—pushing out the curve but not changing its shape. An exception would arise if the transfer is expressed in a fixed amount of the sending country's currency but made in foreign cur-rency. In this case, the demand for foreign exchange to finance the transfer would be unit-elastic.[3]

Adding together the various component autonomous demands for foreign exchange will in all ordinary cases yield an aggregate demand curve of the same general shape as that on goods and ser-vices account alone.

THE SUPPLY OF FOREIGN EXCHANGE

The supply schedule or curve of foreign exchange shows the various quantities of foreign exchange that would be supplied at various rates of exchange, all influences other than the rate of ex-change being held constant. Autonomous sources of supply are the counterparts of the sources of demand: the export of goods and services, capital inflows, and inward unilateral transfers. To a very large extent these sources of supply of foreign exchange depend upon decisions in other countries. How much a country exports depends chiefly upon how much of its goods and services other countries are willing to import; and how much foreign capital and unilateral transfers flow into the country depend upon how much other countries wish to send to it. These decisions, however, are based on precisely the same kind of considerations underlying home decisions with respect to movements in the opposite direction that we have discussed above. Thus, the export of goods and services from one country, which are the same as other countries' imports from it, is a function of exchange rates, for the latter determine the prices in foreign currencies of the export goods and services.

In constructing a supply curve of foreign exchange, it is essential to keep in mind that a change in the exchange rate in one country is accompanied by an *opposite* change in the rate in other countries. We have seen why the demand curve for foreign exchange has a

---

[3] A unit-elastic demand curve is a rectangular hyperbola, with constant rectan-gular areas under each point of the curve. Each such area represents in the case of the demand curve for foreign exchange the product of the exchange rate and the as-sociated quantity of foreign exchange—i.e., the equivalent in domestic currency of that particular quantity of foreign exchange.

negative slope: at a higher rate of exchange import goods and services are relatively more expensive, a smaller quantity is therefore demanded, and a smaller quantity of foreign exchange is required to pay for them. But since a higher rate of exchange in our country is equivalent to a lower rate in other countries, at our higher rates our goods and services are cheaper to other countries. More of our goods are therefore demanded by foreigners at our higher exchange rates, but a smaller quantity of foreign currency is received on the average per physical unit of our exports.

Can we say, then, that the supply curve of foreign exchange *rises* from left to right? Not with the same assurance with which we concluded that the demand curve falls from left to right. While the volume of exports certainly tends to increase with an increase in the rate of exchange, the quantity of foreign exchange received for the exports may or may not increase. The outcome depends upon the foreign elasticity of demand for the country's export goods and services and therefore for its currency.

The quantity of foreign exchange supplied in country A at a given rate of exchange is the same as the amount of foreign currency spent for currency A at that rate of exchange. For example, suppose that at a rate of 20 cents per French franc in New York, equivalent to a rate of 5 francs per dollar in Paris, $100 are demanded in exchange for francs. Since each dollar commands 5 francs in exchange, 500 francs are offered for the $100. Hence, the quantity of franc foreign exchange supplied in New York at the rate of 20 cents per franc is 500. In other words, the supply of foreign exchange in a country is directly related to the demand of other countries for its currency.

To continue the illustration, what would be the quantity of franc exchange supplied in New York if the rate of exchange were 25 cents? In Paris the rate on the dollar would then be 4 francs, and U.S. goods and services would be cheaper to the French. The quantity of dollars demanded in France, therefore, will presumably be greater. But since for each dollar purchased ony 4 francs are offered, whether or not the total amount of francs offered increases depends upon the elasticity of the demand for dollars over the range in rates from 5 to 4 francs per dollar. If the elasticity of the demand is greater than unity, the percentage increase in dollars demanded is greater than the percentage decrease in the franc-dollar rate of exchange, and therefore the quantity of francs supplied increases as the rate changes. Thus, let the increase in the dollar rate on the franc of 25 percent, and equivalent decrease in the franc rate on the dollar of 25 percent, which a change in the rate from $0.20 to $0.25 represents, be accompanied by a 30 percent increase in dollars demanded, from $100 to $130.[4] The total number of francs exchanged for dollars is therefore $100 \times 5 = 500$ at a rate of 20 cents per franc and $130 \times 4 = 520$ at a rate of 25 cents per franc.

Now let us assume that the franc demand for dollar exchange over the range from 25 to 30 cents per franc is unit elastic. In this case, the 20 percent change in rate is associated with an equal percentage increase in the quantity of dollars demanded against francs

FIGURE 15.2

FRANC SUPPLY IN NEW YORK BASED ON DOLLAR DEMAND IN PARIS

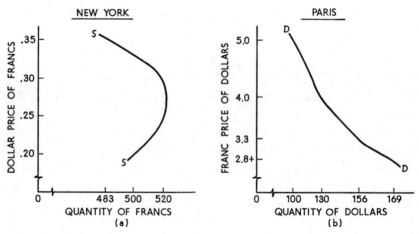

—that is, from $130 to $156. The quantity of francs offered for dollars is then $156 \times 3\frac{1}{3} = 520$, the same as at a rate of 25 cents per franc. General conclusion: When the foreign demand for dollars is unit elastic, the supply of foreign exchange in the United States is zero elastic.[5]

Finally, assume that between a rate of 30 and 35 cents, the franc demand for dollars is inelastic (less than unity). For example, suppose that accompanying the above $16\frac{2}{3}$ percent change in rate, the quantity of dollars demanded increases by only half as much percentagewise—from $156 to $169 ($169 is $8\frac{1}{3}$ percent greater than

---

[4] Percentage changes in arriving at elasticity coefficients are calculated on the lower of the figures as the base.

[5] The elasticity of supply is measured by the percentage change in quantity divided by the percentage in price, exactly as for the elasticity of demand.

$156). The quantity of francs supplied at a rate of 35 cents is then $169 \times 100/35 = 483$, approximately. When the foreign demand for your currency is inelastic, an increase in the rate of exchange causes a decrease in the quantity of foreign exchange supplied.

The preceding conclusions are summarized graphically in Figure 15.2. The supply curve of francs in New York (*SS*) rises from left to right between a rate of exchange from 20 to 25 cents per franc, for over the corresponding franc-dollar rate of between 5 and 4 francs the foreign demand for dollars (*DD*) is elastic. The supply curve of francs is vertical over the range in rate between 25 and 30 cents, because the foreign demand for dollars over the equivalent range in rates of from 4 to $3\frac{1}{3}$ francs per dollar is unit elastic. The supply curve of francs bends backward between rates of from 30 to 35 cents, because over the equivalent rates of from 100/30 to 100/35 francs per dollar the foreign demand is inelastic.

DEMAND, SUPPLY, AND EQUILIBRIUM

We may now place the demand and supply curves of foreign exchange on the same set of axes, as in Figure 15.3. The supply curve has been drawn to rise continuously from left to right, based on the assumption of an elastic foreign demand for the country's currency over all the exchange rate ranges included. In a later discussion, we shall assume that the supply curve bends backward above a certain exchange rate and then explore the consequences.

The first observation to make about the demand and supply curves of foreign exchange in Figure 15.3 is that they are the foreign exchange counterparts respectively of cash autonomous, ex ante debit and credit balance-of-payments transactions during the same period. As noted earlier, not all balance-of-payments transactions are conducted through the foreign exchange market, but those that are show up on the demand side if they are debits and on the supply side if they are credits. However, the demand and supply curves do not reveal what quantities of exchange actually are demanded and supplied until the rate of exchange is specified. Even at a specified rate of exchange, we do not know what the realized quantity of exchange bought and sold will be without further information, for the curves reveal only *desired* actions, which may or may not be realized. Indeed, it is this characteristic of the curves that directly relates to exchange equilibrium or disequilibrum.

The exchange market is in equilibrium only at one particular rate of exchange—the rate at which the quantity demanded equals the quantity supplied. This is called the *equilibrium rate of exchange*. In Figure 15.3 the equilibrium rate is shown as R_e.

If the exchange market is in equilibrium at the prevailing rate of exchange, there is no reason for the rate to change, unless and until one or more outside influences—assumed to remain constant in constructing the demand and supply curves—changes. At the equilibrium rate of exchange all the foreign exchange demanded

FIGURE 15.3

THE EQUILIBRIUM RATE OF EXCHANGE

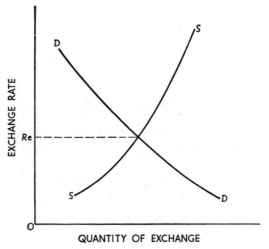

for various autonomous debit transactions in the balance of payments is furnished by various autonomous credit transactions, obviating the need for any accommodating transactions.

But now suppose that an initial equilibrium in the exchange market is disturbed by a change in one of the outside forces mentioned previously. For example, suppose that the national income of the country rises, causing the demand for imports to increase, and thereby the demand for exchange to increase. This shows up in the movement of the whole demand curve upward and to the right, such as to $D'D'$ in Figure 15.4. The initial equilibrium rate R_e is clearly now a disequilibrium rate, for the quantity of foreign exchange demanded at R_e exceeds the quantity supplied at that rate. As a consequence, something has to "give," but exactly what gives depends upon the kind of system prevailing.

The typical free-market response to an excess demand situation is a rise in price. In the case at hand, this would mean an increase in the rate of exchange. If the rate of exchange is free to move in accordance with market forces, it would tend to rise until rate R'_e in Figure 15.4 is reached, for this is the new equilibrium rate, at which equality is restored between the quantity demanded and that supplied.

A rise in the free-market rate of exchange is thus one of the manifestations of disequilibrium. At the same time, it is a major method of restoring equilibrium in the face of disequilibrium.

Most exchange-rate systems, however, prevent the exchange rate from freely responding to market forces. As we shall see, this is the

FIGURE 15.4

THE EFFECTS OF AN INCREASED DEMAND FOR FOREIGN EXCHANGE

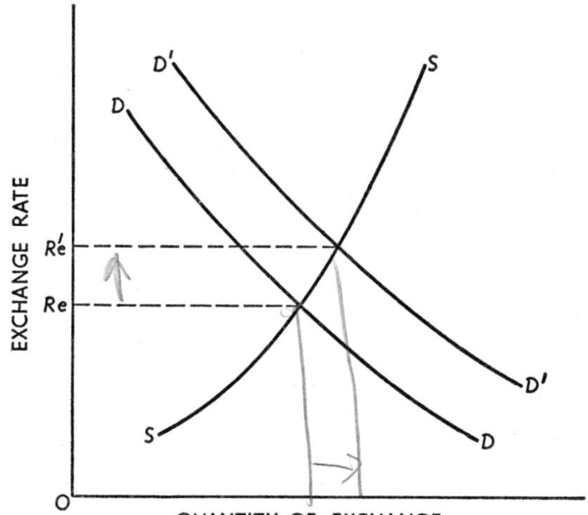

case most notably under the gold standard system, but it is also the practice under other systems as well, including the current one. What, then, happens when disequilibrium develops at the prevailing rate?

One possibility is the introduction of controls to suppress the market demand or to push the supply outward. One type of such controls involves the requirement of licences to import goods and services and to make foreign loans and investments. Other control devices include import tariffs and quotas and export subsidies.

If market forces are to be allowed free expression without inhibiting controls, the maintenance of stable exchange rates in the face of an excess demand for foreign exchange requires the provision of additional amounts of foreign exchange on the market. The extra supply may be furnished through private channels in response to the excess demand situation, or it may be furnished through the sale of foreign exchange by the central bank or other government agency out of official reserves. In either case, the additional foreign exchange is provided by *accommodating* transactions, which serve to fill in the gap between the quantities of exchange autonomously demanded and supplied and to keep the exchange rate stable.

In summary, we have found three signs of a deficit balance-of-payments disequilibrium. The first is a market-induced rise in exchange rates; the second is the imposition of controls over international transactions; the third is the presence of accommodating transactions. In the next chapter we shall pursue the implications of each of these.

RECOMMENDED READING

HABERLER, GOTTFRIED. "The Market for Foreign Exchange and the Stability of the Balance of Payments," *Kyklos,* Vol. 3 (1949), pp. 193–218.

MACHLUP, FRITZ. "The Theory of Foreign Exchange," *Economica* (New Ser.), Vol. 6 (November, 1939, and February, 1940). Reprinted in (American Economic Association) *Readings in the Theory of International Trade* (eds. HOWARD S. ELLIS and LLOYD A. METZLER), chap. v. Homewood, Ill.: Richard D. Irwin, Inc., 1949.

MEADE, J. E. *The Balance of Payments,* chap. i. London: Oxford University Press, 1951.

STUDY QUESTIONS

1. Satisfy yourself that higher rates of exchange are associated with more expensive imports and cheaper exports.

2. Why, in a free market, is a New York rate of exchange of $0.02 on the Belgian franc equivalent to a rate in Brussels of 50 francs per dollar?

3. What do you understand by the statement that the quantity of foreign exchange demanded is a function of the rate of exchange?

4. In constructing a demand or supply schedule of foreign exchange, which variables are admitted and which are excluded?

5. Why is the rate of exchange and the quantity of foreign exchange demanded inversely related?

6. What determines the elasticity of demand for foreign exchange on goods and services account?

7. Why is the elasticity of demand for foreign exchange on ordinary capital account zero?

8. What would cause the supply curve of foreign exchange to bend backwards?

9. If a country wished to increase the amount of foreign exchange supplied in its market through raising the rate of exchange, what foreign demand conditions for its exports would be most favorable?

10. Define the equilibrium rate of exchange.

11. Why are accommodating transactions not included in the sources of demand and supply of foreign exchange in determining the equilibrium rate of exchange?

12. Identify three different manifestations of exchange market disequilibrium.

Chapter 16	DISEQUILIBRIUM AND ADJUSTMENT OF THE BALANCE OF PAYMENTS

We have defined balance-of-payments disequilibrium as existing when, over any given period, aggregate autonomous international payments (debits) and receipts (credits) are not equal. This is an inherently unstable situation, containing forces leading to change in the direction of bringing autonomous payments and receipts into balance. The process through which equilibrium is restored is called the adjustment process.

THE GENERAL NATURE OF PAYMENTS ADJUSTMENT

Balance-of-payments disequilibrium creates the most serious adjustment problem for the country experiencing it when it is of a deficit nature and persists over a prolonged period.

A *deficit* disequilibrium exists when autonomous payments exceed autonomous receipts. If the inequality between autonomous payments and receipts is in the opposite direction, there is a *surplus* disequilibrium. As a rule, a deficit in the balance of payments is more bothersome to a country than a surplus because the burden of adjustment tends most often to lie more heavily on deficit than on surplus countries. However, since one country's deficit is necessarily accompanied by one or more other countries' surplus, they are equally incapable of being sustained indefinitely.

As observed in an earlier discussion, because of the multifarious decision-making entities engaged in international transactions and the diversity of their motivations, the matching of autonomous decisions in an equilibrium pattern is not to be expected as the norm. But more or less continuous disequilibrium does not necessarily imply a constant state of balance-of-payments difficulties. Real problems arise mainly from any tendency of a country's international payments to suffer disequilibrium in just one direction—especially in the direction of a deficit—over a long period. Periodic deficits followed by surpluses, leading to an approximate balance over a period of from, say, two or three years, are not likely to create too serious problems. In practice, therefore, balance-of-payments equilibrium docs not require the continuous balancing of autonomous decisions, which would be an impossible goal, but only their approximate balancing over a reasonable period of time. We shall later indicate the pragmatic basis for determining in any particular case how long a "reasonable" period is.

Since balance-of-payments disequilibrium is a state of imbalance between autonomous international payments and receipts, adjustment implies a change in the relationship between these two sides of the ledger. To remove a deficit, autonomous receipts must expand relatively to payments; to remove a surplus, payments must expand relatively to receipts. For such adjustments to occur, there must be changes in the underlying variables to which autonomous payments and receipts are functionally related. A complete list of these variables would embrace the economic universe, for all parts of an economy are interrelated. However, for theoretical analysis to be illuminating and practically useful, attention must be concentrated on the dominating and key variables. In the case of the balance of payments, these key variables are exchange rates, prices, income, and controls, a change in any one of which will tend significantly to affect the balance of payments because of their strong functional relationship to autonomous balance-of-payments decisions. The following discussion shows how adjustment in the balance of payments may be effected by changes in these variables. For the greater part, we shall assume that disequilibrium is of a deficit variety. Generally, the same principles would apply, operating in reverse, to a surplus disequilibrium.

ADJUSTMENT THROUGH EXCHANGE RATES

Under ordinary circumstances, there is some exchange rate at which, given the other key variables influencing the balance of payments, the balance of payments of a country will tend toward equilibrium. Hence, it follows that if the balance of payments is in disequilibrium at one level of exchange rates, equilibrium adjustment can be accomplished by an appropriate change in that level.

We are familiar with the reason for the power of exchange rates to shape the balance of payments. Other things being equal, the higher exchange rates are in a country, the lower are the prices of its export goods and services to the rest of the world and the more expensive to it are import goods and services. Even though some autonomous transactions, such as capital movements and unilateral transfers, may not be directly influenced by exchange rates, we can be quite certain that in the aggregate autonomous payment and receipts are directly affected.

How responsive the balance of payments is to a change in the exchange rate depends upon the elasticities of the home demand for import goods and services and of the foreign demand for the country's export goods and services. The more elastic these demands are, the greater is the effect of a given exchange rate movement on the balance of payments. The less elastic the demands are, the greater is the degree of rate movement necessary to eliminate a given disequilibrium.

Ordinarily, the effect of a rise in exchange rates is to reduce autonomous international payments and increase autonomous receipts, and vice versa, for a fall in rates. A rise in exchange rates is known as *exchange depreciation,* because the international value of the currency in terms of other national currencies falls as rates on the latter increase.[1] A fall in exchange rates is called exchange *appreciation,* and it involves an increase in the international value of the currency.

For exchange depreciation and appreciation to reduce a balance-of-payments deficit and surplus, respectively, however, certain minimum elasticity conditions are required. This can best be seen in terms of the demand and supply curves of foreign exchange, as described in the preceding chapter. As long as the demand curve for foreign exchange has a negative slope (falls from left to right) and the supply curve has a positive slope (rises from left to right), a rise in the exchange rate reduces the quantity of exchange demanded and increases the quantity supplied, and a fall in the rate has the opposite effects. As we know from an earlier discussion, the demand curve will almost surely have a negative slope and thereby contribute to balance-of-payments adjustment through rate changes. But the supply curve of exchange over some range in rates may have a negative slope—that is, bend backward as in Figure 15.2 (page 300). In this event, a rise in rate *reduces* the quantity of

---

[1] The term *devaluation* also means a decrease in the international value of a currency, but it is properly used only when the currency is valued in terms of gold and the gold content is reduced.

exchange supplied, so that from the supply side, exchange depreciation would increase rather than reduce a deficit.

We recall that the reason for a backward-bending supply curve
of foreign exchange is an inelastic foreign demand for the country's
exports. If such is the case, in order for exchange depreciation to
reduce a deficit and appreciation to reduce a surplus the elasticity
of demand for foreign exchange must be great enough to offset the
negative effects produced on the supply side. Expressed in terms of
the slopes, rather than the elasticities, of the curves, the required
condition is that the supply curve approach the demand curve

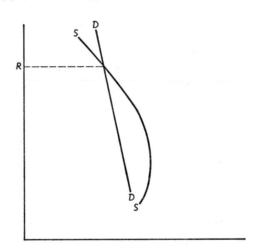

FIGURE 16.1
UNSTABLE RATE SITUATION

above the point of intersection from the right and below the point
of intersection from the left. Figure 16.1 shows a case where this is
not true. A rise in the rate of exchange above R would cause the
quantity of exchange supplied to decrease more than the decrease
in quantity demanded, and a fall in rate would cause the quantity
supplied to increase more than the quantity demanded. This is the
opposite set of reactions to that usually expected from price
changes, with the consequence that usual exchange rate variations
to adjust the balance of payments are not appropriate under such
circumstances. (Another consequence is the instability of the rate,
a matter that is discussed in a later context.)

Apart from the probably rather special case considered above,
exchange depreciation must be regarded as one of the prime methods of correcting a balance-of-payments deficit. Indeed, of all the
methods of adjustment it is the most natural in a free-market sys-

tem. In the absence of any kind of government control or intervention in the market, balance-of-payments disequilibrium would automatically be corrected through exchange rate movements produced by market forces. Earlier we noted that variations in the exchange rate are a sign of disequilibrium; now we may add that they are also a method of balance-of-payments adjustment.

To illustrate how in a completely free market balance-of-payments adjustment would be effected through exchange rate movements, let us assume that a country's initial balance-of-payments

FIGURE 16.2

ADJUSTMENT OF CURRENT ACCOUNT BALANCE TO CAPITAL
OUTFLOW VIA EXCHANGE-RATE CHANGE

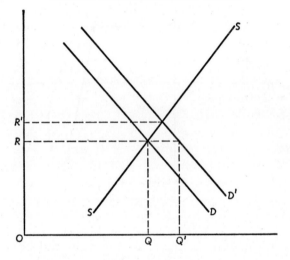

equilibrium is disturbed by an autonomous capital outflow. The situation is depicted in Figure 16.2. Before the movement of capital occurs, the rate of exchange is in equilibrium at R, based on the then-prevailing autonomous demand (D) and supply (S) curves of foreign exchange. The outflow of capital causes the demand for foreign exchange to increase to D'. The immediate impact of the capital movement is a deficit disequilibrium, for at rate R the quantity of foreign exchange demanded exceeds the quantity supplied. In terms of the balance of payments, the disequilibrium is manifested in an excess of autonomous debits over autonomous credits. For equilibrium to be restored, an excess of credits over debits—equal in amount to the capital outflow—must be generated on the combined other autonomous accounts. For example, if prior to the capital outflow all transactions were in goods and services in the current account, equilibrium would require that the current account develop a net credit balance (equal to the surplus of exports over imports) to match the capital outflow. The adjustment mechanism in the present case that brings about the surplus of credits on other accounts is the rise in the exchange rate. At rate R' (Figure 16.2), adjustment is complete and equilibrium is reestablished. It will be observed that the rise in the rate of exchange produces the surplus of credits on other accounts, equal to QQ' and the outflow of capital, in part through contracting debit transactions which use foreign exchange and in part through expanding credit transactions which provide foreign exchange.

Adjustment of the balance of payments through the exchange rate is automatically generated by market forces in a pure market system with respect to international monetary relations. In the next chapter, this will be called a "freely fluctuating exchange rate system." In most historical systems, however, exchange rates are not free to move in response to free-market demand and supply, but are limited in their movement in various ways and to varying extents. But this does not preclude the exchange rate as an instrument of adjustment to be employed at the discretion of the monetary authority. Whether an automatic market response or the decision of the monetary authority, exchange variation has the same kind of influence on the balance of payments. The major difference between automatic and discretionary variations in rate is that the latter is subject to nonmarket desiderata and judgments with respect to the degree and timing of rate changes. The implications of this difference will be discussed in the next chapter.

ADJUSTMENT THROUGH PRICE CHANGES

The exchange rate is a price, but a very special one, for changes in it alter the relationship between the prices of all domestic goods and services and the prices of all foreign goods and services. Exchange depreciation lowers the domestic price level relative to foreign price levels, and exchange appreciation raises the domestic price level relative to foreign price levels. It is evident that the same kind of changes in relative national price levels could be effected with exchange rates held stable through differential rates of absolute price changes at home and abroad. A uniform decrease in domestic prices of 10 percent, foreign prices remaining stable, would have equivalent effects to a 10 percent exchange depreciation so far as relative national price levels are concerned. As we shall see later, however, price deflation and exchange depreciation have quite different effects in other respects.

As in the case of exchange rate variations, the power of price level changes to adjust the balance of payments depends upon the elasticities of demand for imports at home and abroad. If the foreign demand for a country's export goods and services is elastic, a drop in their prices results in an increase in the quantity of foreign exchange proceeds. If the foreign demand is inelastic, the quantity of foreign exchange earned at lower export prices is smaller than at higher prices. On the demand side, lower home prices will nearly always cause a smaller quantity of foreign exchange to be demanded, the decrease being greater the higher the cross-elasticity of demand between imported goods and domestic goods.[2]

Again, as in the case of exchange rate variations, price changes may either be automatically produced through market forces or deliberately brought about through discretionary policy measures. Inflation and deflation of prices are not, however, symmetrical with respect to the ease with which they may be effected, whether through automatic forces or discretionary policies. More will be said on this point in the next chapter.

ADJUSTMENT THROUGH INCOME CHANGES

Autonomous balance-of-payments transactions are a function not only of exchange rates and prices, but also of income. At given and unchanged exchange rates and prices, higher levels of income at home tend to cause a greater volume of imports, and higher levels of income abroad tend to cause a greater volume of exports. (Income levels at home and abroad also probably affect autonomous capital movements, but the relationship here is generally less reliably predictable.) Hence, a balance-of-payments deficit may be corrected through either a decrease in the level of home income or an increase in foreign income.

The responsiveness of imports and exports to income changes at home and abroad is measured by the *marginal propensity to import* or by the *income-elasticity of demand for imports*. The *average*

---

[2] The cross-elasticity of demand between imported and home goods is defined as the percentage change in the quantity of import goods demanded, divided by the percentage change in the price of home goods.

propensity to import is defined as the ratio of imports to the national income, symbolically expressed as M/Y, where M represents imports and Y represents national income. If we wish to investigate effects of a change in income on imports, the appropriate measure is the *marginal* propensity to import, defined as $\Delta M/\Delta Y$, where Δ signifies change. To measure the ratio of *relative* changes in imports to changes in income, the income-elasticity of demand for imports is the most appropriate concept. It is defined as the percentage change in imports divided by the percentage change in income— that is, $(\Delta M/M) \div (\Delta Y/Y)$.

The balance of payments of a country and its national income are intimately interrelated, changes in one causing changes in the other. National income is defined, in real terms, as the aggregate domestic production of goods and services and, in money terms, as aggregate expenditure on domestically produced goods and services. Goods and services exported out of current home production are part of the national income. Imports, on the other hand, even though they are available for domestic use, are not part of the national income, for they are produced elsewhere (and are therefore part of the national incomes of the producing countries). Hence, viewing the national income as aggregate expenditure on home-produced goods and services, foreign expenditure on a country's exports is included, while domestic expenditure on imported goods and services is excluded. This yields the following identity:

$$Y \equiv C + I + X - M$$

where Y represents the national income, C is consumption expenditure, I is investment expenditure, X is exports, and M is imports. (For simplicity, government purchases of goods and services are not separately identified.)

It will be noted that the foreign component of income, $X - M$, consists of the current account of the balance of payments. If the net balance on current account is zero (that is, $X = M$), expenditure on imports, which does not enter the national income flow, is exactly offset by foreign expenditure on the country's exports, which does enter its income flow. In this case, the effect of foreign trade on the country's money national income is neutral. If exports exceed imports (a net credit balance on current account), foreign trade exerts an expansionary influence on the money national income, while a net debit balance on current accounts has a deflationary effect.

The same conclusions can be reached by a slightly different route. Exports stand on the same footing as domestic investment expenditure in their effects on money national income: Each is an "injection" into the income-expenditure flow, swelling the stream of income receipts generated by the purchase of goods and services. They are also alike in that, contrasted to consumption expenditure, they are to a large extent determined independently of the current level of domestic income. In other words, whereas the volume of consumption is mainly determined by the level of domestic income and does not significantly change except in response to a prior change in income, both investment and exports are importantly influenced by other factors. In the case of exports, the chief determining force is the national incomes of *other* countries which provide the markets for the home country's export goods and services.

Imports, on the other hand, have a national income role similar to that of saving. Both are "leakages" in the income-expenditure flow, in the sense that they represent dispositions of income receipts which do not reenter the domestic income stream (although import expenditure does enter the income flow of the exporting countries). They are also similar in both being primarily functions of the national income, their volume and changes in volume being largely determined by domestic income and changes in income.

On the basis of the above relationships it is perceived that if exports change, national income will change in the same direction, and that if income changes—because of variation in exports or for other reasons—imports will change in the same direction. In short, income is an increasing function of exports and imports are an increasing function of income. Hence, starting out in both balance-of-payments and income equilibrium, if the balance of payments is disturbed by an autonomous change in exports, balance-of-payments adjustment will tend to occur through a change in imports induced by the income effects of the change in exports. On the other hand, if the national income changes with exports remaining constant, the consequent induced change in imports will cause balance-of-payments disequilibrium, assuming that equilibrium existed before the change in income occurred.

To give precision to these relationships between the balance of payments and the national income, the conditions of income equilibrium for an open economy need to be stated. First, let us recall the income identity

$$Y \equiv C + I + X - M$$

By deducting the import component of consumption and investment expenditure and of exports separately, the identity may be rewritten as

$$\Upsilon \equiv C_d + I_d + X_d \tag{a}$$

where the subscript indicates production out of domestic resources. We know that the national income is also necessarily equal to the sum of the various possible uses to which income receipts are devoted—namely, expenditure on domestically produced consumer goods and services and on imported goods and services, plus the unspent residual, saving—yielding the identity

$$\Upsilon \equiv C_d + M + S \tag{b}$$

Combining the two identities (a) and (b) and reducing gives

$$I_d + X_d \equiv M + S \tag{c}$$

This last identity states that the sum of expenditure on domestically produced goods, added to the home stock of goods, plus those exported, necessarily equals the sum of expenditure on imports, plus saving.

The terms in (c) may be rearranged as follows:

$$S \equiv I_d + X_d - M \tag{d}$$

This is an extremely useful and revealing relationship. If a country's exports and imports are equal $(X_d - M = 0)$, then domestic investment is limited to home saving. But if imports exceed exports, the identity tells us that domestic investment is greater than home saving by the amount of the import surplus. One very significant aspect of this is the potential role of foreign trade in providing extra resources for economic development when domestic saving is insufficient to finance adequate capital formation. The third possibility is for exports to exceed imports, in which case domestic investment is necessarily less than saving, with the difference equal to foreign investment.

All the above relationships are ex post, referring to realized events of a past period, and necessarily hold by definition of the terms. But they are not necessarily equilibrium relationships. Equilibrium prevails, as we have seen in the concept's application to the balance of payments, when ex ante, or planned, decisions of various groups are consistent with each other, so that the decisions can be carried out harmoniously and with no built-in tendency for change to occur. Applied to national income, equilibrium exists when planned "injections" into the income-expenditure flow equal planned "leakages" from the flow. Since expenditure on domestically produced goods added to capital stock (or investment) and exports are injections, and imports and saving are leakages, when these are all on a planned or ex ante basis the income equilibrium equation becomes

$$I_d + X_d = M + S \qquad (e)$$

The terms are the same as in identity (c) above, except for the important difference that the equality *must* hold for the identity, but holds only in equilibrium for equation (e). Hence, when we use the identity sign $(\equiv)$, reference is made to ex post relationships, while the equality sign $(=)$ indicates an equilibrium relationship.

The condition for income equilibrium may be restated as cor-

$$S = I_d + X_d - M \qquad (f)$$

responding to identity (d) above.

Now we are ready to examine the interrelationship between the current account of the balance of payments and the national income. To simplify the analysis, let us first assume that the net balance on all autonomous balance-of-payments transactions, other than those in the current account, is zero. Therefore, current account balance $(X_d = M)$ is the condition for balance-of-payments equilibrium.

It is at once evident from the income equilibrium equation—either (e) or (f) above—that income equilibrium and balance-of-payments equilibrium need not necessarily coexist. But let us assume that during an initial period income equilibrium and balance-of-payments equilibrium both prevail. Hence, equation (f) above is satisfied under the special assumption that $X_d = M$.

Suppose now that exports decrease. This might occur for any of numerous reasons—a contraction in foreign income, the imposition of tariffs or quotas by other countries, a shift in foreign preferences, and so on. The decrease in exports immediately causes a deficit disequilibrium in the balance of payments. It also immediately causes a decrease in the national income, since exports are a component of income. The question we wish to investigate is what effects the decline in income will in turn have on the balance of payments.

We observed earlier that imports are a function of the national income and defined the relationship between changes in them as the marginal propensity to import, $\Delta M/\Delta Y$. By what amount imports will change as a result of a change in income is discovered by multiplying the change in income by the marginal propensity to import. For instance, assume that $\Delta M/\Delta Y = 2/10$. Then a change in income of, say, $100 causes imports to change, in the same direction, by $20.

Knowing the value of the marginal propensity to import, we need know only the change in national income to calculate the induced change in imports. The first question, then, is how much income changes as a result of an autonomous decrease in exports. Let the decrease in exports be $100. The *immediate* effect on income is to reduce it by the same amount. But this is not the end of the story, for the reduction in income in turn will induce changes in all the variables functionally related to income, with "feedback" effects on income. The result is a series of repercussions manifesting themselves in successive income-expenditure rounds, but in dwindling force, until a new equilibrium level of income is reached. This phenomenon is known as the foreign trade *multiplier* effect.

To illustrate how the multiplier works, let us assume the following values for the variables functionally related to income:

$$\text{Marginal propensity to save:} \quad \frac{\Delta S}{\Delta Y} = 2/10$$

$$\text{Marginal propensity to import:} \quad \frac{\Delta M}{\Delta Y} = 3/10$$

$$\text{Marginal propensity to consume:} \quad \frac{\Delta C_d}{\Delta Y} = 5/10$$

$$\text{Marginal propensity to invest:} \quad \frac{\Delta I}{\Delta Y} = 0$$

The accompanying table shows the series of changes that occur in successive income-expenditure periods, beginning with a decrease in exports of $100 in the first period.

Period	ΔS	ΔM	ΔC_d	ΔI_d	ΔX_d	ΔY
1................					−100	−100
2................	−20	−30	−50	0	0	−50
3................	−10	−15	−25	0	0	−25
4................	−5	−7.5	−12.5	0	0	−12.5
Equilibrium Values:	−40	−60	−100	0	−100	−200

The decrease in exports occurs in period 1, causing income for that period to decline by an equal amount. The decline in income in period 1 induces in the next income-expenditure period a decrease in saving, imports, and consumption, in each case by an amount determined by their respective marginal propensities times the preceding period's decrease in income. Since we have assumed a marginal propensity to invest of zero, no induced changes in investment expenditure occur. It is also assumed that no further changes in exports occur after the initial decrease. The decrease in income during each period after the first equals the decrease in consumption expenditure for that period, for under our assumptions, consumption is the only component of income that is induced to changes by prior changes in income.

It will be observed that saving, imports, and consumption expenditure fall by smaller amounts in each successive period, steadily approaching equilibrium values when further change ceases. These equilibrium values are listed in the bottom row of the table. As indicated, the new equilibrium level of income is $200 less than originally, the decline being accounted for by the autonomous decrease in exports of $100 plus the induced decrease in consumption of $100. The new equilibrium level of saving is $40 less than originally, and imports are $60 less than originally. The income equilibrium equation, $I_d + X_d = M + S$, is satisfied, since, starting from the base of the original equilibrium, $\Delta I_d + \Delta X_d = \Delta M + \Delta S$.

Since the decline in income is twice the amount of the decrease in exports, the foreign trade multiplier in this case is 2. More generally, the value of the multiplier is equal to the reciprocal of the sum of the marginal propensity to save and the marginal propensity to import. That is, letting K stand for the multiplier,

$$K = \frac{1}{\Delta S/\Delta Y + \Delta M/\Delta Y}$$

The chief effect of the decline in income set off by the autonomous fall in exports which we are interested in at the moment is the induced decrease in imports. We see that imports are $60 less than originally, the decrease being brought about by the contraction in income of $200, in conjunction with an assumed marginal propensity to import of 3/10. Hence, a considerable adjustment in the balance of payments has occurred, the deficit of $100 in period 1 being reduced to $40 at the new equilibrium level of income. The adjustment has been effected entirely through the income effects of the decline in exports, working through the multiplier.

However, balance-of-payments adjustment is not complete, a deficit of $40 remaining. What accounts for the incomplete adjustment? Evidently, the failure of national income to decrease by an amount large enough to induce a decrease in imports of $100 instead of only $60. With a marginal propensity to import of 3/10, income would have to fall by $333.33 to induce a contraction in imports of $100 (since $333.33 × 3/10 = $100).

The next question, then, is why income did not fall by a greater amount. The answer is because its fall was "braked" by induced decreases in saving and imports. Referring to the table, we notice that in each period the decline in income is less than the decline in the preceding period by exactly the sum of the decreases in saving and imports. Had the induced changes in saving and imports been smaller, income would have contracted by a greater amount. In other words, the multiplier is greater if the denominator in the formula

$$K = \frac{1}{\Delta S/\Delta Y + \Delta M/\Delta Y}$$

is smaller.

However, the real culprit is saving, for whatever decreases in imports occur directly contribute to balance-of-payments adjustment. For example, suppose that $\Delta S/\Delta Y = 0$ and $\Delta M/\Delta Y = 5/10$. The multiplier retains a value of 2, and the new equilibrium level of income is $200 less than originally, as under the previous assumptions. But in this case imports fall by $100 and adjustment is complete.

The presence of a marginal propensity to save greater than zero prevents complete balance-of-payments adjustment through income effects, unless the income braking caused by saving is offset by the presence of a marginal propensity to invest ($\Delta I/\Delta Y$) greater than zero. Saving is a leakage in the income-expenditure flow, but investment is an injection. Hence, even if saving decreases as income falls, if investment expenditure also decreases by the same amount income will not be restrained in its descent as under our previous assumptions. To put it another way, the multiplier will be greater when the marginal propensity to invest is greater than zero, the formula becoming

$$K = \frac{1}{\Delta S/\Delta Y + \Delta M/\Delta Y - \Delta I/\Delta Y}$$

If

$$\Delta S/\Delta Y = \Delta I/\Delta Y, \quad K = \frac{1}{\Delta M/\Delta Y}$$

Inserting a value of 3/10 for the marginal propensity to import yields a multiplier of $3\frac{1}{3}$, so that the decrease in income set off by a decline in exports of $100 would be $333.33, with an induced decrease in imports of $100. Adjustment is therefore complete.

Unfortunately for a nice, clean adjustment theory, however, there is no reason for expecting the marginal propensities to save and to invest to be equal, since the decisions are made for different motives and largely by different groups. It is just as possible for $\Delta I/\Delta Y$ to be *greater* than $\Delta S/\Delta Y$ as for it to be equal or unequal in the opposite direction. If $\Delta I/\Delta Y > \Delta S/\Delta Y$, *over*adjustment of the balance of payments will occur, for in this case income changes more than enough to restore equilibrium.

Finally, one other element in the adjustment process through income effects needs brief mention. It is called the "foreign repercussion." To illustrate what is meant by this, consider the effects of the autonomous decrease in our country's exports on the incomes of other countries whose imports from our country decrease. If the contraction in the imports of these other countries is autonomous (that is, not induced by a prior reduction in their incomes), it will have the effect of increasing their incomes. As their national incomes rise, there will tend to be an induced expansion in their import demand, depending upon their marginal propensities to import. And part of their greater import demand can be expected to be directed toward the exports of our home country, thus contributing to the adjustment of its balance of payments.

The foreign repercussion can be significant or it can be negligible in the adjustment process, depending upon circumstances in the particular case. One relevant factor is how important a country's trade and national income are in relation to world trade and income. For a country like the United States, with the largest volume of trade and income of all countries, the feedback effect of changes in her income on trade may be considerable. On the other hand, for smaller countries, the foreign repercussion is likely to be much weaker, for the impact of changes in their income or trade on other countries' incomes is negligible.

The general conclusion emerging from the above discussion is that balance-of-payments adjustment through income effects is potentially powerful, but with no assurance that it will not be either insufficient to effect complete adjustment or so strong as to cause overadjustment, and hence disequilibrium in the opposite direction.

The adjustment process we have illustrated is automatic and operates on the assumption that the income changes initiated by balance-of-payments disturbances have free rein to work themselves out, uninhibited by countervailing government policies. However, this does not preclude the government's reinforcing, or substituting for, automatic market forces through appropriate measures. If, for example, automatic income effects are too weak to bring about balance-of-payments equilibrium, further income changes can be fostered through monetary and fiscal policies. In general terms, deflationary monetary and fiscal policies tend to reduce balance-of-payments deficits (or increase surpluses) , while expansionary monetary and fiscal policies tend to reduce balance-of-payments surpluses (or increase deficits) .

Obviously, government also may interfere with automatic adjustment, restraining the income changes which balance-of-payments disturbances produce. The reasons for doing so may be very strong, as is shown in the next chapter.

The Cash-Balance Effect. The conclusion that income effects do not assure that adjustment in the balance of payments may not be under- or overachieved is actually too pessimistic. The model that leads to the conclusion stated is a partial equilibrium model, in the sense that all the variables affecting imports, except for income, are assumed to remain constant. In fact, however, other variables influencing the trade balance cannot remain constant while direct income effects are working themselves out. For one thing, prices are very likely to be affected, as described in the next section. Even more important is the so-called "cash-balance effect," which we shall examine now.

We have seen that with fixed exchange rates a deficit in the trade balance reduces the domestically held supply of money. Unless the monetary authority of the country takes action to offset the impact of a trade deficit on the domestic supply of money, the supply continues to contract as long as the trade deficit continues. But clearly, money supply cannot contract indefinitely, nor will it do so. As the public's holdings of money decline, a liquidity squeeze develops which leads the public to attempt to restore their desired cash balances. Assuming that the monetary authority refrains from satisfying the public's desire to hold more cash through an expansion in money supply, there are in general only two means available to individuals and business firms of acquiring additional cash: (*a*) buying less (or selling more) goods and services, and (*b*) liquidating securities (stocks, bonds, mortgages, and so on). The first method reduces import demand and/or increases exports, thereby directly contributing to the elimination of the trade deficit and drain of the money supply. The second line of action causes a decline in the prices of securities, which is equivalent to an increase in interest rates. Higher interest rates in turn tend to reduce expenditure on goods and services, especially investment expenditure but perhaps consumption expenditure as well, in either case including expenditure on imports. To the extent that the decrease in demand falls on domestic or export goods, the money national income falls (and by a multiple, depending upon the size of the multiplier), inducing a decrease in imports.

Recognition of the cash-balance effects of a trade deficit is important for two reasons. In the first place, it reinforces the "pure" income effects previously identified, and insures that any failure of the latter completely to adjust the balance of payments will be offset by cash-balance effects. Second, the analysis points to the fundamental conclusion that the balance of payments is essentially a monetary phenomenon, with the implication that a deficit disequilibrium cannot continue in the absence of monetary policies working counter to the automatic adjustment mechanism. A balance-of-payments deficit cannot continue persistently unless the monetary authority of a country "feeds" it by replacing the money drained out by the deficit.

Combined Price and Income Effects

As the discussion of the cash-balance effect has shown, the direct income effects of changes in the balance of payments do not work in a vacuum. Separation of price and income effects is convenient for expository purposes, but in reality both are normally present, exerting their influence jointly, sometimes in a complementary fashion, at other times in opposition to each other. However, it remains true that the mechanism of adjustment relies upon *either* price *or* income effects—depending upon the exchange rate system in operation—as the trigger mechanism initiating the adjustment process and as the primary adjustment variable.

An excellent example of the interaction between price and income effects is provided by the adjustment mechanism through exchange depreciation. The initial impact on the balance of payments of exchange depreciation stems from the increase in exports and decrease in imports resulting from the effects of depreciation in lowering export prices (in foreign currencies) and raising import prices (in domestic currency). However, an increase in exports and decrease in imports causes national income to increase, producing secondary income effects on the balance of payments in the direction of inducing a greater volume of imports. The final improvement in the balance of payments is therefore likely to be less than that initially provided by the price effects of the depreciation.

Regardless of the type of exchange-rate system in operation and the trigger mechanism setting off the adjustment process, an improvement in the balance of payments on current account requires a change in the relationship between a country's production of goods and services and its expenditure on goods and services. A convenient framework for analyzing the required change and the role of income and price effects is the so-called "absorption" approach.

The Absorption Approach

As noted previously, the national income equation is

$$Y = C + I + X - M$$

The elements of national income may now be separated into two groups. The first group represents expenditure on goods and services by domestic residents, or the economy's "absorption" of goods and services. It consists of consumption expenditure (C) plus domestic investment expenditure (I), including import components. The second group consists of the trade balance, exports minus imports ($X - M$). Hence, letting A represent absorption and B the trade balance, the income equation is rewritten

$$Y = A + B$$

If the trade balance B is to increase (through either an increase in exports or decrease in imports), clearly either Y must rise, or absorption A must fall, since

$$B = \Upsilon - A$$

(This is equivalent to the proposition implied in our earlier income analysis that for the balance of payments to improve, saving must increase relatively to domestic investment.)

If there are idle resources available to be drawn upon, or already-employed resources can be more efficiently used, an increase in the real national income (output of goods and services) is an avenue for improving the balance of payments, provided that the increase in income is not wholly absorbed domestically. How much extra absorption is induced by an increase in income depends upon the economy's marginal propensity to spend income. If, as normally is assumed to be the case, an increase in income does not induce an equal increase in expenditure or absorption, the balance of payments is improved.

Applying the absorption analysis to exchange depreciation, we observe that the initial impact of depreciation, assuming favorable elasticity conditions and the presence of unemployed resources, is to increase the real national income through expanding the output of export goods and of import-competing goods. The balance of payments improves to the same extent.[3] As a secondary repercussion, the increase in real income induces an increase in absorption and to this extent reduces the initial improvement in the balance of payments. The final net effect of depreciation on the balance of payments thus depends upon the relative magnitudes of the increase in income and the induced increase in absorption. As indicated before, the normal presumption is a favorable outcome, on the grounds that induced absorption tends to be smaller than the increase in real income.

The situation is quite different if balance-of-payments adjustment is to take place in the context of a fully employed economy operating at the outset at capacity. In this case, real income cannot increase, except to the extent that the efficiency of resource use is improved. Apart from the possibility of the latter, the burden of adjustment must therefore fall on reduced absorption.

But how is absorption to be reduced? Exchange depreciation offers slim possibilities. To the extent that reduced import expenditure is accompanied by increased expenditure on home-produced goods, absorption is not contracted. Other possible effects of de-

---

[3] The balance of payments improves by a larger amount if the increase in expenditure on import-competing goods is less than the decrease in expenditure on imports —that is, if absorption decreases.

preciation in reducing absorption exist, but they are extremely tenuous and of limited magnitude.[4]

The moral of the story is that exchange depreciation may not be an effective instrument of balance-of-payments adjustment when the economy is fully employed (though some economists believe that it can be effective through the diversion of resources to the more efficient export sector which depreciation encourages). Instead of, or in addition to, depreciation a policy of expenditure reduction through monetary and fiscal restraints may be necessary to correct a balance-of-payments deficit in a period of full employment. An alternative is the imposition of controls, discussed next.

ADJUSTMENT THROUGH CONTROLS

The last general method of balance-of-payments adjustment is through direct controls over international transactions. This method differs radically from the others in that it seeks directly to suppress market forces rather than working through them. It therefore may be argued that direct controls cannot establish a genuine equilibrium, on the grounds that the latter is a free-market concept which is inherently inconsistent with direct controls. However, this is a semantic issue in which we need not become involved. In an era when government controls over various aspects of the economy are pervasive, controls over international transactions cannot be precluded as a possible method of balance-of-payments adjustment, whether or not one wishes to label the result a "true" equilibrium.

Much more important than the semantic question is whether controls can be *effective* in terms of measured results. Suppose that in an effort to eliminate a balance-of-payments deficit a country introduces exchange controls limiting the freedom to import goods and services and to export capital. Since the controls do not lessen the *desires* of residents to import and send capital abroad (and, indeed, may even stimulate their desires), there is the strong tendency for the controls to be circumvented through extralegal channels. "Black markets" frequently evolve in countries with exchange controls, wherein foreign exchange is illegally bought and sold for purposes not officially sanctioned.

---

[4] Among these effects are the so-called "money illusion," the Pigou effect, and a redistribution of income. For discussion of these, see S. S. Alexander, "Effect of a Devaluation on a Trade Balance," International Monetary Fund, *Staff Papers*, April, 1952.

Even if controls are strictly adhered to, they may not be successful in achieving intended results. For example, if demand for imported goods is not allowed free expression, it may simply be shifted to domestic goods and services, causing a rise in prices and diversion of resources out of export industries. In this case exports fall and the balance-of-payments deficit remains uncorrected.

Notwithstanding such difficulties in successfully adjusting the balance of payments through controls, they must be admitted as a potentially effective method of adjustment when employed in conjunction with other measures. For instance, if the effectiveness of controls is threatened by the diversion of demand to home goods, contractionary monetary and fiscal policies might be employed to avoid adverse repercussions on exports. Of course, in this event one might say that the adjustment is being accomplished through the income effects of these measures rather than through direct controls. However, the controls may well serve to hasten the process.

Most important, in some cases there may be no acceptable alternative to direct controls as a means of handling a balance-of-payments deficit. Market methods may not work because of destabilizing speculative transactions or because of noneconomic forces at work. Thus, as is shown in the next chapter, exchange depreciation may set off an outward movement of capital based on the expectation of further depreciation, rendering this method of adjustment ineffective.

RECOMMENDED READING

MACHLUP, FRITZ. *International Trade and the National Income Multiplier.* New York: Blakiston Division, McGraw-Hill Book Co., 1943.

MEADE, J. E. *The Balance of Payments,* Parts IV and V. New York: Oxford University Press, Inc., 1951.

SCAMMELL, W. M. *International Monetary Policy,* chaps. ii–iv. 2d ed. London: Macmillan & Co., Ltd., 1964.

YEAGER, L. B. *International Monetary Relations,* chaps. iv–vii. New York: Harper & Row, Publishers, 1966.

STUDY QUESTIONS

1. Review the concept of balance-of-payments disequilibrium. Distinguish between deficit and surplus disequilibrium.
2. What are the dominating and key variables with which the balance of payments is functionally related?

3. Define exchange depreciation and appreciation.

4. State the conditions required for exchange depreciation to eliminate a balance-of-payments deficit.

5. Illustrate adjustment of the balance of payments to a capital outflow through exchange rate movement.

6. What makes the exchange rate as the price of foreign currency different from the other prices?

7. Explain why and in what sense price deflation and inflation are comparable in their balance-of-payments effects to exchange depreciation and appreciation, respectively.

8. Define: average propensity to import, marginal propensity to import, income-elasticity of demand for imports.

9. State the national income identity for an open economy.

10. In what respect are investment expenditure and exports similar in their income roles?

11. What is meant by the statement that imports are a "leakage" in the income-expenditure flow?

12. Explain why, ex post, $I_d + X_d$ must equal $M + S$.

13. If a country has an import surplus, what must be true of the relationship between domestic saving and domestic investment?

14. What change in the income identity is required to convert it into an equilibrium equation?

15. Define and explain the determinants of the size of the foreign trade multiplier.

16. Under what conditions will balance-of-payments adjustment through income effects alone be complete?

17. What is meant by the "foreign repercussion," and what role does it have in balance-of-payments adjustment?

18. If the government wishes to reinforce the market process of adjustment through income effects, what monetary and fiscal policies would be appropriate in the face of a balance-of-payment deficit? In the face of a balance-of-payments surplus?

19. Explain the cash-balance effect and how it reenforces the income effect with stable exchange rates.

20. In what sense is the balance of payments essentially a monetary phenomenon?

21. Why is the final effect on the balance of payments of exchange depreciation less than the initial effect?

22. Explain the "absorption" approach in balance of payments analysis.

23. Why is it more difficult to correct a balance-of-payments deficit

when there is full employment than when there are idle resources?

24. On what grounds may it be argued that balance-of-payments equilibrium and direct trade and exchange controls are inconsistent?

25. What difficulties may be encountered in successfully adjusting the balance of payments through direct controls?

Chapter 17

ALTERNATIVE INTERNATIONAL MONETARY SYSTEMS

In the preceding chapter four different general processes of balance-of-payments adjustment were identified: variations in exchange rates, price changes, income changes, and direct controls. One or more of these methods of adjustment must be activated if a country's balance of payments suffers disequilibrium in a given direction for a prolonged period. But which method, or combination, is used depends upon the kind of international monetary system in operation. This chapter examines the major historical systems and discusses their respective advantages and disadvantages. The contemporary system will be reserved for discussion in the next chapter.

CLASSIFICATION OF SYSTEMS

Alternative monetary systems may be classified according to various criteria, the principal ones being (a) the degree of stability of exchange rates and (b) the extent to which market forces are allowed freely to operate. Depending upon the combination of (a) and (b), the third criterion is (c) the balance-of-payments adjustment mechanism associated with the system.

Based on these criteria, there are four "pure" types of system:

1. Stable exchange rates, with market operations free of direct controls, and primary adjustment through automatic price and income changes. We shall call this the pure gold standard system.
2. Freely fluctuating rates, determined by free-market forces, with primary adjustment through exchange rate variations. We shall call this a freely fluctuating rate system.
3. Exchange rate stability, though frequently with exceptions, and direct controls over trade and payments. Primary adjustment

through direct controls. We shall call this an exchange-control system.

4. Short-term exchange-rate stability, but with occasional changes in rate and with government intervention limited to operations in the market, with no direct controls. The primary adjustment mechanism consists of discretionary exchange-rate changes. We shall call this "managed flexibility."

Most actual operating systems contain some mixture of elements from two or more of the above pure types. However, usually there are certain dominating characteristics of an operating system which permit its identification primarily with one of the pure types.

THE GOLD STANDARD SYSTEM

We shall begin the discussion with the gold standard system, for it was the first historical system in modern times and continues heavily to influence the contemporary system.

The dominating characteristic of the gold standard is the stability of exchange rates, within very narrow margins, produced by free-market forces.

The Mechanism of Rate Stability

Exchange rates under the gold standard have fixed par values determined by the gold content of the standard national monetary units. Each country legally defines its standard monetary unit as consisting of a specified quantity of gold. To keep the national currency equivalent in value to its declared gold content, the government stands ready to buy and sell gold in unlimited quantities at the price implied by its relationship to the standard monetary unit. Thus, for example, in 1930, when both the United States and England were on the gold standard, the dollar was defined as containing 23.22 grains of fine gold, and the pound was defined as containing approximately 113 grains of fine gold. The U.S. government freely bought and sold gold at the implied price of $20.67 per fine troy ounce.[1] The British government freely bought and sold gold at the implied price of £3/17s./10 1/2d. per troy ounce, 11/12 fine. The par rate of exchange between the pound and the dollar was equal to the ratio of their gold contents or—the same thing—to the ratio

---

[1] There are 480 grains in a troy ounce, and 480 ÷ 23.22 = 20.67.

of the prices of gold in each country. Hence, in 1930 the par rate between the pound and the dollar was $113 \div 23.22$, or £1 = \$4.86+.

From the above relationships it follows that the actual rate of exchange between two gold standard currencies cannot vary above or below the par rate of exchange by more than the cost of shipping gold (including insurance) from one country to the other. If the rate should rise or fall by more than this margin, dealers can earn profits by exporting or importing gold and selling or buying exchange with the proceeds, until the prevailing exchange rate is brought nearer to the par rate.

Suppose, for example, as was approximately the case at one time, that the cost of shipping 113 grains of gold from the United States to England is 2 cents. In this event, with a par rate of £1 = \$4.86+, the market rate could not continue to fall below about \$4.84 or to rise higher than about \$4.89. If the market rate fell to \$4.84, dealers would buy sterling bills, acquire 113 grains of gold in England for each pound, and sell the gold in the United States at \$4.86+, making a slight profit on the transaction, equal, for each pound bought, to the difference between the \$4.84 paid for the sterling bill plus \$0.02 shipping and insurance charges on the gold, and the \$4.86+ for which the gold was sold. The rate at which it pays to import gold (\$4.84 in this example) is the "gold import point," and at this rate the demand for exchange is infinitely elastic. On the other hand, if the market rate were to rise to \$4.89, it would pay dealers to buy gold in the United States, ship it to England, and sell the sterling proceeds for dollars, since it costs only \$4.86+, plus \$0.02 shipping charges, to get 113 grains of gold to England, where it commands £1. The rate at which it is profitable to export gold is the "gold export point," and at this rate the supply of exchange on the market is infinitely elastic.

In terms of demand and supply analysis, it is precisely because of the infinite elasticity of demand at the gold import point and infinite elasticity of supply at the gold export point that the market rate of exchange is prevented from fluctuating outside this range. This is shown graphically in Figure 17.1.

DZD' is the original demand and *SVS'* the original supply of exchange. The rate of exchange is originally at r. Now let the demand for exchange increase to *DZ'D'*. The rate rises to the gold export point, at which rate the quantity of exchange supplied from the export of goods and services is OQ_s. But at this rate the quantity of exchange demanded to pay for imports is OQ_D. The excess demand,

$OQ_D - OQ_S$, is satisfied from the exchange proceeds of the export of gold which private dealers find it profitable to sell abroad. In terms of the balance of payments, the current account net debit balance is matched by the gold account net credit balance.

It should be noted that the movement of gold through the above mechanism represents an *accommodating* balance-of-payments transaction. That is, gold movements occur only because there is an imbalance between autonomous demand and supply of exchange over

FIGURE 17.1

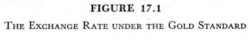

THE EXCHANGE RATE UNDER THE GOLD STANDARD

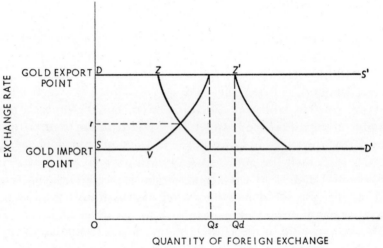

the range in rate between the gold points. As we know, this is a sign of balance-of-payments disequilibrium.

However, gold movements are not the only indication of disequilibrium, for they may be partially or wholly dispensed with through the effects of substitute short-term capital movements. Suppose the market rate of exchange begins to rise toward the gold export point. Exchange dealers are confident that the rate will never exceed that point and will probably sometime fall back toward par. The rise in rate may therefore induce dealers to acquire the currency in exchange for foreign currencies while it is temporarily cheap. (Reminder: a rise in exchange rates means a decrease in the international price of the currency.) The inflow of short-term funds from abroad is an accommodating capital movement which restrains the increase in the exchange rate, perhaps preventing it from reaching the gold export point. In the reverse case of a decline in exchange rate, accommodating short-term capital outflows may absorb the extra supply of foreign exchange and prevent the rate from reaching the gold import point.

We shall see later that a current account balance-of-payments deficit or surplus tends to produce certain monetary effects under the gold standard which also encourage stabilizing short-term capital inflows or outflows. We may summarize, then, by saying that, under the international gold standard, rates of exchange are stable, not only because of automatic gold flows at maximum and minimum rates, but also because of the tendency for short-term capital movements to provide additional exchange when the rate rises and to absorb excess exchange when the rate falls.

Adjustment Process

Accommodating gold and/or short-term capital movements signal disequilibrium in the balance of payments, occurring because autonomous payments and receipts are unequal at the fixed rate of exchange. Such disequilibrium cannot continue indefinitely, for neither gold nor capital movements are inexhaustible means of financing differences between autonomous payments and receipts. This is clearest in the case of a deficit disequilibrium. During a deficit period, a country loses gold from its reserve stock, or experiences either a reduction in its foreign short-term assets or an increase in its foreign short-term liabilities, or a combination of these. Obviously, the amount of gold that can be lost is ultimately limited by the stock on hand. The same is true for the amount of foreign short-term assets that can be drawn upon. While there are no formal limits of a similar nature on the volume of short-term foreign liabilities that can be created, there are effective limits set by the willingness of foreigners to accept further claims against the deficit country. The more serious and prolonged the deficit is, the less willing foreigners are likely to be to accumulate further claims against the deficit country, for the greater becomes the risk that its currency will be forced into devaluation.[2]

If disequilibrium cannot persist, how is balance-of-payments adjustment to be effected? A change in the exchange rate is inconsis-

---

[2] Devaluation of a currency means a lowering of its gold content and a decrease in its international value. Hence, assets denominated in that currency become worth less in terms of other currencies.

tent with the gold standard idea of a fixed gold value of the currency and is resorted to only if it is unavoidable. Direct controls over trade and payments are likewise anathema to the gold standard principle of market freedom. There is left, then, the remaining adjustment mechanism of price and/or income changes.

The classical theory of gold standard adjustment places primary emphasis on price changes which are brought about by what David Hume (1711–76) called the "gold-specie-flow mechanism." A country with a deficit balance of payments loses gold, while a country with a surplus balance of payments gains gold. Under the traditional gold standard, the domestic supply of money is based on gold holdings. Hence, a deficit balance of payments causes a decrease in the domestic supply of money, while a surplus increases it.

According to the quantity theory of money, the price level is a function of the quantity of money in circulation. A balance-of-payments deficit therefore leads to a decrease in the price level, and a surplus leads to an increase in the price level. This in turn causes deficit countries' exports to rise and imports to fall and surplus countries' imports to rise and exports to fall, thereby eliminating the disequilibrium.

The classical theory of the adjustment mechanism is therefore composed of three connecting main stages: the first is the connection between the balance of payments and the supply of money; the second is the connection between the supply of money and the price level; the last is the connection between the price level and the balance of payments.

From the standpoint of present-day theory, classical theory retains much of its validity, but in the light of changed institutional conditions and later theoretical developments, it requires modification. The weakest link in the classical formulation of the adjustment mechanism is stage two above—the relation between money supply and the price level. The relation between money supply and the price level posited by the classical theory is based on the quantity theory of money, which states that changes in the supply of money cause changes in the same direction in the price level. It is outside the scope of this book to evaluate the quantity theory, but two of its underlying assumptions should be noted.

The first is the assumption that there is full employment. In the presence of a considerable amount of unemployment, the chances that an increased supply of money will cause prices generally to rise are much less than if there is full employment, for the physical volume of output may keep pace with increased money expenditure. The classical theory of the adjustment mechanism is less applicable, therefore, when there is unemployment.

The second assumption is that costs and prices are flexible, that is, responsive to a decrease in aggregate money expenditure. If costs and prices are "sticky," a decrease in aggregate money expenditure causes a contraction in the volume of output and employment rather than a decline in costs and prices. Several elements contribute to cost and price inflexibility. Labor is ordinarily resistant to wage cuts, and, if labor is organized in strong unions, the power to resist is strengthened. Some costs (including wages, under collective bargaining agreements) are contractually fixed for given periods. More generally, any type of monopolistic element tends to reduce cost and price flexibility. It is common practice, for example, for firms in an oligopolistic market (a few large firms in the industry) to follow a concerted policy of price maintenance even in the face of declining demand for their output.

To question the universal validity of the quantity theory of money is not equivalent to questioning the very important role of monetary changes in the adjustment mechanism. The decrease in the domestically held supply of money a balance-of-payments deficit automatically causes, and the increase in money supply a surplus causes, are nearly certain to contribute to adjustment, provided that offsetting actions by the monetary authority are not taken. As money supply continues to contract in a deficit balance-of-payments situation and the liquidity of the economy correspondingly is reduced, at some point expenditure decisions will be affected. Consumption and investment, as well as import, expenditure may be reduced as a direct consequence of reduced liquidity. In any event, a lowered money supply is likely to cause interest rates to rise, which in turn has a dampening effect on expenditure.

If costs and prices are flexible and responsive to changes in aggregate expenditure, adjustment would follow along the lines indicated by classical theory. But even if prices do not respond to changes in expenditure, *income* does. And, as we know, income changes also provide a means of balance-of-payments adjustment.

At this point, however, we have left the classical world and entered the world of modern theory with its emphasis on adjustment through income, rather than price, changes. But there is no conflict between classical price and modern income effects. On the contrary, they complement and reinforce each other. As we concluded in the preceding chapter, adjustment through automatic income effects alone will be complete only under special conditions. The monetary effects of disequilibrium tend to strengthen the adjustment process by leading either to price changes or additional income changes or both.

Evaluation of the System

As far as the *effectiveness* of the automatic adjustment mechanism under the gold standard is concerned, combined price and income changes can generally be relied upon to perform an adequate job. Together with the encouragement to international trade and growth given by stable exchange rates, this constitutes a powerful argument in favor of the gold standard system. During its heyday in the latter part of the 19th century and until World War I, the gold standard provided a monetary framework which encouraged and facilitated the vast expansion in output and trade occurring during that era.

However, several conditions favorable to the operations of the gold standard were present before 1914 but have disappeared since. Among these, perhaps the most important was the willingness of countries to accept the basic premise underlying the system—namely, the subordination of the national economy to the dictates of external economic and monetary relations. Simultaneously, to maintain stable exchange rates and freedom of trade and payments requires adjustment of the balance of payments to serious disturbances through the price and income effects previously described. If this adjustment mechanism is resisted or counteracted by monetary and fiscal policies, trouble is bound to develop sooner or later, with the consequence that either fixed gold values of currencies, or freedom of trade and payments—or both—will be abandoned. This is precisely what happened during the 1930's, when one country after another, beginning with Great Britain in 1931, abandoned the gold standard. Why?

The immediate reason was the world economic crisis and the breakdown of confidence that followed it, but more fundamentally the reason lay in the rejection of the internal consequences of the gold standard adjustment mechanism. Price and income deflation is an effective method of eliminating a deficit disequilibrium in the balance of payments, but, in conjunction with downward price and cost inflexibility, unemployment is a frequent accompaniment. On the other hand, unless there is slack in the economy, the gold standard mechanism tends to cause inflation in countries with a surplus balance of payments. But today most countries are committed to full employment and price stability as major national goals. Few are willing to pay the price of internal economic and monetary instability for the sake of external equilibrium.

Conflict between domestic equilibrium at full employment and reasonably stable prices and balance-of-payments equilibrium is most prone to occur in a system of stable exchange rates and freedom of trade and payments. Under such a system the internal and external economy are closely bound together, developments in one directly affecting the other. The effects of autonomous changes in the trade balance on the national income were earlier explored in our discussion of the foreign-trade multiplier and adjustment through income effects. It is appropriate now to consider briefly the reverse relationship—the effects on the balance of payments of independent changes in the national income.

Suppose that a country is suffering from a recession and unemployment but is in balance-of-payments equilibrium. To rid itself of unemployment and restore prosperity, expansionary monetary and fiscal policies are called for. But as income and employment respond to these policies, the demand for imports will tend to increase, leading to a balance-of-payments deficit. Some partial compensation may be forthcoming through the foreign repercussion, but rarely could it be counted upon to prevent a deficit from arising. Thus, to achieve equilibrium at full employment the country is exposed to balance-of-payments disequilibrium. If the country has large gold and foreign exchange reserves it may be able and willing to allow the deficit to continue for a considerable period. But if its international reserves are inadequate to finance a deficit for long, an expansionary domestic policy is inconsistent with its commitment to the rules of the gold standard.

In short, the gold standard imposes constraints upon domestic policies which can be expected at least on occasion to clash head-on with important goals.

FREELY FLUCTUATING EXCHANGE RATES

The dilemma created by the gold standard would seem to have an obvious and easy solution: Let the burden of balance-of-payments adjustment be borne by exchange rates rather than by domestic income and prices. To ease further the problem of maintaining external equilibrium without burdensome constraints on domestic policies, let exchange rates respond freely to market forces of demand and supply. Such a system is, of course, that of freely fluctuating exchange rates.

The above paragraph summarizes in capsule form the outstanding advantage of a freely fluctuating exchange rate system. Some further discussion of it is warranted, both for its own sake and for the light it may throw on alternative systems.

As compared to the gold standard, the chief distinguishing characteristic of freely fluctuating rates is national monetary independence. In a gold standard system, national currencies are linked together through their common tie to gold and are in effect parts of a unified international monetary system. This is the underlying reason countries are not free in such a system to pursue independent domestic policies without regard to the policies of other countries and the state of the balance of payments. In contrast, with freely fluctuating exchange rates, each country's monetary system stands in an independent position, permitting the pursuit of domestic policies without the constraints imposed by balance-of-payments considerations.

This monetary independence is provided by the absorption of external shocks through exchange-rate changes rather than through changes in the domestic supply of money and income. Consider, for example, the effects of an autonomous decrease in exports. Under the gold standard, as we have seen, a deficit in the balance of payments is thereby immediately created, with gold exports and/or accommodating short-term capital inflows providing the means of financing it. Accompanying these is a decrease in the domestically held supply of money. But with freely fluctuating rates, the fall in exports causes an immediate rise in exchange rates which moderate the decrease in exports and causes imports to contract. No accommodating finance is necessary[3] and, correspondingly, the domestic supply of money remains unaffected.

Nor does the country have to undergo price and income deflation as a result of the decline in exports. Imports are reduced through

---

[3] However, accommodating transactions may occur if instantaneous adjustment in the balance of payments through the rise in exchange rate is not effected. For example, a private short-term capital inflow may be induced by the rise in rate, as discussed later, in which case the domestic supply of money is reduced.

the rise in exchange rate automatically caused by the fall in exports rather than through a contraction in income or deflation of prices as under the gold standard.

Notwithstanding these undoubted advantages of a freely fluctuating exchange-rate system, it has not been widely accepted either in practice or in theory. Unfortunately, the other side of the coin is blemished. Corresponding to the advantages of freely fluctuating rates over the gold standard as far as the insulation of the domestic economy from external disturbances is concerned lies their disadvantage as far as external relations are concerned. Exchange rates are key variables in the international economy. When they are stable, as under the gold standard, they provide solid lines of communication among national economies. When they are severely unstable, they make international price and cost comparisons difficult, introduce an extra element of risk and uncertainty, and promote speculative activity inimical to productive effort (though speculation can be beneficial, as we shall see in a moment).

With no official intervention in the market, frequent exchange-rate fluctuations are to be expected. Under favorable conditions, these fluctuations may be mitigated by stabilizing speculative activity. For example, if the exchange rate begins to rise under the impact of a temporary increase in demand or decrease in supply, importers may slow down foreign orders in the expectation that the rate will soon fall back toward its former level. For the same reason, foreigners may accelerate their purchases of the country's goods to take advantage of a temporarily low rate of exchange. Both of these actions serve to restrain the rise in rate—the first by reducing demand for foreign exchange, the second by increasing supply. Short-term capital inflows have the same effect and may be induced by the same belief that the rise in exchange rate is only temporary.

Such stabilizing commodity and capital movements would be normal while a country's balance of payments remains in reasonably stable equilibrium, but should serious disequilibrium develop, speculative actions may become *destabilizing*. Suppose that the exchange rate begins to rise and promises to continue upward. Importers may then wish to accelerate foreign orders to avoid higher costs later, and foreigners may wish to postpone purchases from the country until its currency has depreciated further. At the same time, owners of short-term funds may wish to move them out of the country into other currencies whose international value is rising. Of course, these actions increase the demand and decrease the supply of foreign exchange, causing the rate to rise faster and further.

Apart from the influence of speculative commodity and capital movements, a more basic influence on exchange-rate fluctuations is the elasticities of the demand and supply of foreign exchange. These, in turn, we found earlier to be mainly a reflection of the elasticity of demand for imported goods and services and of foreign demand for the country's export goods and services. The less elastic the demand and supply functions are, the greater the fluctuation in rate caused by any given shift in demand or supply.

The most unfavorable circumstances for the operation of a freely fluctuating rate system exist when both the demand and supply of foreign exchange are highly inelastic. Indeed, in an extreme case, the exchange rate may be in an unstable equilibrium position. This would be the result if the supply curve is backward-bending and intersects the demand curve from above to the left, as illustrated in Figure 16.1 (page 309). Any movement in the rate above or below the point of intersection would set off a cumulative reaction, forcing the rate further in the same direction. Even though eventually the rate would settle in stable equilibrium (because the elasticity of demand is bound to increase as the rate rises), the rate is subject to great fluctuations.

Whatever elasticities the demand and supply of foreign exchange may have over the long run, they will tend to be less in the short run. The production of goods and services takes time to respond to price changes. If the rate of exchange rises, a country's exports cannot ordinarily increase immediately, except to the extent that inventories can be drawn upon. A difficulty under fluctuating rates thereby arises from the lag in resource reallocation in response to rate changes.

Historical experience with freely fluctuating rates has been limited, offering little empirical evidence either to support or reject the system. Most of the little modern experience there has been— in the early 1920's and again for a short time in the early 1930's— generally revealed more of the weaknesses than the strengths of the system.[4] But these were not fair tests, since free rates were adopted only as interim measures during transitional and troubled periods.

---

[4] See League of Nations, *International Currency Experience*, chaps. v and vi (Geneva, 1944).

The Canadian experiment with a "floating" rate, from 1950 to 1961, demonstrated that a free rate can be surprisingly stable. However, again the test was not a fair one because of the close ties between the Canadian dollar and the U.S. dollar. Moreover, Canada decided to abandon the system, returning to a fixed par value in 1962.

Nevertheless, the case for freely fluctuating rates is far from closed. Many economists strongly favor the system. Not least among their arguments is the difficulties with the contemporary system, detailed in the next chapter.

EXCHANGE CONTROLS

Although they are widely different methods of organizing the international monetary system, the gold standard and freely fluctuating exchange-rate systems have in common the reliance upon automatic market mechanisms. In sharp contrast, an exchange-control system is designed to suppress or circumvent market forces.

In a thoroughgoing exchange-control system, all international economic and financial transactions of the country are legally subject to the prior approval of the control authority. All current foreign exchange receipts are required to be sold to the control authority, and all foreign exchange is purchased from it. Sometimes "free" markets for certain kinds of transactions are permitted, but these are limited in scope and are actually a part of the control system.

Typically, exchange rates are fixed at official levels, except for transactions in the free-market sector, if such exists. Typically, also, the official exchange rate overvalues the home currency—that is, the rate is held below the equilibrium level. Were not this the case, the necessity for exchange controls for balance-of-payments purposes would usually disappear.

Various devices may be employed to keep the balance of payments under control. The heart of the system, of course, is the direct control over international transactions. But other, ancillary methods are also frequently used, such as "multiple" exchange rates. This means the setting of different exchange rates for different kinds of transactions. For example, to discourage luxury imports a high rate of exchange can be set on foreign exchange purchased for this purpose, while a lower rate is applicable to imports of raw materials and foodstuffs. As indicated above, there may even be some transactions for which exchange can be bought or sold at free rates.

Exchange controls have been instituted for a variety of historical reasons. One obvious basis is the presence of a centrally controlled economy, with exchange controls being simply a logical extension to the international sector. Apart from this, exchange controls have originated in most cases in one or more of the following circumstances: economic or monetary crisis, associated with the threat or outbreak of war or severe political disturbances; internal economic or monetary instability, in the form either of deep recession or serious inflation; the presence of a persistent and intractable deficit balance of payments; as part of a national program for economic development, with the objective of direct "rationing" of scarce foreign exchange.

Exchange controls in the 20th century first began to flourish during the economic, monetary, and political crises of the late 1930's. They were continued and extended during World War II and, with few exceptions, maintained in the early postwar years. It was not until late 1958 that Western European countries felt stable and strong enough to dismantle most controls and reestablish a large measure of freedom in international payments. Even so, selected controls, especially over capital movements, have been retained by most European countries down to the present day. More extensive controls are commonly found today in the underdeveloped countries of Latin America, Africa, and the Near and Far East.

As we shall learn in the next chapter, exchange (and quantitative trade) controls, with some exceptions, are now outlawed, in principle, among the major trading countries of the Western world. This is in recognition of their generally uneconomic effects. Freedom of trade and payments ordinarily offers the best assurance that resources will be efficiently allocated domestically and internationally. Direct controls tend to distort or destroy the price mechanism guiding resources into their most productive uses.

Nevertheless, exchange controls cannot reasonably be entirely excluded from the arsenal of weapons at the disposal of governments in their search for economic stability. Free-market forces do not always produce optimum results, and in some cases they lead to quite intolerable results. To cite some examples, consider first a country suffering from severe inflation. Until the inflation is brought under control, a freely fluctuating exchange rate system—

the "most free" of all free-market systems—tends to lead to a self-feeding upward spiral of exchange rates and prices. If exchange rates are held stable without exchange controls, the balance of payments may develop a deficit too large to handle with available gold reserves or other accommodating finance. Exchange controls may then be the least undesirable alternative feasible.

A second case for controls arises when a country experiences an outflow of "hot" capital or other large-scale destabilizing capital outflows because of internal political instability, the threat of war, and so on. Exchange depreciation is likely only to aggravate such movements of capital, while the attempt to maintain stable rates could lead to an early exhaustion of the country's international reserves.

More generally, exchange controls can be defended not so easily on their own merit as on the grounds that under some circumstances no more satisfactory alternative is available. A serious balance-of-payments deficit disequilibrium requires *some* method of adjustment. Exchange depreciation or income and price deflation may not always do the job, or may do it with unacceptable consequences. It is then a matter of judgment whether direct controls are preferable.

FLEXIBLE EXCHANGE RATES

The last monetary system to be discussed is a hybrid one, sharing characteristics of the gold standard, freely fluctuating rates, and exchange controls. It may be called a system of "managed flexibility" of which there are two varieties: a flexible-rate system and an "adjustable-peg" system. The latter will be considered in the next chapter.

By a flexible-rate system we mean one in which exchange rates are neither kept at fixed, predetermined levels, nor allowed freely to fluctuate in response to private market forces and yet in which there is freedom of market transactions. This combination is brought about through the operations of an agency of the government—usually called the Stabilization Fund—which indirectly controls movements in exchange rates through sales and purchases of foreign exchange. The Fund is furnished by the Treasury or Central Bank, under whose aegis it operates, with both gold and foreign exchange balances and domestic currency. Domestic currency is used to buy foreign exchange on the market when it is desired to prevent or retard a fall in exchange rates; foreign exchange is used to buy domestic currency when the objective is to prevent or retard a rise in rates or to force rates downward.

The adjustment mechanism depends upon the policies adopted by the monetary authority managing the system. To the extent that the rate is kept stable, even in the face of persistent or basic changes in autonomous demand or supply of foreign exchange, the mechanism is essentially the same as under the gold standard. On the other hand, if the authority were to remain neutral and allow the market to be shaped entirely by private demand and supply, it would become a virtual freely fluctuating rate system.

However, neither of the above policies is normally to be expected, for the presumptive purpose of the system is to avoid the disadvantages of both fixed and freely fluctuating exchange rates. The chief disadvantage of the latter can be avoided by *offsetting temporary fluctuations* in rates through appropriate market operations; the principal disadvantage of fixed rates can be avoided by *allowing the rate to change as a means of* correcting a persistent disequilibrium.

Flexible rates, however, are not panaceas for balance-of-payments problems. Like any system of discretionary management, it is necessarily liable to mismanagement. A major source of mistaken judgment is in determining the "correct" rate of exchange in the face of dynamic changes in underlying conditions behind autonomous transactions. A rate that is set too low overvalues the home currency and leads to balance-of-payments deficits; a too-high rate undervalues the currency and leads to balance-of-payments surpluses.

In attempting to predetermine the equilibrium rate of exchange, the concept of "purchasing power parity" may be applied. This holds that the equilibrium rate is one that establishes equality in the purchasing power of the home and foreign currencies. It is calculated by multiplying a past period's demonstrated equilibrium rate by the ratio of price changes at home and abroad that have occurred since the past equilibrium period. For instance, if home prices have quadrupled on the average while foreign prices have doubled, the equilibrium rate of exchange is now twice as high as formerly.

There are several weaknesses in the purchasing-power-parity doctrine, both theoretically and in practice. A major theoretical defect is its assumption that only relative price changes affect the balance of payments, ignoring possibly equally or more significant changes of a structural or cyclical nature.

However helpful purchasing-power-parity calculations may be in forecasting equilibrium exchange rates, only experience can reveal whether in fact they were. Of course, mistakes can be corrected, but the danger is always present that others will be made in the opposite direction. Too frequent rate changes detract from the potential advantage of rate stability and, moreover, encourage destabilizing speculative activity. Reluctance to allow rates to change, on the other hand, reduces the attractiveness of the system in providing a means of adjustment other than through income and price deflation or direct controls.

Finally, a major weakness of flexible rates, revealed during their period of germination during the 1930's, is their tendency to result in conflicting national policies. Country *A*'s decision to allow or force the exchange rate on *B*'s currency to rise is inconsistent with *B*'s decision to prevent the rate on *A*'s currency from falling. Such conflicts were not uncommon during the 1930's, until cooperation among national monetary authorities was instituted under the Tripartite Agreement (among the United States, the United Kingdom, and France, later adhered to by others) in 1936. This experience played a large role in shaping the postwar monetary system discussed next.

RECOMMENDED READING

Brown, William Adams, Jr. *The Gold Standard Reinterpreted, 1914–1934*. 2 vols. New York: National Bureau of Economic Research, 1940.

Friedman, Milton. "The Case for Flexible Exchange Rates," *Essays in Positive Economics*. Chicago: University of Chicago Press, 1953.

League of Nations. *International Currency Experience*. Geneva, 1944.

Nurkse, Ragnar, "Conditions of International Monetary Equilibrium," *Essays in International Finance*, No. 4 (Spring, 1945). Princeton, N.J.: International Finance Section, Princeton University.

Triffin, Robert. *The Evolution of the International Monetary System: Historical Reappraisal and Future Perspectives*. Princeton Studies in International Finance, No. 12. Princeton, N.J., 1964.

STUDY QUESTIONS

1. What determines par rates of exchange under the gold standard?
2. How does a government maintain a fixed gold value of its currency?
3. Explain in what sense accommodating short-term capital movements are a substitute for gold movements.
4. What limits the ability of a country to remain on the gold standard if it has a persistent balance-of-payments deficit?
5. Explain the gold-specie-flow mechanism.
6. How is the classical theory of the gold standard adjustment mechanism dependent upon the quantity theory of money?
7. How do inflexible costs and prices affect the assumptions of the classical theory of adjustment?
8. What premise underlies the gold standard system with respect to national economic and monetary policies?
9. What is the nature of the objection to the gold standard adjustment mechanism in today's world?
10. Give an example of a situation in which domestic economic goals and balance-of-payments equilibrium are inconsistent.
11. Contrast and explain the difference in the degree of independence of national monetary systems under the gold standard and under freely fluctuating exchange rates.
12. State the objections to freely fluctuating rates from the point of view of international trade and investment.
13. Distinguish between stabilizing and destabilizing speculation, and explain what determines which kind will develop under freely fluctuating rates.
14. Why are inelastic demand and supply curves of foreign exchange unfavorable to the operation of freely fluctuating rates?
15. Define "undervalued" and "overvalued" currencies.
16. What is meant by multiple exchange rates?
17. List some of the conditions under which exchange controls may be justified.
18. Discuss the major objection to exchange controls.
19. How are exchange rate movements controlled in a flexible-rate system?
20. Explain the purchasing-power-parity theory and its weaknesses.
21. What are the main weaknesses of a flexible-rate system?

Chapter 18

THE CONTEMPORARY INTERNATIONAL MONETARY SYSTEM

The present international monetary system, like the flexible-rate system discussed at the end of the preceding chapter, belongs to the category of "managed flexibility." It is, therefore, closely related to the flexible-rate system and similar to it in many respects. However, the system has its own unique characteristics not found in any prior historical experience.

For reasons that will soon become evident, present international monetary arrangements go under the name of an "adjustable-peg" system. It is also known as the Bretton Woods system, for its basic framework was laid in a conference in 1944 at that New Hampshire site.

The creators of the Bretton Woods system[1] were intensely aware of the unsatisfactory monetary experience of the prewar decade. The gold standard, which had been the bulwark of the world economy before World War I, became less and less appropriate in the years following, and finally collapsed early in the 1930's under the impact of the economic and monetary crises set off by the Great Depression. The demise of the gold standard left a vacuum, which was filled by a succession of experiments with freely fluctuating rates, flexible rates, and exchange controls. None of these produced satisfactory results. The hope and objective at Bretton Woods was to create a new system that would avoid the undesirable aspects of its predecessors while capturing their best features. The main things to be avoided were the rigid exchange rates and associated

---

[1] Many experts from different countries contributed to the development of the system over a discussion period of several years. The principals, however, were Lord Keynes of the British Treasury and Dr. Harry White of the U.S. Treasury, each of whom advanced a plan bearing his name. In the end, the White Plan, as it emerged from the process of intense discussion and compromise, won the day and became the basis of the system adopted. However, Keynes' ideas were not buried and have enjoyed a revival in recent proposals for reforming the Bretton Woods system, as shown in the next chapter.

deflationary adjustment mechanism of the gold standard; the instability of freely fluctuating rates; the conflicts of national policies and competitive exchange depreciation of the flexible-rate system; and the repressive and distorting techniques of exchange controls. The features to be captured were the stability of the gold standard, the easy adjustment mechanism and market freedom of freely fluctuating rates, the discretionary control over market forces of the flexible-rate system, and the selective use of controls when necessary, borrowed from the exchange-control system. Finally, entirely new institutions and practices had to be devised to provide the appropriate means of accomplishing these objectives.

Irreducible conflicts are evident from inspection of the above lists of things to be avoided and to be sought. For example, exchange rates cannot be both fixed and flexible, and adjustment cannot be both automatic and controlled. Compromise was therefore unavoidable, and some of the problems of the system as it has operated in practice can be attributed to this. Nevertheless, it is a bold experiment which deserves careful criticism.

THE ESSENTIALS OF THE ADJUSTABLE PEG

The basic notion underlying the Bretton Woods system is that of the adjustable peg. Essentially, this means that exchange rates are kept stable (that is, "pegged") around declared par values, but with the rates subject to repegging at different levels when balance-of-payments considerations justify such actions. In other words, rates are stable but not unalterably fixed. The obvious intent of such a system is to gain the advantages of gold standard stability without having to suffer the rigors of its adjustment mechanism.

Pegging the rate of exchange at a specified level involves two operations. The first is deciding at what rate to peg the currency. Having made this decision, it is implemented by declaring a par value of the currency in terms of some standard. In the current system, the standard is gold. The second operation consists of the methods used to maintain the rate stable at or near the declared par. One method of doing this is for each national monetary authority freely to buy and sell gold at the officially set price. Apart from the United States, which follows this practice in modified form,[2] a different method is generally used. It is the flexible-rate

---

[2] Monetary gold operations of the United States are confined to purchases and sales from and to foreign official institutions. Domestic residents are not permitted to hold monetary gold.

technique of operations in the market by stabilization funds.

In contrast to a flexible-rate system, however, under an adjustable-peg system, countries are committed in principle not merely to eliminate day-to-day fluctuations in exchange rates (beyond small margins around par), but to keep them stable as long as possible, consistent with the achievement of other objectives.

Among these objectives the most important are (*a*) freedom of trade and payments on current account transactions from quantitative restrictions and (*b*) domestic economic stability, including full employment and a reasonably stable price level. If either of these goals is threatened by balance-of-payments pressures, relief through repegging exchange rates at a different level is admitted as a legitimate action.

However, again in contrast to other systems, changing the par value of a currency is not regarded as a prerogative which may be exercised unilaterally and without the prior approval of other countries. In the absence of such an agreement, the commitment to rate stability would be in danger of violation through frequent and unwarranted rate changes.

ROLE OF THE INTERNATIONAL MONETARY FUND

It should be clear from the above discussion of the basic principles of an adjustable-peg system that it cannot operate as intended without international agreement to adhere to its principles and an appropriate institutional framework for their implementation. The International Monetary Fund (IMF) was created to serve these purposes.

The IMF and its sister institution, the International Bank for Reconstruction and Development, were formed in 1944 at the Bretton Woods Conference. The Fund began operations in 1946 and stands today at the center of the current international monetary system, with a membership of over 100 countries, including all the important trading countries of the world outside the Soviet Union and mainland China blocs.

The basic approach of the IMF is to provide machinery for consultation and collaboration among member countries, as well as direct assistance in carrying out obligations imposed by the Articles of Agreement, or constitution. A permanent international organization, the IMF is guided by a policy-making board of governors on which all member countries are represented; the executive directors, who are responsible for day-to-day operations; and a technical staff of international civil servants.

Principles of the Fund

As we have noted, the IMF is based on an adjustable-peg system. Hence, the obligations of members and assistance provided to them are designed to implement the principles of this system.

The first of these principles listed earlier is the stability of exchange rates. This principle is embodied in the obligation of each member of the IMF to declare a par value of its currency in terms of gold and to refrain from changing the par value, except to correct a "fundamental disequilibrium." Market rates of exchange are to be kept within 1 percent of par values. This is accomplished in most cases through the operations in the market of national stabilization funds.

A second principle of the adjustable-peg system is freedom of current account transactions from quantitative controls. The Articles of Agreement of the IMF prohibit such controls, unless special circumstances warrant exception. Controls over capital movements, however, are permissible. The acceptability of capital controls was based on prewar experience with the disrupting influence that erratic and destabilizing capital flows can have.

The obligation both to keep exchange rates stable and to refrain from imposing quantitative controls over current payments cannot be discharged if the means of financing temporary balance-of-payments deficits are not available. Suppose that a member country enters a period of several months, or even a year or two, of payments deficit. The quantity of foreign exchange autonomously demanded exceeds the quantity autonomously supplied. Hence the rate of exchange rises, and unless private accommodating capital inflows occur, the monetary authority is obliged to provide additional foreign exchange on the market to keep the exchange rate from exceeding the allowable upper limit over the par rate. If the country possesses sufficient official reserves of gold and foreign exchange to finance the deficit, this may create no special problem. But if official reserves are inadequate, and arrangements cannot be made to obtain international credit, either the exchange rate will break through the official upper limit or controls on payments must be imposed, or both.

The authors of the IMF were well aware that if its principles were to be operationally meaningful, member countries would have to have access to extra foreign exchange reserves when needed to tide them over temporary periods of balance-of-payments deficit. One of the greatest innovations introduced by the IMF was its creation of a "revolving pool" of credit, available to members for this purpose. In the technical language of the Fund, such credit is known as "drawing rights."

The IMF acquires the resources for lending mainly through member subscriptions. Upon joining the Fund, a member is assigned a *quota,* the size of which determines the amount of subscription it must pay into the Fund, as well as its drawing rights and voting power. Quotas are based on such factors as national income and volume of trade.

Quota subscriptions are payable 25 percent in gold and the remainder in the member's national currency, though the gold portion may be less for countries with small gold and foreign exchange reserves. Additional resources can be mobilized, if needed, through arrangements to borrow from several of the larger members.

When a member "draws" upon the Fund, it receives foreign exchange out of the Fund's holdings in return for an equivalent amount of its own currency paid to the Fund. While this appears to be simply a purchase operation, in reality it is a loan operation. The member is required to repurchase within five years any of its currency held by the Fund in excess of the member's quota, and in the meanwhile interest is charged on drawings outstanding. The repurchase is made with gold or acceptable foreign exchange. The Fund's holdings of a member's currency may be reduced in another way: through its purchase by *other* members. This would normally happen if the member develops a balance-of-payments surplus vis-à-vis other members who then draw upon the Fund to help finance their deficits. Indeed, the Fund's resources are designed to be used in precisely this way—that is, as a "revolving pool" of credit, drawn upon by a given member only occasionally and for short periods of deficit and replenished as deficits give way to surpluses. In short, the Fund extends credit to meet *temporary* balance-of-payments deficits.

Restriction of the Fund's resources to financing short-term, temporary deficits is further assured by limitations, both quantitative and qualitative, on members' drawing rights. The general rule, violated only exceptionally, is that a member may not purchase foreign exchange from the IMF if the purchase would cause the Fund's holdings of that member's currency to increase by more than 25 percent in any 12-month period, or to exceed 200 percent of its quota. Moreover, a member has more or less automatic drawing rights only up to one quarter of its quota—the so-called "gold tranche." Beyond that, drawings are subject to determination by the Fund on the basis of the applicant's balance-of-payments situation and its program for restoring equilibrium.

In the direction of more liberal access to the Fund's credit, "standby arrangements" may be made with individual members, assuring that drawings may be made up to specified amounts and within a specified period, provided that agreed-upon policies are pursued by the member.

Finally, there remains the crucially important question of adjustment to balance-of-payments disequilibrium. As noted previously, the IMF is able to help members ride out short-term disturbances. But persistent disequilibrium is another matter. Any stable-rate, free-market system requires for its successful operation a reasonable degree of balance-of-payments stability on the part of the major trading countries. Periods of short-run disequilibrium are to be expected—indeed, are inevitable. As we have seen, the IMF is prepared to help take care of these. Persistent disequilibrium, however, is neither inevitable nor sustainable. The IMF is unable—and in any event would be unwilling—to finance a member's continuing deficit.

Responsibility for maintaining long-run equilibrium rests primarily with each individual country. A member of the IMF is expected to pursue monetary and fiscal policies consistent with this responsibility. However, occasions may arise when, either because of inappropriate policies or because of forces over which a country has no effective control, persistent balance-of-payments disequilibrium develops. Domestic inflation is a common example of the former; shifts in demand and technological changes are examples of the latter. Moreover, a country may find itself caught in the dilemma of a conflict between domestic stability and balance-of-payments equilibrium. This possibility arises out of the relationship between the balance of payments and the national income, as we found in an earlier discussion. To bring its balance of payments into equilibrium a country may have to accept an underemployment equilibrium level of income.

The authors of the IMF recognized that these kinds of problems would arise. To meet them is the chief purpose of the right given to member countries to change the par value of their currencies— that is, to "repeg" their currencies. This is allowable under the Articles of Agreement to correct a "fundamental disequilibrium." But to safeguard the principle of exchange stability, changes in par must receive the prior approval of the Fund, unless the change is less than 10 percent of the initially declared par.

The Articles of Agreement do not define the "fundamental disequilibrium" which justifies the repegging of currencies at different levels. However, from the context of the nature of the system and from operating interpretations over the years, the meaning is fairly clear. Fundamental disequilibrium can be said to exist when a persistent balance-of-payments disequilibrium is not amenable to correction at prevailing exchange rates except through controls over current transactions or at the cost of serious unemployment or inflation. This is a pragmatic rather than theoretical definition, but appropriately so as a guide to policy decisions. The objective is to avoid both unnecessary exchange rate variations and the worst consequences of rigid rates, the latter consisting mainly of current-account controls and/or domestic instability.

MODIFICATIONS OF THE BRETTON WOODS SYSTEM

If one were to compare the international monetary system today with the model emerging from Bretton Woods in 1944, some marked differences would be apparent. The system has evolved in unforeseen ways, including some important structural changes.

The most significant of these changes has involved a transformation in the direction of an earlier version of the gold standard, in operation during the latter part of the 1920's, known as the "gold-exchange standard." The latter is a system in which one or more currencies are fixed in terms of gold and become "reserve" or "key" currencies to which other national currencies are tied and in terms of which international reserves are in part kept.

The U.S. dollar has acquired the role in today's system of a reserve, key currency. The British pound sterling is in a similar position, though on a more limited scale. Even though the currencies of all members of the IMF have a declared par in terms of gold. the dollar's relationship to gold is regarded as more firmly fixed. While other countries may change the gold value of their currencies, this is mainly only a formal method of changing the *dollar* value of their currencies, for the gold value of the dollar is expected to remain unaltered.

One consequence of these relationships is that the dollar shares with gold the status of an international reserve. As long as there is confidence in the ability and willingness of the United States to convert dollars into gold on fixed terms for official holders, whether a country holds gold or dollars in its reserves makes little difference.

It should be observed that the foreign exchange a country may acquire through drawings on the IMF is ordinarily marginal. The principal means of financing balance-of-payments deficits are the international reserves owned by the deficit countries, and it is only when these are insufficient that recourse to the IMF is had. Adequate reserves to finance temporary balance-of-payments deficits are indispensable for the smooth functioning of a stable-rate system. As the volume of international trade grows, the volume of needed reserves also grows, though not necessarily in the same proportion. Gold production, however, is related not to the need for new reserves, but rather to such factors as costs of production, the exhaustion of old sources and the discovery of new ones, and technological developments. The failure of new gold output (or that portion of it going into monetary uses) to keep pace with the expanding need for reserves has given to the dollar as a supplemental reserve a very important role in the international monetary system, and has led to the creation of a new kind of reserve asset called "Special Drawing Rights" that will be described in the next chapter.

It has also changed in related ways the character of the system envisaged at Bretton Woods. The United States does not have the same status in the system as do other countries. As a reserve center, with billions of dollars held in it by other countries, the United States is much more restricted in its freedom of action. Most notably, it is under great pressure not to change the gold content of the dollar, even in the face of a prolonged deficit in its balance of payments. Were the dollar to be devalued, not only would foreign owners of dollars be subjected to capital losses, but the dollar would probably lose its status as a reserve currency. This would be a heavy blow to the present system and threaten its disintegration.

The transformation of the Bretton Woods system into a type of gold-exchange standard, and the growing shortage of gold and the emergence of the dollar as a major reserve medium have created serious problems that call for a reexamination of the system and proposals for its reform. The next chapter is devoted to a discussion of these problems and proposals for reform.

RECOMMENDED READING

ALIBER, ROBERT Z. *The Management of the Dollar in International Finance*. Princeton Studies in International Finance, No. 13. Princeton, N.J., 1964.

FLEMING, J. MARCUS. *The International Monetary Fund, Its Form and Functions*. Washington, D.C.: International Monetary Fund, 1964.

GOLDENWEISER, E. A., and BOURNEUF, ALICE. "The Bretton Woods Agreements," *Federal Reserve Bulletin,* September, 1944.

INTERNATIONAL MONETARY FUND. *Annual Reports*. Washington, D.C.

SCAMMELL, W. M. *International Monetary Policy*, chaps. v–vii. 2d ed. New York: Macmillan Co., 1964.

TEW, BRIAN. *The International Monetary Fund: Its Present Role and Future Prospects*. Princeton University, Essays in International Finance, No. 6. Princeton, N.J., March, 1961.

STUDY QUESTIONS

1. Justify the inclusion of both flexible-rate and adjustable-peg systems in the category of "managed flexibility."

2. List the characteristics of previous historical systems that the Bretton Woods system seeks to avoid and those it seeks to capture.

3. In what important respects does the adjustable-peg system differ from the gold standard? From freely fluctuating rates? From flexible rates?

4. How do most countries maintain the market values of their currencies at or near par? How does the United States?

5. What rule does the IMF impose concerning quantitative payments controls?

6. What is meant by the IMF's "revolving pool of credit"? In what sense does it "revolve"?

7. Why are drawings upon the IMF in reality the extensions of credit by the Fund?

8. State the limits on the amounts and conditions of drawing rights on the IMF.

9. Why can the IMF not help finance a member's persistent balance-of-payments deficit?

10. Why are adequate international reserves indispensable for the operation of the present system?

11. Under what circumstances may a country justify repegging its currency?

12. Describe a gold exchange standard.

13. What is meant by the status of the dollar as a "key" currency?

14. Why is the dollar generally regarded as being as "good as gold"?

<table>
<tr><td>Chapter
19</td><td># REFORM OF THE INTERNATIONAL MONETARY SYSTEM</td></tr>
</table>

REFORM OF THE INTERNATIONAL MONETARY SYSTEM

It would be difficult to deny that the present international monetary system is a great improvement over the prewar system. Apart from institutional improvements in international monetary arrangements, the most significant advance lies in acceptance of the principle of international cooperation in formulating policies of an inherently supranational concern. Nevertheless, the system has been beset with problems from the beginning. The character of the problems has changed over time but, if anything, they have become increasingly serious, to the degree that the system itself has been called into question.

THE RECORD OF THE PRESENT SYSTEM

The International Monetary Fund, which was to be at the center of the postwar monetary system, began its operations at a very inauspicious time. The extensive physical destruction and economic and monetary disorder that were the legacy of World War II precluded immediate return to any kind of normal international monetary relations. The demands of the time were for massive reconstruction and rehabilitation of war-torn economies—demands which the IMF was not constructed to meet. The United States stepped into the breach with massive economic aid under the Marshall Plan. In the meanwhile, the IMF attempted, with only limited success, to persuade member countries to reduce the maze of controls and restrictions on payments which were in widespread use in the early postwar years and which were contrary to the principles of the system, except as temporary measures during the transition to more normal relations.

In a remarkably short time, the economies of Western Europe and Great Britain, which were an essential part of the world economy and were the most severely disrupted by the war, were restored and a degree of monetary stability was established. By the latter part of 1949, it was decided that it was time to lay the foundations for the creation of an equilibrium pattern of trade and payments without the prop of extensive economic aid from the United States. In September of that year, the principle of currency repegging was applied on a large scale upon the devaluation, with the consent of the Fund, of most European currencies.

During the next several years, progress toward establishing the conditions envisaged at Bretton Woods was steadily achieved. Although Marshall Plan aid was largely terminated by 1950, the United States continued to support Europe financially, with the aim of restoring the international reserves that had been depleted by war and reconstruction. At the end of 1958, the United Kingdom and several other major European countries virtually removed restrictions on current account transactions, thus conforming to one of the basic principles of the IMF.

As the conditions appropriate to the functioning of the IMF were gradually established, it became correspondingly more active. The usefulness of the Fund was dramatically demonstrated during the Suez crisis in 1956. The closure of the Suez Canal and disruption of oil pipelines in the Middle East fields created a sharp, but temporary, balance-of-payments crisis for certain European countries, especially the United Kingdom and France. To help bolster their payments position and to check speculation against their currencies, the Fund made available large credits to these countries. Several similar operations were carried on in subsequent crisis situations, in each case with support from the Fund serving to help prevent an international monetary crisis. In the meanwhile, the Fund has made available credit to many of its members under more normal circumstances.

Paradoxically, as the Fund's participation and influence in the international monetary system grew, a new set of problems arose with which the Fund's ability to cope was questionable. These may be called the problems of confidence, liquidity, and adjustment.[1]

The Confidence Problem

Whenever exchange rates are not rigidly fixed, the possibility of a change in rates is, of course, ever present. In the case of a pegged-

[1] See Fritz Machlup and Burton G. Malkiel (eds.), *International Monetary Arrangements: The Problem of Choice* (Princeton, N.J.: Princeton University Press, 1964).

rate system, such as the present one, the possibility of rate changes becomes one of increasing *probability* if serious balance-of-payments problems persist or if a speculative attack on a currency arises.

A "speculative attack" on a currency refers to a massive, and frequently sudden, outflow of short-term capital from a country whose currency's international value becomes doubtful. An outflow of capital (debit entry in the balance of payments) adds to the demand for foreign exchange, which, if not satisfied through the sale of foreign currencies out of official reserves, results in either a change in exchange rates or the imposition of exchange controls. The expectation of devaluation or exchange depreciation tends to be self-fulfilling in that the outflow of capital motivated by the expectation puts pressure on the exchange rate and may finally force it upward.

Any one or combination of numerous reasons may be responsible for lack of confidence in the future value of a currency. One reason, of course, is a stubborn balance-of-payments deficit. For instance, a continuing deficit in the balance of payments of the United Kingdom, accompanied by dwindling official reserves, suggested in 1967 that the British pound would sooner or later be devalued. The withdrawal of foreign-owned capital from England put additional pressure on the pound, and the expected devaluation was realized in November, 1967.

A much more significant example, from the point of view of the international monetary system, has been the periods of uncertainty with respect to the status of the dollar because of the long and persistent balance-of-payments deficit of the United States. Like Great Britain, but on a much larger scale, the United States is vulnerable to the pressures of massive capital outflows because of the huge amount of dollars owned by foreigners. (As of mid-1970, some $45 billion in dollar balances and short-term claims were held by nonresidents.) These foreign-owned dollars have been accumulated, as explained later, as the consequence of the U.S. balance-of-payments deficit over the years. Willingness to hold the dollars is based on the status of the dollar as a reserve currency, "good as gold."

While other members of the IMF maintain the values of their currencies in terms of the U.S. dollar, the United States fulfills its exchange-rate obligations by keeping a fixed relationship between the dollar and gold. The dollar is kept in a fixed relationship to gold by the Treasury's unlimited offer to purchase and sell gold to official foreign agencies at a price of $35 per ounce. Any increase in the official dollar price of gold would constitute a devaluation of the dollar, each dollar then being worth less in terms of gold. In such a case, foreign owners of dollars would incur a capital loss as measured by the gold value of their holdings of dollars.

Clearly, then, if for any reason the expectation arises that the dollar is going to be devalued, or that its convertibility into gold is going to be discontinued, foreign holders of dollars would be motivated to convert them into gold or other currencies before the expected action occurs. But, like a bank faced with a "run" on it by its depositors, the United States would not be able to convert all foreign dollar balances and claims into gold at its present official price. (Compared to foreign official dollar balances of $13 billion, the gold stock of the United States in early 1970 was $12 billion.) [2]

Confidence in the dollar is thus an essential ingredient in the present international monetary system. Were the confidence to disappear, followed by the attempt of foreigners to convert their dollar holdings into gold or foreign exchange, the consequence would be either the severance of the relationship between the dollar and gold or the imposition of controls on trade and payments. In either case, the blow to the system would be severe, if not fatal.

The probability of such events occurring may be rather small. Nevertheless, it is a possibility which renders the system vulnerable to crises of confidence. The point is forcefully illustrated by what happened in 1968.

A growing belief that the continuing deficit in the U.S. balance of payments and accompanying shrinkage in her stock of gold were going to force devaluation of the dollar reached a critical stage in early 1968. The crisis assumed the form principally of a great increase in the speculative demand for gold in European gold markets, forcing the market price of gold above the official parity price of $35 per ounce. It had been the practice of the United States and other countries to supply gold on the market, out of their reserves, whenever necessary to keep the market price in the neighborhood of the official price. The purpose of such support action was to avoid a *de facto* devaluation of the dollar. Now, however, it became evident that the speculative demand for gold (based on the expectation that the official price of gold was going to be raised)

---

[2] Moreover, private foreign holdings of dollars could be added to the demand for gold indirectly by being withdrawn in a capital outflow and adding thereby to the balance-of-payments deficit of the United States. Indeed, in this manner even dollars owned by U.S. residents could become a source of demand for gold.

was so great that official reserves would become exhausted as the result of continuing to feed the market.

To stop the drain on gold reserves while at the same preserving the official price of gold the United States and the major European countries established a "two-tier" system. The private gold market was to be left alone, with the price of gold free to respond to market forces without official intervention. At the same time, it was agreed that official transactions in gold between governments would be conducted at the established parity price of $35 per ounce. As long as governments were willing to adhere to the agreement and not be tempted to convert their dollar holdings into gold for sale in the private market, the two markets could be effectively isolated from each other and the gold stock of the United States protected from being drained into private hoards. The procedure has, in fact, worked very well. Even though the price of gold in the private market at times reached in the area of $45 per ounce, the official parity of the dollar in terms of gold remained intact. Speculators at last become convinced that the dollar was not going to be devalued after all, the price of gold in the private market returned to near the official price, and the crisis ended—at least for the moment.

Other currencies besides the dollar and the pound have suffered from the confidence problem. An episode of full-blown international monetary crisis occurred during 1968–69. The stage was set by the persistent balance-of-payments *surplus* of West Germany, leading to widespread anticipation of an *upward* revaluation of the mark. As a consequence, huge amounts of foreign short-term capital flowed into Germany, creating an embarrassing accumulation of reserves in the hands of the monetary authority. (The monetary authority was obliged to purchase excess supplies of foreign currencies in order to keep the mark near its official par value.) The counterpart of the inflow of capital into Germany was, of course, an *outflow* of capital from other countries. Especially hard hit was France, whose economy and balance of payments were suffering from the dislocations caused by riots and strikes in the spring of 1968. The already-existing prospect of devaluation of the franc, combined with the anticipation of a higher-valued mark, set off an extensive flow of funds out of France, mainly into Germany. To stem the tide and protect French reserves, the government imposed stringent exchange controls. The crisis cooled, but the final settlement came only after both the mark and the franc were revalued—the former upward, the latter downward.

The susceptibility of the system to periodic crises of confidence has led to the adoption of several different arrangements to prevent a breakdown in such periods. An important role has been played by the International Monetary Fund. Employing the device of special standby arrangements, the Fund has given various members access to large credits beyond normal drawing rights for the purpose of permitting the member countries to support their currencies in the face of extraordinary demand for foreign exchange. In addition, special arrangements have been made with the six largest members of the Fund whereby if the need arises for additional resources their currencies may be borrowed by the Fund.

Paralleling the Fund's efforts, bilateral and multilateral agreements have been concluded by the monetary agencies of the largest countries of Western Europe, the United Kingdom and the United States. So-called "swap" agreements between pairs of countries provide for the temporary exchange of currencies when the need arises. More or less regular meetings of central bankers are held in Basle, Switzerland, under the aegis of the Bank for International Settlements, at which accords for support of currencies under attack are worked out. In the early part of 1970, it was announced that the European Common Market countries are planning to establish a large fund of foreign exchange available for member countries to borrow from in periods of crisis. In these various ways the system has managed to preserve itself, emerging intact, if somewhat bruised.

The Liquidity Problem

The confidence problem may be thought of as a short-run liquidity problem. Liquidity refers to the readiness and ease with which assets can be converted into forms acceptable in making payments. If foreign owners of dollars wish to withdraw them from the United States, the problem is not that the United States has insufficient assets to meet these claims against it, but rather that it may not have sufficient *internationally liquid* assets—that is, gold and acceptable foreign exchange reserves.

From a longer-run point of view, the liquidity problem has a different aspect, namely, insufficient international reserves in the system as a whole to finance a growing volume of international trade and investment. Every country needs international reserves —internationally liquid assets—to cover balance-of-payments deficits when these arise. As the volume of transactions increases, the need for reserves grows, though not necessarily at the same rate.

International reserves in the present system consist mainly of gold and foreign-owned key currency balances. Additions over time to gold reserves depend upon new gold production, less that part of it going into industrial and artistic uses and private hoards. There is little, if any, connection between the need for additional monetary gold and the amount of it forthcoming. Reserves in the form of key currency balances are created when key currency countries incur balance-of-payments deficits. Thus, the huge amount of foreign-owned dollar balances originated from the balance-of-payments deficits of the United States over the last several years.[3]

New gold output entering into monetary reserves has accounted for less than half the growth in reserves over the past several years. This means that the system's need for reserves has been satisfied more from the balance-of-payments deficits of key currency countries than from new gold production. This inherently leads to the following dilemma: As the proportion of key currency reserves to gold reserves increases, the liquidity of the key currency countries declines. The vulnerability of key currency countries is thereby increased, and the further growth of reserves may be stunted by the lessening acceptability of key currency balances and the pressure on key currency countries to eliminate their payments deficits. Hence the system becomes increasingly liable over time to a shortage of liquidity.

The Adjustment Problem

The third problem confronting the present system is that of balance-of-payments adjustment. International reserves serve the function of financing temporary payments deficits, but they cannot serve as a substitute for correcting them.

As we know, the Bretton Woods system was based on the principle of adjustment to fundamental disequilibrium through the repegging of exchange rates. As mentioned earlier, however, the system has evolved away from this principle, in the direction of a gold-exchange standard. Certainly, as far as the United States is

---

[3] Recall that when a country has a balance-of-payments deficit its excess autonomous payments over autonomous receipts are financed through accommodating outflows of gold or inflows of short-term capital. The latter has taken the form of the accumulation of dollar balances by those countries in a surplus balance-of-payments position vis-à-vis the United States.

concerned, as a reserve center it is effectively precluded from changing the gold content of its currency. Most other major countries, too, resist exchange-rate variations, even though some have resorted to it.

If adjustment through the exchange rate is rejected, the market mechanism that automatically takes over consists of the price and income variations set off by disequilibrium. But these, too, are strongly resisted, for they frequently interfere with the domestic priority goals of full employment and a stable price level.

What, then, is left to correct a disequilibrium? The answer was given in a previous discussion: direct controls. But again, except for those on capital movements, direct controls are outlawed in principle by the charter of the International Monetary Fund.

In short, all of the general means of balance-of-payments adjustment theoretically possible are for one reason or another resisted in the present system. The consequence has been the development of a variety of *ad hoc* measures, many of which are simply partial and roundabout ways of exchange-rate changes or controls over trade and payments. In some cases, the medicine of deflation has been reluctantly administered. In any event, no generally satisfactory method of adjustment has developed. The truth of this is no better illustrated than in the failure of the chronic deficit in the U.S. balance of payments to be overcome, as we shall see in the next chapter.

REFORM OF THE SYSTEM

The weaknesses of the present international monetary system have become evident enough to cause a consensus to emerge on the need for its reform. However, there is a wide diversity of opinion as to the kind of reform that would be most desirable. At opposite poles are those who believe the present system is structurally defective and should be scrapped in favor of an altogether different kind of system, and those who feel that the system is basically sound and requires strengthening only in minor respects. In the middle may be found many proposals less extreme than the first group's but more extensive than the second group's.

Alternative Systems

The advocates of replacing the present system with one founded on different principles base their case primarily on the absence of a satisfactory adjustment mechanism through occasional exchange-rate repegging. Critics of the adjustable-peg system contend that it is neither "fish nor fowl" with respect to balance-of-payments adjustment. On the one hand, exchange rates are to be kept stable; on the other hand, they are to be varied when disequilibrium cannot be coped with any other way. The tendency is to postpone rate changes as long as possible, a tendency reinforced by the availability of credit from the International Monetary Fund and through "swap" and other intergovernmental arrangements. As a consequence of postponing adjustment to a deficit disequilibrium, one of two things is likely to happen. Either the automatic adjustment mechanism through price and income deflation begins to operate, leading to a slowdown in the growth rate and to unemployment, or quantitative controls are introduced. Neither of these is palatable or consistent with the principles of the system.

The choice is nevertheless to accept them, in the hope that equilibrium will be restored in the near future, or finally to resort to exchange depreciation.

But if depreciation is undertaken only as a last resort, maladjustments may have accumulated and disequilibrium become deeper, so that the severity of the depreciation required to restore equilibrium is much greater than would have been necessary earlier. Moreover, undue delay in correcting a deficit can easily cause additional pressure on the balance of payments from speculative capital outflows. The longer a deficit continues the more likely becomes an eventual depreciation of the currency. The motive to transfer capital out of the country is strengthened by the virtual absence of any risk of loss through currency appreciation. Hence, the cards are stacked in favor of speculative movements of capital out of the country.

The additional pressure on the exchange market from speculative capital outflows compounds the problem of choosing the equilibrium exchange rate at which the currency should be repegged. There is no reliable method of predetermining equilibrium rates, and the deeper the disequilibrium is, the more difficult the problem becomes. As we observed earlier, the purchasing-power-parity theory—which states that equilibrium rates are determined by relative national price level changes since some prior equilibrium period—cannot be relied upon, especially when structural changes have occurred. In the final analysis, only experience with an exchange rate will reveal whether or not it is an equilibrium rate.

Because of the difficulty in predetermining equilibrium rates of exchange, the risk is great that in repegging a currency the level chosen will either overvalue or undervalue it. An overvalued currency is one with too low exchange rates for equilibrium, leading to a continuing deficit in the balance of payments. An undervalued currency has too high exchange rates on other currencies, causing a balance-of-payments surplus to develop. In most instances, a country unsure of the correct equilibrium rate prefers to err in the direction of undervaluation in setting a new rate to avoid the risk of having soon to repeat the operation. But, of course, this tends to result in a surplus disequilibrium for the depreciating country and a deficit for others. For example, it is probable that the European devaluations in 1949 were excessive and bear some responsibility for the deficit balance of payments of the United States since that time.

The above defects in the adjustment mechanism of the present system could be remedied by abolishing the adjustable-peg principle in favor either of a fixed rate or a freely fluctuating rate system. Each of these alternatives has its advocates, but of the two the preponderance of professional economists would much prefer the second. For a fixed-rate system to operate satisfactorily, a greater degree of cost and price flexibility and of coordination of national monetary and fiscal policies is required than is feasible in today's world. Otherwise, the adjustment process of price and income changes would surely conflict with priority goals of national economic stability.

The greatest attraction of freely fluctuating exchange rates is that balance-of-payments adjustment is automatically brought about by a process that leaves individual countries with a maximum degree of freedom to pursue independent policies. There is no danger of setting incorrect exchange rates, for these are determined by free-market forces. There may be speculative capital movements, but unlike the present system there is no inherent tendency for the movements to be of a destabilizing variety because of an asymmetry in rate variations.

Notwithstanding the advantages of freely fluctuating rates, it is not an alternative which commands the support of either a large number of economists or of practically any monetary statesmen. We are already familiar, from an earlier discussion, with the strongest reasons for this opposition: the damage to international trade and investment which leaving the key variable of exchange rates to fluctuate might cause.

Many economists who accept the theoretical merits of a free-rate system oppose it on practical grounds. With most national economies now subject to extensive management by the government, leaving external monetary relations entirely to the free play of the market would be anomalous. The tendency would be strong for the system to evolve into one that is managed, but without the international coordination provided by the present system.

In any event, the opposition to abandoning stable exchange rates is so strong at the present time by those in policy-making positions that for all practical purposes the door is closed against freely fluctuating rates as an alternative to the present system.

While freely fluctuating exchange rates lie outside the realm of practical implementation at the moment, some sort of compromise system in which exchange rates are given a more important adjustment role than in the present system may have a better chance of being considered. Two varieties of compromise have commanded attention in recent discussions, the "widened band" and the "crawling peg."

The widened band refers to an enlargement of the range within which exchange rates would be free to move without the obligation on the part of the national monetary authority to intervene in the exchange market with support operations. As will be recalled, the rules of the IMF oblige member countries to keep exchange rates within 1 percent of par values. This means, of course, that rates are prevented from exercising any significant adjustment function. If the permissible range within which exchange rates could vary above and below par values were extended, a correspondingly more important part of adjustment could be assigned to the exchange rate. At the same time, the maintenance of par rates of exchange in terms of which limits on the range of fluctuation are set would avoid or mitigate the problems which a system of unlimited fluctuations may present. For instance, if the band were extended to 5 percent above and below the par rate of exchange—permitting the rate to change as much as 10 percent—it is possible that most balance-of-payments disequilibria would be corrected through rate changes as under a freely fluctuating rate system. On the other hand, destabilizing capital movements would be discouraged by the knowledge that rates of exchange could not rise or fall beyond the upper or lower limits of the band.

A second compromise between the rigidity of the present system and the flexibility of a free-rate system would be provided by the so-called "crawling peg." (Other names for essentially the same idea are "gliding parity" and "sliding parity.") In this system a fixed par rate of exchange would be abandoned, but any changes in rate would be limited to small and frequent movements in contrast to the discrete, and large, "once-for-all" adjustments of the peg as in the current system. The objective is to permit balance-of-payments adjustment through exchange depreciation or appreciation, but in such a manner as to avoid the shock of large occasional rate changes with the accompanying invitation to disruptive speculation and risk of over- or underrevaluation. Suppose, for instance, that a country experiences a growing pressure on its balance of payments in the direction of a deficit. Instead of letting the disequilibrium cumulate until reserves are threatened and the setting of a new rate is necessitated, the rate would be permitted to rise gradually—say, by no more than $\frac{1}{6}$ of 1 percent in any one month, or 2 percent per year. Rate changes would be discontinued when equilibrium is reestablished.

It is evident that proposals for reform such as those just described are intended to place on the exchange rate a greater continuous responsibility for correcting payments imbalances while at the same avoiding unnecessary or excessive rate fluctuations. Whether this sort of compromise between the brittle rigidity of the present system and the fluid flexibility of a freely fluctuating rate system will some day become politically acceptable is a moot question. It is significant, however, that the respected Joint Economic Committee of the United States Congress has repeatedly urged in several of its *Reports* that the current system be modified to permit exchange-rate variations to play a greater role in correcting disequilibrium in the balance of payments. The trend of professional thinking is clearly sympathetic to this point of view.

Liquidity and Confidence

In any system in which exchange rates are not completely free to fluctuate, thereby automatically keeping the balance of payments in continuous equilibrium, the potentiality exists of problems arising with respect to confidence and liquidity. The current system, in which exchange rates are kept stable for long periods but are occasionally adjusted sharply, and which relies heavily upon key currencies as reserve media, is particularly susceptible to confidence and liquidity difficulties, as observed earlier.

Both the confidence and the liquidity problem are closely related to the nature of international reserves and the process of their creation. Depending so heavily on the balance-of-payments deficit of the United States to provide it with reserves, the system has a built-in conflict between the need for liquidity and the maintenance of confidence in the convertibility of the dollar into gold. It is safe to say that this conflict has been the major focus of concern of international monetary authorities in recent years and has inspired the greatest amount of effort to find a solution.

Until very recently, the approach has been twofold. Additional reserves have been provided through expanding the credit facilities of the International Monetary Fund. First, this has been accomplished, on a modest scale, by periodic increases in subscription quotas and therewith drawing rights.[4] Second, when particular countries have been confronted with a speculative attack on their currencies and a threatened exhaustion of reserves, a variety of rescue operations has been devised, as mentioned above. These include special additional credit from the IMF, bilateral "swap" arrangements, and *ad hoc* support from the central banks of other major countries.

Clearly, however, such measures as these do not meet head-on the confidence and liquidity problems arising from the use of the dollar and the pound sterling as reserve currencies. A new and more basic approach is called for. Out of the welter of various proposals made to reform the liquidity system, the one finally chosen was the creation of an entirely new reserve asset called Special Drawing Rights—SDR's—popularly referred to as "paper gold."

Special Drawing Rights. After several years of intense discussion, the Board of Governors of the International Monetary Fund approved in 1967 at its annual meeting the proposal to create Special Drawing Rights. This was an historic decision, for it introduced an entirely new approach to the problem of international reserves.

Unlike gold, SDR's are merely bookkeeping entries —hence the rubric "paper gold"—in a special account with the International Monetary Fund. Unlike dollars and other reserve currencies, SDR's are not ordinary money usable in private international transactions but are accounting units the use of which is confined to intergovernmental transactions. Finally, the supply of SDR's does not de-

---

[4] Quotas in the Fund have periodically been increased. The latest proposal again to increase quotas was approved by the Board of Governors at the end of 1969, involving the raising of quotas to approximately $28,900 million. In 1959 quotas were only $9,000 million.

pend upon the mining of gold, nor upon the balance of payments of reserve countries, but is created by the discretionary decision of the IMF with a stroke of the pen.

A decision is to be made periodically on the allocation of Special Drawing Rights during a prescribed forthcoming period. The first such decision called for allocations of approximately $3.5 billion in 1970 and $3.0 billion in each of the two succeeding years. The SDR's are distributed among member countries of the IMF in proportion to their regular quotas in the Fund. Upon receipt of its allocation, a member country will simply have its special account with the IMF credited in the amount of the allocation.

Having acquired a Special Drawing Right account, a country is then free to use it as the need arises to cover a balance-of-payments deficit. The procedure is for the member to acquire foreign currencies from other members in exchange for a transfer of SDR's to the selling countries. Member countries are willing to accept SDR's as payment for their currencies because of the general agreement to do so, and the knowledge, therefore, that such Drawing Rights can always be used for acquiring the currencies of other members.[5]

The most important innovation the SDR system represents is the deliberate creation of a fiat reserve asset to be added to gold, key currencies, and ordinary drawing rights as reserve media. This permits an expansion of international reserves in response to a policy-making decision in lieu of letting the volume of reserves be determined by the vagaries of gold mining in relation to the private demand for gold and by the balance of payments of reserve countries.

From a longer-run point of view, the greater significance of SDR's may lie in their constituting the first step in the direction of creating a world central bank. The evolution of national monetary systems has been toward the substitution of *credit* for commodities as monetary bases, and of discretionary management for the automatic determination of money supply. The same principle applied to the international sector would call for the transformation of the IMF into a world central bank. This institution might have func-

---

[5] Participating countries have the general obligation to accept SDR's in exchange for convertible currencies but in particular cases need not do so unless designated by the International Monetary Fund. Normally, a country will be designated by the IMF for this purpose only when its balance of payments or reserve position warrants such designation. Moreover, no country is obliged to accept SDR's in excess of three times its net cumulrative allocation. The purpose of this acceptance limit is to calm any fear of a country that it may be loaded up with SDR's during the initial trial period before the system has been proven out. However, the acceptance limit is not likely to have much practical significance.

tions on an international scale paralleling those now performed by each country's central bank on a national scale. It would serve as a clearinghouse in settling international payments balances through the debiting and crediting of deposit accounts held by each country in the bank. More important, accounts with the bank would constitute the ultimate international reserve asset—displacing gold in this traditional role—with the volume of reserve accounts regulated in accordance with the liquidity needs of the world economy.

In modified form, proposals for creating an international institution with powers and functions similar to those just described have been advanced and widely discussed. In the discussions and negotiations leading to the formation of the International Monetary Fund, one of the two major plans—that of John Maynard Keynes—envisaged the establishment of an International Clearing Union whose chief task was to be the furnishing and controlling of international monetary reserves in the form of deposit accounts held with the Union by member countries. More recently, Professor Robert Triffin of Yale University has suggested that the International Monetary Fund be expanded and transformed into a similar kind of institution.[6]

Theoretically, both the confidence and liquidity problems could be solved by creating a new international reserve medium in the form of deposit accounts with an international institution endowed with the power to control reserves in this form. Attractive as it is on a rationalistic basis, however, the idea is no doubt too revolutionary to be acceptable in today's world. Any such institution would possess tremendous powers to influence the world economy for good or ill. If excessive reserves were created, the danger of fostering world-wide inflation would result, while a too-restrictive policy could impose a deflationary bias on the world economy. The central problem, then, would be the proper management of the system, and this raises the question of national governments yielding part of their sovereign authority to a supranational institution. It would seem that such far-reaching reform of the system must await a much greater degree of international political and economic integration than now exists. Nevertheless, the acceptance of SDR's is an indication that radical reform of the international monetary system may

---

[6] For the Keynes plan, see "Proposals by British experts for an International Clearing Union," reproduced in *Proceedings and Documents of the United Nations Monetary and Financial Conference*, Vol. II (Washington, D.C.: U.S. Government Printing Office, 1948), pp. 1548–73. For the Triffin Plan, see his *Gold and the Dollar Crisis* (New Haven, Conn.: Yale University Press, 1960).

not be as remote a possibility as one would have though a short time ago.

RECOMMENDED READING

GRUBEL, HERBERT G. (ed.). *World Monetary Reform.* Stanford, Calif.: Stanford University Press, 1963.

HALM, GEORGE N. "Toward Limited Exchange-Rate Flexibility, *Essays in International Finance,* No. 73. Princeton, N.J.: International Finance Section, Princeton University (March, 1969).

JOHNSON, HARRY G. *The World Economy at the Crossroads,* chap. iii. New York: Oxford University Press, Inc., 1965.

MACHLUP, FRITZ. *Plans for Reform of the International Monetary System.* Princeton University, Special Papers in International Economics, No. 3. Princeton, N.J., 1962.

———— and MALKIEL, BURTON G. (eds.). *International Monetary Arrangements: The Problem of Choice.* Princeton, N.J.: Princeton University Press, 1964.

SALANT, WALTER S. "Does the International Monetary System Need Reform?" in J. Carter Murphy (ed.), *Money in the International Order.* Dallas, Tex.: Southern Methodist University Press, 1964.

TRIFFIN, ROBERT. *Gold and the Dollar Crisis.* New Haven, Conn.: Yale University Press, 1960.

WILLIAMSON, JOHN H. *The Crawling Peg.* Princeton University, Essays in International Finance, No. 50. Princeton, N.J., December, 1965.

STUDY QUESTIONS

1. Why was the International Monetary Fund slow in operating as intended in the early postwar years?
2. What is meant by a "speculative attack" on a currency? How does it show up in the balance of payments?
3. Briefly describe some of the reasons that may be responsible for lack of confidence in a currency.
4. Why are the United States and Great Britain especially vulnerable to short-term capital outflows?
5. In what way do attacks on the dollar constitute a threat to the present international monetary system?
6. Describe the "two-tier" gold price system and the reasons for its development.

7. In what manner did the balance-of-payments surplus of Germany contribute to French balance-of-payments problems in 1968?

8. Describe the various devices employed to support currencies under speculative attack.

9. Describe the long-run liquidity problem.

10. What are the sources of new international monetary reserves in the present system?

11. What effect on international reserves would a balance-of-payments surplus by the United States have?

12. Describe the adjustment problem in the present system.

13. What problems does delay in adjustment to balance-of-payments disequilibrium create?

14. Why is it difficult to predetermine equilibrium rates of exchange?

15. Define currency overvaluation and undervaluation. What balance-of-payments effect does each have?

16. State the theoretical and practical arguments against a freely fluctuating rate system.

17. Describe the "widened-band" proposal and its rationale.

18. What is meant by a "crawling peg"? How is it a compromise between exchange-rate rigidity and flexibility?

19. How is there a built-in conflict in the present system between the need for liquidity and maintenance of confidence in the U.S. dollar?

20. Describe Special Drawing Rights. Where do they come from? How do they differ from gold and key currencies as reserve assets?

21. What particular problem are SDR's intended to help solve?

22. How would a world central bank operate to provide international reserves? What are some of the questions it raises?

Chapter 20

THE BALANCE-OF-PAYMENTS PROBLEM OF THE UNITED STATES

The balance-of-payments evolution of the United States since the end of World War II illustrates the problems arising out of international monetary relations and offers us the opportunity to submit the principles we have been discussing to the laboratory of experience.

The U.S. balance of payments has displayed three stages of development since 1945. The first stage, embracing the years 1946–49, was characterized by a huge balance-of-payments surplus and is often referred to as a period of "dollar shortage"; the second stage, 1950–57, was a transition period, characterized by a "planned" deficit; the third stage, beginning in 1958 and continuing to the present time, has been marked by a persistent unplanned deficit and is sometimes called a period of "dollar glut."

DOLLAR SHORTAGE, 1946–49

The immediate postwar years were a period of reconstruction and rehabilitation of war-torn and disrupted economies. Western Europe, including Great Britain, had suffered the most damage, and the economic and political future of the Western world depended upon its speedy rehabilitation.

Europe emerged from the conflict with demands on her resources far in excess of her domestic capacity to meet them. A backlog of consumer wants, plus the requirements for restoring and expanding productive capacity through large investment expenditure, created a heavy demand for imports, while reducing the capacity to export. The ability to pay for imports with large international service income, as in prewar years, was seriously impaired by the war liquidation of overseas investments, the loss of shipping, and the temporary reduction in tourist travel in Europe.

In addition, structural changes in world trade had been produced

374

by the war to the detriment of Europe's international trading position. In the prewar years, Western Europe had a substantial dollar balance-of-payments deficit settled with net earnings in other areas as an integral part of a system of worldwide multilateral settlements. But during and after the war, the position of the United States as a supplier so expanded that nearly all areas of the world became short of dollars, and the basis for the prewar multilateral settlement system was greatly weakened.

Finally, Western Europe was beset in the early postwar years with inflation and, until her currencies were devalued in September, 1949, with overvalued currencies. These monetary sources of disequilibrium served to aggravate the more fundamental real sources of difficulty, and to obstruct the processes of adjustment.

Given these conditions, the prospects for Europe without extraordinary financial aid from the United States were portentous. Without a prolonged and agonizing period of adjustment, the possibility of restoring the prewar standard of living and of reentering a free and multilateral world trading system unencumbered by quantitative trade and payments controls was slim indeed. Politically, there was a great danger that democratic political and social institutions would collapse under the heavy strain of economic hardship and disorder.

In response to these threats, the United States adopted a variety of financial aid programs, the most important of which was the European Recovery Program—more popularly known as the Marshall Plan. Billions of dollars in grants and loans were made available to European countries. This aid undoubtedly provided the extra margin of resources making it possible for Europe to get back on her feet economically within a remarkably short space of time, and gradually to dismantle the direct controls over external trade and payments. Indeed, after a few years' transition, as we shall soon see, the Europe of 1946–49—confronted with economic and political collapse and a massive dollar shortage—was transformed into a dynamic economy of unprecedented prosperity and growth, with a large dollar surplus in her balance of payments.

The phrase "dollar shortage" refers to the fact that Europe did not have enough current dollar earnings and dollar assets to draw upon to finance the import surplus required for her rehabilitation. Hence the role of the extraordinary financial assistance extended by the United States was to fill the gap between Europe's needs and resources.

The counterpart of the rest of the world's (especially Europe's) dollar shortage was the surplus in the balance of payments of the United States. This is shown by the data in Table 20.1, which have been rearranged from the way they are ordinarily presented. Against the current account balance are set the means of financing it. It may reasonably be assumed that the $5.4 billion of private capital outflow and remittances represented autonomous and normal means of financing. This left approximately $26 billion of financing by other means, nearly all of which consisted of U.S. government grants and loans.[1]

Clearly, the export surplus of the United States could not have been nearly so large as it was had the U.S. government not ex-

TABLE 20.1

U.S. BALANCE OF TRADE AND MEANS OF FINANCING IT, 1946–49
(in billions of dollars)

Export of goods and services (excluding military transfers)	$67.0
Import of goods and services	35.1
Excess of exports	$31.9
Means of financing excess exports:	
U.S. private capital (long and short term)	2.9
U.S. private remittances	2.5
U.S. government financing:	
Loans	11.7
Grants (excluding military transfers)	13.1
Liquidation of gold and dollar assets	4.8
Errors and omissions	−3.1
Total Net Financing	$31.9

SOURCES: U.S. Department of Commerce, *Survey of Current Business*, various issues.

tended grants and loans to foreign countries. Indeed, if the U.S. government had refused to extend foreign grants and loans, the rest of the world would have been *incapable* of running such a large current account dollar deficit. What, then, are we to say: that the dollar shortage of the world was *caused* by U.S. government grants and loans? Or that the grants and loans were made as a *result* of a shortage?

The question is largely one of semantics, for either point of view can be defended, depending upon one's perspective. It is quite clear that the financial assistance making possible Europe's import surplus and U.S. export surplus was in response to a huge excess demand for imports by Europe over the means of financing them

---

[1] The $4.8 billion liquidation of gold and dollar assets was offset to the extent of $3.1 billion by "errors and omissions," probably largely representing unrecorded (and for the most part clandestine) capital movements to the United States.

without foreign aid. In this sense, at least, U.S. assistance represented accommodating finance, and the dollar shortage may be regarded as having been an independent phenomenon.

TRANSITION: 1950–57

By the end of 1949, the period of rehabilitation of Europe's
economy was essentially over, and extraordinary American economic assistance under the Marshall Plan terminated. U.S. government foreign grants and loans—apart from military programs—
dropped sharply.

TABLE 20.2

U.S. BALANCE OF PAYMENTS, 1950–57
(in billions of dollars)

Export of goods and services (excluding military transfers)	$156.3
Import of goods and services	134.4
Excess of exports	$ 21.9
Means of financing excess exports:	
Private capital (net)*	10.8
Remittances	4.7
U.S. government grants and loans (net)	20.0
Total financing	$ 35.5
Excess of financing over export balance	$ 13.6
Increase in foreign U.S. balances and short-term dollar claims (net)	8.6
Purchases of gold from U.S. (net)	1.7
Errors and omissions (net)	3.3
Total	$ 13.6

SOURCE: U.S. Department of Commerce.
* U.S. capital outflow, less long-term foreign investments in the United States.

The improved dollar-payments position of the world showed up
clearly in the increase of dollar and gold reserves of foreign countries. Whereas during the years 1946–49 the world drew down its
gold and dollar reserves by nearly $5 billion (see Table 20.1), 1950
marked the beginning of a period of their replenishment. In the
eight-year period 1950–57, the net recorded accumulation of dollar
reserves and gold from the United States by other countries
amounted to over $10 billion, as shown by the balance of payments
of the United States given in Table 20.2.

From these developments it might be argued that not only was
the dollar shortage ended, but that its opposite—a dollar "glut"—
had already begun to develop. By a dollar glut is meant the presence
of a balance-of-payments surplus of other countries vis-à-vis the

United States—that is, a U.S. balance-of-payments deficit. As measured by the increase in foreign-held dollar balances and gold outflow, the United States indeed did incur a balance-of-payments deficit.

Nevertheless, there are good reasons for not regarding the surplus dollar receipts of other countries during this period as evidence of a genuine dollar glut. It will be observed from Table 20.2 that the current account surplus of the United States continued, as in the preceding period, to exceed the net private capital outflow and remittances. Government loans and grants were therefore necessary to finance the excess. But the volume of assistance rendered was considerably greater than the amount needed to cover the dollar deficit of other countries. This was apparently the result of a conscious decision on the part of the U.S. government for the purpose of allowing other countries to reconstitute their international reserves, which had been seriously depleted during the war and early postwar period. Moreover, there remained during the period various quantitative restrictions by most other countries on their dollar payments. Had the market demand for dollar exchange not been held in check by artificial controls, no doubt the surplus dollar receipts would have been significantly reduced, perhaps eliminated.

In any event, it is clear that the world dollar-payments situation was significantly different from that of both the preceding years of dollar shortage and the following years of dollar glut.

DOLLAR GLUT: 1958–?

Let us accept for the moment the so-called "liquidity basis" for defining a balance-of-payments deficit. According to this basis, a deficit is measured by the sum of decreases in official reserve assets plus increases in short-term liabilities to foreigners. Compared to the average annual liquidity deficit from 1950 through 1956 of approximately $1.5 billion, from 1958 through 1969 the deficit reached an annual average of roughly $3.0 billion, or double that of the preceding period.

From a position of having a comfortable margin of gold and other liquid reserves in excess of foreign short-term claims against it, the United States found itself within the space of a few years in the highly unusual position of having less gold than total potential foreign claims for payment in gold. If the United States was a willing participant in the transfer of gold and dollar reserves to other countries during 1950–56, this certainly was not the case after 1957. On the contrary, the balance of payments of the United States, for the first time in memory, became a cause for concern and anxiety to the public and to the government, as well as to foreigners.

Before examining the causes of this sharp deterioration in the balance of payments, let us take a look at the actual balance-of-payments data for the 12-year period 1958–69, summarized in Table 20.3. We have identified the recorded deficit in the balance

TABLE 20.3

U.S. BALANCE OF PAYMENTS, 1958–69
(in billions of dollars)

Export of goods and services *	$392	
Import of goods and services	340	
Balance on current account		+52
Remittance and pensions	−9	
Private capital (net) †	−26	
U.S. government grants and loans	−38	
Balance on capital and unilateral transfer accounts		−73
Errors and omissions		−11
Deficit on combined current, capital and unilateral transfer accounts		−32
Means of financing deficit:		
Increase in liabilities to foreigners, plus decrease in gold and foreign exchange reserves		+32

SOURCES: U.S. Department of Commerce, *Survey of Current Business* and *Federal Reserve Bulletin* (April, 1970), Table 1, p. 316.

* Excluding transfers under military grants.

† U.S. private capital outflow less foreign capital inflow, excluding reserve transactions and liabilities to commercial banks abroad.

of payments as the difference between net capital outflows plus unilateral transfers and the balance on current account. However, there has been excluded from the capital flow figure the movement into the United States of foreign short-term capital which took the form of liquid claims against domestic institutions. These claims consisted mainly of deposits in U.S. banks and holdings of U.S. government obligations. Instead of such capital movements being included in the regular capital account—where they would appear as a credit offset to the outflow of U.S. capital—they have been placed under "means of financing deficit." The reason for this lies in the assumption that the accumulation of short-term liquid claims against the United States represents *accommodating* finance rather than an autonomous capital inflow. In short, the claims are regarded as the result of the deficit and serve as a substitute for gold outflows.

On the other hand, the $26 billion figure for net private capital outflow includes *all* U.S. private capital flows, liquid short-term as well as other forms. In other words, U.S. short-term capital movements are presumed to be autonomous rather than accommodating.

The rationale for the asymmetrical treatment of foreign and U.S. short-term capital movements lies in their different implications for the international liquidity position of the United States. Even though short-term private claims against foreigners contribute to the overall liquidity of the economy, they are not assets available to the government for drawing upon to settle payments balances. On the other hand, foreign short-term liquid assets in the United States constitute a potential claim against the government for conversion into gold. It can be argued that this line of reasoning is not valid and that it leads to an overstatement of the deficit in the balance of payments. However, it has the virtue of bringing out in sharp relief the potential liquidity problem which the continuing deficit in the U.S. balance of payments has created.

Alternative bases for measuring deficits can give a sharply different impression of the balance-of-payment position. One alternative measure is the so-called "official reserves transactions basis." The major difference between this and the liquidity basis is that it treats only increases in *official* foreign short-term claims against the United States in the measure of the deficit and excludes increases in private claims. The rationale here is that the obligation of the United States to convert dollars into gold extends only to foreign official holders of dollars and that private foreign claims against the United States should be treated no differently from private U.S. claims against foreigners.

The difference that may arise between the liquidity and official reserve transactions measure of the United States balance-of-payments position was dramatically demonstrated during the year 1969. On the liquidity definition, the balance of payments showed a *deficit* of over $7 billion, while on the official reserve basis there was a *surplus* of $2.7 billion! Obviously, there was a huge inflow into the United States of foreign private short-term capital, accompanied by a reduction in foreign official dollar holdings.[2]

---

[2] It appears that the inflow of private capital was to a large extent due to borrowings by U.S. commercial banks in the so-called "Euro-dollar" market because of tight money conditions in the United States.

There are some economists who maintain that there is no way of meaningfully identifying a deficit or surplus in the U.S. balance of payments. A discussion of this point of view will be postponed until the next chapter. In the meanwhile, we may investigate the reasons for the deficit as conventionally defined.

CAUSES OF THE U.S. DEFICIT

In seeking an explanation for the remarkable transformation in the U.S. balance of payments from a position of huge surplus in the early postwar period to chronic deficit since 1957, the data in Table 20.3 yield an important general clue. We observe that, in contrast to more usual deficit situations, the current account has displayed a large net credit balance. Obviously, the deficit has been the result of net debit balances on the capital and unilateral transfer accounts exceeding in total sum the current account credit balance. Given the very large outward movement of private capital, combined with the continuation of government foreign loan and grant programs, equilibrium required that the current account develop a larger surplus than was realized in fact. One way of stating the cause for the deficit, then, is in terms of the failure of the current account fully to adjust to changes in the capital and unilateral transfer accounts. This relates to what is known as the "transfer" mechanism, which is the adjustment process by which *monetary* tranfers—capital movements and unilateral payments—are converted into *real* transfers in the form of the net movement of goods and services.

As a first approach to the reasons for the failure of the U.S. balance of payments to reach an equilibrium adjustment, let it be noted that the strains placed upon it have been of an extraordinary nature. The strains have been of two kinds. First is the sheer magnitude of the capital movements and unilateral transfers to which the current account must respond for equilibrium to prevail. A net outflow of capital plus U.S. government foreign grants and loans totaling over $60 billion for the 12-year period 1958–69 must be regarded as an unusually heavy burden for the balance of payments to bear.

Second, a high proportion of total U.S. foreign payments has been motivated by political and military considerations having little or no connection with market forces. In addition to government foreign loans and grants, included in this category are military expenditures abroad which averaged $3.0 billion per year during

1960–64 and $3.7 billion during 1965–67, and reached $4.5 billion in 1968 and $4.9 billion in 1969. Since equilibrium adjustment in the balance of payments is largely dependent upon market decisions with respect to the import and export of goods and services, the presence of such large nonmarket transactions can be presumed to complicate the problem of adjustment.

In view of the huge size of the U.S. economy, there is no question of its physical *capacity* to produce an export surplus sufficient to match outward movements of capital and unilateral transfers. The problem, rather, has been that market forces have not been strong enough in the right direction to generate a matching surplus. Indeed, the trend at the end of the 1960's was toward a large reduction in the current account surplus of the United States, from an annual average of nearly $6.0 billion during 1960–67 to only slightly more than $2.0 billion in 1969.

The market forces determining the amount of an export surplus include as major elements aggregate demand and supply at home and abroad, price competitiveness, and the commodity pattern of trade. The influence exerted by each of these elements has varied during different periods.

An important structural factor was the changed supply situation in Westrn Europe as compared to the early postwar years. For the first few years following the war, Europe's productive capacity remained far below the demands upon her economy, while the U.S. economy, physically intact, easily was able both to meet pent-up domestic demand and to furnish extensive aid to other countries. The remarkable recovery and expansion of European productive capacity not only relieved the United States of the burden of continued massive assistance but transformed Europe from the status of a deficit supply area to that of a dynamic competitor of the United States in world markets.

This switch in the relative positions of Europe and the United States was fostered by several other developments. Accompanying Europe's economic expansion—and partly responsible for it—was rapid technological advances, while many American industries were operating with outmoded equipment and techniques. As a result of the improved efficiency of its industries and the lag in U.S. industries, productivity per man-hour in Europe increased during the 1950's at a more rapid rate than in the United States. A similar favorable differential was enjoyed by Japan which, like Europe, was undergoing an extraordinary economic expansion.

The competitiveness of other countries in world markets was strengthened by price factors. All countries suffered inflation during and after the war, but the inflation in Europe was more severe than in the United States. This was an important contributing reason for the dollar shortage. The situation was radically changed in 1949 by a wave of exchange depreciation. The pound sterling was devalued by 30.5 percent. Others followed suit, though devaluing by a smaller percentage, until countries accounting for four fifths of world trade (excluding that of the United States) had realigned the dollar value of their currencies. Whereas previously European currencies generally had been clearly overvalued in relation to the dollar, this was no longer true. Indeed, for some countries the devaluation may have been excessive, leaving their currencies *undervalued*.

In any event, the major countries sharing world markets with the United States became increasingly capable after 1949 of competing with the United States in terms of price. American industry was no longer in a world "sellers' market," limited in its export sales only by the availability to other countries of dollar exchange. The competitiveness of other countries was sharpened by the vigorous efforts of their industries to expand export sales. Depending as a rule on exports to a much greater degree than their American counterparts, European and Japanese manufacturing firms display a responsiveness and adaptability to foreign demand for their products that is outside the tradition of most U.S. firms. Among other ways, this manifests itself in export pricing policies. Even though in their domestic operations foreign firms are generally no more competitive than U.S. firms, in the export field they are.

By the beginning of the period of the dollar glut in 1958, however, and for the next several years, the combination of a high degree of price stability in the United States and the resumption of inflationary trends in Europe still permitted, notwithstanding the adverse factors described above, the United States to realize a large export surplus. This situation abruptly came to an end in 1964. Starting in that year and progressing through 1969, inflationary forces in the United States gathered momentum under the impact of a declining rate of unemployment and rapidly expanding aggregate demand. A not surprising accompaniment was a shrinkage of the export surplus, as noted previously.

Observing the trade position of the United States over the entire postwar period, it becomes clear that a deterioration has occurred.

The long-term tendency has been for the volume of world trade to expand at a faster rate than world production. While U.S. imports have followed this pattern, its exports have not. This contrasts sharply with the experience of certain other countries, especially West Germany, Japan, and Italy, whose exports over the years 1961–69 have expanded 25 percent, 80 percent, and 100 percent, respectively, more rapidly than world output. To put it in other terms, the U.S. *share* of world exports has decreased in recent years.

Aside from the factors already mentioned as contributing to this result, certain structural changes have been at work reinforcing the trend. One of these is the declining U.S. share of agricultural products in world trade. Since agricultural products account for roughly 15 percent of U.S. exports—a much higher proportion than for most other industrial countries—the effect has been to brake the expansion of total U.S. exports.

A similar adverse effect has been producd by the fact that while world trade in agricultural products has been relatively declining, trade in manufactured consumer goods has undergone the greatest expansion. The United States, however, is not a major exporter of such goods, nor has the proportion which they bear to U.S. total exports (about 12 percent of nonagricultural exports) changed over the last decade. On the other hand, the U.S. import demand for consumer goods has risen—to over 25 percent of total imports as compared to 17 percent in 1960.

In summary, the deficit in the U.S. balance of payments has been the consequence of the failure of the current account to develop a credit balance sufficiently large to cover the net debit balance on autonomous capital and unilateral transfer accounts. This failure in turn is the result of changes in supply conditions, a declining price competitiveness of the United States in world markets, and structural changes in the pattern of trade unfavorable to the U.S. position.

RECOMMENDED READING

HARRIS, SEYMOUR E. *The Dollar in Crisis.* New York: Harcourt, Brace & World, Inc., 1961.

A collection of papers on various aspects of the balance-of-payments problem of the United States.

KINDLEBERGER, C. P. *The Dollar Shortage.* New York: John Wiley & Sons, Inc., 1950.

LARY, HAL B.   *Problems of the United States as World Trader and Banker.* New York: National Bureau of Economics Research, 1963.

MACDOUGALL, DONALD.   "The Dollar Problem: A Reappraisal," *Essays in International Finance,* No. 35. Princeton, N.J.: International Finance Section, Princeton University (November, 1960) .

STUDY QUESTIONS

1. What is meant by dollar "shortage" and dollar "glut"?

2. Argue pro and con that the dollar shortage was not an independent phenomenon, but was the result of U.S. foreign aid to Europe.

3. What circumstances during the period 1950–57 support the conclusion that the U.S. balance-of-payments deficit during that period was not an indication of balance-of-payments disequilibrium?

4. How are U.S. short-term capital movements treated differently from foreign short-term capital movements in constructing the U.S. balance of payments? What is the justification for this practice?

5. Review the implications of the U.S. balance-of-payments deficit for its international liquidity position.

6. Explain the meaning of the "transfer" problem.

7. State the requirements for balance-of-payments equilibrium when a country has net autonomous outward capital movements and unilateral transfers.

8. In what way did the economic recovery and expansion of Europe and Japan contribute to the shift from dollar shortage to dollar glut?

9. How did the widespread currency devaluations in 1949 affect the U.S. balance of payments?

10. What is meant by the statement that the devaluation in 1949 may have left European currencies "undervalued"?

11. What is the nature of the special strains placed on the U.S. balance of payments over the past several years?

Chapter 21

RESTORING EQUILIBRIUM IN THE U.S. BALANCE OF PAYMENTS

Two different points of view have developed concerning the U.S. balance-of-payments experience of recent years. The more or less official view of the U.S. government, and one that conforms to the conventional analysis of academic economists, is that the deficit in the balance of payments, as described in the preceding chapter, is a serious problem demanding corrective measures. The basis for this viewpoint is twofold.

First, continuation of the deficit may increasingly hamper policies for domestic economic stability and growth. As the international liquidity of the United States shrinks, the necessity for avoiding measures which might have adverse effects on the balance of payments grows more compelling. For example, it may be thought desirable domestic policy to foster an expansion in residential construction, which has suffered a marked slowdown for a long time. An important part of such a policy would be an easing of credit conditions and lowering of interest rates. However, this might well lead to an outflow of capital from the United States in search of higher rates of return abroad, thereby aggravating the deficit in the balance of payments. Were the balance of payments in a "strong" condition, there would be little cause for concern.

Second, restoring equilibrium may be regarded as essential for the viability of the international monetary system. Because of the special role of the dollar, as previously described, the future of the whole system is bound up with the future of the dollar. To look upon it in the most pessimistic way, suppose that the U.S. deficit were to continue for several more years. As gold and foreign exchange reserves shrink further, a crisis of confidence, accompanied by large-scale withdrawal of foreign-owned assets, would become ever more probable. In any event, at some point the ability of the United States to convert dollars into gold or acceptable foreign currencies would disappear. As a consequence, either the dollar's tie to gold would have to be severed or restrictions on trade and payments would have to be imposed. In either case, this would mean the breakdown of the present system. Moreover, reform of the system to relieve the dollar of its special status and vulnerability is much less likely to be undertaken if the dollar is in a weak and threatened position than if it were in a strong and secure position. At the same time, eliminating the U.S. deficit would make reform of the system even more pressing, since the supply of additional reserves to other countries furnished by the deficit would dry up.

A quite different point of view of the U.S. balance-of-payments position, based on a different analysis of the role of the dollar, can be adopted. The point of departure of this approach is the denial that there is any meaningful way of identifying disequilibrium in the balance of payments of a country like the United States that serves as an international financial center as well as commercial center. Especially unreliable in this view is the "liquidity" basis of defining disequilibrium, according to which an increase in any foreign short-term claim against the United States is interpreted in the same light as a decrease in the international reserves of the country.

The reason given for objecting to this measure of deficit is that an international financial center can be expected to receive large amounts of short-term capital from other countries as a normal part of its operations. Foreigners *wish* to hold dollars, not only as working balances in the conduct of international commercial relations but also as liquid assets that are at once safe and yield a return. In this latter respect, the United States is like a bank, with international depositors holding short-term claims against it. While a bank needs reserves to meet net cashing of claims against it, the reserves necessary are only a fraction of its deposit liabilities, since only in crisis situations will the exercise of claims be more than a fraction of the amount of deposits outstanding. So, too, it is argued, the United States need not have international reserves (in the form of gold, foreign exchange balances, and IMF Drawing Rights) that are more than a fraction of its foreign short-term liabilities.

Consistent with the above perspective is the opinion that, at the very least, the disequilibrium in the U.S. balance of payments is grossly exaggerated by the conventional measures of the deficit. The deficit measured on the "liquidity" basis, for example, increases if Europeans accept short-term dollar claims in exchange for long-term U.S. investments in Europe. Yet this may be simply the result of credit conditions in the two areas and of portfolio preferences, rather than an indication of disequilibrium in the balance of payments.

The widely disparate results obtained from different measures of the U.S. payments position (recall the $7 billion deficit for 1969 according to the liquidity basis, as compared to the $2.7 surplus according to the official reserve transactions basis) suggest that there is indeed merit to the criticisms that have been levied against these measures. This does not necessarily mean, however, that the United States is in balance-of-payments equilibrium and need not be concerned with its international monetary position. While admitting that international reserves need not be as large as short-term foreign liabilities, one may still insist that there are limits to the spread beyond which the monetary order is threatened. At the end of 1969, U.S. foreign short-term liabilities had reached a total of $42 billion, while its official monetary reserves stood at $17 billion. This compares to liabilities of $22 billion and reserves of $19 billion in 1960. The spread, in other words, increased over the decade from $3 billion to $25 billion. Regardless of whether this development should have been regarded with concern in the past, we may doubt whether it can continue unabated in the future without important implications for the international monetary order. One possible implication is examined toward the end of this chapter.

In any event, the official position of the U.S. government, shared by the governments of most other industrial countries of the Western world, is that the balance of payments of this country must be corrected, with the deficit as conventionally measured eventually eliminated. The central question, however, is through what processes or methods the correction can be effected. It is to this topic that we now turn.

CORRECTIVE MEASURES ATTEMPTED

We may begin the discussion with the policies that have been tried. It was not until around 1960 that the government evidenced sufficient worry about the balance of payments to take measures for its relief.

Operation Twist

One of the most interesting early policies adopted went by the name of "operation twist." The basic idea here was to allow short-term interest rates to rise while holding long-term rates steady. The hope was that higher short-term rates would make dollar holdings more attractive to foreigners, while keeping long-term rates low would favor domestic economic growth. The policy was successful in keeping the intended differential in rates over the first half of the 1960's, but thereafter inflationary pressures pushed both short- and long-term rates upward, with the spread between them disappearing except for a brief period. In any case, the policy could not be expected fundamentally to change the balance of payments; its primary purpose was to reduce the conversion of dollars into gold —that is, to change the form in which the deficit in the balance of payments was expressed.

Capital Controls

A second major policy decision was reached in 1963. This was to restrict the outflow of capital from the United States. The first implementation of the decision was the imposition of a so-called "interest equalization tax," under which U.S. residents who purchased foreign securities have to pay a tax of up to 15 percent of the purchase price.[1] By thus making the net return on foreign securities less attractive, the outflow of capital in this form was discouraged.

Capital controls were extended in 1965 through a program of voluntary restraint on the part of American firms and banks and business firms with overseas investment and loan operations. Three years later, the voluntary program was transformed into a mandatory program accompanied by a considerable tightening of restrictions on capital outflows in the form of direct investments abroad. At the same time, new and more restrictive guidelines on the extension of foreign credits by banks and other financial institutions were instituted by the Board of Governors of the Federal Reserve System.

That the capital-control program of the United States had some success in reducing the payments deficit below the level it would have otherwise reached is fairly clear. However, the program has always been regarded as only a temporary device, and in his economic message to the Congress in 1969, the President affirmed the administration's intention to relax and ultimately remove restrictions on capital movements.

---

[1] The tax was 15 percent for equity shares and for bonds maturing in 15 or more years, with lower rates applicable on bonds of shorter maturity. Securities of underdeveloped countries and of Canada were exempted.

The rationale of capital controls as a method of reducing the U.S. balance-of-payments deficit is straightforward. As indicated in the preceding chapter, the outflow of private capital from the United States spurted around the middle of the 1950's to a new high level and became the largest monetary transfer debit item in the balance of payments.

It is incorrect to assume that a dollar's payment on capital account contributes a dollar to the balance-of-payments deficit. Some capital movements, in fact, involve no foreign exchange expenditure at all and are self-transferred in real terms. The chief example are direct investments in which plant and equipment are sent from the United States for installation in foreign branch plants. In such cases, the balance-of-payments deficit is unaffected. Foreign investments are also frequently accompanied by other kinds of transactions which provide additional foreign exchange receipts. Foreign firms with connections with U.S. firms may, because of the connections, purchase equipment from the United States, thereby expanding her exports. Another example are license agreements under which foreign firms are permitted to use patented processes in return for royalty or copyright payments to the American firm holding the patent or copyright.

Even when a particular capital outflow is unaccompanied by any direct return flow of receipts as in the preceding examples, there is an indirect feedback effect tending partially to compensate for the foreign expenditure. Over the long run, the most important feedback is the payoff from the loan or investment in the form of interest and dividends. The significance of this for the U.S. balance of payments is indicated by the magnitude of interest and dividend receipts from past foreign loans and investments. In 1969 these receipts were close to $9 billion.

Interest and dividend receipts are not the only feedback from foreign loans and investments; the transfer adjustment mechanism works in the direction of expanding a country's export of goods and services in response to capital outflows. The mechanism consists mainly of increasing the income—and perhaps price level—of the countries receiving the capital, leading in turn to increases in their demand for imports. To the extent that the capital-sending country participates in satisfying this increased demand, its balance of payments adjusts to the capital movement.

Notwithstanding the above favorable feedback effects of capital outflows on the balance of payments, it is highly probable that such

outflows have a net adverse effect on the balance of payments over
the short and medium term. The payoff in interest and dividends
takes several years to equal the initial principal amount of capital
outflow. The transfer mechanism, as we explained in an earlier discussion, operates imperfectly and, in any event, slowly. The conclusion is that, while a dollar's capital outflow certainly does not
add a dollar to the balance-of-payments deficit, it almost surely adds
some significant part of a dollar. It follows that a reduction in capital outflow from the United States reduces the country's balance-of-
payments deficit during the period in which the reduction occurs.

Nevertheless, there are strong objections to controls over capital
movements, as there are to trade controls. First, they interfere with
the most efficient use of resources, leading to allocative distortions
which sap international trade and investment of their full potential
benefits. Second, the United States, together with the other major
trading countries, is committed to the principle of freedom of trade
and payments, unless exceptional circumstances warrant a temporary deviation. The leadership of the United States in establishing
this principle makes its own adherence to it all the more important.
Third, as indicated above, capital controls are more in the nature
of a temporary palliative than a method of fundamental correction
of payments imbalance, since over the long run, interest and dividend receipts decline as a result of restricting capital outflows.

Redistribution of the Burden of Defense and Economic Aid

Comparable to the reduction of private capital movements as a
means of relieving the balance of payments is the reduction of public capital and unilateral transfer outflows for overseas economic
and military aid. This could be accomplished by unilateral action,
but since foreign aid is an instrument of foreign policy, it is not
easily amenable to significant change on balance-of-payments grounds.
Alternatively, an effort could be made to maintain the total of foreign aid while reducing the share borne by the United States, requiring, of course, an increase in the share of aid contributed by
other countries.

The United States in recent years has relied principally upon the
second approach. Even though it has unilaterally reduced the
amount of foreign economic aid, its foreign military aid has increased. On the other hand, a concerted effort has been made
through diplomatic channels to obtain the acquiescence of allied

countries to assume a larger share of foreign aid. How successful the campaign has been is difficult to determine. However, according to the published data, the aggregate volume of government loans and grants, excluding military grants, has remained relatively stable over the last several years at an annual volume close to $4 billion.

Ad Hoc Measures

The measures described are the most general that the United States has adopted to date to relieve its balance of payments. Other actions have been confined to a hodgepodge of piecemeal *ad hoc* measures of doubtful effectiveness and questionable justification. Among these are the following: a reduction in the duty-free goods American tourists are allowed to bring into the country; a program to encourage foreign tourists to visit the United States and Americans to see America first; the "tying" of foreign aid to U.S. goods— that is, requiring recipients of aid money to spend it in the United States; a tightening of "buy American" provisions in government procurement, discriminating further against foreign suppliers; and an export-promotion campaign directed toward business firms. It is doubtful that these measures yield any significant benefit to the balance of payments. At the same time, some of them (such as "buy American" practices and tied loans) constitute a disguised depreciation of the dollar and violate principles of trade and payments freedom to which the United States is committed.

OTHER APPROACHES

It is evident that the various policies adopted by the government to improve the balance of payments have not enjoyed any great success. This raises the question of what other policies, if any, might be more effective.

Deflation

The classical prescription for a balance-of-payments deficit is deflation—that is, bringing down the internal price level to an equilibrium relationship with external prices. The classical method of accomplishing deflation is monetary contraction. Alternatively, the price level can be reduced with sufficiently strong fiscal policies (lowering of government expenditure, increasing taxes) designed to reduce aggregate demand.

Over most of the period since the balance of payments of the United States has become a matter of concern, the classical prescription has been eschewed. Whereas in the classical model a decrease in gold or other reserve assets calls forth a concomitant reduction in domestic money supply, in actuality the money supply of the United States continued to rise over the years of deficit in payments and loss of gold. Not until 1969 was a vigorous and persistent policy of monetary restraint pursued by the Federal Reserve authority. This policy may have been adopted in part because of the balance-of-payments situation, but the chief motive was to rid the economy of the ill effects of a growing inflation.

As in the case of monetary policy, fiscal policy has not been generally employed to correct the balance of payments. If it had been so employed, increases in taxes and/or decreases in government expenditure to restrict aggregate demand would have been the guiding principles. Instead, for the greater part of the period, again with the exception of the year 1969 and continuing into the early part of 1970, expanding government expenditure in excess of increased tax collections was the rule.

The reason for the failure to apply monetary and fiscal brakes on the economy is not difficult to apprehend. While undoubtedly effective as a means of improving the balance of payments, unfortunately such policies tend also to cause a slowdown in economic growth and unemployment. If restriction of money supply and aggregate demand had the effect only of reducing the price level while maintaining full-employment production, it would be a much more acceptable method of correcting the balance of payments. In fact, however, the downward inflexibility of wages and prices causes a contraction of aggregate demand to have its primary impact on output and employment rather than on prices. Full employment has such a high priority among national economic goals that its sacrifice for the sake of the balance of payments is not often acceptable. This is all the more so in view of the relatively large reduction in national income required to reduce imports. With a marginal propensity to import on the order of 5 percent, it would require a contraction in income of $20 to reduce imports by $1.

Reduction of Sectoral Costs and Prices

The risks attending general deflation do not extend to reducing costs and prices in particular sectors of the economy, for this is consistent with—and indeed contributive to—the maintenance of high growth rates and full employment. While there is no convincing evidence that the balance-of-payments deficit has been caused by a more rapid rise in the general level of prices in the United States than in export-competing countries, the evidence is strong that in certain sectors relative price increases have been important contributing causes of the deficit. As mentioned in the preceding chapter, the share of the United States in world exports of manufactured goods has declined. Weighing heavily in this decline have been non-electrical machinery, transport equipment, metals, and metal manufactures. The U.S. prices of these products have tended to rise more than average, and it must be assumed that this bears a heavy responsibility for the loss of overseas markets.

One way of improving the balance of payments, then, is through reducing costs and prices in industries whose exports are important in total exports. But how is this to be done? Since most manufactured goods exported are produced in oligopolistic industries, characterized by downward price rigidity, a change in their pricing policies in the direction of greater flexibility would be helpful. If it is unduly optimistic to count upon a voluntary change in oligopolistic pricing practices, various means are available to encourage a greater willingness to lower prices in the face of an eroding international market. One would be to inject stronger competitiveness in markets through vigorous enforcement of antitrust laws. A second, and perhaps more effective method, is to stimulate cost-saving investments and technological improvements through tax concessions, such as has been done already on a limited scale. It would also be helpful, of course, for wage demands by strong labor unions to be kept within the limits of productivity increases, as set out in guidelines such as those established by the Johnson Administration.

Exchange-Rate Adjustments

As a substitute for or supplement to deflation, exchange rate adjustments are the second general method of correcting balance-of-payments disequilibrium without direct controls over trade and payments. Were it not for the special position of the dollar in the international monetary system, devaluation would be perhaps the most logical and satisfactory method for the United States to adopt to eliminate its payments deficit. However, for reasons explained on several previous occasions, devaluation of the dollar is practically precluded except as a last resort.

An alternative to devaluation of the dollar would be the *appreciation* of the international value of certain other currencies. This would have the advantage over dollar devaluation of being more selective in its impact and of avoiding depreciating the dollar in terms of gold.

It is a nice question whether the dollar glut was a problem of a deficit in the U.S. balance of payments, or of a *surplus* in the balances of payments of other countries. Obviously, a U.S. deficit vis-à-vis another country has its accounting equivalent in the dollar surplus of that country. *Both* the United States and the other country have balance-of-payments disequilibrium. There is, however, a big difference between a *deficit* disequilibrium and a *surplus* disequilibrium. Ordinarily, the pressure to adjust the balance of payments falls primarily on the deficit country. A country may be willing to accumulate gold and foreign exchange reserves indefinitely; a country is not capable of sustaining a deficit indefinitely.

But this does not necessarily mean that the deficit country is primarily *responsible* for the balance-of-payments disequilibrium, nor that from the point of view of the world's trade and payments system it is always preferable for the brunt of the adjustment process to be placed on the deficit country.

A reasonable case can be made for the proposition that the deficit in the U.S. balance of payments has not been its sole responsibility and that, in any event, measures to relieve the payments situation should not be confined to the shores of the United States. The foreign payments of the United States have been heavily loaded with items of an international public character, contributing not only to the country's own national interests but to the interests of the free world as a whole. As we observed in the preceding chapter, such nonmarket transactions have placed an unusual strain on the balance of payments.

The essence of the balance-of-payments problem of the United States was to develop an *export surplus* of goods and services large enough to effect the transfer in real terms of these huge foreign monetary transfers. But to develop an export surplus of given amount, other countries have to accept an *import* surplus from the United States of equal amount. As a group, other countries obviously did not do this, but instead used part of their dollar receipts to purchase gold and build up dollar balances.

One approach to easing the payments problem of the United States therefore lay in measures by those countries with a surplus in their balance of payments to reduce their exports or, preferably, to increase their imports. Several actions would help to accomplish this, including expansionary monetary and fiscal policies and more rapid increase in wage rates. Since, however, the chief payments surplus countries were at the time also enjoying a domestic economic boom, such policies would have threatened to cause inflation, and were therefore resisted. An alternative measure not having undesirable internal monetary effects was appreciation of exchange rates on the dollar.

The outstanding example of a country in a strong payments surplus position and able to ease the deficit of the United States through exchange appreciation was West Germany. What came to be known as the "miracle" of West Germany consisted of an extraordinary economic recovery and then expansion, taking hold after a currency reform program in 1948. As her economy gained in strength, Germany's balance of payments displayed an increasing surplus.

Evidence that the German mark was undervalued relatively to the dollar (and most other currencies as well) was very strong. Pressure on Germany to revalue the mark upward was insistent, and in March, 1961, the gold parity of the mark (and simultaneously of the Dutch guilder) was raised by 4.75 percent. Again, in 1969, the mark was revalued, this time by 9.3 percent. While such actions contribute to relieving the U.S. balance of payments, it is to be noted that only these three upward currency revaluations have been made, with a corresponding limited quantitative significance for the United States. Moreover, over the same period, several currency devaluations have occurred (such as the British action in November, 1967, of reducing the value of the pound from $2.80 to $2.40 and the devaluation of the French franc in August, 1969, from 4.94 francs to 5.55 francs per U.S. dollar).

A POSSIBLE ULTIMATE SOLUTION: A DOLLAR STANDARD

The experience of the United States with its intractable balance-of-payments deficit serves to emphasize the absence of satisfactory means of adjustment in a regime of fixed exchange rates. If adjustment through either changes in prices and incomes or in exchange rates is rejected, no other general satisfactory method of adjustment remains.

This leaves the United States in a dilemma: What can be done if the deficit in the balance of payments continues until finally her stock of gold and other reserves is exhausted? As indicated at the beginning of the chapter, the consequence would be a drastic change in at least the formal properties of the present international monetary order. The commitment of the United States to maintain a fixed relationship between the dollar and gold would, of course, have to be abandoned. However, this would not necessarily entail the advent of freely fluctuating exchange rates. One strong possibility is that the dollar would continue to be a key, anchor currency, even though no longer tied to gold. The determination of exchange rates between other currencies and the dollar would be at the discretion of other countries (either under IMF rules or independently). If, for example, the United States incurred a deficit in its balance of payments, those countries with surplus dollar receipts would have the choice of either accumulating dollar balances or letting the values of their currencies in terms of the dollar appreciate. In any event, the United States would no longer have to be concerned about balance-of-payments problems, since she would assume a passive role with respect to exchange rates.

In effect, provided other countries wish to maintain stable exchange rates, this would create an international dollar standard. Instead of gold serving as the ultimate standard of value in international transactions, the dollar would assume that function. By severing the tie between the dollar and gold, gold would be demonetized and become merely a metal for use in the arts and industry.

Unless exchange rates are to be left free to fluctuate in accordance with market demand and supply, some kind of standard in terms of which international currency values are expressed is required. If the traditional gold commodity standard disappears, either a new international money could be created or an existing national currency be adapted to serve the role of standard of value. Since the short-run prospects for the creation of a true international money are remote (the recently created Special Drawing Rights by the International Monetary Fund are only a reserve asset the value of which is expressed in terms of the dollar), the use of a national currency for the purpose is the only practical alternative.

The choice of the U.S. dollar as an international standard is natural. In the first place, the dollar in actual practice has already very nearly achieved this status. It is the commonly used "vehicle currency"—that is, the currency employed by most other countries for official intervention in the foreign exchange markets for the purpose of keeping exchange rates within prescribed limits. More than this, the dollar is the primary international transactions currency —that is, the currency most widely used in private commercial transactions—and international investment medium. Finally, the United States is a world banker and international financial center. Foreigners had already accumulated $42 billion in balances and other liquid dollar assets by the beginning of 1970 (not to mention an additional $49 billion in nonliquid dollar claims). Ready access to the large, well-organized financial markets of the United States assures creditworthy foreigners the ability further to acquire dollars through borrowing.

It may seem strange, if not presumptuous, for the United States to react to its balance-of-payments situation by in effect declaring it to be no longer a policy target. However, if those who believe that the U.S. balance of payments is not really in deficit disequilibrium, but rather is merely a reflection of the special position of the United States as world trader and banker, are correct, the establishment of a dollar standard is not only logical but is little more than a formal recognition of a *de facto* situation.

Whether other countries would willingly accept the above view of the role of the dollar is another question. For political as well as economic reasons, other countries may well be reluctant to formalize an international monetary system with the dollar as its core.

RECOMMENDED READING

HANSEN, ALVIN H. *The Dollar and the International Monetary System.* New York: McGraw-Hill Book Co., 1965.

JOINT ECONOMIC COMMITTEE, U.S. CONGRESS. *The United States Balance of Payments,* Part I, "Current Problems and Policies," and Part II, "Outlook for United States Balance of Payments." Washington, D.C.: U.S. Government Printing Office, 1963.

————. *The United States Balance of Payments—Perspectives and Policies.* Washington, D.C.: U.S. Government Printing Office, 1963.

KINDLEBERGER, C. P. "Measuring Equilibrium in the Balance of Payments," *Journal of Political Economy,* Vol. 77, No. 6 (November-December, 1969).

MCKINNON, RONALD I. "Private and Official International Money: The Case for the Dollar," *Essays in International Finance,* No. 74 (April, 1969). Princeton, N.J.: International Finance Section, Princeton University.

STUDY QUESTIONS

1. Give the principal reasons, one domestic and one international, why a solution to the U.S. balance-of-payments problem may be regarded as important.

2. What is the basis for the thesis that the United States may not actually be in balance-of-payments disequilibrium?

3. Describe "operation twist" and indicate what consequences it was intended to have.

4. What feedback effects on the balance of payments can be expected from capital exports?

5. Why would a dollar's decrease in capital outflow probably reduce the balance-of-payments deficit, but by less than a dollar?

6. What are the main objections to controls over capital movements?

7. How would an increase in the foreign aid programs of other countries contribute to reducing the payments deficit of the United States?

8. Describe the classical remedy for correcting the balance of payments. Why is it resisted?

9. How might sectoral reduction in costs contribute to relieving the U.S. balance of payments?

10. What connection have antitrust laws with the balance of payments?

11. State the case for currency appreciation by payments surplus countries rather than devaluation of the dollar.

12. What is meant by an international "dollar standard"?

13. What are the bases for creating a dollar standard?

14. Why would the United States assume a passive position with respect to exchange rates if a dollar standard were established?

PART IV

The International Economics
of Development

The concluding part of this book is devoted to the urgent problem of economic development of the less developed countries. While development is mainly a national problem for each of the countries concerned, it cannot be divorced from the international economy in the framework of which it occurs. Our principal interest, of course, is in the international aspects of development, and in particular with the roles of "trade and aid."

Chapter 22   THE CHALLENGE OF
                ECONOMIC DEVELOPMENT

The vast majority of the world's population is living close to the perilous border of bare subsistence. This no doubt has been the case for a long, long time, but only recently has it commanded the interest and attention it deserves. Today, the poverty in which the great mass of peoples live stands high, perhaps at the very top, of world economic problems demanding solution. The impoverished countries themselves place economic development first on the priority list of goals. Equally significant, developed countries, individually, and collectively through various international organizations, have joined the battle and declared their intention to help raise the standard of living of the poorer countries.

The reasons for the tremendous interest in economic development are several and varied. On the part of the less developed countries, there are the natural desire to participate in the fruits of economic progress so manifest elsewhere and an emerging consciousness that poverty is not an immutable state but a condition amenable to change through deliberate measures. For many countries with a newly acquired political independence and escape from colonial status, accompanied by the emergence of nationalist pride, economic growth is both a sign and prerequisite of independence.

Developed countries, for their part, have been motivated to accept the growth of less developed countries as an important goal and to help in its realization for humanitarian, political, and economic reasons. Of these, the political motivation has probably been dominant. On a general level, it has come to be widely believed that world peace and stability cannot be firmly established with the bulk of the world's population suffering from deprivation and seething with discontent, while the remainder of the world lives in relative affluence. On more particular levels, the economic development of certain countries is regarded as an important instrument of the foreign policy of the major powers. The interest of the United States in Latin America, of France in parts of Africa, and of the Soviet Union in Cuba are examples.

Whatever the motives are, the important fact remains that economic development has become a major concern of the contemporary world.

THE MEANING AND EXTENT OF UNDERDEVELOPMENT

It has become common practice to refer to certain countries of the world for whom economic growth is of paramount importance as "less developed countries," or LDC's, while others are labeled "developed countries." As the term implies, less developed is a relative condition. All countries, including the most advanced, are less

TABLE 22.1

ESTIMATED PER CAPITA NATIONAL INCOME FOR
SELECTED AREAS AND COUNTRIES, 1968
(U.S. dollar equivalents)

Regions and Selected Countries	Per Capita Income (For the Year 1968 unless Otherwise Noted in Parenthesis)
World* (1965)	610
North America	3,454
Europe	1,440
Africa (1965)	130
Congo	52
Ghana	198
Kenya	107
Morocco	185
Tanzania	67
Uganda	80
Latin America (1967)	370
Bolivia	147
Chile	449
Ecuador	196
Guatemala	276
Mexico	511
Peru	246
Middle East (1965)	290
Asia (excluding Japan) (1965)	100
Burma	67
India (1967)	73
Indonesia	86
Pakistan	121
Thailand	137
Republic of VietNam (1967)	155
Japan	1,306

SOURCE: United Nations, *Statistical Yearbook*, 1969, pp. 557–61.
* Excluding U.S.S.R. and the Soviet bloc countries, mainland China, and Yugoslavia.

developed than they are capable of becoming. There is, therefore, a considerable amount of arbitrariness in classifying countries as either "developed" or "less developed."

However, there is no useful purpose served in attempting to draw fine distinctions. The pragmatic basis for identifying the LDC's is per capita real national income. If the mean of the world's per capita income is taken as the line dividing the less developed from the developed countries, approximately two thirds of the world's population belong to the LDC's. The range of variation in income is huge: the per capita income of the richest country in the world is more than 60 times that of the poorest! Nearly one half the world's population has an average per capita income of less than $100. Though there are enormous statistical difficulties in measuring and comparing real incomes of different countries, the margin for error without essentially changing the picture this figure evokes is wide.

Whatever income level is reasonably adopted as the criterion, it is clear from the data presented in Table 22.1 that the great majority of countries in Asia, the Middle East, Africa, and Latin America falls into the category of LDC.

THE MEANING AND PURPOSES OF DEVELOPMENT

If per capita real income is taken as the criterion of the state of economic development, the corollary is that *growth* in per capita real income is the measure of success in attaining the goal of development.

The emphasis on per capita real income derives from its being the single best, though by no means the only, measure of the economic welfare of a country. Real income consists of the flow of produced goods and services. The quantity of goods and services available for current consumption, investment, and government use is limited to the quantity domestically produced (plus any net inflow from other countries). Other things being equal, the standard of living or level of consumption in a country therefore depends upon the real income it produces. The standard of living of LDC's is low mainly because their real income, in relation to their population, is low.[1]

[1] Per capita income, of course, is an average figure which conceals the extent of variations above and below. If income within a country is very unequally distributed, the mass of people may have a very low standard of living even though average income is at a respectable level.

It should also be noted that income levels may be a poor indicator of living

It is observed that it is not the total national income, but income per head of population, which we have adopted as the chief indicator of the state of economic development. If the population of a country grows at the same rate as its national income, the base determining the standard of living remains unchanged. The presumed goal of economic growth, therefore, is an increase in real national income proportionately greater than any accompanying increase in population.

Because the rate of population growth in most less-developed countries is high—and tends to increase as the death rate is lowered through improved medical conditions and nutrition—the difficulty of realizing growth is compounded. The average annual rate of population growth for the less developed countries is in the neighborhood of 2.4 percent. If the national incomes of these countries were to grow at a rate of 5 percent, per capita income would increase at an annual rate of only 2.6 percent. At this rate it would take 80 years for the less developed countries to reach the current level of per capital real income of Western Europe, and an additional 40 years to reach the U.S. level. For the least developed countries, having one half of the population of the LDC's, the time required to reach Western European levels would be on the order of 200 years![2]

No wonder "The rate of growth of 5 percent per annum . . . can in no sense be considered fully satisfactory."[3]

If more rapid economic growth is to be experienced, obviously either population growth must be reduced or national growth must be accelerated. For the reasons to be examined in the following pages, the obstacles to the rapid expansion of the national incomes of most less developed countries are formidable.

THE PROCESS OF ECONOMIC GROWTH

Economic growth is a complicated and many-sided process which defies simple analysis. We cannot pretend, within the space of a few pages, to do more than indicate briefly some of the major elements

---

standards because of claims on output other than for current consumption. For example, to the extent that a country diverts its income to maintaining a military establishment, the availability of consumer goods and services is correspondingly reduced.

[2] See United Nations, *Towards a New Trade Policy for Development* (New York, 1964), p. 5.

[3] *Ibid.*

of economic growth, for the purpose of providing background for the understanding of the problem of developing economically backward areas.

Sociopolitical Elements

Experience in recent years with attempts at economic development in various parts of the world is leading to wider acknowledgment than formerly that the process of economic growth is not only —and perhaps not even mainly—an economic problem. It can more properly be described as a social phenomenon, with cultural, political, and economic aspects.

A propitious social environment is indispensable for economic growth. A strong desire for an improvement in material living conditions and a reasonable prospect that energy devoted to this end will yield rewards are prerequisite conditions. To material-conscious Americans this may appear to be a far-fetched obstacle. But in many parts of the world, cultural values traditionally de-emphasize economic welfare. In part, the lack of drive for material betterment may be the product of a historic poverty, from which escape has only rarely been found on the part of individuals and which has come to be accepted as an immutable part of the natural order of things. Contacts with other cultures with a higher standard of living —whether through movies, tourists, radio, or GI's—tend, however, to weaken the hold of parochial cultural values and fatalistic acceptance of the status quo. But there probably has never been such a widespread urge to acquire higher living standards as there is today.

Still, economic development implies a plasticity of attitudes and institutions which cannot be created overnight. The illiterate peasant is not easily persuaded to change his timeworn methods of cultivation; the practice of having large families—as a means of providing old-age security or larger household earning power or, in some cases, as the result of religious or moral tenets opposing birth control—is not subject to sudden reversal; the social and sometimes legal barriers to occupational mobility may be formidable.

On a broader scale, governmental organization and administration in less developed countries are frequently outmoded and inefficient. Resistance to political changes is notoriously strong, especially when, as frequently is the case, nepotism and corruption have become standard practices. Reform of monetary, banking, and fiscal systems is particularly important in creating the basis for economic development. And in those not uncommon cases where landownership is concentrated in the hands of a few wealthy, absentee landlords, a reform program for the redistribution of land tenure may be required to give the incentive to greater productive effort.

Other examples could be cited of the social changes, often of a revolutionary character, in the habits, institutions, and general outlook of the people which economic development involves. Such considerations could easily lead to an extremely pessimistic outlook on the prospects of development in most of the presently less developed countries. There are several reasons, however—while fully admitting the difficulties and complexities of the sociocultural adaptations required for economic growth—for not adopting a defeatist attitude as to possibilities.

One reason is historical experience. After all, every developed country today was at one time itself underdeveloped. And in each case the beginning and progress of economic growth involved deep social and cultural changes. We need only remind ourselves of the static, tradition-bound, nonmaterialistic-oriented societies of Western Europe in the precommercial and preindustrial era or of the feudalistic social organization in Japan just prior to the beginning of its rapid economic development to realize that social and cultural matrixes extremely uncongenial to the changes implicit in economic growth need not constitute an insuperable barrier.

Second, there is no clearly defined causal sequence in which cultural change precedes and economic growth follows. Though in the present state of our knowledge of the process of economic growth, ignorance far outbalances firmly established principles, one point seems incontrovertible: the process is a *total* one, involving interaction among a multitude of economic, social, political, and cultural forces. Economic growth is itself a powerful source of change in the noneconomic aspects of society. Two of the most nearly universal characteristics of economically developing societies are industrialization and urbanization, and perhaps no two more potent forces affecting the ideology and social structure of a society can be found.

Finally, it may well be that apparent resistance to social change is a function of lack of opportunity to gain from change. Social psychology teaches that man's wants and desires are to some extent shaped by the means available for satisfying them. If, then, there is opened up the prospect of economic growth and higher standards of living, resistance to the necessary sociocultural adaptations may be greatly reduced. This is one of the chief underlying justifications for a committed program of external assistance to less developed countries by developed countries—a point to be discussed more fully later.

Limitations of space forbid any more extended consideration here of the crucially important sociocultural aspects of economic growth. In what follows we shall concern ourselves primarily with the economic aspects of growth.

Economic Elements of Growth

Economic growth, in the sense in which the term is employed here, refers to the long-run or secular increase in *per capita* productivity. Per capita productivity is a function of the volume and quality of productive resources in relation to the size of the population, the state of technological knowledge, and the efficiency with which resources are combined. One, or a combination, of the following is a necessary, though not always a sufficient, condition for economic growth: (*a*) that the quantity of capital or of utilizable land be increased relative to population, (*b*) that the health, education, skills, and similar elements determining the productive qualities of the population be improved, (*c*) that technological knowledge be increased, and (*d*) that the economic efficiency of resource use be improved.

The above-listed elements are in good measure interrelated, so that, once started, economic development contains within itself the seeds of self-generation. An increase in per capita real income ordinarily leads to an increase in the volume of savings, which, in turn, are the means of financing the creation of a new capital and a further increase of income and savings, and so on in a mutually stimulating fashion. Rising per capita income is also accompanied as a rule by better health, broader education, and greater economic security, thus enhancing the physical and mental capacity of the population and its productivity. Rising per capita income creates a larger volume and new patterns of consumer wants, opening new markets and fields of profitable investment opportunity.

The first and most important step in economic development, therefore, is to get started. This is not meant to imply that, once begun, development will proceed inexorably or automatically. Indeed, one of the great dangers of plans for economic development is that they will be attempted before the proper environment is created or on a too ambitious scale, resulting in failure and frustration. But, given general social and economic conditions favorable to growth, a beginning has the great virtue of creating the basis for further progress in a cumulative fashion.

"The Takeoff." The "mysteries" of the growth process pertain largely to this initial stage, the breakthrough from the state of economic stagnation to the dynamics of growth. This has aptly been called the "takeoff" stage.[4] What exactly happens to cause the "takeoff" is not known, except that the causes are to a greater or lesser extent unique for each country. The history of England's development in the 18th and 19th centuries differs markedly from that of Japan in the last part of the 19th century and of the Soviet Union in the 20th. For example, England's development was largely unconscious and unplanned, while Japan's and the Soviet Union's were both the result of deliberate and organized effort on the part of the government. It would appear in any event, however, that some force, or forces, must come along, fortuitously or otherwise, to trigger the mechanism of growth. In 17th- and early 18th-century England, such things as the enclosure movement and the discovery and invention of new methods and techniques of agriculture were among numerous important "preconditions" for the takeoff into growth.[5] Schumpeter has emphasized the crucial role of entrepreneurship and innovation for growth.[6] But Japan, which within less than half a century preceding 1914 was transformed from an isolated and stagnant society into a dynamic industrial society, was apparently pushed into growth by the fear of its leaders (newly come to power in the Meiji restoration of 1868) that otherwise she would fall under the domination of a foreign power.[7]

So far as generalizations can be made concerning contemporary LDC's, the awakening of strong desires to raise living standards, the belief that growth can be deliberately brought about, and upsurging nationalistic pride and anticolonialism are together perhaps the most powerful propellants operating to take off into growth. This does not mean, of course, that the takeoff will occur; an economy, like an airplane, needs lifting power as well as speed down the runway to accomplish takeoff.

---

[4] See W. W. Rostow, "The Take-Off into Self-sustained Growth," *Economic Journal*, March, 1956.

[5] See Norman S. Buchanan and Howard S. Ellis, *Approaches to Economic Development* (New York: Twentieth Century Fund, 1955) , pp. 126 ff.

[6] See J. A. Schumpeter, *The Theory of Economic Development* (Cambridge, Mass.: Harvard University Press, 1949) .

[7] See Buchanan and Ellis, *op. cit.*, p. 181.

What are the sources of the "lifting power" required for takeoff? Again, no simple answer of universal applicability is presently known. Certain elements, however, are nearly indispensable. One of these is access to additional capital—either out of increased domestic savings or from loans, grants, or investments from abroad. If, as is the case in nearly all LDC's today, the population is growing, there must normally be net additions to the capital stock merely to keep the standard of living from falling.

For the total output of an economy to grow by 1 percent per year, net new capital formation of around three to four times this amount may be necessary. Suppose that the population is growing at an annual rate of 2.5 percent. In this case, it takes net new capital formation of from 7.5 to 10.0 percent of the national income to keep the standard of living from falling. However, in the typical stagnant LDC, the volume of domestic saving is hardly sufficient to support such a rate of investment, let alone to support the higher investment required for growth. It has been suggested that at least 15 percent of the gross national product must be devoted to capital investment for an economy to "break out of the vicious circle of poverty and underemployment."[8]

While additional capital formation is almost certainly a necessary condition for takeoff into growth, it is rarely a sufficient condition. New plant and equipment are of little use if the raw materials, the technical knowledge, the manpower with proper training and skills, and the managerial and supervisory personnel are not present as complementary parts of the production process. Moreover, adequate markets for the increased output made possible by enlarged productive capacity must be found if it is not to be wasted. These are some of the reasons why a survey of the economy's resources and possibilities, together with a well-worked-out program of investment expenditure, is essential to avoid false starts and unbalanced developments.

The Stage of Self-sustaining Growth. It was indicated before in a general way that the hardest part of growth is in the initial breakthrough out of stagnation. Once well started, growth contains self-generating and self-sustaining elements. What some of these are we shall now discuss.

One of the most important may be of a social-psychological char-

[8] See *The Role of Foreign Aid in the Development of Other Countries,* A Study Prepared at the Request of the Special Commitee to Study the Foreign Aid Program, U.S. Senate, by The Research Center in Economic Development and Cultural Change of the University of Chicago (Committee print; Washington, D.C.: U.S. Government Printing Office, 1957), p. 4.

acter: "Nothing succeeds like success." With observable improvements in the economy and new opportunities for still greater advances, sources of human energy and ingenuity lying dormant for want of stimulation may be released. Particularly important is the release of entrepreneurial and innovating propensities, for growth is, above all, characterized by the application of new methods and techniques, requiring imagination and daring.

More substantively, growth in per capita productivity and real income creates both the incentives for additional investment and the means of financing it. Growth in one sector of the economy creates markets for the output of other sectors, thus encouraging expansion throughout the economy. Increasing real incomes allow greater savings to be made at the same time that consumption is also modestly increased. Thus, even though total savings may be in the neighborhood of only 15–20 percent of the gross national product, at the *margin* savings might be as high as 50 percent, still leaving half of increases in total output for additions to consumption. This is the familiar process of "plowing back" into further investments a substantial part of income increments, comparable on an enlarged scale to the process by which business firms often expand their operations.

Moreover, economies already in the process of development may have opened to them other sources of capital besides that furnished from their own savings—namely, the inflow of private capital from abroad. As we shall note later, stagnant economies do not easily attract private capital from other countries, except in some cases of the so-called "colonial" type that may not contribute too much to the development of the domestic economy. By contrast, a country with an expanding internal market offers investment opportunities that have a better chance of attracting private foreign capital for investment of a kind that directly contributes to the growth of the domestic economy.

SOME SPECIAL PROBLEMS

We have emphasized the important fact that economic growth is a total process, involving the interaction of a host of elements. This does not deny, however, the strategic and critical significance of particular elements in the overall process. In this section, let us look briefly at some of these particular elements that often exert a powerful influence on the process or potentialities of growth.

Industrialization versus Agriculture

One of the chief questions confronting a country embarking on a planned program of growth is to what extent new investments should be directed into the creation of new manufacturing industries as compared to the expansion of agricultural output.

Economic development and industrialization are commonly regarded as synonymous. The validity of this concept appears to be strengthened by the observation that nearly all industrialized economies are relatively well developed, while nearly all underdeveloped countries are mainly agricultural. From this it does not follow, however, that the only or best way of raising per capita real income is through industrialization. The economies of some countries falling into the higher per capita income groups are based on agricultural specialization, though they do not fall into the category of "agricultural" countries as technically defined earlier. Australia, New Zealand, and Denmark are outstanding examples.

Much of the confusion between economic development and industrialization stems from the failure to realize the part that geographic specialization and international trade have to play in the process of development. Starting with the proposition that a high standard of living is impossible without the availability of manufactured products, the conclusion is reached that, therefore, the economy must be industrialized. But this overlooks the possibility of *importing* manufactured goods in exchange for primary products. Because of international trade, the shortest cut to development is through specialization in those commodities and services in which an economy has the greatest natural comparative advantage.

Whether a given country should attempt to industrialize cannot, therefore, be determined except within the context of its particular situation. Countries like Brazil and Uruguay, with a relatively large supply of land, are much less dependent upon industrialization for an increase in real per capita income than are countries like India and China. It must be granted, however, that most of the less developed areas of the world have so little land area relatively to population that the escape from poverty cannot ultimately be achieved except through some industrialization. The amount of capital in agriculture and the methods of its employment in less developed countries leave a wide margin for potential improvement. Irrigation, the use of more fertilizers and better seeds, scientific cultivation and crop rotation, and similar projects and techniques would raise tremendously the per capita output of farm products. But, then, where does this leave those previously employed in agriculture—unless new industries are being created, or old ones expanded, that will absorb them?

The absorption of those engaged in agriculture into other occupations is especially important where there is a large amount of "underemployment" or "disguised unemployment." By this we mean that the amount of usable land area and capital per family is so small that there is insufficient work available to keep everyone productively employed full time. (Where workers are wage-employed, rather than self-employed, an insufficiency of land and capital leads to outright unemployment.) Underemployment or chronic unemployment is generally characteristic of the least developed countries and constitutes a waste of human resources as well as a source of potential productive capacity.

We may conclude that, except perhaps in those cases where there is unutilized land area available that is potentially productive, economic development requires both an improvement in agricultural output and some industrialization. This does not mean that less developed countries can, or should, create large-scale manufacturing industries on the model of the United States or Western European countries. For a long time to come, less developed countries are likely to remain relatively labor-abundant and capital-scarce. Their available investment capital, therefore, can ordinarily be more advantageously spread among many light and small-scale manufacturing industries, where the labor-capital ratio is relatively high, than concentrated in a few large-scale heavy industries. Exceptions to this general rule include investments in certain strategic projects which may be essential to further development, such as transportation facilities and hydroelectric plants. Another element that is relevant in determining the kinds of industry which can appropriately be encouraged is the local availability of raw materials. If, for example, a particular industry requires raw materials that must largely be imported, and especially if the materials are costly to transport, it would be unusual for a country to have a comparative advantage in that industry.

Specific Obstacles to Growth

Each country has its own peculiar problems to solve before the process of growth can get started or, once started, be maintained. The extent and seriousness of these problems are not, however, uniform among all LDC's. In some countries the potentialities for growth are much greater than in others. Indeed, particular areas of the world may, in the present state of knowledge at least, have *zero* potentialities. Without attempting an exhaustive survey, let us examine a sample of specific obstacles to growth that most LDC's face to a more or less serious degree.

Lack of Natural Resources.   If a country is fortunate enough to be well endowed with an abundant supply of natural resources and of land area possessing favorable attributes of soil, climate, and topography, the base for economic growth is laid in advance by nature. The economic history of the United States offers an outstanding illustration of these advantages.

Many less developed countries of the world are handicapped at the outset by the small amount or poor quality of natural resources available per head of population. Agricultural development may be limited by such factors as poor soil, adverse climatic conditions, lack of sufficient rainfall, or rugged topography. The development of particular industries may be precluded, on an economic basis, by the paucity or inaccessibility of domestic raw materials, especially if the raw materials are weight-losing and costly to transport.

We must be cautious, however, not to exaggerate the limitations on growth potentiality set by the quantities or qualities of natural domestic resources. There are outstanding examples of countries with relatively high standards of living, yet poor in natural resources, either quantitatively or qualitatively. Switzerland and the Netherlands, for example, fall into the upper range of per capita incomes; yet they are both among the countries of the world with the least amount of arable land per capita and without any important domestic sources of industrial raw materials.

Moreover, natural resources of economic value are not absolutely fixed. On the contrary, they are in good part a function of technology. The Netherlands has expanded its supply of arable land through walling off areas from the sea. What is today regarded as worthless rock may tomorrow become a valuable source of minerals or energy, as the history of uranium has dramatically shown. It will probably be only a matter of time before salt water can be cheaply converted into fresh water, at which stage enormous areas of land now too arid to be useful will become potentially rich and valuable for agriculture.

Nor must it be forgotten that various inputs are generally substitutable over a considerable range in producing a given output. Both capital and labor may often be substituted for land or other natural resources. Even food can be grown chemically, and an acre of land can be made to yield several times greater output through the use of fertilizers, hybrid seeds, and so on.

Finally—and this is a point of particular interest in international economics—necessary resources not available domestically may be imported. Japan has very limited domestic supplies of industrial raw materials, including coal; yet she is a manufacturing nation. Great Britain is one of the greatest industrial countries in the world, yet she possesses no oil or nonferrous metals. But, of course, countries that are dependent on foreign supplies of raw materials or other goods must have the ability to pay for them.

In summary, we may say that the lack of an adequate supply of land and other natural resources can be a serious, though not always an insuperable, obstacle to economic growth. It is clear that, other things being equal, a country endowed by nature with plenty of fertile land and rich deposits of iron, coal, and other minerals has a greater growth potential than countries niggardly endowed. The absence of generous natural endowments does not, however, necessarily preclude economic growth.

Labor Resources. Production requires labor, a productive resource with which the vast majority of LDC's appear to be exceedingly well endowed. The raw statistics of numbers in the working population give, however, an entirely misleading picture of this aspect of economic growth, for several reasons.

First, more important than sheer numbers of workers are the qualities of the labor force. Second, since it is per capita and not aggregate output that determines the standard of living, it is possible to have too much labor in relation to the amount of land and capital available. And, third, the future growth of population may be much more relevant to economic growth than the size of population at any one time. Let us consider each of these points in turn.

One of the most important reflections of a stagnant economy with low per capita income is a working population plagued with malnutrition and ill-health, illiteracy, lack of initiative, inadaptability to new ideas and new processes, indifference to self-betterment, and similar inabilities and attitudes, constituting a hard core of resistance to economic growth. This is indeed one of the main reasons for the "self-breeding" character of deep poverty. For most LDC's, it is hardly an exaggeration to say that the first step toward a higher standard of living is improvement in the health, physical stamina, and level of education and skilled training of the mass of people. The dilemma, as always, is how to get started—with lack of facilities and, especially, lack of teachers. One possibility, that we shall explore further later, is through technical assistance from abroad.

Apart from the qualities of the population and working force, most LDC's simply have too many people in relation to their endowments of natural resources and supply of capital. This, in fact, is one of the chief explanations for a state of underdevelopment. As we have stated many times before, per capita productivity and real income are in part a function of the ratio of land and capital to population. Other things being equal, the lower this ratio is, the lower will be the standard of living. To put it another way, with given supplies of land and capital and a given state of technology, there is some population number that is "optimum." The concept of an optimum population is tricky to handle, but, however refined the definition, hardly anyone would deny that the typical less developed country today has a population in excess of the optimum. We have already considered one aspect of this in our previous discussion of the prevalence of "disguised" unemployment and underemployment.

From a static point of view, the "solution" to an above-optimum population is to increase the supply of capital. But, unfortunately, this may not be enough, for populations are not static, especially in the face of increased production. The third problem with respect to labor supply and population, then, relates to their future growth.

If, in a particular area of the world, the population is relatively sparse, an increase in population may have a favorable impact on economic development by providing a widening market and opportunities for a greater degree of specialization within the economy. The United States in the 19th century and Canada and Australia still today offer excellent examples of the favorable effects of growing populations.

In countries already highly overpopulated, the situation is different. Overpopulated areas generally have both high birthrates and high death rates. An improvement in hygienic conditions and nutrition—perhaps essential for increasing labor productivity, as suggested earlier—has the immediate effect of reducing the death rate without, however, correspondingly lowering the birthrate. Indeed, the birthrate may even rise, because of better health and care of expectant mothers, a decrease in the practice of abortion, and so on.

The consequence is a tendency for the population to increase in response to economic progress, thereby threatening to make the progress only temporary. In many countries this may prove to be one of the greatest stumbling blocks on the road to a higher standard of living. Because of the admixture of economic, social, political—and often religious—aspects entering into the determination of the birthrate, only carefully worked-out policies, appropriate to the particular cultural complex of each country, can hope to succeed in solving the problem. It is for this reason that India's efforts to solve the population problem will be watched with interest all over the world. For perhaps the first time in history, a country is trying on a national scale, as part of a planned program of economic growth, to overcome the "Malthusian specter" by disseminating information and propaganda on family limitation.

Limited Markets. The profitability of private investment in an industry depends upon the existence of an adequate market for its product. But in low-income countries the domestic market for anything but the most elemental types of commodities is, simply because of the low level of per capita income, exceedingly narrow. Even though the creation of additional industries would generate additional income and purchasing power, no *single* industry is ordinarily able in itself to create an adequate demand for its own product. On the other hand, the simultaneous development of many industries tends to raise the level of income and demand enough to provide an adequate market for each. In effect, the workers and other factor owners in each industry constitute a market for the products of all other industries.

The balanced expansion of the economy in many sectors at the same time would be the most direct way of breaking the stalemate just described. This may not be possible, however—in which case the initiating force must come from another source. Two sources of special importance might be mentioned.

The first is an expansion of the internal market through more extensive communication and transportation facilities. The investment in these public or quasi-public facilities would in itself create additional income and demand and widen the market for the products of agriculture and industry. In addition, isolated village and regional markets would be expanded under the influence of broader and cheaper contacts with other areas within the country.

The second source of demand is external. With international trade, a new industry need not be stymied by the lack of a market at home, provided that the product is of a quality and price that make it competitive in the world market and provided that its transport costs are not too high. It is for this reason, among others mentioned earlier, that a country would be well advised to heed the principle of comparative advantage in its efforts to develop its economy.

Deficiency of Savings. Finally, we come to what is perhaps the ultimate quantitative barrier to the economic development of impoverished countries: the deficiency of domestic savings.

In our previous discussion in this chapter of the "lifting power" required for "takeoff" into growth, it was noted that savings in less developed countries rarely are sufficient, with current rates of population growth, to support the investment required to keep per capita productivity from declining. Growth depends, then, upon increasing the rate of new capital formation above the level that current rates of domestic savings are able to support.

This immediately leads to a dilemma. Savings are a function of per capita income. When the latter is very low, there is little margin for refraining from consumption. To expect a family with an annual income of $300 or $400 to save a part of its income—that is, not consume all of it—is equivalent to expect the family to be willing to starve. If per capita income could be raised, then it would be reasonable for a large fraction of the *increase* to be devoted to savings. But here, of course, is precisely the dilemma: to raise per capita income in the first place, higher savings to finance greater capital formation are necessary; but higher savings are extremely difficult to realize if per capita incomes do not increase first.

There is one obvious way out of this dilemma—namely, to borrow, or receive as gifts, part of the savings of other countries that are already developed. We shall reserve discussion of this possibility to a later point. Barring this alternative, what are the other possibilities?

One approach is to *force* larger domestic savings through governmental action. Increased taxation, the proceeds devoted to public capital investment, and the financing of such investments through inflationary means are examples. The rapid industrialization of the Soviet Union has been accomplished by such means. Needless to say, however, extreme measures of compulsory savings and lowered consumption are hardly consistent with a democratic society. Even if they succeed, few would agree that the accomplishment is worth the price paid in human suffering and loss of freedom.

Although probably of limited effectiveness, other measures are available to encourage a greater volume of savings. Maintenance of stable monetary conditions and confidence in the government and the creation of media and institutions into which savings can safely be placed might in many cases result in larger voluntary savings, especially on the part of the higher-income groups.

Equally important is the mobilization of what savings are made and their direction into useful and productive channels. It is characteristic of less developed economies for a large part of savings to be put into gold and foreign exchange hoards or into such domestic projects as luxury apartment buildings, so that they contribute very little to the development of the economy. Again, any improvement in this situation depends in part upon the establishment of monetary stability and confidence in the political future of the country.

Finally, there is one other possibility of creating new savings through the use of unemployed or underemployed labor. It can be argued that where large amounts of underemployed labor exists, there are concealed potential savings that might be tapped.[9] For example, if for some countries a certain number of farm laborers could be removed from agriculture without reducing total output, in effect these redundant workers (not individually identifiable) are being supported by the rest of the population. If this excess labor were put to work building dams, irrigation systems, roads, and the like, they could continue to receive the same income as previously, provided that the consumption of the remaining agricultural population were kept from rising. But the capital thus created would, of course, be additions to the national income not consumed—that is, saved. Concealed potential savings—and, correspondingly, concealed potential capital investment—would thus be realized.

There are, no doubt, formidable practical difficulties in realizing these potential savings and investments—such, for example, as preventing the consumption of the remaining agricultural population from rising. But it is an interesting idea and one that may be surprisingly fruitful in certain countries where the social atmosphere is favorable to cooperative efforts at improvement.

CONCLUSION

It must be clear from our preceding brief discussion of some of the elements inherent in economic development and of the obstacles likely to be encountered that the burden and responsibility for de-

---

[9] On this point see Ragnar Nurkse, *Problems of Capital Formation in Underdeveloped Countries* (New York: Oxford University Press, Inc., 1953), pp. 36 ff.

velopment necessarily rest primarily on the less developed countries themselves. Yet the problem transcends the individual countries immediately concerned. Development can take place only with exceptional difficulty in national isolation; if it takes place at all, it is more likely to be within the framework of an international economy.

In the next chapters, we shall investigate in some detail the role of other countries in promoting the economic growth of underdeveloped areas.

RECOMMENDED READING

BUCHANAN, NORMAN S., and ELLIS, HOWARD S. *Approaches to Economic Development,* Parts I and II. New York: Twentieth Century Fund, 1955.

HOSELITZ, BERT F. (ed.). *The Progress of Underdeveloped Areas.* Chicago, Ill.: University of Chicago Press, 1952.
  Especially useful in giving historical and cultural aspects of economic development.

KINDLEBERGER, CHARLES P. *Economic Development.* New York: McGraw-Hill Book Co., 1958.

KUZNETS, SIMON. "Toward a Theory of Economic Growth," in ROBERT LEKACHMAN (ed.), *National Policy for Economic Welfare at Home and Abroad,* pp. 12–77, and discussion in following pages. Garden City, N.Y.: Doubleday & Co., Inc., 1955.

LEWIS, W. ARTHUR. *The Theory of Economic Growth.* London: George Allen & Unwin, Ltd., 1955.

NURKSE, RAGNAR. *Problems of Capital Formation in Underdeveloped Countries,* chaps. i–iii. New York: Oxford University Press, Inc., 1953.

RESEARCH CENTER IN ECONOMIC DEVELOPMENT AND CULTURAL CHANGE, UNIVERSITY OF CHICAGO. *The Role of Foreign Aid in the Development of Other Countries.* Special Committee to Study the Foreign Aid Program, U.S. Senate. Committee print. Washington, D.C.: U.S. Government Printing Office, 1957.

UNITED NATIONS, DEPARTMENT OF ECONOMIC AFFAIRS. *Measures for the Economic Development of Underdeveloped Countries.* New York, May, 1951.

VINER, JACOB. *International Trade and Economic Development,* chap. vi. New York: Free Press, 1952.

STUDY QUESTIONS

1. What is meant by the term "less developed area"? Canada has vast unrealized economic possibilities. Do you include her among the less developed countries?

2. Explain the statement that "the process of economic development is not only—and perhaps not even mainly—an economic problem."

3. List the chief economic changes which, separately or in combination, are required for an increase in per capita productivity.

4. Show how economic growth, once begun, contains within itself elements of self-generation.

5. Is industrialization always necessary for economic development? How does the existence of international trade affect the answer to this question?

6. Under what particular conditions does economic development nevertheless depend upon some degree of industrialization?

7. Explain what is meant by "disguised unemployment," or "underemployment."

8. In those cases where some degree of industrialization is necessary or desirable for economic development, what types of industry are likely to prove most satisfactory?

9. What part would you say that favorable natural conditions played in the economic development of the United States?

10. Did the rapid growth in the population of the United States during the 19th century aid or hinder economic development? May this conclusion be legitimately applied to the role of population growth in underdeveloped countries today?

11. How may the obstacle to economic development of limited internal markets be approached?

12. Why does poverty tend to be self-perpetuating?

13. Through what methods may the volume of domestic savings be increased in underdeveloped areas? What is the ultimate limiting factor on the volume of domestic savings in these areas?

| Chapter 23 | THE ROLE OF INTERNATIONAL TRADE IN DEVELOPMENT |

As stated at the conclusion of Chapter 22, the economic development of a country normally evolves within the framework of the international economy. The question of interest to us now is what part the external economic relations of a country have to play in its development. In this chapter we shall examine the role of trade, in the next the role of capital movements and technical knowledge.

In classical thought, trade was regarded as an "engine of growth" —that is, it provided the opportunity and the stimulus for a country to become economically developed. This classical view has been strongly challenged.[1] The gains realizable from trade in accordance with the principle of comparative advantage are not denied but are regarded as irrelevant for economic growth. The theoretical reason given is that trade theory is static, based on given resources and techniques, whereas development is a *dynamic* process inherently involving changes over time. Thus, for example, while it may be rational for a less developed country to specialize in primary products from the viewpoint of static efficiency, from the standpoint of economic development it may be wiser to deviate from the principles of free trade in order to stimulate manufacturing industry. This theoretical argument is buttressed by appeal to historical experience. For many LDC's, participation in international trade has not served as an engine of growth. On the contrary, the poor countries remain poor, and the gap between them and the rich nations has widened.

---

[1] Among the principal dissenters to the classical proposition are W. H. Singer (see his "The Distribution of Gains between Investing and Borrowing Countries"), *American Economic Review, Papers and Proceedings,* May, 1950; Paul Prebisch (see his report, as Secretary-General of the United Nations Conference on Trade and Development, *Towards a New Trade Policy for Development* [New York, 1964]) ; and Gunnar Myrdal (see his *Rich Lands and Poor* [New York: Harper & Row, Publishers, 1957]) .

Since the challenge to the traditional view of the role of trade in development has important policy implications, an examination of the bases of the traditional view and of the challenge to it is warranted.

GROWTH THROUGH TRADE: THE CONVENTIONAL VIEW

One of the means of increasing productivity and real income referred to in the preceding chapter is improvement in the efficiency of resource use. As demonstrated in the earlier chapters of this book, by specializing in the production of those goods in which it has a comparative advantage and engaging in trade, a country achieves a higher level of efficiency than would be possible in isolation. To put it simply, through trade given resources can be transformed into a larger quantity of output than if the resources were used to produce domestically all goods consumed.

However, while trade can lift a country from a lower to a higher level of efficiency, *with given resources and techniques,* it is a once-over change. That is to say, the efficiency of the economy does not continue to improve in a cumulative fashion but remains on the same higher plateau reached through trade. Hence, if trade is to stimulate growth over time, it must release other, dynamic forces in addition to the static efficiency effects.

One of these forces is the "spillover" effect of growth in developed economies. As income and demand rise in developed countries, increasing pressure is exerted on their natural resources and supplies of foodstuffs and raw materials. This tends to cause an increased demand for the primary products of less developed countries and to create additional linkages between the two groups of economies. As incomes rise in the LDC's in response to the growth in external demand for their export products, profitable opportunities arise for manufacturing at home imported goods not subject to marked economies of scale. Some of these goods, such as textiles, may eventually become export goods.

In a similar fashion, LDC's may find increasing opportunities for production and trade as a consequence of increasing real wage rates in developed countries. In effect, LDC's tend to acquire a comparative advantage in a wider range of products as real wages rise in other countries. This is especially true, of course, for labor-intensive products employing the less skilled and less highly trained types of labor.

Foreign trade also serves as a transmission line through which technical information and know-how flow from the more developed to the less developed economies, while the competition of foreign producers forces local firms to become more efficiency minded and innovative.

Finally, foreign trade permits the escape from the domestic limitations of resources and markets. If a country does not possess supplies of raw materials required for the manufacture of certain goods, it may still manufacture the goods with imported materials or import the finished goods themselves. If the domestic market is too limited to allow the economical production of goods subject to marked economies of scale, trade opens the possibility of enlarging the market through exporting.

The above is a thumbnail sketch of how trade may theoretically promote the development of countries. It is a model, however, which some critics contend is unrealistic and irrelevant for contemporary LDC's. Several charges are levied against the model.

CRITIQUE OF THE CONVENTIONAL VIEW

Perhaps the central thesis of the critics is that, for a variety of reasons, free international trade does not transmit to less developed countries their fair share of the fruits of progress enjoyed by developed countries. One of the principal reasons is the alleged secular deterioration in the terms of trade of the LDC's. This deterioration is attributed both to the nature of their export products and to institutions and policies of the developed countries.

The exports of LDC's consist chiefly of foodstuffs and raw materials, plus a few lightly manufactured goods. But these are products for which the income- (as well as price-) elasticity of demand is low. This means that demand does not keep pace with the growth in income. The situation is aggravated by the tendency in developed countries to create synthetic import substitutes for natural raw materials. In addition, the developed countries are accused of deliberately restricting their demand for the imported goods of which the LDC's are the principal suppliers, through tariffs, quotas, and taxes. This charge will be discussed below.

On the other side of the coin, it is alleged that while export prices of primary products are determined by worldwide competitive forces and reflect cost conditions, the prices of manufactured goods exported by developed countries are set in monopolistic markets and do not respond to decreases in costs of production.

If it were true that the long-run trend in the terms of trade of LDC's is seriously unfavorable, this would indeed be a potent argument against the view that free trade is a stimulant to growth. However, all the major empirical evidence indicates the absence of any such trend. That the terms of trade may, and do, fluctuate is not to be denied; nor is it to be denied that during periods of deteriorating terms a less developed country may be faced with a serious problem deserving some kind of ameliorative action. But this is quite different from the unsupported allegation that trade hampers development because of a persistent deterioration in the terms of trade.

A second complaint is that free trade leads to an unbalanced, "dual" economy in less developed countries, with a relatively well-developed but small export sector and a large undeveloped domestic sector. (Moreover, the export sector tends to be established and dominated by foreign investors—a point considered in the next chapter.) The result is that the economy becomes highly dependent upon the export of a few primary products to pay for its varied imports, making the country vulnerable to sharp changes in the terms of trade and to external economic conditions and policies. Meanwhile, diversification of the economy through development of industry is discouraged by the competition of foreign producers who have the advantage of established economies of scale and an advanced technology.

The first response to the above indictment is to question whether the lack of development in the domestic sector is actually attributable to the creation of a primary-goods export sector. The presumption is strong that an expansion in any part of an economy tends to have favorable effects on other parts. If in fact this does not occur, the explanation must lie in the absence of those *internal* conditions which favor the carry-over of development from sector to sector. If the stimulus to development emanating from trade falls on infertile ground, its force will necessarily be weak.

Second, the virtues of a "balanced" economy can easily be overrated, while the costs of achieving it may be very great. It is true that a high degree of dependence on exports renders an economy liable to disturbances from the outside world and that the greater the concentration on a few export goods, the greater is the exposure to such disturbances. However, this is saying no more than that the economies achieved through specialization inevitably are accompanied by an interdependence of the specialized parts. Independence is bought at the cost of inefficiency; at the limit, independence is maximized by self-sufficiency, at a maximum cost.

There may be a valid case for LDC's to adopt special measures to encourage the development of certain industries. Caution in doing this, however, is warranted, and in any event the rationale is not based on the desirability of reducing the role of foreign trade.

PROPOSALS FOR NEW TRADE POLICIES

The case for development within the context of free international trade is theoretical, in the sense that the conditions assumed in the model are only very incompletely fulfilled in the contemporary world. The validity of the criticisms of the conventionally conceived role of trade in development is therefore much stronger when it is directed toward actual prevailing conditions than when it is directed toward the theoretical model itself. There is general agreement on the part of nearly all observers that changes in the trading relations of LDC's are highly desirable. However, divergence of views reappears once the question of what specific changes should be made. Those who accept the underlying validity of the theoretical model find it difficult to accept many of the proposals advanced by those who reject the theoretical model.

The viewpoint of the LDC's was crystallized at the United Nations Conference on Trade and Development (UNCTAD) held in 1964, with a second session convened in 1968. At these conferences —among the largest and most widely represented ever held—existing trade practices and institutions of the developed countries were subjected to a searching criticism. Although many different facets of these were considered, the two main areas which emerged as central were the obstacles to an expansion of exports from the LDC's, and instability in primary commodity prices. Correspondingly, the proposals advanced to solve these problems consist of trade preferences for LDC's and international arrangements to stabilize commodity prices.

Trade Preferences

Notwithstanding the doubts of many spokesmen for the LDC's as to the validity of the traditional view concerning the role of trade in development, trade is assigned a central place in their thinking, provided the conditions under which it occurs are modified. Trade is regarded as highly important by the LDC's as a principal potential means of stimulating their industrialization.

This was not always the case. The general approach adopted by the LDC's has been typically to promote industrialization through diverting resources into the production of import-substitute goods. The means employed to this end include taxation of agricultural products, the allocation of the bulk of investment funds to industry, protective tariffs against manufactured goods, the maintenance of overvalued currencies and associated trade and payments controls, and so on.

The defects of attempting industrialization through import substitution, however, are serious and eventually manifest. The chief objection is the higher costs of domestic substitutes as compared to imports. The discrepancy becomes increasingly wider as the substitution extends to the production of goods for which domestic resources and technology are less and less suitable. Associated with the higher costs incurred and the protectionist measures necessary is the insulation of national markets from external competition, with the consequent weakening of the incentives to produce efficiently.

Rational policy would seem rather obviously to call for the development of export industries in which a country has, or can reasonably expect to acquire, an internationally competitive position, rather than the artificial creation of inefficient import-substitute industries. Spokesmen for the LDC's agree but legitimately cite the serious obstacles to this procedure imposed by the policies of developed countries.

In our earlier discussion of commercial policies (see Chapter 8), we noted the significant movement toward a reduction in trade barriers, formally expressed in the General Agreement on Trade and Tariffs (GATT). However, the LDC's complain—and with a great deal of justice—that the trade policies embodied in GATT are mainly directed toward and relevant to trade among the developed countries. Even though trade for the latter countries has been greatly liberalized in the postwar years, the exports of the LDC's remain severely handicapped by a variety of protectionist devices.

As for primary products—accounting for over four fifths of the export earnings of LDC's—import quotas on certain products are commonly imposed by developed countries as part of their programs of domestic price supports or, as in the case of petroleum, for example, in pursuit of national security interests. Tariffs are also levied on certain primary products to protect domestic producers. Even in the case of commodities not produced at home—such as tropical foodstuffs—import demand is frequently limited by high consumption taxes.

Most primary products used as raw material inputs in making other products are subject to low or zero tariffs. On the surface, this would seem to suggest that importing countries are giving free rein to the export of such materials by the LDC's. Actually, however, from the standpoint of the total export earnings of LDC's, an accurate assessment of the effects of low duties on raw materials cannot be made without taking into account tariffs levied on the processing of the materials. Typically, the more highly processed a material is and the higher the stage reached in the production of the final output, the greater is the tariff imposed. As a consequence, low tariffs on raw materials increase the protective effect of the tariffs on products processed from the materials. (The point here is the distinction between nominal tariffs and effective rates of protection, discussed on pages 147–48.) For instance, if $1 of imported raw material, duty-free, is processed into a product worth $2 on which a 25 percent tariff is levied, the effective rate of protection on the value added by the processing is 50 percent. The net result is to reduce the import market for processed materials and prevent the less-developed exporting countries from realizing potential export earnings from this source.

The fact that the tariffs of developed countries are generally higher on goods the more advanced are their stages of production, together with the significant difference that may exist between nominal and effective rates of protection, are also important considerations in determining the access of LDC's to the markets in developed countries for manufactured goods. The successive rounds of negotiations for lower tariffs under GATT, described in Chapter 8, have reduced the *average* nominal tariff on manufactures to a markedly lower level than previously prevailed. However, nominal tariffs on manufactured products which the LDC's have the greatest ability to export—in particular, labor-intensive, light manufactures—tend to be considerably higher than the average, while the effective rates of protection are frequently a great deal higher than the nominal rates.

The difficulties encountered by LDC's in increasing their export of manufactured goods to developed countries are not limited to the tariffs of the latter. Whenever the import of particular goods into the developed countries appears to affect adversely domestic competing industries, additional restrictive measures are often taken or threatened to be taken. A prime example is cotton textiles, the prototype of manufactured products in which many LDC's have a comparative advantage and which they are able to export, even over tariff walls. As noted in an earlier discussion, the United States and other developed countries have responded to the increased inflow of foreign cotton textiles by threatening to impose quotas if the exporting countries do not "volunteer" to restrict the volume of their exports. The overt imposition of import quotas has been avoided so far (the possibility of their use in the future is always present) only through an international agreement severely limiting cotton textile exports to developed countries by the LDC's.

If developed countries wish to open the way for an expansion in the exports of less developed countries, a reduction in the trade barriers described above would be an obvious route to take. The conventional free-trade approach consists simply of removing tariffs and quantitative restrictions on all goods. In the framework of currently accepted rules of conduct as embodied in GATT, however, any reduction in tariffs is supposed to be on the basis of negotiated *reciprocity* and applied in a *nondiscriminatory* manner. On both counts, the less developed countries have other ideas.

The principle of reciprocity is opposed on the grounds that it would lead to the perpetuation of the traditional pattern of trade, with the LDC's continuing to produce and export mainly primary products and to import manufactured goods. The goal of industrialization would therefore be ill-served. The LDC's insist that trade concessions to them should be *unilateral* and extend in particular to manufactures and semimanufactures.

The principle of nondiscrimination is opposed on the grounds that what LDC's need to foster their industrialization is an initial period during which industries can have a chance to develop without the competition in export markets of already well-established industries in developed countries. The central idea here is mainly infant-industry protection, but afforded by the developed countries rather than by the less developed countries themselves through their own tariffs or subsidies. Hence, the proposal is for developed countries to extend *preferential* treatment to the products of LDC's. For example, if the United States were to maintain a tariff of 20 percent on shoe imports from other developed countries, it might reduce the tariff to 10 percent or some other level less than 20 percent on shoes imported from LDC's.

Unilaterally granted, preferential trade treatment for the LDC's has been accorded a rather cold reception by the largest potential grantor, the United States, which has taken a stand in favor of the more traditional methods of trade liberalization. (Though the practices of the United States are far from consistent with its proclaimed principles.) Moreover, there are numerous and bothersome operative problems that would be encountered in any attempt to implement the proposals of the LDC's—such as deciding what commodities from what countries would be extended preferences, for how long a period, the degree of tariff discrimination by commodity and by country, and so on. However, our chief interest here is in the principles which should serve as the guide to policy formulation.

From a theoretical point of view, most economists are opposed to preferential trade policies. The principal objection is the distortion they cause in price relationships, leading to a mis-allocation of resources. However, a vast amount of price distortion already exists, and it can be argued that the real issue, therefore, is whether trade preferences for less-developed countries would be productive in stimulating development, rather than whether they would have ideal allocative effects.[2]

The alternative to preferential treatment for the manufactures of LDC's is removal of the hindrances to their export imposed by the developed countries. This approach has many advantages over trade preferences.

In the first place, it would obviate all the cumbersome, costly administrative machinery and possible conflicts in policies that preferences would entail. Second, it would avoid conflicting with the hard-won code of liberal conduct in international economic relations embodied in GATT. Third, it would encourage the development of those industries in LDC's in which they have or can acquire a genuine comparative advantage and which can survive free competition in world markets. (If infant-industry protection is justified, this can best be afforded through subsidies provided by the individual country concerned.) It is highly improbable that a preference system could be devised to yield a rational pattern of stimulation to the industries of the LDC's.

Notwithstanding the theoretical advantage of the trade liberalization approach over a preference system, it would be unfortunate if disputation over their relative merits were to result in no effective

---

[2] This argument is supported by the theory of "second best," which shows that when ideal conditions do not prevail throughout an economy, the optimum policy with respect to any sector may require deviation from the ideal.

action of any kind being taken to expand the markets of the LDC's. In comparison with the present situation, trade preferences for the LDC's would undoubtedly improve their prospect for development.

Commodity Price Stabilization

The second major proposal emanating from the UNCTAD meetings related to the problems less developed countries face with respect to the instability in the world prices of primary products.

Exports of primary products account for over 80 percent of the foreign exchange earnings of LDC's. It has become standard practice to assert that LDC's are hindered in their development by two problems arising out of this dependence on primary products. The first is the alleged secular decline in export prices compared to import prices—that is, deterioration in the terms of trade. We have already briefly considered this allegation above, pointing out the lack of evidence to support it. The second problem is the *instability* in the prices of primary products, causing fluctuations in foreign exchange earnings and difficulties in planning development.

Various devices may be employed in an effort to stabilize commodity prices. One is the use of *buffer stocks*. An agency would buy and store commodities during periods of price decline, and sell them during periods of price increase. Such a scheme is feasible only for products that are storable at a reasonable cost. More important, the procedure suffers from the serious weakness of tending to set prices that are either too low or too high. If the price is set below the long-run equilibrium level, stocks will become exhausted and therewith the ability to keep prices down. In the more probable case in practice, prices would be set above equilibrium levels, resulting in the accumulation of stocks and the eventual necessity of ceasing further acquisition.

A second variety of stabilization schemes is *production* or *export restriction* for the purpose of maintaining prices above their free-market levels. This can be done through production or export quotas for supplying countries, but to be effective it requires that major importing countries agree to enforce the quotas through their import policies.

Like buffer-stock programs, output or export restrictions suffer from the difficulty of projecting future equilibrium conditions, in the latter case demand conditions. Moreover, the supply side is likely to prove resistant to control, since there is always the temptation for individual producers to escape from the program and sell larger quantities than they are supposed to. Finally, restrictive measures protect inefficient producers and foster a misallocation of resources.

Other schemes, such as multilateral contracts between producing and consuming countries and price-compensation arrangements have been used or proposed as methods of stabilizing prices or export earnings. The history of international commodity agreements, however, is replete with failures.[3] Even if successful in stabilizing prices, moreover, this would not be tantamount to stabilizing *export earnings* of the LDC's. To the extent that price fluctuations arise from shifts in supply, stabilizing prices can have the effect of aggravating the instability of earnings.

An alternative approach to the problem of price instability for the exports of LDC's is *compensatory financing*. If a country suffers from a temporary decline in its export earnings, the impact on its economy could be softened by giving the country access to credits or outright grants. The former system is already in operation under arrangements introduced in 1963 by the International Monetary Fund. Under the IMF program, less developed members may borrow 25 percent of their IMF quotas if their export earnings fall short of the recent average. This arrangement has been criticized at UNCTAD, however, as being inadequate. Whether some more satisfactory method of evening out short-run fluctuations in export earnings of the LDC's can be devised remains to be seen. (There is no lack of proposals.)

SUMMARY AND CONCLUSIONS

There are sound theoretical reasons for believing that international trade provides channels for the transmission of stimulants to the development of national economies. In addition to permitting a higher level of static efficiency to be attained in the use of given resources, trade releases dynamic forces which foster national development.

The less developed countries, however, are deeply dissatisfied with present trading arrangements—a dissatisfaction forcefully expressed

---

[3] International commodity agreements were first tried in the 1920's, with the Great Depression of the 1930's causing a breakdown of most of them. Since World War II, only five agreements have been concluded—for wheat, sugar, coffee, tin, and olive oil. The sugar and olive oil agreements are no longer effectively operative, the wheat agreement has little imporance, and the remaining two agreements have encountered serious difficulties.

at UNCTAD. The experience of most LDC's does not square with theoretical expectations. In part, this is attributed to alleged defects in the theory itself, which is said to be applicable to trade among developed countries but not to the trade of less developed countries. In the opinion of most economists, the grounds for this charge are extremely weak. Trade cannot assure development, but only provide an impetus to it. If the response to the impetus is weak, the reason must lie in the absence of the internal conditions necessary for the exploitation of opportunities for development.

On firmer ground is the charge that the development of the LDC's is inhibited by the prejudicial policies of the developed countries. Tariffs, quotas, and other restrictive devices fall with especial severity on the products of the LDC's. This much must be admitted. Controversy arises, however, as to what changes in policy would be most appropriate.

The LDC's insist that a simple reduction in trade restrictions in accordance with prevailing procedures under GATT is not enough. The claim is for nonreciprocal and preferential trade arrangements in order to foster the industrialization of the LDC's, and for commodity price stabilization in order to prevent deterioration in their terms of trade and instability in export earnings. Most economists regard these proposals with scepticism, being concerned with both their theoretical soundness and their practicability. On pragmatic grounds, however, it may be that some such devices will prove to be the most effective means of increasing the role that trade can perform in promoting the growth of the less developed countries.

RECOMMENDED READING

BHAGWATI, JAGDISH. *The Economics of Underdeveloped Countries,* chap. xxv. New York: McGraw Hill Book Co., 1966.

JOHNSON, HARRY G. *Economic Policies Toward Less Developed Countries,* chaps. ii–vi. Washington, D.C.: Brookings Institution, 1967.
   By far the most extensive and balanced treatment of the topics considered in this chapter.

MEIER, GERALD M. *The International Economics of Development,* chaps. vii–ix. New York: Harper & Row, Publishers, 1968.

PINCUS, JOHN. *Trade, Aid and Development,* chaps. iv, vi, and vii. New York: McGraw-Hill Book Co., 1967.

UNITED NATIONS CONFERENCE ON TRADE AND DEVELOPMENT. *Towards a New Trade Policy for Development.* New York: United Nations, 1964.

STUDY QUESTIONS

1. Describe the various ways in which international trade may serve as an "engine of growth."

2. Distinguish between the static efficiency effects and the dynamic effects of trade.

3. Why does a less developed country tend to acquire a comparative advantage in certain products as the result of increased real wages in developed countries?

4. What is the basis of the allegation that the terms of trade of the LDC's tend to deteriorate over the long run? Is there any evidence that this is true?

5. What is meant by a "dual economy"? How is trade alleged to be responsible for its existence?

6. What in the view of the LDC's is the principal role of trade in their development?

7. Describe and evaluate the policy of import substitution as a means of development.

8. Describe the various ways in which developed countries inhibit the import of primary products. Of manufactured goods.

9. Review the distinction between nominal tariffs and effective rates of protection.

10. What are the objections raised by the LDC's to the principle of reciprocity in trade negotiations? To the principle of nondiscrimination?

11. What are the objections that can be raised against trade preferences?

12. Describe buffer-stock and output restriction schemes for stabilizing commodity prices. What are the objections to them?

13. What is meant by "compensatory financing," and how might it aid less developed countries?

Chapter 24

THE ROLE OF CAPITAL MOVEMENTS AND FOREIGN AID IN DEVELOPMENT

In Part I of this book, we saw that the substantive content of international economic relations embraces two components: trade and factor movements. Each of these has an important influence on development. We have already examined the influence of trade on development, and now we turn to the role of factor movements.

Even though factor movements include labor as well as capital, we shall concentrate on capital. Our neglect of labor migration is not based on theoretical considerations but rather on the pragmatic consideration that in the present world, international labor movements have little practical relevance for the growth of the vast majority of less developed countries. Such was not always the case, as the role the vast influx of persons into the United States during the 19th century played in its development attests. Theoretically, population movements could still exert a major influence on development in the contemporary world. For instance, one possible avenue for the diffusion of American economic affluence would be the migration of labor from low-wage, less developed countries into the United States. However, for various familiar reasons, it is obvious that this route is effectively closed, with practically no chance of ever being reopened except for a negligible trickle of traffic.

The story with respect to capital is altogether different. Capital is not only inherently much more mobile than labor, its movement is also subject to many fewer obstacles. The trend in recent years has been toward a dismantling of artificial barriers to the international movement of capital, increasing thereby the opportunity for the theoretical effects of such movement to be expressed in actuality.

TYPES OF CAPITAL MOVEMENT

Capital may move from one country to another in response to two different sets of motives and under two different sets of conditions.

With respect to motive, the movement may be in response to market forces, or it may be in implementation of a public-policy decision. The distinction may be conveniently drawn in terms of private versus public capital movements.

With respect to conditions, the movement of capital may be reversible, in the sense that the initial direction is later reversed, or it may be a once-and-for-all movement in one direction, or *unilateral transfers*. "Reversible" movements are the norm when private capital is involved, since private lenders and investors expect to recapture the principal of their loans and investments as well as earned interest and profits. Public capital may also be of the reversible variety, as in the case of loans, but alternatively it may take the form of unilateral transfers under which repayment is not expected.

From a long-run point of view, it makes a great deal of difference whether capital moves to less developed countries in the form of loans and private investments from which returns are expected, or in the form of unilateral transfers. In the latter case, *foreign aid* is extended to the recipient country. In the former case, no aid in the strict sense of the term is involved, unless and to the extent that the capital is loaned or invested on more favorable terms than obtainable in private markets.

Although, as we shall see, the distinctions between private and public capital movements and between ordinary and foreign aid capital are important, in the short run they all share the basic function of providing extra resources to recipient countries and in this manner contribute to economic development. Let us see how this function is performed.

CAPITAL INFLOW AND DOMESTIC INVESTMENT

Foreign trade may contribute to a country's development, as we have seen, through increasing the efficiency of resource use and through releasing dynamic forces which encourage the growth of production. However, trade itself does not provide additional resources to a country. As long as a country is constrained to pay for its imports of goods and services with exports of equal value, the total flow of goods and services available to it is limited to its national product or income.

The only way a country can obtain a flow of goods and services greater than its national production is to receive an excess of imports over exports. This can be formally expressed in terms of the following equations:

$$Y = C + I + X - M \tag{1}$$
$$A = C + I \tag{2}$$

Equation (1) is the national income identity, familiar from an earlier discussion (see pages 313–14), where Y represents income, C consumption, I investment, X exports, and M imports. Equation (2) shows the current flow of goods and services available to the domestic economy (A) for consumption (C) and investment (I). Clearly, A can exceed Y only if M is greater than X.

We observed in Chapter 22 that a principal constraint on growth in less developed economies is inadequate saving to finance the rate of investment required for an increase in per capita productivity. The problem is how to increase investment (I in the above equations) at a given level of national income and current volume of consumption. The solution is indicated by rewriting equation (1) as:

$$I = S + M - X \tag{3}$$

This is equivalent to equation (1), since saving (S) is definitionally equal to income (Y) minus consumption (C).

From equation (3) it is clear that if investment is to exceed domestic saving, imports must exceed exports. We arrive, then, at the same result as before, except that now it is expressed in terms of the crucial saving-investment relationship rather than in terms of the overall availability of resources.

Since the typical less developed country is faced with the barrier to growth arising out of the insufficiency of domestic saving, it follows that one way of hurdling the barrier is to realize an import surplus over a period of some years. Provided that the extra resources thus rendered available are devoted to investment in productive capacity (rather than used to increase current consumption), an important contribution to development is made.

An obvious question now suggests itself: How is a country to finance an import surplus over an extended period? The answer is furnished by our earlier analysis of the balance of payments (see Chapter 14). To avoid balance-of-payments disequilibrium, an import surplus of goods and services must be accompanied by an autonomous inflow of capital. To put it the other way around, a net autonomous inflow of capital is transferred in the form of a net movement of goods and services into the capital-receiving country.

The significance of the distinction between an inflow of capital in

the form of ordinary loans and investments and in the form of foreign aid should now be apparent. Interest and amortization payments on foreign loans and remittances of profits on foreign investments are charges (debit items) on a country's balance of payments.
This means that in order to make such payments, a country must
have a surplus of international receipts on other accounts. If new
capital is not continuing to flow into the country from abroad, the
surplus must be generated on the goods and services account—that
is, an *export surplus* is required. In this case, the extra resources
provided by the initial capital inflow are later returned to the lending and investing countries. In order for a country to continue to
receive extra resources from abroad, new capital inflows must continue to exceed in amount the repayment and servicing of earlier
capital inflows. In the case of foreign aid, on the other hand, resource
transfers are permanent, entailing no future charges on the country's balance of payments and resources.

While dollar-for-dollar foreign aid capital provides over the long
run more resources to a country than do foreign loans and investments, the fact remains that the latter is an important means through
which less developed countries might acquire resources for additions
to its stock of capital. The presumption is that capital yields a net
product over and above its cost. It is not a question, therefore, of
the capital-receiving country enjoying only an ephemeral benefit
from foreign loans and investments which disappears with repayment, any more than a private company which borrows money for
capital improvement expects to receive no net benefit. Moreover,
private capital, especially in the form of direct investments, carries
with it certain side effects helpful to development, as we shall see
in the next section.

PRIVATE CAPITAL MOVEMENTS

In the traditional view, private long-term capital movements perform a function parallel to that of trade in fostering the development of countries. In the absence of artificial impediments, developed countries tend to be net capital exporters, the less developed
countries net capital importers. The mechanism bringing this about
consists of differential rates of return on capital investment. Developed countries, almost by definition, are relatively capital-abundant,
while less developed countries are relatively capital-scarce. As a consequence, marginal rates of return on investment and interest rates

tend to be low in developed economies and high in less developed economies. In seeking maximum returns on their investible funds, private individuals and business firms are led to seek outlets in less developed areas. Not only are additional resources thus provided to the latter, but managerial skills and technical know-how are transmitted.

The idealized picture thus drawn was more or less closely approximated in actuality in the late 19th century and the early part of the 20th century. Great Britain, France, and Germany—the most developed economies of that era—were large providers of capital to the rest of the world and unquestionably contributed to the rapid growth of many countries.

World War I marked the end of an era with respect to foreign investment as well as so many other things. In the interwar years, the international flow of capital diminished to a fraction of the earlier volume, completely ceasing during the depression decade of the 1930's.

In recent years, a resurgence of private foreign investment has occurred. However, even though the absolute magnitude of long-term capital movements has become quite large, relatively to the volume of world income and trade it has not reached the pre-1914 level.

As with respect to trade, so with respect to private capital movements the less developed countries are critical of the theory and dissatisfied with experience. Several reasons for dissatisfaction can be identified.

To begin with, foreign investment in LDC's is strongly associated in the minds of many persons with past imperialistic exploitation and colonial dependence.

Second, foreign investment in LDC's has been highly concentrated in extractive industries and the primary export goods sectors. As a consequence, it is charged that a "dual" economy has been fostered, with a developed foreign-dominated enclave surrounded by an undeveloped native sector.

Third, it is alleged that the gains in output produced by foreign investments are withdrawn from the local economy, and transferred to the investing country in the form of remitted profits.

Finally, quite apart from the above objections, the total volume of private capital flowing into LDC's is regarded as entirely inadequate to furnish the external assistance needed for development.

These criticisms contain an admixture of valid and questionable points. The fear of foreign imperialist domination is understandable in the light of history, but it can be alleviated through such devices as requiring a minimum local participation in the management and ownership of enterprises. The dual-economy argument is perhaps misplaced. Concentration of foreign investment in primary export industries is mainly due to the absence of profitable opportunities in other sectors of the economy. There is little reason to believe that other sectors have been deprived of growth because of development in the export sector, rather than because of the absence of the internal preconditions for growth in the former. The charge that the gains from foreign investment are withdrawn from the local economy overlooks the net productivity of capital and the benefits accruing to the indigenous population in the form of enlarged employment opportunities, higher wages, acquisition of new skills and exposure to more advanced techniques, and increased tax revenue. The final objection that private foreign capital is inadequate in amount is perhaps the most telling, though not without certain reservations. This objection will be examined in some detail.

There is probably quite general agreement among economists that private capital flows into LDC's have a very significant part to play in the latter's development. Nevertheless, there is also general agreement that private capital cannot meet the needs of LDC's, especially in the early stages of their growth. Private capital moves, and should move, in response to the profit motive. For those countries still in the very early stage of growth and even more for those countries not yet started on the road to growth, profitable investment opportunities are extremely limited. The returns on investments depend ultimately upon the volume of consumer demand. With their extremely low incomes, impoverished countries offer very limited markets, and the markets that do exist are "narrow"—i.e., are largely confined to food and basic necessities. This is surely one of the chief reasons why so great a part of the foreign investments that are made in LDC's is directed into mineral exploitation and other extractive industries oriented to export markets.

In effect, what we are saying is that economic growth requires not only an adequate supply of capital but also an effective *demand* for it[1] and that the private market supply and demand are interrelated. Private capital is not attracted if investment opportunities are

---

[1] This point has been especially emphasized by Ragnar Nurkse, *Problems of Capital Formation in Underdeveloped Countries* (New York: Oxford University Press, Inc., 1953).

poor; and investment opportunities are poor, in part because of the lack of capital. Again, we come back to an aspect of the "vicious circle" of poverty breeding poverty.

It is no answer to the above dilemma to cite the historical evidence that the circle *was* broken by private capital and entrepreneurship in the early development of now-developed Western industrial countries. A parallel cannot legitimately be drawn between, for example, the situation of early 18th-century England and early 19th-century America, on the one hand, and 20th-century Asia, Africa, and South America, on the other.

In the context of the situation now prevailing in LDC's, part of the answer to the dilemma described above lies in the creation of what is described as "social overhead" capital. This means investment in such things as roads, harbors, irrigation systems, hydroelectric plants, training schools, health institutes, and similar projects of a public utility nature. The function of social overhead capital is to prepare the way for expansion in agriculture and industry— to increase the "absorptive capacity" of the economy. A better transportation and communication system, the availability of adequate and cheap power, a supply of trained workers and administrative personnel, the expansion of arable land supply, and so on, all work in the direction of opening up profitable investment opportunities for private capital.

If this is the case, why does not private capital undertake investment in such social overhead projects? The chief reason is that the direct market return on investments of this kind is likely to be very low and recoverable only over a very long period of time—this notwithstanding the fact that the indirect *social*-economic return may be immense. The greatest social-economic benefits of a network of roads, for example, may lie in the creation of new markets and the stimulation to increased specialization.

The concepts involved here is that of "external economies," individual firms benefiting from social developments over which they have no control and for which they are not responsible. For example, each firm would benefit from the spread of training and technical knowledge among workers. But it may not pay an individual firm to attempt such training on its own, the cost being excessively high in relation to the returns. Yet if such training is provided socially by the government (or by all firms acting jointly and cooperatively), the aggregate returns might be very great in relation to costs.

We have just concluded that not much can reasonably be expected of private capital at the critical *initial* stages of growth, when the preconditions for growth are being created and "takeoff" into growth is not yet firmly established. After, however, growth has been well begun, it can be expected that private capital will be attracted by expanding investment opportunities. The social function of private capital is then to accelerate growth, reinforcing the self-sustaining movement toward ever higher levels of production and income.

In some less developed areas of the world, the stage at which private capital flows have the greatest contribution to make is already reached or being closely approached. It is important, therefore, that the institutional, political, and psychological barriers to private international long-term capital flows be reduced, so that, as situations ripen favorably for private capital movements, they be encouraged to respond.

PUBLIC ASSISTANCE

If private capital flows are insufficient to provide the extra margin of resources the less developed areas of the world require to realize their potential for growth, there is a case for the provision of external *public* assistance. For the various reasons mentioned in Chapter 22, most developed countries have adopted assistance to less developed countries as a major instrument of their foreign policies. Several major issues are involved in public foreign assistance programs.

The Magnitude of Foreign Assistance

Perhaps the first question to be addressed is, How much capital and technical assistance from the developed countries is required to make possible a reasonable rate of growth in the less developed countries of the world? (Note that the question is not how much aid will *assure* growth—for no amount of aid can do that.)

There are several facets to the question just asked. One obvious facet is the meaning of "reasonable" rate of growth. In the industrial, developed countries of the world, annual rates of growth in net national product generally amount to from 3 to 4 percent. If the average rate of growth in national output is maintained at 3 percent a year, it requires less than 24 years (with the growth compounded) to *double* output. But, of course, this does not mean that per capita income rises as rapidly if population is also growing. Thus, if the annual rate of population growth is 1.5 percent, growth in aggregate net output of 3 percent per year would double per capita output in about 47 years. Obviously, the higher the rate of population growth, the greater is the rate of output growth required to increase per capita output.

During the last several years, the average annual rate of increase in the gross national product of developing countries has been around 5 percent. On a per capita basis, the increase has been on the order of $2\frac{1}{2}$ percent per year. This must be counted as significant progress. Needless to say, however, it is too slow to satisfy the understandable desire of the people to raise their living standards within a short space of time.

A second point to be considered is the "absorptive capacity" of less developed areas to use additional capital productively. It is often observed that many LDC's are not "ready" to use additional capital —they lack a development program, they do not have sufficient trained administrative personnel or skilled labor supply, markets for increased output do not exist, and so on. For such countries, large amounts of external assistance would be wasted. On the other hand, a certain amount of foreign aid—devoted to providing technical assistance, raising the level of literacy and skills of the population, and increasing investment in social overhead capital—may serve the crucial function of helping to create the preconditions for growth.

There is no way of determining with precision how much external capital and technical assistance the LDC's could use productively. There is considerable evidence, however, that an increase in the amount of assistance rendered in recent years would be amply justified. Some years ago a rule of thumb that developed countries should contribute a minimum of 1 percent of their national incomes to foreign assistance for LDC's was generally accepted as a target. In fact, this target has never been reached, and the recent trend is away from it rather than toward it. In the case of the United States—by far the largest provider of foreign assistance—the amount of aid is on a downward trend, both absolutely and relatively to the national income.

Apart from the adequacy of past and current levels of assistance, the downward trend in its volume is disturbing. The presumption is that the ability of LDC's productively to absorb capital *increases* as development progresses up to the point of self-sustaining growth. For most LDC's this point clearly has not yet been reached. A reduction in the volume of assistance at the present stage of development might not only seriously threaten the prospects for a continuation of growth; it might well result in destroying much of the progress made to date.

Forms and Terms of Assistance

Foreign assistance is extended in several different forms and under varying terms which are by no means equivalent to each other. The principal forms of assistance are loans, grants, and commodity transfers.

Loans, bearing interest and requiring repayment, are not foreign aid in the strict sense of the term, except to the extent that they carry concessionary terms. In calculating the amount of foreign aid represented by a loan, the present discounted value of future interest and amortization payments must be deducted from the amount of the loan. Many loans made to LDC's by governments and international organizations contain foreign aid elements in the form of lower-than-market rates of interest, deferred repayment schedules, and so on, while other public loans may have no aid component.

Grants differ from loans in that they entail no obligations of repayment or interest. Accordingly, the entire amount of a grant constitutes foreign aid, though its true value may be considerably less than its nominal value, depending upon the number and nature of "strings" attached.

Commodity transfers are a special form of foreign assistance, the outstanding example of which is the program of the United States under Public Law 480. Under this program, surplus agricultural commodities are sold to certain countries for local currency, called "counterpart funds." Technically, these funds are available for the U.S. government to spend locally (for example, to pay the local expenses of junketing congressmen), but in practice the largest portion is transferred as grant aid or allowed to accumulate unspent. From the donor's point of view, the opportunity cost of surplus commodities sent to foreign countries may be close to zero. From the receiving country's point of view, aid in the form of specific commodities may be much less valuable than equal dollar amounts in more general forms.

The conclusion to be drawn from the above observations is that if the nominal quantity of external assistance is insufficient, as most economists believe, the shortfall is actually much greater than apparent on the surface. This conclusion is strongly reinforced when account is taken of the various inefficiencies in the distribution of aid.

Inefficiences in the Distribution of Aid

The first source of inefficiency is the practice of "tying" aid. This means requiring the receiving country to spend aid funds, in whole or in part, on the goods of the donor country. The practice is sometimes justified on balance-of-payments grounds, but we may suspect that a large element of subsidy to donor countries' industries is also involved. In any event, the effect of tying aid is to force recipient countries to purchase goods which frequently are not as suitable or as cheap as those available elsewhere.

Besides being tied to the donor country, aid may also be tied to specific projects. This means that a given loan or grant is designated for a particular use. One reason for such specification is that it allows the donor and recipient countries to observe the concrete results of aid, with attribution of the assistance properly identified. A second reason is the desire to prevent aid resources from being frittered away on useless projects or ending up in the pockets of corrupt politicians.

Project tying has as serious defects as country tying. It encourages "showcase" investments which may be politically attractive but not sensible from the point of view of the recipient country's development. More fundamental, it is fatuous to suppose that effective use of aid resources can be assured through directing them into specific projects. The amount of resources provided by aid is always a small fraction of the total resources of the recipient country. If the objective is general development, it is how total available resources are employed that matters. Moreover, it makes little sense to try to separate aid resources from domestic resources, for they are to a large extent substitutable for each other.

The above considerations strongly support aid being extended on a general-program basis rather than on a specific-project basis.

Bilateral versus Multilateral Assistance

Foreign assistance to the less developed countries is predominantly bilateral in character. Bilateral aid is given on the basis of an agreement between each donor and recipient country. Multilateral aid, on the other hand, is channeled through international organizations, avoiding the country-to-country relationship of bilateral programs.

One drawback of bilateral programs is the opportunity they offer for the interjection of national political considerations into the aid-giving process. While it is naïve to believe that political motives can be kept out of aid programs, the multilateral approach removes the opportunity for expression of the more virulent forms of nationalism and, moreover, reduces the fear of the LDC's of foreign domination.

The economic weaknesses of bilateral program stem first of all from the difficulties of rational development planning when aid is being received from numerous donor countries, each with its own demands as to the proper use of aid resources. These difficulties are compounded when, again as a characteristic of bilateral programs, aid is tied, by either country or by project, or both.

One method of minimizing the problems created by a collection of separate bilateral aid agreements is the formation of a *consortium* among the countries extending aid to a particular less developed country, under which assistance is coordinated within the framework of a total development plan. The Aid India Club is an example of this approach, and other consortia, as well as less formal coordinating efforts, have become established, with the World Bank assuming an important role in their spread.

The surest way of avoiding the difficulties associated with bilateral programs, of course, is the provision of aid multilaterally through international organizations. Several such organizations have been created, with generally satisfactory records.

The World Bank. The prototype of international assistance institutions is the International Bank for Reconstruction and Development (IBRD), popularly known as the World Bank. Created at the Bretton Woods Conference in 1944 as a specialized agency of the United Nations, the Bank is a twin sister of the International Monetary Fund. While the IMF was designed to bring order and cooperation in international monetary relations, the IBRD was designed to help in reconstruction and development after World War II.

The central activity of the World Bank consists of making loans to less developed member countries.[2] In the first 23 years of its opera-

---

[2] The original idea was for the Bank to stimulate *private* foreign capital movements through its powers to guarantee and participate in private loans and investments. As it turned out, the Bank has confined itself to making direct loans, while the role of participation with private investors has been assumed by the International Finance Corporation, discussed on pages 449–50.

tions, begun in 1946, the Bank loaned a total of more than $12 billion. In general, its loans are relatively small in amount and extended to numerous member countries.

The bulk of the loan funds of the IBRD is obtained through bond issues in private capital markets. To this extent, the Bank serves mainly as an intermediary between less developed countries and private investors in developed countries. The intermediation is necessary to acquire private capital at close to market rates of interest, for the credit standing of the Bank is high, its obligations being fully guaranteed by its member governments.

The major complaint that can be raised against the World Bank is the limited and somewhat rigid operations it is obliged by the terms of its charter to follow. It is enjoined to avoid making loans in the absence of reasonable assurance that the borrower will be able to repay and meet service charges. Further, it is stipulated that loan funds be used only for specific projects approved. In these and other ways, the Bank is guided by essentially commercial bank criteria, thereby limiting its contribution to the development of countries the requirements of which are not capable of satisfaction in accordance with such criteria.

However, the IBRD was never intended to meet all the capital needs of development, and its conservative approach has probably had a salutary influence in encouraging careful planning and rational calculation of costs and benefits. Moreover, it has avoided the inefficiency of the country tying of assistance by prohibiting this procedure, and has performed valuable services in the form of technical assistance and advice, expert studies of development problems, training programs, and the coordination of aid. Finally, the limitations imposed by the Bank's conventional frame of reference have been partly overcome by the creation in 1960 of an affiliate organization, the International Development Association (IDA).

The International Development Association. IDA was formed with one central objective in mind: to provide "soft" loans to less developed countries, on more favorable terms than those of conventional loans, including World Bank loans. Credits are extended for long periods (up to 50 years), are repayable in easy stages after a 10-year period of grace, and carry no interest except for a three fourths of 1 percent service charge. Because of these concessionary terms, IDA loans contain a large element of grant aid.

The justification for establishing IDA was the belief that less developed countries had reached the stage where, in the words of IDA's First Annual Report, "the need for, and the ability to make effective use of, outside capital is increasing faster than the ability to service conventional loans." The role of IDA has assumed greater importance as the burden of service payments on outstanding loans weighs increasingly more heavily on developing countries. By mid-1968, the external public debt of developing countries had reached the staggering total of over $47 billion, with annual service payments exceeding $4 billion.

The financial resources of IDA are derived from capital subscriptions of its members (all of which must also belong to the World Bank). However, in fact the overwhelming bulk of operating capital is furnished by developed members (called Part I countries as distinguished from less developed members, called Part II countries). The organization has suffered from a shortage of resources, though the recent trend has been toward frequent replenishment of funds, including grants from the World Bank. By mid-1969, credits totaling more than $2 billion had been extended by IDA.

The International Finance Corporation. The IFC is the third institution which, together with the IBRD and IDA, form the triad now known as the World Bank Group.

The purpose of the IFC is to further economic development in its less developed member countries by investing directly in private enterprises, in association with private investors. Government guaranties are not accepted. The International Bank discovered through experience that government guaranties have effects just the opposite of those intended. Instead of encouraging private investments, they discourage them, because of the fear that government guaranties will lead to government controls or restrictions.

Not only does the IFC reject any kind of government guaranty, it will not invest in undertakings government owned and operated or in the management of which the government participates to any significant extent.

Since the purpose is directly to stimulate private investment, the IFC does not go into business "on its own." Indeed, it will not cover more than half the total investment cost of an enterprise. The remainder must be furnished by private capital, and the actual management and operation of the enterprise are left in the hands of the private owners. The IFC is empowered to make investments in whatever forms it may deem appropriate in each particular case. But it does not make conventional fixed-interest loans without the right to participate in profits. Since an amendment to its charter adopted in 1961, the IFC may make straight equity investments.

Finally, the IFC is anxious to "revolve" its capital by selling its investments as soon as they prove sufficiently successful to attract private interests.

The funds which the IFC invests are obtained mainly from paid-in capital from member countries and the sale of equity stock and portions of loans acquired in its operations. Additional resources are obtainable in the form of loans from the World Bank. In toto, the resources available to the IFC are small. From its establishment in 1956 to 1969, its gross commitments came to only $365 million. However, it was never intended that the IFC should engage in large-scale operations (as evidenced by the limit on its authorized capital of $110 million). Rather, its function is conceived to be that of a catalyst to private investment in less developed countries. As stated by the president of the organization ". . . the primary significance of our operations is not the amount of our funds employed, but their multiplying effect in supplementing and attracting larger amounts of private capital."

The IFC has enjoyed a not inconsiderable success in meeting this objective. In 1969 total commitments to development projects assisted by IFC since its inception had reached a total of over $2 billion. Perhaps its most important function is to demonstrate the possibility of finding profitable investment opportunities in less developed countries, and, through this demonstration, stimulate the flow of a larger volume of private capital into such countries.

Other Multilateral Institutions. Numerous other international organizations are involved in assistance programs. The United Nations itself has undertaken to coordinate the provision of technical assistance under its Expanded Program of Technical Assistance. Various regional organizations, such as the Inter-American Development Bank and the European Investment Bank of the European Common Market, provide multilateral assistance to certain regions.

Clearly, it is not the lack of administrative machinery which stands in the way of expanding the multilateral portion of development assistance programs.

SUMMARY

The principal role in development of foreign capital, whether private or public, furnished at market terms or as aid, is to supplement the limited capacity of LDC's to create additional capital out of their own resources. While private foreign capital may be attracted to LDC's because of high marginal rates of return, in the early stages of growth private investment opportunities are often limited even though opportunities exist for high-yielding social investment. The rationale for foreign public assistance is to fill the gap between the amount of external capital the LDC's need for exploiting their growth potential and the amount furnished through private capital flows.

While a large amount of external assistance has been extended to the LDC's since the end of World War II, the recent trend in the volume of assistance provided is downward. Moreover, the true value of foreign assistance to LDC's is less than the nominal value, because a considerable portion of aid is in the form of repayable loans, bearing interest charges, and another part is in the form of specific commodities less contributive to development than their nominal value. In addition, the effectiveness of aid is reduced by various inefficiencies in its distribution, such as its being tied by country, project, or both, and its predominantly bilateral character. The World Bank Group and other agencies for the multilateral distribution of external assistance are operative, and in the judgment of most observers, the extension of their role would be desirable.

RECOMMENDED READING

American Enterprise Association, Inc. *American Private Investment, Foreign Economic Development, and the Aid Programs.* Prepared for Special Committee to Study the Foreign Aid Program, U.S. Senate. Washington, D.C.: U.S. Government Printing Office, 1957.

International Bank for Reconstruction and Development. *Annual Reports.*

International Development Association. *Annual Reports.*

International Finance Corporation. *Annual Reports.*

Little, I. M. D., and Clifford, J. M. *International Aid.* Chicago: Aldine Publishing Co., 1966.

Meier, Gerald M. *The International Economics of Development,* chaps. v, vi. New York: Harper & Row, Publishers, 1968.

Mikesell, Raymond F. *The Economics of Foreign Aid.* Chicago: Aldine Publishing Co., 1968.

National Planning Association. *Agricultural Surplus Disposal and Foreign Aid.* Prepared for Special Committee to Study the Foreign Aid Program, U.S. Senate. Washington, D.C.: U.S. Government Printing Office, 1957.

Research Center in Economic Development and Cultural Change, University of Chicago. *The Role of Foreign Aid in the Development of Other Countries.* Prepared for Special Committee to

Study the Foreign Aid Program, U.S. Senate. Washington, D.C.: U.S. Government Printing Office, 1957.

ROSENSTEIN-RODAN, P. N. "International Aid for Underdeveloped Countries," *Review of Economics and Statistics,* Vol. 43 (May, 1961).

STUDY QUESTIONS

1. Distinguish between private and public capital movements, and between ordinary movements and unilateral transfers.

2. What is the criterion for determining whether and to what extent a foreign aid element is present in any particular foreign assistance program?

3. Describe the only way a country can obtain a flow of goods and services in excess of its current national production.

4. In a closed economy, the saving and investment of a national economy must be equal; in an open economy they need not be equal. In the latter case, what must account for any difference between saving and investment?

5. Why do foreign grants represent, dollar-for-dollar, more aid than loans? Nevertheless, what is the basis for the presumption that private capital inflows contribute to the development of a country?

6. Discuss the criticisms leveled by less developed countries against foreign private capital as a source of development.

7. For what reasons may private capital movements not be attracted into LDC's on a scale justified by the requirements of the latter?

8. What is meant by the "absorptive capacity" of a country? How does it relate to foreign assistance?

9. Describe the principal forms of external assistance and the manner in which they represent different amounts of foreign aid.

10. Define "tied aid," distinguishing between country and project tying. What are the objections to these practices?

11. What are the weaknesses of bilateral assistance programs?

12. Review the nature of the operations of the World Bank, IDA, and IFC.

| Chapter 25 | THE PRESENT AND THE FUTURE OF THE INTERNATIONAL ECONOMY |

This concluding chapter proposes that we take stock of the international economy as it has evolved since World War II, identify its dominant current problems, and consider its prospects for the future.

THE BLUEPRINT OF THE POSTWAR WORLD

The 19th century witnessed the development of a vigorous international economy, with a rapidly expanding volume of national production and income in significant measure being the result of international trade and factor movements. The role of trade and factor movements was made possible by the creation of a stable international monetary system and the large measure of freedom in international economic relations.

World War I dealt a severe blow to the 19th-century system; it never fully recovered. The attempt during the interwar years to return to the "normalcy" of the prewar years created serious strains which, under the impact of the Great Depression during the 1930's, followed by Word War II, became irreparable structural cracks in the system.

Responsible statesmen were determined that a new international order be established in the postwar years. Corresponding in the economic sphere to the new political framework provided by the United Nations were new principles and institutions designed to avoid the catastrophic economic and monetary experiences of the 1930's—the competitive currency depreciations, "dog-eat-dog" trade practices, widespread trade and payments restrictions, treatment of underdeveloped countries as colonial appendages, and so on.

Three institutions were to be created to serve as the central core for the organization of the postwar international economy: The International Monetary Fund, (IMF) the International Trade Organization (ITO), and the International Bank for Reconstruction and Development (IBRD). Each of these institutions was designed to cope with a critically important problem area. The IMF was to provide the framework for a stable monetary order to replace the chaotic monetary disorder of the 1930's. The ITO was to provide the framework for international trade free of quantitative controls and discriminatory practices and for the negotiation of reductions in the level of tariffs. The IBRD was to mobilize public capital for the reconstruction of war-torn economies and, over the longer term, to assist underdeveloped economies to raise their productivity and standards of living.

One must stand in respect, and even awe, at the imagination and boldness of the architects who drew up this blueprint of the postwar organization of the world economy. However, the interesting and relevant question now is how well the plans have worked out.

THE DISILLUSIONMENT OF EXPERIENCE

First, in all fairness it should be said that, compared to the prewar system it was designed to replace, the new order has been highly successful. But from the perspective not of the past but of the present and the future, a less favorable judgment cannot be avoided. The system at the present juncture of the world economy displays weaknesses and inadequacies in each of the three problem areas toward which it is oriented.

If a general explanation for this is to be sought, it perhaps can be found in the tendency of institutions inadequately to adapt themselves to changing circumstances and needs. As we have noted, the new postwar institutions were designed to overcome the problems of the prewar period, but today's problems are of a quite different character and consequently demand a different approach.

The Monetary System

Consider the international monetary system. The IMF was constructed on the implicit assumption that national currencies have equal status and member countries have equal rights and responsibilities. As it has turned out, however, the dollar and, to a lesser extent, the pound sterling, have acquired a special status, and the United States and the United Kingdom have acquired special responsibilities. The basic principle which was to guide the system—stable exchange rates subject to occasional adjustment—has been replaced in operating practice by the principle of one or two reserve currencies with fixed values in terms of gold at the center, with other currencies tied more or less firmly to the reserve currencies. This, as we know, is the structural characteristic of a gold-exchange standard, such as operated in the 1920's, the defects of which were to be removed by the postwar reformation.

The basic reason for the corruption of the system as originally conceived probably lies in its failure to sever historical ties with gold. The assumption underlying the system is that gold is the primary international monetary reserve medium, with credits from the IMF having only a residual, marginal role. But experience has clearly shown that gold cannot fulfill its assigned function and that supplementary reserve media are needed if world trade is not to be hampered by a shortage of liquidity. The introduction of Special Drawing Rights—"paper gold"—into the system opens the door to a more rational provision of reserves, but how well this will work in practice remains to be seen.

While insufficient liquidity imparts a deflationary bias to the world economy, from a more fundamental point of view the critical weakness of the international monetary system is the absence of a satisfactory balance-of-payments adjustment mechanism. This weakness stems from the very structure of the Bretton Woods system, in which stable exchange rates are a primary principle. Some encouragement may be found in the recent attention being given by monetary authorities to proposals for increasing exchange-rate flexibility. However, resistance to deviating from the entrenched notion that stable exchange rates are necessary for a stable world economy is strong.

Neither the goal of freer trade nor of economic development can avoid being adversely affected by an inadequate international monetary system. Insufficient liquidity imparts a deflationary bias to the world economy, making it more difficult to cope with the adjustments necessitated by the removal of trade barriers and the easier access to world markets of the products of less developed countries. The absence of an efficient balance-of-payments adjustment mechanism fosters the use of restrictive trade and payments devices.

The Trade System

Let us now compare experience with plans as to the postwar system of international trade.

As indicated above, the failure of the international monetary system to work as anticipated has placed a handicap on the creation of a liberal trading system. However, other developments have also contributed to frustration of the original plans.

A heavy blow was dealt early to the system by the abortion of the International Trade Organization. The severity of the blow was mitigated by the General Agreement on Tariffs and Trade (GATT), which has continued in existence as a substitute for the ITO. Nevertheless, the refusal of the U.S. Congress formally to accept a permanent international trade organization, and its passive tolerance rather than positive approval of the GATT, has had at least unfavorable psychological effects on the trading system.

Of more substantive significance, while the intention to create a world trading system free of discrimination and quantitative controls and with gradually reduced levels of tariffs has been partially realized, fulfillment has been blocked in several ways.

First, we note that experience demonstrates that protectionist sentiment is not easily exorcised simply by the declaration of the principle of free trade. While notable progress has been made in successive rounds of tariff negotiations under the aegis of GATT, barriers to trade remain formidable.

The widespread practice of quota limitations on imports of agricultural products, in violation of the principles embodied in GATT, keeps national markets in these products largely insulated from each other and severely handicaps expansion in the exports of less developed countries. Quantitative restrictions on imports for balance-of-payments purposes and in the interest of national security are also widely practiced. Moreover, quotas for strictly protective reasons, exemplified by textile arrangements, are employed to some extent and perennially threatened to be extended.

Apart from quota restrictions, nontariff barriers and disguised protectionism exist in profusion. Cumbersome customs porcedures and formalities, "Buy American" discrimination, and tied loans are examples.

The principle of nondiscrimination—a keystone of the planned postwar trading system—has been derogated by the exception permitted for countries forming a customs union. The creation of such unions on a regional basis, however beneficial they may (or may not) prove to be to the participating members, is clearly a move in the opposite direction to the blueprint of a nondiscriminating world trading system.

In addition to the deviations in practice from the principles set out in the GATT, the principles themselves are deficient in at least one important respect: They do not take sufficient account of the trade problems of developing countries. The technique of reducing trade barriers through bargaining leaves most developing countries on the sidelines. Small countries with limited import markets have very little bargaining power. At the same time, developing countries' exports consist predominantly of the primary products and labor-intensive manufactured goods for which the developed countries are least willing to negotiate tariff and quota reductions. The policy of the European Common Market severely to discriminate against agricultural imports is the most salient recent example of how the interests of developing countries (except for former colonies and dependencies of Common Market countries having an associate membership in the Market) can be injured within the framework of the present GATT.

In summary, the vision of a postwar trading system free of the hampering and distorting effects of tariffs, quotas, and discriminatory practices has been rather blurred by experience. Instead of developments in the direction of an integrated world economy implicit in the envisaged system, in actuality the tendency has been strongly in the direction of the formation of economic (and political) blocs, standing in a state of tension toward each other.

Economic Development

The third pillar of the postwar international economic order—the development of the low-income economies containing the overwhelming majority of the world's population—has also suffered strains and cracks. Not only are the impoverished still with us, but the gap between them and the developed areas of the world is widening.

The basic reasons for the failure to realize expectations here are the infinitely more complicated nature of the problems of development than was realized earlier and the consequent insufficient provision of necessary means.

It is clear by now, after two and a half decades of aid programs, that real progress in lifting the economies of less developed countries onto the road of self-sustaining growth cannot be achieved without a concerted, massive, and long-term effort on the part both of the affected countries and of the developed countries. This conclusion is contrary to the optimistic expectations held earlier.

From the point of view of the passive attitude of prewar days, when the economic development of impoverished areas of the world was generally regarded as a matter of the gradual working of market forces, the postwar efforts to hasten the process are impressive. But from the standpoint of the actual requirements for significant progress, the efforts have fallen short. Deficiencies have become apparent in several different respects.

First, despite the tens of billions of dollars of financial assistance extended to developing countries since the end of the war, there has not been enough, nor on the proper terms, to serve its intended role. The notion that the World Bank would furnish the external capital necessary to serve as a catalyst and attract the additional capital needed from private sources early was shown to be overly sanguine. This was quickly recognized, the resources of the World Bank were expanded, and numerous other sources of assistance were created. As a consequence, the net flow of official financial resources from the developed market economies to less developed countries rose from an annual average of less than $2 billion dollars in the early 1950's to an average of over $6 billion dollars in the 1960's. However, the flow leveled off during the 1960's and has even tended recently to contract. A few additional billion dollars of aid each year for the next several years might well constitute the difference between mediocre progress (or perhaps in some cases deterioration) and a marked acceleration of the rate of growth of developing countries.

Apart from the inadequate volume of aid, the manner and conditions under which it is extended have reduced its effectiveness. The failure to commit assistance in specified amounts for reasonably long periods has made it difficult to plan and implement balanced investment programs. Burdensome service payments on loans increasingly reduce the margin of current capital flows available for domestic capital formation. The tying of aid funds to the purchase of the goods of the grantor and lending countries and the use of aid as a device for disposing of surplus products reduce the effectiveness of the aid.

Most unfortunate of all, however, has been a breakdown of the principle of multilateralism. Three quarters or more of economic aid is extended through bilateral programs. The result is twofold: (1) waste of resources from duplications and lack of coordination and (2) the infusion of political and military elements. The extension of the nationalistic rivalries and power plays among the developed countries into programs of assistance to developing countries inevitably carries with it diversion from the goal of growth. The strong desire of recipient countries for assistance to be channeled through the United Nations and its specialized agencies is a reflection of their dissatisfaction with bilateral arrangements.

Finally, insufficient attention has been given to aspects of economic development other than the provision of capital and technical assistance. The premise that the growth of less developed areas would be forthcoming merely by furnishing them capital is based on a simplistic, if not naïve, concept of the growth process. In fact, growth is a highly complicated, multifaceted process, involving social as well as economic transformation. Failure to appreciate this has led to disappointment at the slow pace of progress and premature judgments on future potentials.

However, the most important aspect of the overconcentration on the role of financial and technical aid has been the neglect to provide the international trade framework within which development could proceed in the optimum fashion. Development should be conceived as taking place in the context of an integrated world economy, rather than on the basis of inward-looking national economies. But for this to occur developing countries must have assurance of access to the markets of the developed countries. Lacking such assurance, resources will be assigned to the development of uneconomic sectors. The tendency to promote import-substitution industries through protective devices, rather than to encourage the expansion of capacity according to comparative cost advantages, is the most evident example. This brings us back full circle to our earlier discussion in this chapter of international monetary and trade organization, indicating the interdependence of the three international economic problems which the postwar blueprint was designed to solve.

CONCLUSION

If the preceding discussion gives an impression of bleakness of outlook it is because it has concentrated on unresolved problems rather than on the measures of progress achieved in many respects. There is a basis of restrained optimism in the widespread recognition and discussion of the problems we have identified. But for fruitful results to emerge, less nationalistic and more internationally cooperative attitudes than exist at present must be engendered. Solutions are not likely to be found if political divisiveness does not give way to a unity of purpose transcending narrowly conceived national aims.

Two lines of cleavage in the international political structure have direct relevance for the problems we have been discussing. The first is between the European Common Market countries, (under the leadership of France), on the one side, and the United States and England, on the other side. This cleavage bears especially on monetary and trading relations. Until it is healed, the prospect for creating a rational international monetary system and integrated trading system is dim indeed.

The second cleavage is between the developed and the developing countries. Increasing resentment by the latter of what they regard as a disguised imperialism and colonialism is creating a disaffection which threatens to prevent their integration into the world economy and to retard their progress toward economic growth.[1]

If and when these lines of political division are erased, the early postwar vision of a stable and prosperous world economy may be realized.

RECOMMENDED READING

JOHNSON, HARRY G. *The World Economy at the Crossroads.* New York: Oxford University Press, Inc., 1965.
    A lucid and perceptive essay on the three problem areas considered in this chapter, upon which the discussion has drawn heavily.

STUDY QUESTIONS

1. In what major respects has the international monetary system evolved away from the concepts originally embodied in the International Monetary Fund?

2. Review your understanding of the principal characteristics of a gold-exchange standard.

3. How does a gold-exchange standard interfere with liberal and non-discriminatory trade policies?

4. Why are domestic price-support programs inconsistent with the GATT principle of outlawing quantitative restrictions on trade?

---

[1] Cutting across both of the above is a third cleavage separating the communist bloc from the noncommunist world. We have paid little attention to the contribution this cleavage has made to the problems of the international economy. Suffice it to say that a truly integrated world economy embracing all countries is not possible without a political *modus vivendi* between the Soviet Union and the United States. (A developing fourth cleavage, between the Soviet Union bloc and the mainland China bloc, adds still another dimension, with uncertain implications for the future.)

5. How do customs unions conflict with the principle of nondiscrimination?

6. Why are the developing countries said to be on the "sidelines" in tariff negotiations?

7. Why has the World Bank not proven to be sufficient as an instrument for furnishing financial assistance to developing countries?

8. What are the objections to bilateral as compared to multilateral aid programs?

9. How is economic development related to the international trade system?

10. Why are solutions to the major international economic problems dependent upon international political developments?

INDEX

This book has been set in 11 and 10 point Baskerville, leaded 2 points. Part numbers and titles, and chapter numbers are in 16 point Helvetica italic and chapter titles are in 16 point Helvetica. The size of the type page is 27 by 46½ picas.